MORE...
extraordinary
uses for
ordinary things

Metric Conversion Charts

Lumber

Builder's Slang	Actual Size (US-inches)	Actual Size (Metric-mm)
2 x 2	1-1/2 x 1-1/2	38 x 88
2 x 4	1-1/2 x 3-1/2	38 x 89
2 x 6	1-1/2 x 5-1/2	38 x 140
2 x 8	1-1/2 x 7-1/4	38 x 184
2 x 10	1-1/2 x 9-1/4	38 x 235
4 x 4	3-1/2 x 3-1/2	89 x 89
4 x 6	3-1/2 x 5-1/2	89 x 140

Weights

US (Pounds)	Metric (Grams)
1/4	125
1/2	250
2/3	300
3/4	375
1	500
2	1 kg (kilogram)
3	1.5 kg
5	2 kg

Liquid Volume

US	Metric (mL)
1 teaspoon	5 mL
1 tablespoon **or** 1/2 fluid ounce	15 mL
1 fluid ounce **or** 1/8 cup	30 mL
1/4 cup **or** 2 fluid ounces	60 mL
1/3 cup	80 mL
1/2 cup **or** 4 fluid ounces	120 mL
2/3 cup	160 mL
3/4 cup **or** 6 fluid ounces	180 mL
1 cup **or** 8 fluid ounces **or** 1/2 pint	240 mL
1-1/2 cups **or** 12 fluid ounces	350 mL
2 cups **or** 1 pint **or** 16 fluid ounces	475 mL
3 cups **or** 1-1/2 pints	700 mL
4 cups **or** 2 pints **or** 1 quart	950 mL
4 quarts **or** 1 gallon	3.8 L

* Non-precise conversions may be rounded off for convenience:
1 cup=250 mL
1 pint=500 mL
1 quart=1 L
1 gallon=4 L

Length

US	Metric
1/8 inch	3 mm
1/4 inch	6 mm
1/2 inch	13 mm
3/4 inch	19 mm
1 inch	2.5 cm
2 inches	5 cm
3 inches	7.6 cm
4 inches	10 cm
5 inches	13 cm
6 inches	15 cm
7 inches	18 cm
8 inches	20 cm
9 inches	23 cm
10 inches	25 cm
11 inches	28 cm
12 inches or 1 foot	30 cm

MORE...
extraordinary
uses for
ordinary things

1,715 ALL-NEW Uses for Everyday Items

Reader's
Digest

The Reader's Digest Association, Inc.
Pleasantville, NY | Montreal

Project Staff

Associate Editorial Director
Elissa Altman

Project Editor
Fred DuBose

Writers
Stephen Brewer, Martha Hailey,
Robert V. Huber, Beth Kalet,
Steven Schwartz,
Sharon Fass Yates

Canadian Contributing Editor
Pamela Johnson

Designers
Michele Laseau, Rich Kershner

Copy Editor
Marcia Mangum Cronin

Indexer
Cohen Carruth Indexes

Photography
© Ellen Silverman, Kevin Norris

Prop Stylist
Paul Lowe

Illustrations
© Tania Lee

Reader's Digest Home & Health Books

President, Home & Garden and Health & Wellness
Alyce Alston

Editor in Chief
Neil Wertheimer

Creative Director
Michele Laseau

Cover Designer
George McKeon

Executive Managing Editor
Donna Ruvituso

Associate Director, North America Prepress
Douglas A. Croll

Manufacturing Manager
John L. Cassidy

Marketing Director
Dawn Nelson

The Reader's Digest Association, Inc.

President and Chief Executive Officer
Mary Berner

President, Consumer Marketing
Dawn Zier

ISBN 978-1-60652-051-2 (hardcover)
ISBN 978-1-60652-021-5 (paperback)

Previously published in hardcover as *Baking Soda, Banana Peels, Baby Oil and Beyond* (ISBN 0-7621-0556-4)

We are commited to both the quality of our products and the service we provide our customers. We value your comments, so please feel free to contact us:
The Reader's Digest Association, Inc.
Editor in Chief, Books
Reader's Digest Road
Pleasantville, NY 10570-7000

For more Reader's Digest products and information, visit our website:
www.rd.com

Printed in the United States of America

3 5 7 9 10 8 6 4 (hardcover)
5 7 9 10 8 6 4 (paperback)

Note to Our Readers
The information in this book has been carefully researched, and all efforts have been made to ensure its accuracy and safety. The Reader's Digest Association, Inc., and the individual contributing consultant-writers do not assume any responsibility for any injuries suffered or damages or losses incurred as a result of following the instructions in this book. Before taking any action based on information in this book, study the information carefully and make sure that you understand it fully. Observe all warnings. Test any new or unusual repair or cleaning method before applying it broadly, or on a highly visible area or a valuable item. The information in this book should not be substituted for, or used to alter, medical therapy without your doctor's advice. For a specific health problem, consult your physician for guidance. The mention of any brand or product or Web sites in this book does not imply an endorsement. All prices and product names mentioned are subject to change and should be considered general examples rather than specific recommendations.

Welcome to the world of

Clever Ingenuity...

where ordinary items from baking soda to panty hose
SAVE YOU **TIME** and **MONEY!**

Step inside for more than 1,700 tips and hints

Clean your coffee grinder with rice

Don't bother with fancy tools and brushes. Running a cup of uncooked
rice through the grinder will give it an unbeatable scouring.

Spray away fresh carpet stains

A spray of non-gel shaving cream on a fresh carpet stain
will make it a cinch to clean up.

Make your brass candlesticks glimmer with ketchup

Put them in a pan, cover with ketchup, and bring to a boil
for a spectacular shine.

Keep seedlings happy with aluminum foil

Place a sheet of aluminum foil underneath
container seedlings to promote growth … they love the warmth.

Cure your headache with coffee

Caffeine constricts blood vessels and alleviates
headache discomfort.

Simple!

Clever!

Creative!

Fresh!

contents

Introduction
The Joy of Old-Fashioned Smarts 8

Smart!

Easy!

Ingenious!

Fast!

The Joy of Old-Fashioned Smarts

Plastic CD cases make great **photo frames!**

It's amazing just how clever television commercials have become. There they are—happy, pretty people cleaning their homes, cooking their dinner, grooming their gardens, and using the most *ingenious* new contraptions and solutions, all specially available to you now at this one-time, amazing low price.

"*Hmmm,*" you can't help but think, "maybe if I bought *that* thing, then cleaning my kitchen floor might be easier!"

We've coined a word for this phenomenon: Contraptionism. You name the task—from planting a plant to chopping vegetables to cleaning a shower—and you can find a clever contraption created to get it done faster and easier. And why not? Entrepreneurs make great livings selling clever gizmos meant to make our lives better.

But there are problems with contraptionism. These gadgets usually just accomplish one task. They're either too expensive (crush garlic easier for just $40!), or too cheap (flimsy plastic that bends with the wind). They accumulate in our closets and drawers, often going unused. And they often have a short life—either you need to buy refills, or they break. Sure, on occasion, you come across that one gadget that really does deliver on its promise. But mostly, contraptionism has a not-so-happy ending.

So let us tell you about some of *our* favorite contraptions. An old pair of panty hose. A banana peel (without the banana). A strand of uncooked spaghetti. A roll of duct tape.

These tried-and-true devices for easy living are options that are wiser, smarter, more frugal, a tiny bit old-fashioned, and nearly always a lot more fun to use. Because if you could wash your windows, clean your floors, shine your kitchen tiles, tenderize your meat, poach your eggs, remove old wallpaper and unclog a drain all with the same bottle of inexpensive vinegar, you'd do it … wouldn't you?

And this is what *More Extraordinary Uses for Ordinary Things* is all about: finding the fun in the ordinary and the ingenious in the everyday. And by doing so, saving yourself incredible amounts of time and money.

How We Put This Book Together

We sent our intrepid team of researchers and writers out to talk with chefs, landscapers, grandmothers, herbalists, pet-store owners, carpenters, decorators, and so many more everyday experts. Their task: Find their very best tips and tricks for getting things done quicker, easier, cheaper—and by only using items already available around the house.

What they came back with was thousands of ingenious hints and tips on most every subject imaginable. We honed the list down to 1,715 of the best, and they fill the pages ahead. Now, we've covered similar terrain in other Reader's Digest books, so we worked extra hard to make sure that everything in *More Extraordinary Uses for Ordinary Things* is new and different. And we most assuredly succeeded!

These tips will take you on a wide-ranging tour through your everyday life. We'll visit your kitchen, den, closets, and bedroom; we'll tour your garden and yard; we'll even be with you in your car and on vacation. We'll also be there with you as you take on the tasks of everyday living: cooking, cleaning, mending, sorting the mail, remedying a cut or a cold, rejuvenating those droopy geraniums.

We've asked for help from people you'll recognize, like that great-aunt or uncle who may be getting older, but who still knows how to remove a splinter with an onion, de-gunk a skillet with baking soda and borax, or use an ordinary plastic bag to clean a shower head. Pet owners share their tricks for getting their finicky dogs to eat; homemakers show us how to organize a drawer with an egg carton; creative parents teach us how to remove crayon from a wall with shaving cream.

While ingenuity is priceless, it's also got other benefits: It's usually accomplished without chemicals (and is therefore healthier for you, your family, your home, and the environment). It's parsimonious (who needs contraptionism when you can buy just one thing, like baking soda, to accomplish a multitude of tasks?), and, well, it's just a lot more fun.

Great Advice Ahead!

The thirteen chapters in *More Extraordinary Uses for Ordinary Things* each focus on an integral part of everyday life:

For the cooks of the house, we've gathered hundreds of ingenious cooking tips and tricks using everyday ingredients. What's the one secret ingredient that will turn a supermarket tomato from marginal to magnificent? How can you extend the shelf life of vegetables and other perishables? What's the most tried and true method for baking bread, that goes back thousands of years but is as close as your own garden shed?

For the housekeepers of the house, we've given you more ideas for faster, easier cleaning than you can shake a broomstick at.

What two ingredients can you blend together in seconds to make a wonderful cleaner for a wooden floor? What everyday lunch treat can you use to get something sticky out of a carpet?

For the groggy person standing in front of the bathroom mirror at 7 a.m., we tell you surprising ways to look and feel refreshed. What early morning drink is a great soother of puffy eyes? What everyday breakfast food is a natural lipstick stain-remover?

For the handyman (or woman) of the house, we show you incredibly fast and easy fix-its for many common problems. What does virtually every woman have in her medicine cabinet that does double duty removing scratches and dents in wood? What's the easiest way to remove ancient wallpaper?

For the neat freak in every home, we show you the very best ways to conquer clutter without big investments in fancy boxes and shelves. Don't toss those old egg cartons and milk jugs! Use them instead of buying prefabricated, pricey store-bought clutter contraptions!

As they searched out clever ideas for better everyday living, the writers and researchers of *More Extraordinary Uses for Ordinary Things* often discovered that necessity was the mother of invention. One expert for the home repairs chap-

Let us tell you about some of our favorite contraptions: an old pair of panty hose, a **banana peel** (without the banana), a strand of uncooked spaghetti, a roll of duct tape.

ter replaced the old, wood-frame windows in his house only to discover the new ones drafty enough to chill his family to the bone in winter. His solution? Thick strips of folded paper towel held in place by masking tape.

More exciting was another expert's serendipitous discovery. Trying to revive his dog's interest in dry food, this fast-fixes maven decided to mash a banana and stir a bit of it into his dog's bowl. The pooch ate it like there was no tomorrow and finickiness is now a thing of the past.

The author of the cooking chapter struck gold when she asked family and friends about unusual ways of accomplishing common tasks. She quickly learned about buttering the lip of a pitcher to help stop dribbles, and using a garlic press to crush sugar cubes. One expert revealed that instead of buying a pricey electric sandwich press, he uses a heavy cast-iron skillet for even better results. This clever approach to everyday living is what 21st century "folk wisdom" is all about.

More Extraordinary Uses for Ordinary Things also provides a goldmine's worth of special features that inform, instruct, and entertain: **What's the Story?** brings you the surprising histories of household items new and old.

Make Your Own offers up simple, natural recipes for everything from dog biscuits to nasal spray to natural insecticides for your plants.

Household Superstars! details some of the many uses for the most useful and popular home ingredients, like baking soda, duct tape, petroleum jelly, plastic bags, salt, vinegar, and WD-40.

Curiosity Corner lets you dip into a veritable grab bag of curiosities of all stripes, from how many ingredients it took to build the world's

largest sandwich, to how to estimate air temperature by the frequency of a cricket's chirp, and to understand why a candle can be used to unstick a stuck drawer.

So whether you thrill at the possibility of discovering new ways to use everyday things, or simply want ways to save a few dollars and do things better, this anticontraption bible is for you. Dip into it and dip out, peruse the chapters with a fine tooth comb, or read it from beginning to end … no matter how you use it, this will become the busiest book in the house (and the garage, the garden shed, the lavatory, the playroom, and pretty much everywhere else). And remember, the busier this book is, the more money and time you will save!

—*The Editors*

Chapter One

Cooking and Serving Shortcuts

Are the microwave and a fridge full of frozen meals the best dinner companions you've ever had? Or do you find yourself standing over a hot stove for a few precious hours each night after a long day at work to make a meal for your family?

Whether you love to cook or you find it just another chore, there are easier, faster, and simply smarter ways to kitchen happiness that will not only save you time, but will make daily dinner drudgery delicious!

Not every hint in this magician's bag of cooking tricks will save you time, though. But money-saving, creative solutions to kitchen problems are shortcuts to worry-free cooking, and that's what this chapter is all about!

If your soup is too salty, add a drop of sugar. If your curry is too spicy, applesauce will cool it down. Run out of oil to grease a pan? Use the cut-side of a potato. The hints that follow give you dozens of great ideas and in many cases get you out of a pretty pickle. So let's get cooking!

Fruits, breads, and vegetables make terrific *edible bowls!*

Fast Fixes

Counteract salt with sugar
Did you oversalt Grandma Kate's famous beef stew as it burbled away on your stove? Save it with a teaspoon of granulated sugar, which will absorb excess salt and help balance the taste. No sugar handy? Stir in a teaspoon of honey.

Degrease gravy with baking soda
Sometimes the cooking juices you've used in your gravy are so greasy that they look like an oil slick. Counteract the problem with a pinch or two of baking soda, stirred into the juices just enough to absorb the grease. (Be careful, though: If you overdo it, you'll taint the flavor, and it'll taste metallic.)

Curry sauce too spicy?
Tone it down with applesauce. Add ⅓ cup applesauce for each cup of curry sauce, then taste. If necessary, continue stirring in a bit of applesauce until the curry is acceptable.

Two more for dinner (surprise!)
You cooked the perfect-sized roast for a small get-together, and guess what? Meat shrinks when cooked, so you've got a third smaller entree than you started out with, and *then* the doorbell rings.

What to do? Carve the entire roast into thin strips, toss that large salad you were planning on, top with the beef, and you'll have just ratcheted up the size of your main course.

Rescue a cracked egg
You're boiling an egg and the shell cracks. No reason to throw it out if you have white vinegar in the cupboard. Simply add 1 teaspoon vinegar to the cooking water to coagulate the egg white and stop it from seeping out.

Salsa too hot?
Stir in a drop or two of vanilla extract. Whether it's the vanillin, sugars, or amino acids in vanilla that takes the heat down a notch or two, vanilla extract is the coolest condiment for the job.

Soup too garlicky?
Pack a mesh pouch, gauze bag, or metal tea ball with dried parsley flakes or fresh parsley sprigs and drop it into the pot. After 5 minutes or so, the flakes will absorb some of the taste of the offending ingredient. Once the garlic taste has been adequately toned down, remove the parsley and discard it.

ADD SWEET FLAVOR TO OUT-OF-SEASON SUPERMARKET TOMATOES
Those commercially grown pink tennis balls that pass for tomatoes do have flavor hiding deep inside: Just drizzle tomato slices with a little **rice vinegar** (on supermarket shelves everywhere). You'll be amazed at the difference it makes!

Fat Catchers!

Do you skim the fat off your simmering stew, soup, or sauce with a teaspoon? Stop! Here are three easy and effective ways to reduce artery-clogging fat in the pot:

1

Float a large lettuce leaf on the surface and it will draw the fat right in. Repeat the process with fresh leaves as necessary.

2

Float two or three ice cubes on the surface and you'll soon see fat globules clinging to them. Scoop the cubes out (before they melt!) and continue cooking your now-healthful dish.

3

Slip an uncooked egg white onto the simmering soup or stew or sauce. Left alone for a few minutes, it will absorb the fat as it cooks; simply scoop out the solidified egg white with a slotted spoon, and discard it.

Poultry Prescriptions

Simple skinning

Want to make skinning a piece of poultry or even a whole bird a snap? Put it in the freezer until it partially freezes (generally 1½–2 hours). You'll be able to pull the skin off with no trouble.

Chicken money-saver

Buy whole birds and cut them up with poultry shears. Freeze the pieces in portion-size freezer bags. If chicken is your family's favorite dish, you'll make up the cost of the shears (under $20) in a few weeks!

Butter(milk) up chicken cutlets

To tenderize chicken cutlets and pack them with flavor, rinse the breasts, pat dry, and marinate them in buttermilk for 2–3 hours, in the fridge, before cooking.

Stuffing stopper

Want to make sure stuffing doesn't fall out when you roast a bird? When cooking a stuffed bird of any size, just plug a raw potato into the cavity and the stuffing will stay put.

Tea-riffic flavor

To give chicken or turkey breasts or thighs a light, smoky flavor and help them retain moisture as they cook, brew 2 strong cups of your favorite spice-flavored tea blend. Once the tea cools, add seasonings of choice—black pepper, salt, paprika, and garlic—to taste, pour into a large self-sealing plastic bag, and add the chicken or turkey pieces. Put in a shallow dish and marinate in the fridge for at least 2 hours before cooking.

Carrot and celery rack

Forget hard-to-clean, traditional roasting racks! Instead, crisscross whole carrots and celery stalks on the bottom of the roasting pan, and top with your chicken or turkey. Once it's done, your bird will emerge from the pan without a hitch, and the pan gravy will be enhanced by the vegetables!

Simple roux starters for gravy

Combine excess pan fat with enough all-purpose flour until you can roll it into small balls about half the size of a walnut, and freeze on a cookie sheet covered with a paper towel. When frozen, transfer the balls to a plastic bag and store in the freezer for future use. The next time you need to make gravy, pluck out a roux starter ball from the bag and melt it in the saucepan before stirring in the other ingredients. Is your already-cooked gravy too thin? Drop in a roux starter, whisk well, season to taste, and serve.

GLAZE WITH VERMOUTH

About 15 minutes before you're ready to take your chicken or turkey out of the oven, brush the skin with **white vermouth.** It will take on a rich brown color, thanks to the sugars in the fortified wine.

Double-Duty Kitchen Tools

Some of the most ordinary kitchen gadgets and tools come in handy in ways you never imagined, in some cases making them worth a lot more than you paid.

Vegetable peeler

Run a peeler along the corners of a block of cheese or chocolate to create hearty ribbons to use as a garnish.

Colander

Use as a steamer for vegetables. Fill a stockpot with 2–3 inches of water, bring to a boil, put a heatproof or metal vegetable-filled colander inside, and cover.

Garlic press

Turn sugar cubes into granular sugar by placing one cube at a time into a garlic press and squeezing it shut. One cube equals 1 teaspoon of sugar.

Melon baller

Use smaller ballers to core apples and pears and scoop cookie dough onto a baking sheet. Use larger ones to scoop ice cream into a bowl.

Ice cream scoop

Lightly coat an ice cream scoop with cooking spray and use it to spoon even amounts of batter into cupcake or muffin tin liners. The sweeping release arm will help clean all batter from the scoop, and you won't waste a drop.

Pizza cutter

The sharp wheel on a pizza cutter makes cutting through all kinds of other foods a breeze. Use the cutter to separate waffle segments and to neatly slice a grilled cheese sandwich.

Tongs

Sturdy metal tongs measuring about 16 inches long are like having an extra set of heatproof hands. Use them to turn chops frying in a skillet, to toss salads, to mix pasta with sauce, and to rotate cake and pie pans in the oven.

Empty wine bottle

Don't have a rolling pin or a meat pounder handy? Use an empty wine bottle as a stand-in rolling pin (flour it first) or as a meat pounder to flatten chicken or veal cutlets for more even cooking.

Go Fish

Something's fishy

Before preparing fresh fish, halve a lemon and rub both hands with the cut ends to help keep your hands from absorbing the fishy odor. (If you didn't know you had a tiny scratch or cut on your hand, you will now!) If frying is your cooking method of choice, wash the pan you used and pour in ½ inch white vinegar; the acetic acid should banish any lingering fish smell.

Ease scaling with vinegar

To make scaling a fish less of a chore, rub white vinegar on the scales and let sit for about 10 minutes. The scales will come off so easily that they may make more of a mess than usual, so put the fish in a plastic bag before you do this. Just scale the fish in the bag with one hand while holding the fish by the tail with your other hand.

Keep poached fish firm

When poaching fish, squeeze fresh lemon juice into the poaching liquid to help the fish cook evenly. For each pound of fish, use the juice of half a lemon.

Foil moisture loss when baking

Low-fat fish like bass, flounder, grouper, halibut, and red snapper can easily dry out as they bake. To seal in the moisture, simply wrap each fillet or whole fish in aluminum foil before putting it into the oven.

Freezing fresh-caught fish

When you bring more fish home from the lake than you can eat, here's the smartest way to freeze them. Take an empty milk carton large enough to hold the fish, place the fish inside, and fill the carton with water. Seal the opening with tape and place the carton in the freezer. When you thaw the fish, you won't have to worry about scraping off ice crystals or pulling off some of the flesh with the wrapping.

Cool down shrimp

To ensure tender, well-textured meat, place shrimp in the freezer for 10–15 minutes before

you cook them. Just be sure not to overcook them because you think they need time to warm up in the boiling water. (They don't.)

Make oyster-shucking easier

Soaking oysters in club soda for 5–10 minutes will make it easier for you to open the shells.

Stop lobster squirts

When cracking and twisting the legs and claws off a whole lobster, guard against the occasional squirt by putting a napkin between the crustacean and your hand. Any squirts will hit the napkin, not your silk blouse sleeve or starched white cuff (or dinner companion's sweater).

Improve canned seafood

If you detect a slight metallic taste in canned seafood, soak it as directed below, drain, and pat the seafood dry with paper towels.

- **Water-packed tuna** Soak in a mixture of cold water and lemon juice for 15 minutes (2 parts water, 1 part juice).
- **Canned crab** Soak the crabmeat in ice water for 5–10 minutes.
- **Canned shrimp** Soak the shrimp in a mixture of 2 tablespoons vinegar and 1 teaspoon dry sherry for 15 minutes.

Cut the salt in anchovies

If you like the taste of anchovies but wish they weren't quite so salty, soak them in ice water for 10–15 minutes, and then drain them well before tossing them in a Caesar salad or arranging them on top of a pizza.

make your own
Salt Substitute

Here's a delicious, all-purpose, low-sodium seasoning that will enhance fish, meat, and poultry dishes. Make it in large batches to always have it on hand.

Who-Needs-Salt Mix

Sour salt, arrowroot, and powdered orange peel in this recipe may sound unusual, but they can usually be found in supermarkets.

1 tablespoon celery seeds
1 tablespoon onion powder
1 tablespoon freshly ground black pepper
2¼ teaspoons cream of tartar
1½ teaspoons garlic powder
1½ teaspoons sugar
1½ teaspoons arrowroot
1½ teaspoons powdered orange peel
¾ sour salt (citric acid powder)
½ teaspoon white pepper
½ teaspoon dried dill
½ teaspoon dried thyme, crumbled
⅓ teaspoon powdered lemon peel
¼ teaspoon cayenne

1. Place all ingredients in a blender or food processor. Grind for 8–10 seconds or until the mixture is fine.

2. Use a funnel to fill a glass salt shaker with the mixture.

3. Put the rest of the mixture in an airtight jar and store in a cool, dark place.

From Reader's Digest Great Recipes for Good Health

Red Meat? Read On!

Hamburgers with a difference

To flavor and moisten hamburger patties, add ¼ cup finely minced onion and 2 tablespoons barbecue sauce. Blend the ingredients into the ground beef or turkey with your hands (which you've washed with antibacterial soap, of course!), taking care not to overwork the mixture.

Variations of the ingredients are endless—you can add everything from minced garlic or celery or other crisp vegetables paired with chili sauce, ketchup, Worcestershire sauce, or steak sauce. You could also mix a teaspoon of chili powder or cumin (or ½ teaspoon of both) into the meat to give the patties a hint of Tex-Mex flavor, or even a drop of curry powder to add some Indian spice.

Speed defrosting with salt

Defrost frozen meats quickly and safely by soaking them in cold salt water for several hours. Mix ¼ to ½ cup kosher salt or any other coarse-grain salt with 2 quarts water, then submerge the meat and refrigerate it. Once the meat has thawed, just discard the salt water and get cooking!

Making better burgers

Your last backyard barbecue was a big success, and your hamburgers certainly passed muster. But you can notch up a burger's wow quotient with a few easy tricks.

- **Keep 'em juicy** For a juicer grilled burger, add ½ cup cold water to the ground meat, and shape patties as you normally would. Prepare the patties shortly before you grill them.

- **Flash freeze** Keep hamburger patties from breaking during grilling by freezing them for 5 minutes just before they go on the grill.

- **Poke dents** Use your forefinger to make two or three dents in the center of a patty before placing it on the grill. This speeds even distribution of heat so the burger will cook faster.

- **Toast herbs** You can easily flavor and scent grilled burgers by giving your hot coals an herbal treatment. Place leafy fresh herbs like basil, savory, and rosemary directly on the coals.

BASTE WITH A PAINTBRUSH

A clean paintbrush dipped in vegetable or canola oil is perfect for making your grill nonstick before slapping on burgers or any other meat. Season your steak, chicken, or fish with the same brush, now dipped not in oil but in grilling sauce.

Bake your bacon for a streak o' lean that's crispier, meatier, and less greasy.

Bathe flank steak in ginger ale

Lend flank steak an Asian touch by marinating it in ¾ cup of ginger ale mixed with 3 minced garlic cloves, ¾ cup orange juice, ¼ cup soy sauce, and ½ teaspoon sesame oil. Cover and keep in the refrigerator for 4–8 hours. This recipe makes enough marinade for 1½ pounds flank steak.

Wake up brisket with coffee

Barbara's Brisket (Barbara being an innovative home cook who resides in New Jersey) uses coffee and chili sauce to give brisket a new twist. To enjoy this twice-cooked dish for yourself, combine 2 cups brewed coffee with 1½ cups store-bought chili sauce in a mixing bowl. Stir in 1 chopped onion, 2 tablespoons brown sugar, and salt and freshly ground black pepper to taste.

Place a 5-pound brisket in a roasting pan, then pour the bowl of sauce over the meat. Cover tightly with a lid or foil and bake for 2 hours in a preheated 325°F oven. Remove the pan from the oven and transfer the meat to a platter to cool. Now slice the meat, lay slices in the sauce in the pan, and cover again. Bake at 325°F for another 2 hours or until the brisket is fork-tender.

Meatloaf in a bag

Put all the ingredients for a meatloaf into a large self-sealing plastic bag and squish it with both hands to evenly distribute the seasonings throughout the meat. Turn the bag inside out into a prepared loaf pan, gently press it into shape, and bake. No messy hand, no bowl to wash!

Keep meatloaf moist

Spritzing the top of the loaf with water will keep it from cracking and drying out as it cooks. Open the oven door and brush tomato sauce or ketchup over the top of the loaf about 15 minutes before it has finished cooking.

Easy slices without tearing

To slice thin steaks or stew cubes from a roast prior to cooking, wrap the meat in heavy-duty plastic wrap and freeze for 10 minutes. This

10 Kitchen Uses for Salt

1 Sprinkle on a whole chicken 24 hours prior to roasting, for the most flavorful and juicy clucker you've ever eaten.

2 Release juices in meats by seasoning them with salt an hour before cooking.

3 Prevent pancakes from sticking to the griddle by wiping the griddle between batches with coarse salt wrapped in cheesecloth.

4 Prevent cheese mold by wrapping the cheese in a paper towel dampened with salt water.

5 Clean dirt and grit from leafy greens by soaking them in cold salt water for up to 15 minutes, then rinsing the greens thoroughly under cold running water.

6 Keep apples, pears, and potatoes from browning as you slice them by dropping each new slice into a bowl of lightly salted cold water.

7 Keep hardboiled eggs intact and make them easier to peel by adding a pinch of salt to the cooking water.

8 Make milk last almost twice as long in the refrigerator by adding a pinch of salt each time you open a new carton.

9 Neutralize bitter coffee that's been sitting on the warmer too long by adding a dash of salt to your cup.

10 Enhance the flavor of cocoa drinks and desserts with a pinch of salt.

method works for every cut, from London Broil to inexpensive chuck roast.

Quick 'n' easy pork glaze

If you have apricot jelly, soy sauce, and powdered ginger in your pantry, you've got the makings of a simple but delicious glaze. Just whisk together ¼ cup apricot jelly, 2 tablespoons soy sauce, and ¾ teaspoon ginger and brush it onto a pork tenderloin or rolled pork roast before cooking. If you're pan-cooking pork chops on top of the stove, glaze the browned top of the chops after you've flipped them over once.

Ham too salty?

Give ham bought as "fully cooked" a taste test before warming the slices. If the ham's on the salty side, place the slices in a dish of low-fat milk for 20 minutes before heating them. (Once you remove the slices from the milk, rinse them under cold running water and pat dry with paper towels.) The ham won't pick up the taste of milk but will lose some of its saltiness. Soak whole precooked hams in milk for an hour before heating (just remember to drain, rinse, and pat the meat dry).

Baking bacon!

Laying bacon over a wire rack set on a rimmed baking sheet and baking it at 375°F has two advantages: 1) It makes the slices less greasy because the fat drips onto the sheet, and 2) the bacon stays flat and tastes meatier. If you prefer your bacon fried, prevent it from curling and splattering grease by dipping the slices in cold water before you fry them.

Cup o' joe for lamb

To give lamb stew a beautiful dark color and great flavor, add 1 cup black coffee to the stew pot about halfway through the cooking process.

Perfect Pasta, Right-on Rice

The ideal meal stretcher

You invited six friends over for a buffet dinner, and one couple shows up with two out-of-town friends, another with their strapping teenage son. Help! Make a beeline for the cupboard and pull out a box of pasta—your best bet as a filling meal stretcher. Dig around your pantry and look for a can of tomatoes or condensed soup. Boil the pasta while your friends mingle and snack, heating up the soup (undiluted) or tomatoes at the same time. Drain the cooked pasta, dump it into a large bowl, and toss it with the soup or tomatoes and plenty of grated hard cheese, preferably Parmesan or Romano. (If you have no soup or tomatoes, toss the pasta with a little olive oil and grated hard cheese—a surprisingly delicious combo.) Add the steaming bowl of pasta to the buffet table, and your guests—with the possible exception of Tyler, high school football team center—will have their fill.

Stop spaghetti showers

You're rummaging through a kitchen cabinet for a can of beans and accidentally knock over the half-used box of spaghetti—and the dried strands rain down on the floor. How to keep it from happening again? Save an empty potato chip can (tall and cylindrical and lidded) and recycle it as a dry pasta canister.

Carrot ribbon pasta

Carrots add more nutrients and some vibrant color to a simple pasta dish. Clean and peel the carrots, then use your peeler to shave wide carrot ribbons. Sauté the ribbons in butter and seasonings, such as ginger, black pepper, and salt, then add to cooked and drained pasta. Forgo the red sauce and toss with Parmesan cheese.

Keep pasta pots from boiling over

Before adding water to your pasta pot, coat the interior lightly with nonstick cooking spray. The water won't boil over, even when you add the pasta. If you have no spray on hand, add a teaspoon of olive oil to the water as it cooks. This trick works for boiled rice as well.

Toss leftover pasta...

But don't throw it out! Toss it in a stickproof, ovenproof pan with a teaspoon of olive oil, pour two beaten eggs over it, sprinkle with cheese, and bake until golden brown. Slice the frittata into wedges and have it for another dinner with a small green salad! Money saving, simple, and delish!

Jazz up rice

Instead of boiling your rice in plain water, use chicken or beef stock, tomato juice, or even equal parts orange juice and water. Or just sprinkle dried oregano, cumin, turmeric, and any other herb or spice into the water before adding the rice. You could also add minced onion, garlic, or lemon or orange zest to turn rice from the same-old, same-old into a brand new dish each time it's set on the table.

Fluff it up!

It's easy to keep rice grains from sticking together as they cook. Try one of these methods to ensure you'll spoon out the fluffiest of servings.

- Soak the rice in a bowl of cold water for 30–60 minutes before cooking. Soaking will also make the rice cook faster. Drain and rinse before cooking.

- Put the rice in a colander and rinse it under cold running water several times to remove the surface starch that makes the grains stick together.

- Add the juice of half a lemon to the cooking water. Grating the lemon rind and adding the zest will give rice another taste note and a bit of visual interest.

Fun with chow fun!

Before being cooked, rice noodles need to soak in room-temperature water for several hours (1 hour at least). If you can't cook the noodles immediately, keep them moist by sandwiching them between damp paper towels.

Curiosity Corner
The Great Spaghetti Tree Hoax!

What's said to be the world's greatest April Fools' joke was pulled on the banger-and-mash loving, fish-and-chips munching British public on April 1, 1957. The BBC news show *Panorama* reported on a bumper spaghetti crop in southern Switzerland, the result of an unusually mild winter.

"The spaghetti harvest here in Switzerland is not, of course, carried out on anything like the tremendous scale of the Italian industry," the respected anchorman Richard Dimbleby intoned, as a rural Swiss family was shown harvesting spaghetti from tree limbs and tucking it into baskets. "Many of you, I'm sure," Dimbleby continued, "will have seen pictures of the vast spaghetti plantations in the Po Valley. For the Swiss, however, it tends to be more of a family affair."

Dimbleby also explained the mystery of tree-grown pasta coming in uniform lengths, calling it "the result of many years of patient endeavor by past [plant] breeders who succeeded in producing the perfect spaghetti."

At the time, spaghetti was rarely eaten in Great Britain, which in those days was slow to embrace foreign food. How many of the audience fell for the joke and how many recognized it instantly for what is was is unknown. What *is* known is that hundreds of viewers called the BBC to inquire about the segment, many of them asking how they could grow and cultivate their own spaghetti trees. Staying in character (and impeccably so), BBC customer service representatives replied, "Place a sprig of spaghetti in a tin of tomato sauce and hope for the best."

Eggs and Cheese

Enrich omelets and scrambled eggs

Hot sauce and salsa, shove over: make your scrambled eggs and omelets silken and sinfully rich by whisking in 1 tablespoon of prepared mayonnaise of any type for each egg.

No more cracks

Keep the shells of hardboiled eggs intact by rubbing them with a lemon before cooking. The shells won't crack and will be much easier to peel once they're cool. Achieve the same result by adding 1 teaspoon lemon juice or a small wedge of lemon to the cooking water.

Devilishly easy

When preparing deviled eggs, take these two steps toward perfect alignment: Keep yolks centered as the eggs boil by stirring the water nonstop. Cut a thin slice off opposite sides of the hardboiled eggs to make the halves stuffed with filling sit up perfectly straight on the serving platter.

Perfect slices

Make hardboiled egg slices neat and clean by lightly wiping or spraying the knife blade with vegetable oil or cooking spray. No oil or spray on hand? Run the knife under cold running water just before slicing.

Spray before grating

A cheese grater is no fun to wash clean, but you can make the job easier by taking action in advance. Just spray the grater with cooking spray or use a clean rag to rub it with vegetable oil.

What's the Story?
The Real Word on Cheese Mold

Some cheeses, like Roquefort, Danish Blue, and Stilton, are moldy by design. But that block of Cheddar in the back of your fridge is moldy because fungus spores have invaded it. The good news is that you can save it. Just cut the moldy area plus at least 1 inch of mold-free cheese off and discard it. If you spot mold on Brie, goat cheese, or another soft cheese, it can't be rescued—so throw it out or you'll risk getting violently ill.

You may have heard that you can "treat" mold on cheese by rubbing a vinegar-soaked rag over the mold. Not true. Nor is the advice to put moldy cheese in a plastic bag with a few sugar cubes, mistakenly said to draw out mold. That's the word from the HomeWise Web site from the University of Idaho. The Web site quotes Dr. Sandra McCurdy, University of Idaho Extension food safety specialist. "By the time you see mold spots in cheese," she reports, "the mold has already begun to put down its invisible 'roots.'" That's the reason deep cuts are necessary to remove mold from hard cheese.

Dr. McCurdy says that cheese mold "just happens" in the home refrigerator. So play it safe. Don't leave cheese out of the fridge for more than two hours, and always keep your eye peeled for even the tiniest spot of mold.

Vegetables and Fruits

Rescue wilted veggies

Revive wilted vegetables by soaking them for an hour in 2 cups water mixed with 1 tablespoon apple cider vinegar. Pat dry and prepare as usual. Alternatively, plunge limp veggies into hot water, remove, and then plunge them into a bowl of ice water mixed with a little cider vinegar.

Easy-cheesy creamed spinach

If you like creamed spinach, you'll go for this recipe. Sauté 1 clove finely minced garlic in 1 tablespoons butter for 30–40 seconds. Add about 20 ounces prewashed spinach leaves and toss until just wilted. Stir in ¼ cup ricotta cheese and salt and freshly ground black pepper to taste, then enjoy a rich and flavorful twist on a favorite side dish. For a low-fat version, use reduced-fat ricotta.

Liven up green beans

Flavor steamed green beans and give them a little kick to boot by tossing them in this mixture: 2 tablespoons melted butter, ½ teaspoon chili powder, and a dash or two of garlic powder.

Got milk?

Adding milk to the cooking water can enhance certain vegetables. Two examples:

- The whiteness of cauliflower becomes all the whiter when you add ⅓ cup milk to the cooking water.
- Sweet corn-on-the-cob gets even sweeter when milk is added to the water.

"Almost the real thing" vegetable lasagna

Here's a recipe that may fool even the most die-hard carnivore. Replace the meat in a lasagna recipe with a mixture of diced zucchini, lentils, and ground walnuts—a combination that closely resembles ground beef. Then just follow the recipe and enjoy a high-protein lasagna that tastes much like the classic meat version.

Quick-bake potatoes

Cut baking time in half (without microwave help!) by choosing smaller potatoes and standing them up in the cups of a muffin tin before putting them in the oven. To reduce baking time for a full-size spud by 15 minutes, insert a long nail into the flesh. This will distribute the heat through the potato more speedily.

Muffin tin hint redux

Stuffed green peppers sometimes lean to one side while cooking in the oven. Give them firm

COFFEE CAN LID AS FRUIT KEEPER

Instead of wasting plastic wrap, try this method of storing a half grapefruit or cantaloupe in the fridge. Simply set the fruit cut-side down on a clean plastic **coffee can lid.**

Store your
lemons in water
to make them
jucier!

footing by setting each pepper in the cup of a muffin tin sprayed with a little nonstick cooking spray to ensure easy removal.

Cola-caramelized onions

To ease the work of caramelizing onions, you need only three ingredients: 2–3 sweet Vidalia onions, steak sauce, and cola. Slice the onions about ¾ inches thick and set in a microwavable 9-by-13-inch dish. Pour cola over the onions to cover. Stir in 2 teaspoons steak sauce and microwave at 50 percent power for 30 minutes. No trouble, great taste!

Save those veggie tops!

Beet greens? Fennel fronds? Carrot tops? Don't throw them out! Cut them away from their respective vegetables, wash and dry them well, chop them, and sauté them in a bit of olive oil with garlic to taste for a healthy side dish. Or mince them fine and mix them together with scrambled eggs, salad greens, or leftover pasta.

Toothbrush as veggie cleaner

Use a soft-bristled toothbrush to clean mushrooms and other sensitive vegetables before cooking. A medium- or hard-bristled brush is more suitable for potatoes.

How to slice dried fruit

Have you ever tried to cut dried fruit into small bits only to have your knife stick on the fruit? Simply squeeze a lemon section over the fruit you're about to cut or sprinkle the fruit with a few drops from your pre-squeezed lemon juice. Your knife will slice through with ease.

Juicier lemons

Store your lemons in a sealed jar of water, and when it's time to squeeze them, you'll get twice as much juice. Another trick is to prick the skin once or twice with a sharp knife and then microwave it on medium power for 15 seconds before slicing and squeezing.

Soups and Salads

Quick fix for bland soup

Does your soup lack something … like, say, *taste*? Kick up the flavor by dissolving a beef or chicken bouillon cube in hot water and whisking it into the soup.

Soup stretchers

If you're heating up leftover soup for two or more people and it looks a little skimpy, stir in some cooked rice or pasta. Pearl barley is also a good soup stretcher, and instant or quick-cooking barley will cook in the simmering broth in less than 15 minutes.

In the bag

As you cut salad ingredients, put them in a small plastic garbage bag (fresh from the box, of course). When you've finished, hold the bag closed with your hand and shake. The ingredients will be thoroughly tossed, and you can refrigerate them in the bag until serving time.

Hold the tomatoes

When making green salads ahead of time, add sliced tomatoes only after the salad is on the plate. The greens in your salad bowl will stay crisper in the fridge sans tomatoes, which contribute to lettuce wilt.

"Fast Italian" Broccoli Salad

It's sexy, all right, and easy. Toss room-temperature steamed broccoli florets in a dressing made with ½ cup plain marinara spaghetti sauce, 2 tablespoons olive oil, 1 tablespoon red wine vinegar, 1 tablespoon chopped Italian parsley, and salt and freshly ground black pepper to taste. Buon appetito!

Straight-to-the-Pot Soup Thickeners

To thicken a soup, add …

Frozen spinach While your soup is cooking, put clumps of frozen spinach into the pot. If you prefer, defrost the spinach in the microwave and drain off excess liquid.

Sweet potato Prick a few holes in a small sweet potato and microwave it on high for a few minutes until it's partially cooked. Slice into quarters, mash with a fork, and then add the lumpy pulp to the pot. As the soup cooks, use a fork to mash the pulp further, if necessary.

Bread As the soup cooks, remove the crust from a slice or two of bread and dice the bread into small cubes. A hearty multigrain will work like a charm, and rich white bread will do the job, too.

Mashed potatoes or instant potato flakes Don't want to change the flavor of your soup? Then add either of these two forms of potatoes.

Oatmeal Toss a small amount of uncooked plain, quick-cooking oatmeal or even leftover cooked oatmeal into the pot. Because it's bland, oatmeal shouldn't affect your soup's flavor—but to counteract the blandness you may need to add more seasoning.

Keep it fresh

A chef's trick to saving lettuce for up to two weeks is a snap! Pull the leaves off the core, dry them well, fill a sink with cold water and submerge them for 20 minutes. Remove, dry thoroughly, wrap in paper towels, and store in your lettuce keeper.

Clean Hands, Dry Eyes

Any cook knows how hard it can be to get food stains and smells off hands and to chop eye-stinging onions. Fight back with these helpful hints.

Stain-Free Hands

Rub with lemon juice. Berries and beets are notorious stainers. Remove stains by rubbing them with 1–2 teaspoons fresh lemon juice and then washing your hands with soap and water.

Rub with a potato. Even chopped carrots, red bell peppers, and pumpkin can leave their marks. Rub a raw potato on your fingers to help remove the stains.

Odor-Free Hands (onions, garlic, fish)

Rub on stainless steel surface. This strange-but-true chef's trick works: rub garlicky hands repeatedly on a flat stainless steel surface, and they'll be fresh as a daisy.

Rub with rosemary. Rub your hands with sprigs of fresh rosemary to rid them of garlic and onion smells.

Rub with vinegar. Use a little white vinegar as a hand balm. To avoid oniony hands to begin with, rub vinegar over your hands *before* peeling onions.

Rub with salt. Sprinkle table salt into your palm and rub your hands together to remove smells of garlic and onions. Rinse and dry.

Scrub with sugar. Pour 1 tablespoon sugar in your palm, wet it with 1 teaspoon liquid soap, and rub your hands and fingers together as when washing them. Rinse and dry.

Scrub with toothpaste. Handling fish can leave your hands with an odor that just won't quit. Squeeze toothpaste on a washcloth wetted with cold water, then scrub to remove the smell.

Rub with lemon. Cut a lemon, squeeze a good bit of its juice over your hands, and rub hands and fingers together as when washing them. Rinse under running water.

Tear-Free Eyes

"Bread" your knife. Cut a small piece of bread and insert your chopping knife partway down to the hilt. As you slice the onions, the bread will absorb some of the fumes.

Toss onions in the freezer. Freeze onions for 10–15 minutes before slicing them. The cold helps minimize the fumes that cause tears.

Chop near a stove burner. If you can safely position your cutting board on a gas range stovetop, chop onions with one or two of the burners turned on low. The heat attracts onion fumes and neutralizes them.

Light a candle. Burn a candle near your work area to burn off some of the fumes emanating from sliced onions.

Run the faucet Bring your cutting board over near the sink, and run the faucet on cold while you slice your onion; the chemicals released are actually drawn to dampness (hence their ability to make your eyes tear), and will choose a running stream of water instead of your peepers.

Boons for Bakers

Flour taste test

Can't remember whether flour in your canister is all-purpose or self-rising? Taste it. If it's salty, it's self-rising flour, so called because it contains baking powder and salt to make it rise.

Is your baking powder fresh?

You're not sure how long that can of baking powder has been in your pantry, but you can easily learn whether it's still viable. Scoop ½ teaspoon of the powder into a teacup and pour in ¼ cup hot water. If it bubbles up a storm, it's okay to use; if it fizzes only barely, it's time to buy a new can.

Speed dough's rise

Heat makes dough rise more quickly. Still, if it rises too quickly the flavor will suffer—something that cooks who've tried microwaving dough for a few minutes on low power could probably tell you. Instead, position the bowl or pan over the pilot light of a gas stove or on a heating pad set on medium heat.

Keep hands clean

When working with dough, don't flour your hands to prevent dough from sticking to your skin. Instead, pour a few drops of olive oil into your palm and work it into your hands as you would hand lotion.

Easy greasing

Save the waxy wrappers of margarine and butter and put their buttery residue to good use. Store them in a plastic bag in the refrigerator. When a recipe calls for greasing the pan, press one or two of the wrappers into service.

Muffin release

Muffins or cupcakes stuck to the bottom of the metal muffin tin? While the pan is still hot, set it on a wet towel. The condensation in the bottom of the tin will make the treats easier to remove.

Ice in the oven?

Yes, if you're baking bread and want a better loaf. When you put the bread in the oven, put a second pan holding 6–8 ice cubes on one of the oven racks. The resulting steam will help the bread bake more evenly and give it a crispier crust.

Lighten up quick breads

If your favorite special banana-nut bread, cinnamon coffee cake, or carrot-zucchini muffins are super-tasty but heavy, substitute buttermilk for the milk in the recipes; it will lighten the texture of any quick bread you bake. Experiment to find what gives you the best results: all buttermilk, equal parts buttermilk and milk, and so on.

Butter replacement

If a baking recipe calls for so much butter that you feel your arteries clogging just reading it, substitute a 50/50 mixture of unsweetened applesauce and buttermilk. Best used in light-colored or spiced baked goods, this substitute imparts a slightly chewier texture—the reason you'll want to replace all-purpose flour with pastry flour or cake flour.

A honey of a cookie

Honey will help home-baked cookies stay softer and fresher longer. Replace sugar with honey cup for cup, but decrease other liquids in the recipe by ¼ cup per 1 cup honey.

Flowerpot Cookery

Clay pot cookery is a kitchen tradition that goes back thousands of years. Even a simple, unglazed terra cotta flowerpot will work perfectly! Simply wash your unglazed, unpainted, pot in hot soapy water and air-dry. Oil the pot's interior and lip with vegetable oil until the clay will absorb no more. Place the pot on a baking sheet topped with aluminum foil, and place in a cold oven. Heat to 400°F and turn off immediately. Repeat oiling and heating one more time, and your pot is ready to use.

Baking the bread:

1
Lightly grease the interior of a 6-inch flowerpot with vegetable oil or cooking spray.

2
Prepare your favorite bread recipe as usual and roll 12 ounces of dough into a ball. Place in flowerpot and let rise according to the recipe.

3
Bake at 350°F for 25–30 minutes or until the top is golden brown. Let the bread cool on a wire rack and then gently thwack the bottom of the pot to remove it.

How Sweet It Is

Easy creaming

This important step in many a cake recipe—creaming the butter and sugar—can be a tedious and lengthy task. If the butter is cold, you can speed up the creaming process by warming the sugar a bit on the stovetop or in the microwave.

One-egg replacement

If you're baking a cake that calls for one more egg than you have on hand, you can substitute 1 teaspoon of cornstarch.

Or go fruity

Replace one egg in a cake or sweetbread recipe with one small mashed banana or a half-cup of applesauce. For chocolate cakes, try substituting mashed prunes.

Spaghetti cake tester

If you don't have a wire cake tester, use an uncooked strand of spaghetti. Gently push the spaghetti into the center of the cake and pull it out. If your spaghetti comes out clean, the cake is done.

Improvised cake decorator

Use a clean plastic mustard or ketchup squirt bottle as a cake decorator. Fill it with icing and then pipe scallops, flowers, and other designs onto cakes with ease. Or use it to make squiggles of pesto or sour cream on top of soups or chocolate on desserts.

Pie bubbling over?

If a pie starts bubbling over as it bakes, cover any spills with salt. You'll prevent the spill from burning and avoid that terrible scorched smell.

Lick a Yogurtpop!

Lollipops and Popsicles may be fat-free, but they're also mostly sugar. A custard-style frozen yogurtpop, on the other hand, is full of healthful stuff—and to most palates, a lot tastier.

Making a yogurtpop couldn't be simpler. Just spray unflavored cooking spray into a small paper cup (the kind dispensed at water fountains), spoon in your favorite yogurt, and freeze. In about a half hour, insert a sturdy plastic spoon in the middle, bowl side first.

Depending on the temperature of your freezer, the pops should be ready in about an hour. For a pop that will remind you of the old Creamsicle of your youth, blend vanilla yogurt with softened frozen orange juice concentrate and freeze as directed above.

Best of all, the treated overflow will bake into a dry, light crust that you can wipe off easily when the oven has cooled.

Make piecrust flakier

Flaky piecrusts are the talented baker's hallmark. You can improve flakiness by replacing 1 tablespoon ice water in your crust recipe with 1 tablespoon chilled lemon juice or white vinegar.

Fruit piecrusts too soggy?

To keep the juice in fruit from seeping into the crust of a baking pie, crumble up something to absorb it. A layer of plain, crisp flatbread will absorb the juice and introduce a savory note to the pie, while biscotti or amaretti cookies will keep it tasting sweet.

Slice meringue with ease

Your knife will glide through a meringue-topped pie if you butter it on both sides before slicing. A 10-second solution, if that!

Thrifty chocolates

If you're a chocoholic, have extra freezer space, and are always looking for ways to pinch pennies, this hint may be tailor-made for you. Buy chocolate Easter bunnies and Santas after the holidays when prices are slashed. Store them in the freezer, and then melt them or shave off chocolate curls for use when cooking. Or, if you prefer, just thaw Old Saint Nick and gobble him up whenever you need a chocolate fix.

Turn coffee into granita

Use a yogurt cup to make this refreshing icy dessert, similar to Italian ice. Pour freshly brewed coffee into several clean yogurt cups or similar small-size containers to freeze. Remove and then plop the frozen coffee into the food processor. Process on the frappe setting until crystals form. Spoon the crystals into the cups and freeze for about a half hour before serving.

Homemade granita options: Add milk and sugar (or sugar substitute) to your coffee before freezing or just go with black. Good toppings for granita include whipped cream and a sprinkling of cinnamon.

No cake tester?
Use a strand of
raw spaghetti instead!

Smart Solutions, Easy Improvements

Marinate in plastic bags

You can eliminate washing bowls, spoons, and even pots by marinating meats and poultry in large self-sealing plastic bags. Open the bag and pour in the liquids and seasonings—soy sauce, ketchup, ground ginger, black pepper, crushed garlic, herbs, and so on. Zip the bag shut and shake it to blend. Now add the meat, zip the bag, and shake. Refrigerate 6–8 hours or overnight. Occasionally take the bag out of the fridge and shake it to redistribute the marinade.

Butter stops the dribbles

Dab a bit of butter onto the spout of your creamer or milk pitcher and you'll put an end to the drips and dribbles.

Oil your measuring cup

Sticky liquids like honey and syrup are tough to measure and pour, and a little always remains behind. Oiling the measuring cup will make it harder for viscous liquids to stick and will give you a more accurate serving.

Keep salt on popcorn

Want salt to stick better to hot-air popcorn? Give it something to cling to by lightly coating just-popped corn with vegetable-based cooking spray. Avoid olive oil cooking spray because the flavor can overpower popcorn's taste.

Add tang to sauce with ginger ale

Ginger ale will perk up tomato sauces, but be careful not to overdo it. A third of a cup of ginger ale added to a medium-size saucepan of marinara or a tomato juice–based beef stew will subtly enhance the flavor.

Brighten the taste of OJ

For fresher flavor in orange juice, add the juice of 1 lemon per half gallon. By the glass, squeeze in the juice of a quarter lemon, then set the rind on the rim for a bit of flair.

Flavor plain chips

Bet you didn't know how easy it is to make your own garlic-flavored potato chips. Just place a peeled garlic clove in a bag of plain chips, fasten the bag shut with a clamp or clothespin, and let sit for 6–8 hours; shake the bag occasionally to even out the flavor. Open the bag, discard the clove, and crunch away.

Dress up pancake syrup

Adding chopped strawberries and a little lemon zest to syrup will make it a lot more interesting. Combine ½ cup pancake syrup, ½ cup strawberries, and ½ teaspoon grated orange rind in a microwavable bowl and heat on high power for 30–60 seconds. Top pancakes, waffles, or French toast with the syrup and dig into what's now a tastier and more healthful dish. (Strawberries are packed with vitamin C and manganese.)

Savvy Substitutions

No lemon?

When a recipe calls for lemon juice and the one you thought was in the fruit bowl has flown the coop, a lime is obviously your best bet should you have one on hand. If not, use the same amount of white wine.

Salt mimic

A chef's trick for reducing the amount of salt in a recipe is to replace it with half as much lemon juice. If a recipe calls for ½ teaspoon of salt, substitute ¼ teaspoon lemon juice and shelve the sodium.

Vanilla imitators

If you run out of vanilla just as the batter recipe calls for it, substitute an equal amount of maple syrup or a liqueur such as Frangelico or Baileys Irish Cream.

Powder for powder

Cake recipes often call for baking powder, but if you're without it, try this: For each teaspoon called for, substitute a mix of ½ teaspoon cream of tartar and ¼ teaspoon baking soda. The mixture won't store well, so make it fresh should you ever need it again.

Ersatz bread crumbs

Making a meatloaf or meatballs, but you're running short of bread crumbs? Substitute oatmeal, crushed unsweetened cereal, crumbled crackers, or instant mashed potato flakes.

A surprising pan prepper

You've got the vegetables chopped, the meat ready, and you're about to fire up your skillet when you discover that you're out of oil. Rub

Caught Without Cookware?

You loaned your cake pans to a neighbor, she's on vacation, and you want to bake a cake. Or you're the one who's on vacation, and the supposedly fully equipped cabin in the woods you've rented can't even cough up a loaf pan for the carrot-zucchini bread you crave during your back-to-basics stay. Here are great solutions when you don't have the pot or pan or small appliance you need:

Ceramic bowls Use an ovenproof ceramic bowl in place of a cake pan, or try ovenproof cereal bowls for individual cakes. Just be sure to place them on a baking tray before putting them in the oven; bowls can be too hot to handle even with hot pads or a dishtowel.

Coffee can A quick bread will bake just fine in a coffee can. Be sure to spray the interior with nonstick cooking spray and dust with flour.

Dutch oven If you don't have a slow cooker, a Dutch oven will do the job just as well. Combine the ingredients for your stew or braised dish in the pot, cover, and cook in a slow oven (250–350°F) for 3–4 hours or until any meat in the dish is fork-tender.

the skillet with half of a potato, and your food won't stick.

Sour cream stand-in

To make a substitute for 1 cup sour cream, blend 1 cup cottage cheese, ⅓ cup buttermilk, and 1 tablespoon lemon juice until smooth. The lemon juice will sour its creamy partners.

Practical Advice

Stop the drip

Wrap a terry-cloth sweatband, headband, or bandana around a bottle of olive oil to prevent drips. When your wrap becomes too oily, just toss it in the washing machine.

Elbow grease aid

Trouble twisting off the lid of a new jar of spaghetti sauce, applesauce, or such? Turn the jar upside down and give it a thwack with the heel of your hand; you should hear a popping sound, signaling the release of air. Now turn the jar over, and you may be able to twist off the lid with ease.

Separate packaged bacon

Before opening a package of bacon, curl the package up with your hands a few times, turning it over each time. When you open the package, you'll find it easier to peel away individual slices.

Keep wooden tools in good shape

Sprinkle your wooden salad bowls and cutting boards with salt and then rub them with a lemon to freshen them. The salt-and-lemon treatment will help your salad bowl to impart freshness, not smells, to the ingredients. And when you chop, slice, and dice, your knife won't lift any dried wood bits from the board.

"Micropeel" garlic

Here's a tip to make working with garlic a snap. Microwave garlic cloves for 15 seconds and the skins will slip right off, allowing you to slice, mince, and chop without delay. Bonus hint: As you chop garlic, juices released make the tiny

Flatten That Cookbook!

You're following a recipe in your favorite cookbook—a big book chock-full of pages. But every time you turn your back to add a new ingredient or stir the batter, the pages flip and you lose your place. It's enough to make your blood boil like a bubbling stockpot! To call a truce in the book battle, you could buy a Plexiglas cookbook holder or you could use something you already have: a clear glass baking dish. Just turn to the page where your recipe is printed and flatten the book with the dish. It will not only keep your cookbook open but also will give you a crystal-clear view of the type.

pieces stick to your knife. Sprinkling a bit of salt on both the cutting board and the garlic will go a long way toward solving the problem.

Super lid opener

Too-tight lids on jars can make you feel like a weakling when they just won't budge. A simple way to get them open? Don a pair of rubber dishwashing gloves. With your grip secured, the lid will twist off with minimal effort.

Don't forget the ice cube tray!

Whether you're preparing baby food, storing leftover sauces, or making perfect-sized portions of no-cook fudge, the flexible plastic ice cube tray is your invaluable multitasker. It's a versatile kitchen aid you don't want to forget.

Who'da Thunk It Helpers

Hair dryer as salad green dryer
You've rinsed and spun your salad, but those green leaves are still wet. Don't waste paper towels to dry each one; instead, set your hair dryer on low/cool and gently wave it over the greens.

Teaspoon as a ginger peeler
Finding it impossible to peel ginger without losing some of its precious flesh? Here's a chef's secret: If you're a righty, hold the ginger in your left hand, and using a teaspoon, firmly scrape the edge of the spoon along the knob with your right. The papery skin will peel right off.

Dental floss as slicer
Held taut, floss slices layer cakes, tender quick breads, soft cheeses, butter, and plenty of other soft foods even better than a sharp knife.

Plastic soda bottle as funnel
Cut off the top third of the bottle and turn it upside down. Now you can easily funnel leftover sauces, gravies, kidney beans, or even grease into containers for storage or trash.

Handsaw as rib separator
A sharp (and rust-free) handsaw works wonders when you're serving those juicy racks of ribs at your annual summertime gathering. Slip the blade between the bones, give it one or two good saws, and the result will be perfectly separated ribs.

Coffee filter as gravy strainer
Beef and poultry drippings from a roast make the most delicious, flavorful gravy base but are often small grease bombs. Save the flavor and kill the fat by straining the cooking juices through a paper coffee filter.

Scissors as herb chopper
Use clean household scissors to snip fresh herbs and green onions into salads or mixing bowls. Scissors are also perfect for cutting steam vents in the top crust of a pie about to be put in the oven.

Flowerpots as kitchen tool caddie
Store serving spoons, whisks, tongs, and other kitchen tools in flowerpots set at the back of a countertop. To make the pots more decorative, paint each one in a different pastel color.

Wood rasp as lemon zester
A clean, fine metal rasp from your toolbox or workshop is the perfect zester for lemons, limes, oranges, and virtually any other citrus fruit. Its tiny raised nubs scrape the fruit's skin and leave zest of a perfect granularity that would please the fussiest chef.

SHOEHORN AS CORN KERNEL REMOVER
A clean **shoehorn** has at least two uses in the kitchen. Scrape the wide end along a corn cob to remove the kernels, and use the narrow end to gently release baked muffins from their tin.

Storing Fresh Food

A surplus of spuds?

If you find you've peeled too many potatoes for a potato salad or casserole, don't toss the uncooked extras. Put them in a bowl, cover with cold water, and add a few drops of vinegar. Now they will keep in the fridge for 3–4 days.

Brown-bag your lettuce

Lettuce will keep longer if you transfer it from a plastic bag to a roomier paper bag before storing it in the refrigerator. Lettuce likes a little air, but don't think that calls for removing the limp and discolored outermost leaves; they may not be pretty, but these leaves help keep the inner leaves crisper.

TLC for contents of crispers

Line the crisper drawer of your refrigerator with paper towels, which will absorb the excess moisture that does no favors for the veggies inside. Replace the towels as they become damp. Another way to dehumidify the drawer is to tuck two or three brand new clean kitchen sponges among the vegetables, squeezing moisture out over the sink as needed.

Toast freshens lettuce

Keep lettuce crisp in your refrigerator by storing it in a sealed plastic bag with a slice of almost-burned toast. The toast will absorb some of the excess moisture that would otherwise wilt the lettuce. As long as you replace the toast when it gets soggy, the lettuce should stay crisp for up to two weeks.

Keep greens fork fresh

Keep kale, collards, mustard greens, and other greens fresh longer by storing them in the refrigerator with a stainless steel fork or knife. Just open the storage bag, slip in the utensil, and reclose.

Celery Care 101

Celery is all about crispness, so when it starts to go soft, you may as well throw it out. Right? Not necessarily. Try this first: Put limp stalks in a bowl of cold water with a few slices of raw potato. After an hour or so in this starchy bath, the stalks may deliver the crunch you expect.

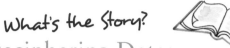

What's the Story?
Deciphering Dates on Food Packages

The packages of most perishable foods are marked with a date indicating how long you may consume the product. But guess what? Except for infant formula and some baby foods, there are no federal regulations governing product dating in regard to safety. The best you can do is understand the three types of dating that food manufacturers stamp on their products.

The sell-by date tells a store how long to keep a product on the shelves, but the period for safe use of the product is longer. Exactly how much longer, however, is uncertain.

The best-if-used-by date is the last date the product will be at its peak quality or flavor and has nothing to do with food safety.

The use-by date gives the last day the manufacturer recommends you should use the product, and therefore may be the most helpful.

Even crisp celery may turn brown, but you can stop browning before it starts. Before storing the stalks in the fridge, soak them for 30 minutes in 1 quart cold water mixed with 1 teaspoon lemon juice—a trick that will also crisp celery just before it's served.

Get the most out of a lemon

When a recipe calls for a few drops of lemon, don't slice the lemon and squeeze. Simply puncture the rind with a toothpick and gently squeeze out the small amount of juice you need. Then cover the hole with a piece of tape and store the lemon in the fridge for later use. Waste not, want not!

Oiled eggs

Prolong the life of fresh eggs by dipping a paper towel into vegetable oil and rubbing the shells before storing the eggs in the fridge. The oil will keep the eggs fresh for an additional 3–4 weeks!

Vinegar and cheese

To keep cheese fresh, wrap it in a piece of soft cloth dampened with vinegar. It should come as no surprise that cheesecloth is ideal for the purpose.

Store potatoes with ginger

Unused potatoes will last longer if you add a piece of fresh gingerroot to their storage bin. It's said that one root vegetable helps keep another root vegetable fresh—and a potato tuber is a root of sorts.

Longer-lasting milk

If you buy more milk than you can use before the expiration date, extend its life with couple of pinches of baking soda. Baking soda reduces milk's acidity, thus staving off spoilage.

Storing Baked Goods

Cookies on tissue

Keep crisp cookies crisp by crumpling tissue paper (the kind popular as gift-wrap) and placing it in the bottom of the cookie jar. It will help absorb any moisture that seeps in.

The birthday cake's in the bag

If you want to bake a cake for a special occasion down the road—like your daughter's 21st birthday or your parent's golden wedding anniversary party—you can actually bake it several months ahead of time and freeze it. The trick is to triple-wrap the layers. Here's how:

1. After taking three layer pans out of the oven, let the layers cool completely.

2. Wrap each layer separately in plastic wrap and then in aluminum foil, making each package as airtight as possible.

3. Pop all three layers into a large freezer bag and seal it, squeezing out the air as you do.

When the big day arrives, defrost the layers before removing the wrap. Then assemble the cake and frost it, secure in the knowledge that your creation will taste as fresh as if it were baked yesterday.

Instant cake dome

If you don't have a fancy cake plate with a glass dome, keep your cake fresh and the frosting intact by covering it with a large bowl turned upside down.

Well-bread cake

Once you cut into a scrumptious three-layer cake, the exposed part of what's left gets stale quickly. Here's a way to slow drying. Place a slice of bread over the cut surface of the cake and hold it in place with a couple of toothpicks. As the bread dries out, the cake will stay moist for later enjoyment.

A trick for store-bought pies

You've eaten two slices of a luscious peach pie and start to wrap it with plastic wrap. Not so fast! If you cover the pie first with an upside down paper plate or aluminum foil pie plate and then wrap it in plastic, the pie will have a little breathing room and stay fresh for a week or more.

Storing a meringue-topped pie

When storing the remains of a meringue pie in the fridge, how do you cover it without ruining the meringue? Rub a large piece of plastic wrap with a stick of butter, making sure it's greased completely. Fit it over the pie plate butter-side down. The next time you want a slice of pie, the wrap will peel off without sticking.

A crisp bread freshener

To keep sliced bread fresh longer, just stick a small, fresh stalk of celery in the bag with the bread. Celery has a high water content but stays dry on the outside, so what better moisturizer could you find?

An apple every two days

The moisture from an apple will keep soft cookies soft. Just place the cookies in an airtight tin and put an apple slice (skin side down) on top before closing it. Replace the apple slice every two days if any resident cookie monsters haven't already polished off the contents.

Freeze Breeze!

That big icy compartment above (or below) your refrigerator can do far more than just store meats and instant waffles. Here's how to use it to make everyday items (including ice cubes!) go the distance:

"Instant" tea

When you brew a full pot of tea and have a lot left over, pour the tea into ice cube trays and freeze it. Later, you can use the tea cubes to chill a fresh batch of iced tea without diluting it, or melt the cubes in the microwave instead of brewing a fresh pot. You can freeze surplus coffee in the same way.

Freeze eggs?

Yes, but only raw yolks and whites. Just break eggs into an airtight plastic container and add 1 teaspoon of salt or honey for each cup of eggs. (About five whole eggs make a cup.) Cover the container and mark it with the additive you chose so you'll know whether to use the thawed eggs in a sweet or savory recipe.

Brown-bag ice cubes

Keep ice cubes from sticking together by storing them in your freezer inside a paper bag. (It'll keep you from cursing as you wield an ice pick or hammer.)

Crystal-free ice cream

When you serve only part of a package of ice cream and return the rest to the freezer, ice crystals tend to form on the surface. You can prevent crystals from forming by tucking a layer of plastic wrap onto the surface of the ice cream before closing the carton and putting it back in the freezer.

Breathe Life into Leftovers

Surplus grilled tuna or salmon

If you grilled too much salmon or tuna for that dinner party, you have the base for a tasty salad. In a large bowl, combine 1½ cups cooked tuna or salmon, a 15-ounce can of white beans, 3 thinly sliced green onions, 2 tablespoons Italian parsley, 1 minced garlic clove, and ⅓ cup of your favorite Italian dressing. Toss and enjoy!

Long life for veggies

Save all leftover veggies for up to a week. Dice them; lightly sauté your mixture in olive oil with savory seasonings such as oregano, basil, and black pepper. Add leftover rice or other grains. Use as filling for a quiche or to fortify a meatloaf.

Get a head start on gravy

Whirl almost any kind of leftover soup that has no bones in a blender or food processor to make a quick sauce or gravy for vegetables or meat.

Jazz up salsa

Add leftover corn kernels to your jarred salsa. Stirring in corn will not only make for a more colorful presentation but will also tone down a salsa you find too hot for your taste.

Oatmeal muffins

Don't toss out the unserved cooked cereal left in the pot when breakfast is done. Instead, use it in batter when making muffins. Add the baking powder, eggs, and other ingredients as the recipe directs, and you may find you like the result.

Beware of the Great Thaw

If there's a power outage in your home while you're on vacation, it's essential for you to know about it before you return home and go foraging in your freezer. If your electric power was off for a long time and the food in the freezer thawed and refroze, the entire household could come down with food poisoning.

How to know whether the power goes out when you travel? Before you leave, place a plastic bag full of ice cubes in your freezer, and check it when you return. If the cubes have become a solid block, a power outage of some duration occurred. If the ice cubes are as you left them, all is well.

Overripe fruit = great smoothies

Don't relegate overripe fruit to the compost or trash. Freeze it and call on your frozen bananas, strawberries, and peaches to make a delicious smoothie with yogurt or your liquid of choice. Your smoothies may even taste better, thanks to the concentrated sugars in overripe fruit.

Leftover wine makes great salad dressings

Don't pour that leftover red or white down the drain! Put it in an airtight jar and store it in the fridge. When it's time to make a vinaigrette, you can combine the wine even-steven with vinegar for a dressing with extra punch.

Freeze leftover wine

If a few inches of pinot grigio or zinfandel remain in the bottle at the end of a party or meal, don't let it go to waste. Pour it into an ice cube tray, and the next time you're making a sauce, a casserole, soups, or stews that call for a splash of white or red, you'll have it handy. The cube will melt quickly, so no defrosting will be required.

Red wine as meat tenderizer

If you have some leftover red wine, put it to work as a meat tenderizer and marinade. Simply put the meat in a self-sealing bag or lidded container and pour the leftover wine over it. Whether cooked on the grill or under the broiler, the meat on the plate will have a juicy, tender texture.

Remember the croquette

How much leftover chicken do you have on hand? Make too much ham for the holidays? Talking too much turkey? Never fear..the croquette is here! Mince the offending leftover very finely to make 2 cups, add a tablespoon or two of prepared white sauce and a beaten egg, shape into tightly packed, small logs, and refrigerate for an hour. Remove the croquettes from the fridge, roll in fine breadcrumbs, heat up a few tablespoons of vegetable oil in a stickproof frying pan, and lightly fry until golden brown. The best news? If you don't finish these leftovers, they'll freeze perfectly … for up to six months! Talk about going the distance!

Leftover sauce from pot roast?

Turn it into a homemade ragu so good that your family will think that a real chef is in the kitchen! Chop up small pieces of leftover pot roast, return it to its sauce, add 2 cups of red wine and 2 cans of crushed tomatoes. Blend well, bring to a simmer, cover, and continue to cook for 30 minutes.

Household Superstar!
10 Cool Uses for Resealable Kitchen Storage Bags

1 Speed the ripening of fruit by sealing it in a bag.

2 Crush graham crackers for piecrust by putting them in a bag and running a rolling pin over it.

3 Crush nuts by placing them in a plastic bag and pounding them with a hammer.

4 Put the ingredients for meatloaf in a plastic bag, seal it, and gently massage the bag.

5 Seal frozen poultry in a plastic bag and submerge it in cold water for several hours for the safest way to thaw chicken, turkey, and game birds.

6 Marinate meat and poultry in a large plastic bag placed in a shallow bowl in the refrigerator.

7 Knead dough in a large plastic bag to keep your hands from getting sticky.

8 Turn a plastic bag into a pastry bag by snipping off a small corner.

9 Protect the recipe card you're using from splatters by enclosing it in a plastic bag.

10 Use a plastic bag as a glove when the phone rings and your hands are oily or covered in flour.

Setting the Perfect Table

Mini bouquets
When your garden is in bloom, cut small bouquets and arrange them in empty jam jars, glass water bottles, or clean mustard pots. If you have a long table, line them up in the center for a centerpiece your guests will remember.

Color coordinate your vases
Add another dimension to the floral arrangements you use as a centerpiece. A few drops of food coloring in the water of a clear glass vase will make a pretty setting prettier.

Can it
Some products, including Italian plum tomatoes and espresso, come in especially artful cans. Once you've consumed the contents, use the cans to create a centerpiece. Set small leafy green plants of different heights in three cans and arrange the colorful planters in the center of the table.

The sit-down test
Before your guests arrive, make sure that your centerpiece isn't so tall that it will block their line of vision: place your centerpiece in the middle of the table, pull out a chair, and take a seat. If the tallest flowers or other decorative items are taller than face height, shorten them so that guests can make eye contact.

You've been framed!
Use small picture frames (matched or unmatched) as place cards holders. If you're a practiced calligrapher, write each guest's name on a piece of good-quality paper cut to fit the frame, or simply choose a nice computer font and print out your guests' names. Slide each "card" into its frame.

Mix and (mis)match?
When good friends are coming over for a dinner party, make things more interesting and unexpected by varying the place settings—a brightly colored Fiesta Dinnerware plate here, a rose-patterned fine china plate there. The result is not only eclectic, but also a great conversation starter.

Use Grandma's silver
Gone are the days when silver was hauled out only on special occasions; use it for everyday casual dinner parties as a reminder of that great woman. Don't worry if it's tarnished … it'll lend the table a bit of retro character!

Ready to Serve

No time to dust?

Let low mood lighting help out! Make a beeline for all the candles you own and place them (carefully, and not near drapes) around the living room and dining room—votive candles on windowsills, candelabras on the mantelpiece, pillar and jar candles here and there. If the lights in both rooms have dimmers, set the light to barely there and bask in the complexion-enhancing, dirt-hiding glow.

No-stick napkins

How to keep napkins from sticking to the bottom of your drinking glasses? Press the bottom of each glass in a plateful of salt, then shake off excess salt. However scant, the salt should break the bond and keep napkin and glass separated.

Chill wine in a hurry

Here's a foolproof way to quick-chill champagne and other white wines. Place the bottle in an ice bucket or other tall plastic container, and add just enough ice cubes to make a 2-inch layer on the bottom. Sprinkle the ice with a few tablespoons of salt and continue to layer ice and salt up to the neck of the bottle. Now add cold water until it reaches the top of the ice. After only 15 minutes (about half the time it would take in a freezer), you'll be able to uncork the bottle and pour properly chilled bubbly for your guests.

Wine bottle cork won't budge?

Run hot water over a towel and wrap the towel around the neck of a stubborn wine bottle. This easy treatment will help the glass neck of the bottle expand just enough to make the cork easier to pull out.

Serve Food in Food

Fruits, breads, and vegetables all make terrific edible receptacles and pretty presentations.

Hard rolls Slice the top off a sourdough roll or other hard roll and remove bread from the interior. Then fill with individual portions of tuna or chicken salad for each guest at your table.

Bell peppers Hollow out red, yellow, or green bell peppers, slice a bit off the bottom so they'll stand straight, and use as condiment "dishes" on your buffet or picnic table.

Pineapple After you carve the fruit out of a pineapple, the shell makes a lovely serving platter—especially for a tiki party! Halve the rind lengthwise and be sure to leave the leaves on.

Melons Hollow out a cantaloupe or honeydew melon half, and serve honeydew chunks in the cantaloupe shell and vice versa. Clever!

Martini-style salads

Dress up the simplest of salads by lining martini glasses with lettuce leaves and add a scoop of chicken, tuna, or egg salad. Pierce an olive with a toothpick and set it in the salad at an angle, à la the classic martini.

Dine alfresco

Why stay inside on a nice evening? Move dinner outside! Cover your patio table with a simple bedsheet (fancy or not), bring your chairs outside, light some candles, and create an instant moveable feast!

Chapter Two

Canny Kitchen Cleanups

The kitchen is the heart of the home, but let's face it: It can also be the messiest room in the house. The unwashed dishes, the overstuffed cabinets and cupboards, the splattered stove top—if you have little time on your hands or a large family, you might think that a dirty kitchen is just a fact of life. Guess again!

The good news is that to keep a kitchen clean, you don't have to spend money on those overpriced or supercheap miracle cleansers and gizmos advertised on TV. To keep your kitchen organized, you don't need a bachelor's degree in organizational management, either. All it takes is a bit of resolve and a good browse of the following pages packed with timesaving, money-saving hints and tips on how to make your kitchen a clean, calm oasis.

Wipe away
pencil marks with

rye bread!

Wash Up, Wipe Down

Add vinegar to your mop water

Add a few drops of white vinegar to your mopping bucket to remove soap traces. If the floor is linoleum or vinyl tile, add a little baby oil to the mop water to bring a soft gleam to the surface—a mere 1 or 2 capfuls at most, or you'll turn the floor into a skating rink.

Bleach painted walls

Mix a solution of 1 gallon water and ½ cup chlorine bleach to give your kitchen walls a brightening sponge-down after frying or sautéing.

Erase pencil marks with rye bread

Remove your young Picasso's kitchen wall pencil sketches with a slice of fresh rye bread (seeded or not). An art-gum eraser can also erase the marks, without the thrill.

Wash away wallpaper grime

If your kitchen walls are covered with waterproof wallpaper, remove excess dirt with a vacuum cleaner, then wash the walls with a solution of ½ cup lemon juice, ½ cup dishwashing liquid, and 1 quart water. Before starting, wash a tiny section in an out-of-sight place to make sure the paper will tolerate the mixture.

Keep stainless steel stainless

Stainless steel kitchen sinks aren't quite as immune to ugly marks as their name suggests. Here are some solutions to various problems:

- **Rust marks** Rub the area with a drop of lighter fluid, and then clean it with non-abrasive scouring powder and water.

Red Alert

It's easy to accidentally turn on the switch that activates the garbage disposal when you really meant to flip a light switch. The resulting racket and grinding action can be startling—and even dangerous. To stay on the safe side, paint the disposal switch with some bright red nail polish so there's no mistaking which switch is which.

- **Water marks** Rub with a cloth dampened with rubbing alcohol.
- **Other marks** Rub marks with white vinegar or club soda, both of which are excellent polishers.

Lemon stain lifter

Getting that tomato sauce stain off your countertop or cabinet is easier than you think. Simply wet the stain with lemon juice, let sit for 30 minutes or so, and then sprinkle baking soda on the abrasive side of an all-purpose kitchen sponge and scrub the discolored area. Most stains will vanish, and your kitchen will smell fresher.

Sterilize your sink

Germs can hang around in your sink on microscopic food particles. To kill them off, fill a spray bottle with full-strength rubbing alcohol. After you finish washing dishes, spray the sink with alcohol and then rub it down with a clean dishtowel or paper towel.

Tea thyme for porcelain

Charming though they are, porcelain sinks are hard to clean because abrasive cleaners dull (and often scratch) porcelain surfaces. Take the gentle route and clean your sink with fresh lemon thyme tea. Place 4–5 bunches of fresh lemon thyme in a 3-gallon metal bucket and fill it with boiling water. Steep for 5–6 hours and strain. Stop up your sink, pour in the tea, and let it sit overnight. When you drain it the next morning, you'll find a gleaming white sink that smells fresh as, well, a sprig of lemon thyme.

Almost-free all-purpose cleaner

Why buy an antibacterial spray cleaner if you can make one in less than five minutes? Combine 1 cup rubbing alcohol, 1 cup water, and 1 tablespoon white vinegar in a spray bottle. Spritz on kitchen surfaces including tile and chrome, wipe off, and watch how quickly the germ-killing polish evaporates.

Dynamic grease-busting duo

The chemistry between baking soda and vinegar is so powerful that this combo can flush grease out of kitchen drains. Just pour ½ cup baking soda into a clogged drain and follow it with ½ cup white vinegar. Cover the drain for a few minutes as the chemical reaction dissolves the grease—then flush the drain with warm water. A caveat: Never use this method after trying a commercial drain cleaner; the cleaner could react with vinegar to create dangerous fumes.

Ice-cold disposal degreaser

Degrease your garbage disposal by occasionally grinding five or six ice cubes along with ½ cup baking soda. The ice congeals the grease, priming it for attack by the fast-acting sodium bicarbonate and sending it down the drain. To flush out any residue, fill the stoppered sink with 2–3 inches hot water and run the water through the disposal.

Household Superstar!
10 Nonbaking Uses for Baking Soda

1 Remove stains from plastic utensils and rubber spatulas with a baking soda paste rubbed on with a sponge or scouring pad.

2 Protect stained enamel cookware, which can be scratched by abrasive cleaners, by coating the stain with a baking soda paste—then wipe it off after an hour.

3 Add 2 tablespoons of baking soda to your dishwashing liquid to clean greasy dishes.

4 Deodorize your dishwasher by pouring in half a box of baking soda and running the empty washer through the rinse cycle.

5 Dip a damp cloth in baking soda and rub it on china to remove coffee stains.

6 Shine stainless steel by sprinkling it with baking soda and rubbing with a damp cloth.

7 Moisten grease stains on your stovetop with water, cover them with baking soda, and wipe clean with a damp cloth.

8 Clean your coffeemaker by brewing 1 quart of water mixed with ¼ cup baking soda.

9 Loosen burned-on food from cast iron skillets by adding 2 tablespoons baking soda to 1 quart water and boiling the solution for 5 minutes.

10 Remove residue from a thermos by putting in ¼ cup baking soda and 1 quart water and letting it soak overnight.

Kitchen Odor Chasers

Borax in the bin

Garbage cans are great incubators for odor-causing mold and bacteria. To fend off accumulations of these microscopic marauders, sprinkle ½ cup borax in the bottom of your garbage can and renew it with every emptying.

Cabbage as culprit

Boiled cabbage is one of the most healthful foods around, but the odor it gives off as it cooks is a major turn-off. To sweeten the air (and perk up cabbage's flavor at the same time), add half a lemon to the cooking water.

Bake a batch of brownies

There's no better natural kitchen deodorizer than a batch of baking brownies. Doesn't matter if they're homemade or out of a box, and your family will thank you for it.

Bake an air freshener

Don't buy an air freshener when you can get rid of kitchen odors at a fraction of the cost with baked lemon. Simply slice 2 lemons, put them on a foil-lined cookie sheet, and bake them in a preheated oven at 225°F for 60–90 minutes. To prolong the cleansing effect once the heat's turned off, open the oven door and leave the lemons on the rack for a few hours.

Odor-killing drain cleaner

Using salt and baking soda to unclog a drain will put an end to bad drain odors at the same time. Pour 1 cup salt into the drain followed by 1 cup baking soda. Pour a kettle full of boiling water down the drain and let all that hard-working sodium get busy.

Disposal deodorizers

Wherever food gets ground up every day, odor-causing bacteria follow, thriving in the cracks and crevices deep inside a garbage disposal. To keep unpleasant smells from wafting out of your disposal, try grinding any of these odor busters:

- Citrus peels—lemon, lime, orange, or grapefruit
- Two or three bunches of fresh mint

SPICE IN THE AIR

When kitchen air gets stale, liven it up by simmering a handful of whole cloves, 3–4 whole nutmegs, 4–5 **cinnamon sticks**, and perhaps a few **orange** or lemon **peels** in a large pot of water for an hour. But don't just pour this bubbling deodorizer down the drain! Instead, strain the cooled liquid into spray bottles and use it in the kitchen and elsewhere whenever the air could use a little freshening.

Debugging the Kitchen

Store flour and rice with bay leaves

Tiny sawtooth grain weevils, rice weevils, and other bugs can enter paper or cardboard containers of flour, rice, oatmeal, and breakfast cereal through the tiniest of cracks. Keep them at bay (so to speak) by putting a few dried bay (also known as laurel) leaves in the containers.

Freeze the buggers

Some bug eggs are in the containers before you bring your groceries home and have yet to hatch. Kill off any eggs by keeping your products in the freezer for the first day or two.

Two other bug chasers

One or two whole nutmegs buried in a sack of flour or box of rice or such will help keep weevils and other tiny invaders out. Some people claim to have successfully repelled bugs by placing sticks of spearmint gum (unwrapped) at different points on the floor of the cabinet where susceptible foodstuffs are stored.

Pop goes the weevil

If your dried beans or peas are under attack by hungry weevils, add a bit of dried hot pepper to the storage container. They'll hotfoot it out of the box or bag in a flash.

Ants hate grits

It's not that ants don't like to eat this dried-corn breakfast food; they just don't like crawling over powdery or grainy substances. When you see a line of ants on the march in your kitchen, spoon a long thin line of grits in their path and watch them beat a retreat.

make your own Flypaper

Houseflies gravitate to the kitchen because—you got it—that's where the food is. Take a cue from housekeepers of old and trap flies with flypaper, which you can easily make all by yourself.

Sticky-Icky Flypaper

Hang these sticky strips underneath top cabinets, in doorways, and from window frames. No hooks needed—just secure the string hangers with masking tape or duct tape.

> 1 brown paper grocery bag
> String
> Tape
> ⅔ cup sugar
> ⅔ cup light corn syrup
> ⅔ cup water

1. Cut the bag into strips 1½ inches wide and 1–3 feet long. Cut 5-to-6-inch pieces of string and secure them to the top of the strips with transparent tape.

2. Combine sugar, corn syrup, and water in a heavy 2-quart saucepan and bring the mixture to a boil over high heat.

3. Reduce the heat to medium and cook until the liquid thickens.

4. Use a pastry brush to coat the strips with the liquid, and then hang them wherever flies congregate.

Keep bugs out of your grains with **bay leaves!**

Spicy ant repellents

If you know where ants are entering your kitchen from the outside, sprinkle a good bit of cayenne pepper or ground cinnamon outside their door as an unmistakable "not welcome" mat. Ants have an aversion to both the powdery texture and powerful smell of these spices.

Fend off fruit flies

No need to keep the fruit bowl empty on the kitchen countertop just because these unwanted guests tend to help themselves. Send them packing with one of the following:

- **Mint or basil leaves** Scatter a few mint or basil sprigs near fresh fruit when you set it out; fruit flies hate the smell and will stay clear.

- **Rubbing alcohol** Rub a little alcohol on a counter next to a bunch of bananas or a ripening melon, tomato, or avocado.

- **Apple cider** Pour cider into a jar or bowl, and fruit flies will be drawn to the sweet-smelling liquid, only to drown.

Build nonpoisonous roach motels

Wrap the outside of an empty jelly jar with masking tape, and rub the inside of the jar with petroleum jelly. Pour in an inch of beer and top it with a few small pieces of ripe fruit and 4–5 drops of almond extract. Place the unlidded jar under the sink or anywhere else cockroaches lurk. Roaches will be drawn to the appetizing aroma, climb into the jar (the tape gives them traction), and drop inside to feast—but thanks to the slippery walls, they'll be unable to escape. To dispose of the tipsy roaches, fill the jar with hot water and flush the contents down the toilet.

Borax on high shelves

Cockroaches like to roam any high spots they can reach, so fetch a stepladder and sprinkle borax on the top of your kitchen cabinets. (Side benefit: The borax will be out of reach of children and pets.) Roaches poisoned by the borax will take it back to the nest, where their fellow roaches will start dropping like flies.

Caring for Your Fridge

Keep it clean

The surface of white refrigerators and freezers gets dirty more quickly than you'd like, especially around the handles. Even the hardware shows fingerprints and spotting. Make your fridge or freezer gleam in one of these ways:

- Scrub it with equal parts ammonia and water.
- Rub it down with club soda, which cleans and polishes at the same time.
- For a glossier finish, wash and rinse the surface, then apply car paste wax and buff it to a shine with a clean soft cloth.
- Polish any chrome trim with a cloth dipped in rubbing alcohol.

Keep a tight seal

The flexible rubber or plastic gasket framing the inside edge of your refrigerator door seals cold air in and warm air out. When cleaning your refrigerator, don't neglect it! Wipe grime off with a soft cloth dampened with rubbing alcohol and finish by rubbing the gasket with a little mineral oil to prevent cracking.

Scrub with salt

You're cramming today's groceries on a high shelf of the fridge and a small bowl of leftover sauce in the back gets wedged in at an angle and begins to leak. To get rid of the gummy mass, sprinkle it with salt. Then dip a plastic scrubber or abrasive sponge in hot water and rub the stain vigorously. Repeat until it's gone, each time wiping the area with a wet paper towel.

Litter box lesson

If cat litter can absorb the really pungent odors in Fluffy's litter box, it can certainly soak up the lesser odors that so easily arise in your fridge. Keeping a small, uncovered bowl of natural clay cat litter on a shelf of the refrigerator will block odors before they take hold.

Deodorize with a spud

A food that will absorb food odors? Indeed! To diminish refrigerator smells, peel a raw potato,

CHARCOAL BRIQUETTE ODOR EATERS

Store three or four **charcoal briquettes** in your refrigerator. Simply put them in a small mesh bag (the kind that holds supermarket onions) and stick them on a fridge shelf. After a month, refresh the briquettes by dumping them into a heavy stainless steel pot and warming them; ventilate the kitchen well while doing this. Once the briquettes are cool, put them back in the bag and return them to the fridge.

cut it in half, and place each half on a small saucer. Now place the potato halves on different shelves in the fridge. When the cut surface of a potato turns black, trim the black part away and return the potato to the fridge with its absorbent powers restored.

Lemon-fresh fridge

Mold and mildew can grab on to your refrigerator and not let go—and banishing the odors takes drastic action. Squeeze a lemon into a cup of water and throw the peel in with the mixture. Unplug the fridge and empty it (we said it was drastic!), nestling ice cream and other meltable items in a tub, sink, or ice chest filled with ice. Then, microwave the lemon water to almost boiling and place it inside the empty refrigerator.

Close the door and let the deodorizer sit for half an hour. The citrus fumes will freshen the smell and soften any food accumulations.

Remove the bowl, wash the fridge's interior, and restock it with your food and beverages.

Two ways to speed defrosting

If you have a freezer that isn't self-defrosting, you can speed defrosting to keep frozen foods from spoiling or going soft. Hasten the process by aiming a stream of hot air at the ice with a hair dryer. Another trick is to boil water in a couple of saucepans, place them in the freezer (on trivets if the floor is plastic), and close the freezer door to trap the steam. In no time at all you'll be able to pry off large slabs of ice with a dinner knife (carefully, of course).

Use your oven when defrosting

If you have a self-cleaning oven, you can use it to store frozen foods as you defrost the freezer. These ovens are so well insulated that they'll keep foods frozen for hours. Just don't turn it on!

Curiosity Corner
Salted Superstitions

In ancient times, salt was so coveted as a preservative and medicine and flavoring that it hastened the advance from nomadic to agricultural life, spurred the opening of new trade routes, and influenced religious rites and rituals in almost every culture. In the Roman Empire, salt was considered so essential that Roman soldiers were given a salarium (salt allowance) as part of their pay.

(Salarium is the origin of the word salary.)

Not surprisingly, all kinds of superstitions swirled around this precious commodity. A vial of salt worn around the neck was thought to keep evil spirits away, though vampires were repelled only by direct assaults with salt. According to Irish folklore, a bag of salt tied onto children's nightgowns kept them from being stolen by fairies in their sleep.

The best known (and still current) salt superstition is found in cultures around the world: "Spilling salt brings bad luck." And its second page: "Toss a pinch of spilled salt over the left shoulder to keep the bad luck at bay." Spirits who brought misfortune were thought to stand behind a person to the left, and a pelt of salt in the eyes would make them flee.

Hot Tips for Stove Cleaning

Keeping your stove's sides tidy

If you have crumbs, spills, and stains sticking to the sides of your stove, pick up inexpensive T-shaped plastic gaskets from a home-improvement store. Slipping them between your freestanding stove and the adjacent countertops will keep goo and gunk from sticking to the stove's sides. When gaskets get soiled (and boy, will they get soiled), simply remove them, wash them, and reinstall them.

Baked-on grates

If your stovetop grates are cast iron, and something has baked onto them, wipe them with nontoxic oven cleaner, and place them in your oven the next time you self-clean it. Remove and wipe clean.

Salt a grease spill while cooking

If grease spills over in your oven while you're roasting meat, sprinkle salt over the grease before it has a chance to bake on. Close the oven door and let the cooking continue. By cleanup time, the spill will have transformed itself into an easily removed pile of ash.

A poultice for broiler pans

Broiler pans with burned-on food are a major pain in the neck to clean. To make the job less of a chore, heat the pan and sprinkle laundry detergent over the affected area. Now cover the detergent with wet paper towels, wait 15 minutes, remove the towels, and you'll see how much easier it is to scrape and scrub the gunk off.

In-the-bag rack cleaning

A typical way to wash a dirty oven rack is to submerge it in soapy water in the bathtub to loosen the grime—but who wants to clean a greasy tub afterward? Instead, put the rack in a large, heavy-duty plastic trash bag and add ⅓ cup dishwashing liquid, 1 cup white vinegar, and enough hot water to almost fill the bag. Seal the bag and place it in a bathtub full of warm water for an hour. Then remove the rack from the bag and scrub, rinse, and air-dry.

CLEAN A GAS RANGE WITH AN ICE SCRAPER

If you can't budge baked-on food on your stove, turn off all the burners and pilot lights, spray the area with WD-40, and let it sink in. After a few minutes, scrape the mess off the stove using a **plastic ice scraper**. Then wash the burner in hot soapy water and wipe it dry with a dish towel.

Ease a rack's slide

When you clean your oven racks, don't forget to clean the oven wall ridges they slide in and out on. Scrub with soap-filled steel wool pads, rinse off the soap and dry the ridges, then wipe them with vegetable oil to keep the racks gliding smoothly.

A scrub for exhaust filters

Once a month, take the filter off the hood above your stove and spray it all over with WD-40. After an hour, scrub with a toothbrush and then put it in the dishwasher for a final cleaning.

Microwave cleanup shortcut

The quickest way to clean a microwave oven is to throw a handful of wet paper towels inside and run it on High for 3–5 minutes. You don't need a science lesson to know that the steam from the towels will soften the grime. Once the towels cool down, use them to wipe the oven's interior.

Carpet a dirty microwave floor with baking soda

To remove cooked-on spills from the floor or turntable of a microwave, make a paste of 2 parts baking soda to 1 part water and apply it to the hardened goop. After 5–6 minutes, wipe up the baking soda with a wet sponge or cloth and remove any residue with a paper towel.

Make a mini steam bath

The easiest way to melt the nasty gunk that accumulates on the walls of your microwave (and ours) is to fill a heatproof glass bowl with water, nuke on High for 2 minutes, don't open the door for another 2 minutes, and then wipe with a soft rag. The steam will have reconstituted the icky, caked-on muck, making it a cinch to wipe off.

What's the Story?
The Invention of the Microwave Oven

Like a number of other machines, medicines, and modern necessities, microwave ovens were invented by accident. In 1945, a self-educated Raytheon company engineer named Percy Spencer was visiting the lab where magnetrons were being tested (magnetrons are the power tubes of radar sets). As he stood next to one of the machines, he suddenly felt the chocolate peanut bar in his pocket begin to melt.

His curiosity piqued, Spencer sent an assistant out for a bottle of popcorn kernels—and when he held the kernels near a magnetron, popcorn kernels exploded all over the lab. The next morning, Spencer brought in a kettle, cut a hole in the side, and put in an uncooked egg. He then moved a magnetron next to the kettle and switched it on. A skeptical engineer peeked into the hole just in time to catch a face full of egg; the egg burst because the yolk cooked faster than the egg white.

Spencer had discovered that food can be cooked with high-frequency radio waves, and in 1946 he patented the Radar Range, an oven the size of a refrigerator and costing $3,000 (almost $35,000 in today's money). In the years that followed, the concept was refined, and rare is the modern home, office, or restaurant that isn't equipped with the machine that revolutionized the way we cook.

Dishwashers (Hands, Too!)

Wash your dishwasher

After washing load after load of greasy dishes, your dishwasher gets dirty, and its interior gets coated with grease that will show up as film on plates and glassware. Assuming you do NOT have a septic tank, you can keep your dishes film-free by taking the two simple steps below. (You may have to repeat the process once or twice to make sure the washer's innards have been cleansed of all grease.)

- Pour 1 cup liquid bleach in a bowl and place on the bottom rack of the dishwasher. Then run the machine on the wash setting only.
- With the first washing complete, open the washer and pour a cup of vinegar into the same bowl and run the machine through a full cycle.

Clip dishwasher spray-arm debris

If your dishwasher seems to have fallen down on the job lately, the spray arms could be clogged with mineral deposits or other debris. Open the washer and take a peek at the top of the three-pronged spray arms to see if the holes look clogged (in most washers, one three-pronged spray arm sits under the top rack and the second arm sits on the dishwasher floor). Test for clogging by sticking a wooden toothpick into one of the holes; if it shows signs of dirt when pulled out, the holes need cleaning.

Unfasten the clips or screws holding the spray arms in place and put the arms in the kitchen sink. Then unbend a paper clip and insert the long end into each spray hole, moving it around to dislodge the blockage. Finish the job by rinsing the spray arms under the faucet and fastening them back in their proper places. Dishwasher back up to speed!

A cleansing (and colorful) drink

After washing grease and miniscule food remains off plates and pots and pans over and over again, a dishwasher can begin to take on an unpleasant odor. To freshen it up, put some powdered orange or lemon drink mix into the detergent dispenser (same amount as your dishwasher detergent) and run the washer through a full cycle. This wacky-but-wise cleaning trick will not only degrease the dishwasher but also help remove rust stains.

Get a jump on odors

A way to keep odors out of your dishwasher in the first place? Just add ½ cup lemon juice to the detergent receptacle each time you use the machine.

Give it the old-fashioned scrub

Save a few bucks on your electric bill and get super-clean dishes in the process. Fill up your sink with warm water, add a few squirts of natural dish soap, pull on your rubber gloves, and have at it. If your dishes are really a mess, let them soak for 10 minutes in lemon juice-infused hot water; if they're still sticky, sprinkle them with kosher salt and dish soap, before rinsing them until they're squeaky clean.

Washing Dishes by Hand

Who says washing dishes in the sink is drudgery? Only people who don't appreciate the simple satisfaction of doing things the old-fashioned way, if only occasionally. Some people see standing over the sink washing dishes as much-welcome "quiet time," ideal for thinking or perhaps listening to music or talk radio. And there's something to be said for watching that beautiful china plate sparkle like new as you move it from the sink to the dish rack.

There's surely no need to tell you how to wash dishes, but we're happy to offer three hints that may be new to you:

Sanitize with a short soak.
If you're so germ-shy that even antibacterial dishwashing liquid isn't enough to put your mind at ease, soak washed dishes in a sink in a solution of 1 tablespoon household bleach to 1 gallon water. After 5 minutes, rinse well with fresh water and air-dry.

Keep rubber-gloved hands odor free.
Unlined rubber gloves may leave an odor reminiscent of auto tires on your hands. How to prevent it? Rub lotion on your hands before slipping on the gloves. No rubbery smell and a hand moisturizing treatment as you wash!

Clear up cloudy glass.
Ovenproof casserole dishes of clear glass may be marred with large cloudy spots even though they're clean as a whistle. Eggs, milk, cheese, and other proteins are the culprits, and none can stand up to white vinegar. All removal takes is rubbing the spots with a vinegar-soaked sponge or cleaning cloth.

About Those Small Appliances

De-bitter your coffee grinder with rice

When you grind your own coffee beans, it's almost impossible to brush all of the residue out of the grinder when you're done—and accumulated residue can make coffee taste bitter. To get rid of the residue, run a cup of raw white rice through the grinder once every month. The rice will clean the grinder and sharpen the blades at the same time.

Hold the spices

If you ever use your coffee grinder to grind spices, be sure to clean all of the remnants out of the grinder before switching back to coffee beans. How to go about it? By grinding two or three slices of cut-up, plain white bread in the machine.

Grind bread, clean meat grinder

Before cleaning a meat grinder, run a piece of bread through it to clean fatty meat particles out of the feed screw. A regular washup of the parts is rarely enough to get the feed screw truly clean.

Purge coffee stains from a carafe

Over time, caffeine will discolor the glass carafe of your automatic coffeemaker, but you can easily make it look like new. Here's how:

1. Fill a quarter of the carafe with water.
2. Cut a lemon into 4 wedges, squeeze the juice of 2 of them into the water, and drop all 4 lemon wedges into the carafe.

3. Add 2 tablespoons salt and swirl the carafe around for 2–3 minutes.
4. Empty the carafe and scrub the inside with soapy water. Rinse and dry and return the crystal-clear carafe to its base.

Clean your toaster with a toothbrush

If your toaster is clogged with hard-to-reach crumbs, unplug it and loosen the crumbs with a small paintbrush or soft toothbrush. Avoid damaging the machine's heating elements by brushing very lightly. Once you've broken the stubborn crumbs apart, turn the toaster upside down, hold it over the kitchen sink, and gently shake out the debris.

Clean your toaster oven window

If the window of your toaster oven gets so caked with grime that you can barely see inside, try one of following fixes:

- Open the oven door and the spray the glass with a solution of 2 parts hydrogen peroxide, 2 parts white vinegar, and 1 part dishwashing liquid. Let stand for half an hour.
- Wipe the window with household ammonia and let stand for 20–30 minutes.

Wipe off either substance with paper towels. If any residue remains, scrape it off with a plastic (not metal) windshield scraper. Finally, clean the oven window with a spray of vinegar or commercial glass cleaner.

Give uncooked **rice** a whirl in your coffee grinder to clean it!

Melted plastic on your toaster?

If you inadvertently leave a plastic bag or plastic wrap so close to a toaster that it touches the metal surface, the plastic will melt onto it when you toast bread—and it won't come off with normal washing. To get rid of it, let the toaster cool and try one of these removal methods.

- Rub the melted plastic vigorously with a damp sponge coated with baking soda.

- Coat the blob with petroleum jelly and then toast a slice of bread. The heated jelly will soften the plastic and make it easier to wipe off with a soft cloth. When the toaster cools, scrub away residue with baking soda and a damp sponge.

- Spray the plastic with WD-40 and let it soak in for a few minutes. Then wipe the goop off with a damp cloth.

Easy blender cleaning

Sure, you always flush out the blender jar under the kitchen sink faucet, and sometimes you even give it a proper washing. But that's hardly enough to keep it hygienically correct. Pour 1 cup water and ¼ cup vinegar into the jar and add a squirt of dishwashing liquid. Put on the jar top and blend the mixture for 1 minute. Now rinse the jar and wipe it dry, and your blender will be ready to whir germ-free.

Hose out stuck food

If food gets lodged in your food processor or blender and trying to remove it is driving you nuts, take the machine's bowl or jar outside—no, not to smash it with a sledgehammer, but to direct a strong stream of water from your garden hose to the gummed-up works. Take a newspaper with you and set the machine on it so it won't get soiled.

Keep appliances dust-free

Sometimes it seems that dust gathers more quickly on countertop appliances than any-where. If this happens to you, cover the appliances with dish towels or—if you're always looking for still one more way to use panty hose—a stocking leg cut to size.

Brush away espresso

If you're a fan of espresso, you're also familiar with how finely ground Italy's favorite coffee is. To keep it from clogging up the filter screen on your espresso maker, scrub the screen gently after each use with a soft toothbrush. If any bits remain, remove them with a straight pin.

Rack it up to prevent toaster oven fires

One of the leading causes of toaster oven fires is the greasy, grimy rack (and you know you have one, same as us). Think about it: the baked cheese dripped cheddar, which burned. The cinnamon bun dripped sugar, which also burned. Maybe the glob dripped onto the heating element and set off a spark. What to do? The next time you clean your (real) oven, wipe the toaster oven racks down with non-toxic oven cleaner and simply place them inside your oven to be cleaned.

De-pulp your juicer

It's easy to forget that electric juicers are traps for all manner of fruit (and therefore, food) particles. Keep it clean as a whistle to prevent bacteria buildup (and illness!) by cleaning it thoroughly: disassemble it, wipe out the pulp and discard it, and fill your kitchen sink with hot, soapy water. Soak everything but the motor casing for 10 minutes, remove the pieces from the sink, and scrub with a soft toothbrush. Dry well, reassemble, and juice for all you're worth!

Household Superstar!

9 Practical Kitchen Uses for Vinegar

1 To clean your refrigerator, wipe it inside and out with a 50/50 mixture of white vinegar and water (and don't forget the door gasket).

2 Prevent mildew in the fridge's vegetable bins by washing them with full-strength vinegar.

3 Steam clean your microwave oven's interior by putting a bowl with ¼ cup vinegar and 1 cup water inside and microwaving it on High for 5 minutes.

4 Disinfect a wooden cutting board by wiping it with full-strength white vinegar after each use.

5 Sanitize and deodorize your garbage disposal by grinding ice cubes made with half vinegar, half water.

6 To make drinking glasses gleam, add 2 tablespoons vinegar to your dishwasher as the rinse cycle begins.

7 Remove coffee stains from china cups by scrubbing them with equal parts vinegar and salt.

8 Clean a coffeemaker by running 2 cups vinegar and 1 cup water through a brewing cycle (hold the coffee!).

9 Eliminate mineral deposits in a teakettle by boiling 3 cups full-strength white vinegar in it for 5 minutes, then letting it sit overnight.

Cleaning Cookware

Choice cast iron cleaners

Both coarse salt and borax (sodium borate) are more cast iron–friendly than dishwashing detergents, so use either to get burned food off a treasured pan that may have been passed down from your grandmother. Just sprinkle the crystals into the pan and scrub with a wet sponge or paper towel. Then rinse with fresh cold water and dry immediately (cast iron is quick to rust).

A cast iron DO

Rub vegetable oil on the inside of a cast iron skillet to keep it seasoned—and do it after each wash and any other time you please.

A cast iron DON'T

Soaking a cast iron skillet in soapy water can deplete the fat that seeps into the porous surface and seasons the skillet—and an unseasoned skillet is a recipe for frustration. You'll be contending with food that sticks and burns and seems almost impossible to clean off.

Scrub away scorched milk

Yikes! You left the milk you were heating on the burner too long, and it began to simmer and fill the air with a scorching smell. How to get rid of it? Wet the bottom of the pan and sprinkle it with salt. Let the salt sit for about 10 minutes and then wash the pan as you usually do. Cleaned pot, vanished odor.

Boil burned-on food

If burned food won't come off a pot, fill the pot with water and add a squirt of dishwashing liquid and 1 tablespoon salt. Bring the water to a boil and then turn off the heat. After about 15 minutes, discard the mixture and use a plastic scraper or scrubber to remove the loosened gunk.

Two aluminum restorers

When aluminum pots and pans become discolored after extended use, revive the luster with either cream of tartar or vinegar and then wash and dry as usual.

- **Cream of tartar** Fill the pan with hot water and add cream of tartar (2 tablespoons powder to 1 quart water). Bring to a boil, then reduce heat and let the mixture simmer for 10 minutes.
- **Vinegar** Combine equal parts white vinegar and water in the pan and simmer for 10–12 minutes.

Note: Avoid using alkaline cleaners like baking soda and bleach on aluminum, which may discolor it even more.

Rub out rust with a potato

With regular use, metal pie pans can rust. To get rid of rust, cut a potato in half, dip the exposed flesh into scouring powder, and rub the rust with your spud "sponge."

Toothpaste for stainless cookware

Fingerprints all over your nice, sparkling new stainless cookware? No problem? Dampen it with lukewarm water, apply an inch of low-abrasion toothpaste, and brush away those unsightly marks. Rinse, dry, and ogle your new shiny cookware again.

Four Ways to Clean Copper Pots

Copper cookware is beautiful—and it darn well should be, considering what it costs. To keep it looking like all it's worth, try these out-of-the-ordinary cleansers.

1
Salt and vinegar

Fill a spray bottle with vinegar and 3 tablespoons salt, shake until the salt dissolves, and give the copper a good spray. Let the pots sit for 10–12 minutes and then scrub them clean.

2
Lemon juice and cream of tartar

Mix these into a paste that's thin enough to spread but thick enough to cling. Apply to copperware with a clean cloth, and let it stand for 5 minutes before washing with warm water.

3
Worcestershire sauce

Yep, you heard right. Soak a sponge with the sauce and rub it over the surface of copper pots and pans. Let it sit 1–2 minutes and then wipe clean. Rinse well and dry.

4
Half a lemon and salt

If you find stubborn stains on your copperware, dip lemon halves in salt and rub the stains away.

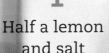

Cleaning China, Glassware, and Utensils

No-spots glassware

To prevent spotting on glass pitchers, candlesticks, drinking glasses, and any other everyday or special occasion glassware, soak a piece for 3–4 minutes in a bath of 2 gallons water and ½ cup white vinegar. Shake off any water droplets and then dry and polish the piece with a clean soft cloth.

Protect a teapot

When you store your treasured china teapot at the back of a cabinet for a long time, chances are it will be banged by the dishes up front at some point. To protect the spout, slip a toilet paper tube over it and secure the tube with masking tape. Or sheathe the spout with the thumb from an old leather glove or thick mitten. You'll also want to use one of these sheathes when you're packing the teapot for a move.

Remove invisible film

Though drinking glasses, mugs, and everyday plates and bowls might look clean after a washing, they could still be covered with a thin film of grease, invisible to the naked eye. See for yourself by making a thin paste of baking soda and water, dipping a sponge into it, and rubbing the glass or china surface well. Rinse, dry with a soft cloth, and your dishes may sparkle as never before and even feel different to the touch.

Tea for crystal

If residue dries inside a crystal pitcher that won't tolerate hard scrubbing without being scratched, fill it with a mixture of 2 parts strong black tea and 1 part white vinegar. After it sits overnight, discard the solution and wash the pitcher with a soft cloth dipped in soapy water.

Cleaning etched crystal

If you have deeply etched crystal, use an old-fashioned shaving brush or large make-up brush to work soapy water into the ridges and crevices at cleaning time. These brushes are rigid enough to root out dirt without scratching the crystal. To rinse, hold the piece under running water.

Smooth out nicks and scratches

If you notice a small nick on the edge of a drinking glass, use an emery board to smooth it out. To eliminate a scratch on a glass, rub it out with non-gel white toothpaste on a soft cloth, then rinse. The mildly abrasive toothpaste will smooth the glass just enough to make the scratch invisible.

Despotting stainless

If you think that vinegar and a paper towel are all you need to rub spots off stainless steel knives, forks, and spoons, guess again! The spots will come clean only if you dip the vinegar-soaked paper towel into a saucer of baking soda. After rubbing off the spots, wash the utensils as you usually do and dry them thoroughly right away.

Whiten bone handles

In time, bone-handled knives begin to yellow. Unless you love the antiqued look, wrap a yellowed handle in a piece of flannel moistened with hydrogen peroxide. Let it sit for a day or so, then unwrap. Rinse and dry a knife, and the handle will be good as new.

Easy waxing for wood

To keep your wooden spoons and salad sets looking like new, wash and dry them and then rub them down with wax paper. The thin coating of wax will help keep wood from drying out.

Scrub that butcher block

Putting your wooden cutting board in the dishwasher is a no-no, as is letting it soak in your sink. That said, keep it clean and you'll avoid bacterial mishaps and the not-so-pleasant illnesses that are related to them. To clean your wooden cutting board, scrub it well with a lightly-abrasive cleansing powder and a nylon scrubbing pad, and wipe it down with hot, soapy water. Rinse, dry it well, and be safe.

Wrap silver in plastic

When putting away silverware, wrap each utensil in two layers of plastic wrap to shut out air. Exposure to air causes the oxidation that tarnishes silver.

Oil Stein, Drink Brew

So you bought a colorful beer stein on your trip to Germany or to one of the faux German villages so often found in alpine areas here and there. You even occasionally drink from it instead of just letting it gather dust on the mantelpiece. But there's trouble in Löwenbräu City: The stein's lid will barely budge when you exert thumb pressure. What a pickle!

Never fear. Simply spray the lid hinge with WD-40 and let it sit for 12–15 minutes. Then wipe off the oil with a soft cloth and give the stein a good washing. Now get out the bratwurst and Muenster cheese and toast your quick fix with an easy-to-down cool one.

NO SMOKING (STAINS) ALLOWED

When you throw a party and you're tolerant enough to let smoking guests puff away on the patio, you may find cigarette stains on a piece of china as you collect all of the post-party dishes. To make short work of the stains, dip the **cork from a wine bottle** into salt and use it to scour away the tobacco tar.

Odds 'n' Ends

Shake it freely

Salt and pepper shakers tend to clog up in humid whether. To keep the moisture out of your salt, add a few grains of raw rice or some crumbled saltine crackers to the shaker. To keep ground black pepper from clogging, add a few black or white peppercorns.

Keep brown sugar from hardening

Prevent brown sugar from turning into a brick by putting either a few dried prunes or a 1-by-3-inch strip of orange peel in the box. Then tape the box closed and store it in a sealed plastic bag—preferably in the freezer.

Keep olive oil fresh

Unless you use olive oil in large quantities, try this trick to make your supply last: add a drop of sugar to the bottle and it will stay fresher longer. And keep it away from your stove, where the heat will turn it rancid.

Storing things within things

If your kitchen storage space is sparse, store items in containers you rarely use. One neglected container is the picnic cooler that sees use only in the warm months. Likewise, that stockpot in the back of the cabinet could hold napkins and other items bought in quantity at your local warehouse store.

Number your containers

If you have lots of plastic containers, you know how frustrating it can be to match them to their lids. A simple solution? Label both container and lid with a number. It's much easier to match a 2 with a 2 or a 5 with a 5 than repeatedly trying lids on for size.

Tame your stray grocery bags with a *pants hanger!*

Hang paper bags

If you're a natural-born hoarder but have no place to store all those brown paper bags you've brought home from the supermarket, clamp them together with an old pants hanger and hang them from a hook on the pantry or mud-room door.

Clean that can opener

To loosen the grime on an electric or manual can opener, spray the blade and gears with WD-40 and let it sit for 6–8 minutes. Then brush away the grime with an old hard-bristle toothbrush. You could also tackle the blade and gears with a toothbrush dipped in hot soapy water—the soap of choice being antibacterial dishwashing liquid.

Storing a thermos

Empty thermoses tucked away in cabinets tend to take on a sour smell, but you can guard against odors after washing and drying a just-used thermos:

- Drop a few denture cleaning tablets into the thermos and fill it with water. Let it sit for an hour or so, then wash, rinse, and dry.

- Put a teaspoon of sugar in the thermos and screw the lid on tightly. The sugar will absorb unwanted odors.

Keep your board from sliding

To keep your cutting board from slip-sliding away while you're trying to chop on it, try this simple trick: dampen a small piece of paper towel and place it between the bottom of the board and the countertop. Press down, and your board won't budge.

Cleaning cutting boards

Freshen both the look and smell or a stained or greasy cutting board by sprinkling it with salt

Sanitizing Kitchen Sponges

When a sponge starts to smell like a dead animal, it's time to throw it away. What's not so obvious is that even slightly odoriferous sponges have seen their day. These innocent-looking germ hotbeds can quickly become one of the filthiest things in your kitchen—the reason you should sanitize seemingly okay sponges every three or four days at the very least. Two courses of action:

- Soak a sponge overnight in a mixture of 1 cup hot water, ½ cup white vinegar, and 3 tablespoons salt. The next day, rinse and squeeze the sponge several times to rid it of all of the cleaning liquid.

- Put a wet sponge (emphasis on wet) in the microwave and heat it on High for 2 minutes. Stay there until the microwave beeps because there's a chance (though an extremely slight one) that the sponge could burst into flames.

and rubbing the board with the cut side of half a lemon. If a wooden cutting board won't come clean, try sanding the entire surface with very fine-grit sandpaper (160–240), pressing lightly. When the board is smooth, coat it with mineral oil or olive oil to keep the wood from drying and to give the board a nice sheen.

Keeping garlic fresher longer

The papery peel from fresh garlic does a lot more than cover it; left in the canister in which you store your garlic (on your countertop, not your fridge please), it releases enzymes which help keep your garlic fresher for longer. So after you peel a clove, put the skin back in the storage container with the rest of the bulb. Amazing!

Chapter Three

Creative Housekeeping

The miraculous housecleaning products found on store shelves today—everything from labor-saving devices like self-propelling vacuum cleaners to flashy washing machines—are astonishing in their breadth.

But, some of our favorite twenty-first century housecleaning methods were tried and true hundreds of years ago: salt, tea, vinegar, lemon, and any number of other all-natural items cut through grime just as well now as they did in days long past.

Lifting grease off wallpaper with a slice of bread, polishing bronze with a wedge of lemon, scattering tea leaves on the floor before sweeping—such simple techniques are timeless. This isn't to say, of course, that modern science hasn't advanced housekeeping in ways that make it infinitely easier. Still, supplementing commercial products with the no-nonsense cleaning and laundering methods found in the coming pages is more than worthwhile. As you try them, you'll discover the pleasures of self-sufficiency and spare your pocketbook in the bargain.

Polish your silver with *banana peels!*

Cleaning Floors and Walls

Wipe scuffs off hardwood floors

Head into the bathroom to arm yourself with the tools to remove scuff marks. First, try squeezing a little toothpaste (the non-gel, non-whitening kind) onto an old toothbrush, scrub the marks gently, and wipe up the paste with a damp cloth. If that doesn't do the job, dab some baby oil or petroleum jelly onto a dry cloth and rub the mark, then remove any residue with a rag or paper towel.

Protect floors when rearranging furniture

Need to move heavy furniture out of the way to clean? Rearranging the living room for a big party? Protect your precious hardwood floors—and save yourself the trouble of dealing with scratches later—by pulling heavy socks over furniture legs and securing them with masking tape. This trick will also make it easier to push heavy furniture around. For everyday floor protection, consider putting adhesive bandages or moleskin patches on the bottom of furniture legs. If you have a rocking chair, affix a long strip of masking tape to the bottom of each rocker to help keep hardwood floors unmarred.

Take down waxy buildup

If you wax a vinyl or linoleum floor, you know all too well how wax builds up over time. Here are two easy ways to remove it:

- **Club soda for vinyl** Working in sections, pour a little club soda onto a vinyl floor and scrub it with the abrasive side of a kitchen sponge. Let the soda sit for

The Dirt on Garage (and Basement) Floors

They're often the least thought-of floors in (and out) of the house, but garage and unfinished basement floors take a lot of hard knocks, on a daily basis. Never mind your car: if you store your lawn mower, leaf blower, or string trimmer in this space, you're bound to experience all manner of oil and grease spills here. And if your floor is made from porous, unsealed cement—and it probably is—the surface will absorb odors like a brand-new sponge. The simplest way to remove odors is to head to the nearest pet supply shop, and pick up a large pail of non-clumping kitty litter.

1. Blot any oil or grease from the surface with newspaper; the floor should be fairly dry.

2. Spread a healthy amount of kitty litter on the stain, and using a broom, sweep it over the area until it's covered.

3. Let stand for 24 hours, and sweep or vacuum up the litter. Magic!

5 minutes, then wipe up the loosened wax with a wad of cheesecloth or panty hose.

- **Rubbing alcohol for linoleum** Mop a linoleum floor with a solution of 3 cups water to 1 cup rubbing alcohol. Use a sponge mop to scrub it in well, then rinse it thoroughly.

Buff that scuff with *toothpaste!*

Liquidate heel marks on vinyl

Vinyl floors are highly susceptible to heel marks, especially from rubber heels. An easy way to wipe the marks off? Just spray them with WD-40, let sit for 5–6 minutes, and then rub the marks with a soft cloth.

Vinegar for tile and linoleum

These materials are practical choices for flooring in kitchens, bathrooms, and mudrooms—all of which receive some of the most punishing wear in the house. Keep your frequent cleanups of these areas simple by mopping with a solution of ½ cup white vinegar to 1 gallon warm water.

A clean sweep with tea

Rural Japanese housekeepers traditionally strewed still-damp tea leaves over the floor before sweeping—and some no doubt still do. Dust and dirt cling to leaves and are easier to push into a dust pan. You can then throw the contents into a garden bed or compost pile.

MORE VINEGAR FOR STONE AND BRICK

These tough flooring materials can stand a larger dose of **acidic vinegar**, so scrub stone or brick floors with a solution of 1 cup vinegar in 1 gallon water. The operative word is "scrub," since the most effective way to clean is to get down on your hands and knees and work with a stiff scrub brush.

(Talk about an eco-friendly cleanser!) Just don't use tea leaves on unbleached wood or carpeting, since tea may stain.

Erasing crayon marks from walls

Junior may be a real Rembrandt, but even so, you probably don't want him defacing your walls with crayons. Try these techniques to clean up surprise murals.

- Lightly rub the area with a clean, dry fabric softener sheet.
- Rub vigorously with a clean art-gum eraser—or ask your young artist do it.
- Squirt shaving cream on the markings and scrub with a toothbrush or a scrub brush.
- Soften the markings with a hair dryer and wipe them off with a cloth moistened with a little baby oil.

Cleaning wood-paneled walls

Most wood paneling needs only a good dusting every once in a while, but you can give it a more thorough cleaning with a simple homemade solution—one best applied with panty hose, whose texture is perfect for abrasive yet gentle scrubbings. Combine 2 cups water, 1 cup white vinegar, and ¼ cup lemon juice in a pail and mix well. Dip a handful of wadded panty hose in the solution and wipe the paneling, working from the bottom of the wall upward so you won't have to deal with drips.

Wallpaper washups

How can you restore luster to dingy washable wallpaper? First fill a pail with 1 quart water and mix in ½ teaspoon dishwashing liquid. Then dip a soft cloth in the liquid and wring it out until no excess water remains. Gently rub the wallpaper with the cloth and blot it dry with a lint-free towel.

make your own
Floor Cleaner

Clean a hardwood floor with herbal tea? You bet, as long as it's combined with a few other ingredients. The tannic acid in some herbs—in this case, peppermint—attack dirt without damaging the floor finish. As with any mopping, wring the mop several times as you clean; letting the floor get too wet could warp the floorboards.

Pep-It-Up Floor Wash

To make the peppermint tea good and strong, use 6 tea bags to 1 quart water and let the tea steep for at least 2–3 hours.

> 1 quart water
> 6 peppermint tea bags
> 1 quart white vinegar
> 2 tablespoons baby oil
> 1 teaspoon dishwashing liquid

1. In a large saucepan, boil 1 quart water, remove from heat, and add 6 peppermint tea bags. Let steep 2 hours.

2. Pour tea in a mop pail and add vinegar, baby oil, and dishwashing liquid. Stir with a large kitchen spoon to mix.

3. Dip a clean mop into the solution, wring or squeeze it out, and mop away.

If wallpaper is soiled with a greasy stain, try one of these remedies:

- Brush talcum powder onto the stain, let sit for at least half an hour, and then brush it off; repeat as necessary.
- Fold a brown paper bag and hold it over the stain. Press a warm iron to the spot so that the grease is drawn into the paper. Repeat as necessary until the spot is gone, repositioning the bag each time.

Caring for Carpets

Baby your carpet

Cooking fumes, cigarette and cigar smoke, and other odors can cling to carpeting and make your house smell musty. When a little freshening is in order, spread a liberal coating of baby powder over the carpet using a flour sifter. Leave the powder in place for a few hours or overnight, then vacuum it up. Baking soda will do the job, too, though you may want to throw in a bit of ground cinnamon or nutmeg to sweeten its smell (if you have a darker carpet).

Steam away furniture footprints

When you move a piece of furniture in a carpeted room, its footprints stay behind. The tools to raise the crushed fibers? Your iron and a fork. Put the iron on the steam setting and hold it about ¼ inch above the carpet, then fluff out the steamed fibers with the fork tines.

Inexpensive homemade carpet cleaner

Before spending money on commercial carpet-cleaning solutions, mix 1 part white vinegar to 10 parts hot water, or if you choose, ½ cup household ammonia in 2 cups hot water. Use either in a carpet-cleaning machine or apply with a scrub brush and elbow grease. Rinse the cleaned carpet with a damp cloth. To help dissipate any lingering odors, open your windows and, if necessary, place an oscillating fan in the room.

It's all in the alum

Alum, or potassium aluminum sulfate, does a great job cleaning carpet when combined with water and vinegar. (You can find alum in pharmacies and some supermarkets.) To make your own cleaner, pour 2 gallons hot water into a

Choose Your Rug Wisely

It happens all the time: that stunning rug calls out to you at the store, and you plunk down a pretty penny for it, imagining that those luscious golds and reds and creams will lighten up your living room or den (and they probably will). You bring it home, put it down, and you were right: it's *gorgeous!* Unfortunately, Fluffy and Fido are *just* as drawn to it as you are, and like a big vomit magnet, it seems to attract your furry friends at the precise moment that they need to hack up a hairball or barf up a biscuit. (Sound familiar? It's remarkable!) Remember this the next time you go rug or carpet shopping, and plan accordingly. You'll still have to clean it, but your stain woes will be much less serious if you don't buy that light-colored rug of your dreams!

large pail and add 2 cups alum, 1 cup white vinegar, and ¾ cup cinnamon tea (for scent). Now dip a sponge mop into the solution, squeeze out the excess, and mop one section of

Peanut Butter to the Rescue

Peanut butter as a carpet cleaner? It's a nutty idea, but nutty in a *good* way. Peanut butter helps remove chewing gum from a carpet.

First, heat the area with a hair dryer to loosen the gum. Press the area gently with a plastic bag, which should lift at least some of the gum; you could also try scraping it up with a plastic spatula. Some gum will remain in the carpet, which is where the peanut butter comes in: Its natural oils help the carpet fibers detach from the gum.

Rub a small dollop of peanut butter into the spot, let it sit for 5 minutes, and then wipe it up with a damp cloth. Now dab the spot with warm water mixed with 1 teaspoon dishwashing liquid. The final step? Have a little "chat" with the family member whom you suspect put you to so much trouble.

carpet at a time. Be sure to rinse the mop in fresh water after each cleaning as you work your way around the room.

Clean up paint spills with vinegar

Don't waste time crying over spilt paint on your carpet. Instead, spring into action before it sets: mix 1½ teaspoons vinegar and 1½ teaspoons laundry detergent into 2 cups warm water. Now sponge away the paint (a task that takes time and a lot of elbow grease), and rinse with cold water. If you're lucky, what might have been an unwelcome (and permanent) decorating touch will be gone.

Beat a rug

Dust and dander collect daily on (and in) area rugs, so shake 'em out the old-fashioned way: Hang the rug over a rail or taut clothesline and beat it. Your beater? A tennis racquet.

Flip the pricey ones

Did Fido relieve himself on your priceless Peshawar that you inherited from Aunt Mabel? No need to cry! Scoop up the mess, turn the rug over, place a bucket under the offending spot, and pour water—repeatedly—through the underside of the stain and into the bucket until the spot is gone. This will clean the delicate fibers without the need for scrubbing.

Baby it!

Yet another great use for mild baby wipes is as a simple carpet stain cleaner. Blot up a spill with a damp (but not soaking wet) baby wipe. This will lift out the stain before it sets.

Shaving cream to the rescue

To clean a stain that hasn't yet set, squirt non-gel shaving cream directly onto the stain and wipe clean with a damp rag or sponge.

Club soda with a twist

Every waitress and bartender knows how reliable a stain remover club soda is. To use it on a stained carpet, pour it onto the stain, leave it for 3 minutes, and dab it up with a paper towel or sponge.

Ammonia reliever

To clean tougher stains, mix 1 cup household ammonia in ½ gallon warm water, sponge it onto the stain, and dab it until the stain disappears.

Clobbering Common Carpet Stains

Below are treatments for five common carpet stains—treatments that work on upholstery as well. Your follow-up after removing as much of the stain as you can is to rinse the wet spot with warm water, then lay a heavy cloth towel or several layers of paper towels on top. Weigh this blotter down with heavy books or pots and pans and leave it in place until the treated spot dries.

Red wine

Liberally pour salt onto the stain and dab with a cloth dipped in club soda. Or blot the spill with a paper towel, pour a little white wine onto the stain, and scrub with a damp cloth. If neither method works, mix 1 teaspoon dishwashing liquid with 1 cup warm water and pour a little onto the stain; then blot the stain with a paper towel and repeat with a solution of ⅓ cup white vinegar and ⅔ cup water.

Fruit and fruit juice

Pick up any solid pieces of fruit, then stir 1 tablespoon laundry detergent and 1½ tablespoons white vinegar into 2 cups water. Work the solution into the stain and blot.

Grease or oil

Accidentally drop that family-size bucket of takeout fried chicken on the den carpet? Sprinkle the grease spots liberally with cornmeal or cornstarch, let sit for several hours, and vacuum it up. Or work shaving cream into the stains, let it dry, and rub it off with a damp soft cloth.

Coffee and tea

Choose one of these three methods and act fast. Pour club soda liberally onto the stain and blot, repeating as necessary. Or blot with a solution of equal parts white vinegar and water. Or beat an egg yolk, rub it into the stain, and blot it.

Ketchup

Jump right on this one because once a ketchup stain sets, it won't come out (ever). Grab the salt and sprinkle it over the spill, let sit for a few minutes, and vacuum. Sponge up any residue and continue salting and vacuuming until the stain is completely gone.

Sprucing Up Furniture

Double-duty dusting formula

Here's a duster that's also good for moisturizing dry wood. In a teacup, mix ¼ cup linseed oil with 1 teaspoon lemon balm tea. Dip your dusting cloth into the mixture (soaking up only a small amount at a time) and rub it vigorously into the wooden surface to be cleaned. Use a soft clean cloth to wipe away any residue.

Removing stuck-on candle wax

If your candlelight dinner party ended with hot wax dripped onto your nice mahogany table, here's how to remove it without scratching the wood. Put a few ice cubes in a plastic bag and rest the bag on the wax until it becomes brittle. Then gently lift the wax with the edge of a spatula or credit card. Gently rub a soft cloth dampened with a solution of 1 part apple cider vinegar to 10 parts warm water to take care of any residue.

Three wood surface fixes

You don't have to look any farther than the kitchen or bathroom when you need to take care of these three problems.

- **Stuck paper** To remove paper stuck to a wood surface (say, because the kids were busy doing crafts projects), pour a few drops of olive oil over the paper, wait about 20 minutes as the oil softens it, and then use a clean dry cloth to remove the paper and oil. (Not only is olive oil harmless to wood, but it may do it some good.)

- **Burn mark** If a wood surface suffers a slight burn from a mislaid cigarette or a lit match, rub a little mayonnaise into the burn, let it sit for a few minutes, and wipe

it off with a clean damp cloth. Mayo also removes crayon marks from wood.

- **Tape** If adhesive tape is stuck to a wood floor or piece of furniture, don't just yank it off or you may remove some of the finish. Apply a little rubbing alcohol to the tape, then rub the area with a cloth dipped in a solution of 1 teaspoon dishwashing liquid and 2 cups warm water.

Get rid of water rings and spots

It's bound to happen: A party guest doesn't use a coaster, and her glass leaves a white ring or

Blast from the Past

Stripped pine furniture may be thought of by interior decorators as "so seventies," but what's wrong with lending a touch of hippie chic to a room? A stripped hutch or table or armoire can look like a million dollars to the right eyes.

Stripped wood furniture may be fashionably retro, but it's also quick to dry out. Besides regular dusting and the occasional wipe-down with soapy water, it needs a little oil—and here's how to make a moisturizer and apply it:

Stir ½ teaspoon lemon oil into 1 cup mineral oil (not to be confused with mineral spirits, a paint thinner). Put only a drop or two of the mixture on a soft cloth and rub it onto a small area of the wood with a circular motion, repeating until all surfaces are oiled.

Now step back and admire your spruced-up sideboard or hutch—so handsome that you may decide it's just the place to display your mood ring and Led Zeppelin LPs.

spots on a wood table. The unsightly marks will disappear like magic if you dampen a cloth, apply a dab of toothpaste, and rub the area gently. For a stubborn spot, add a little baking soda to the toothpaste. Dry the area and then polish the surface as usual; if you're lucky, all traces of the damage will vanish.

Homemade furniture polish

A simple polish made from two kitchen staples will leave wooden furniture with a nice shine and pleasant smell. Combine 2½ cups vegetable oil with 1½ cups lemon juice, mix well, and pour the solution into a 16-ounce spray bottle. Spray on finished wooden surfaces and polish with a soft cloth.

Because the polish contains lemon juice, you'll have to store it in the fridge, where it will keep for up to six months. Non-hydrogenated oil won't congeal, so the polish will never need "thawing."

Caring for vinyl upholstery

Though vinyl upholstery is durable, it has a weakness—body and hair oil can cause it to harden and even crack. To keep vinyl-covered furniture in good shape, clean it regularly, especially when it gets a lot of use. Dampen a cloth in water, dip it in white vinegar, and gently wipe the vinyl surfaces to cut through oils. Now add a few drops of mild dishwashing liquid to a bucket of water, stir well, and wash the vinyl with a soft cloth dipped into the soapy water. Rinse with a damp cloth and dry.

Foam away dirt

For spot cleaning dirty sofa cushion corners, upholstered chair arms, and the like, whip up some foam. First, make sure the fabric can be safely cleaned with water-based agents (check the cleaning instructions tag). If it can, vacuum the soiled fabric thoroughly to remove loose dirt. Mix 1 part mild laundry detergent with

Give melted-on candle wax the freeze!

4 parts distilled water in a bowl. (Distilled water doesn't leave watermarks on fabric.) Using a hand mixer, beat the solution until a good head of foam builds. Carefully apply foam to the upholstery, working in small sections and using a clean sponge or cloth. Let dry, then wipe it off with a cloth dampened with white vinegar diluted with distilled water (1 part vinegar to 6 parts water).

Removing stains from vinyl furniture

To remove stubborn marks from vinyl furniture (tablecloths, too), try rubbing the stain with a cloth dipped in milk. (Whether the milk is 1 percent, 2 percent, or whole doesn't matter.) Then wash with soapy water as directed above and dry.

Scorch mark on upholstery

Whether someone was smoking on the sly or accidentally dropped a match on your fancy jacquard chair is irrelevant: you've now got an expensive repair to deal with. Don't despair! You may be able to blot out the char with paper towels. Wet a paper towel with distilled water and dab it on the mark (don't rub). Now blot it with a dry paper towel. If that doesn't work, put a drop of mild liquid laundry detergent on a wet paper towel and treat the spot. After a minute or two, blot up the detergent with a wet paper towel and then blot the area one last time with a dry one.

Touching up leather

Though leather is hard to stain, it can easily sustain watermarks. Just wipe these away with white vinegar—but only after testing on an out-of-sight area of the upholstery. To get rid of scuff marks, rub them with a pencil eraser.

Take a lesson from Flicka or Willie Mays

If you're lucky enough to own a sofa or club chair made of heavier, saddle leather, take care of it not with expensive and fancy leather cleaners, but with old fashioned saddle soap or baseball mitt softener. Treat once or twice a year, depending on how dry or humid your home is.

Make Glass and Metals Shine

Keep glass tabletops sparkling

If you have a glass table, you're used to cleaning it often to remove smudge marks. To add a nice shine every time, squeeze the juice of a halved lemon onto the surface and rub it with a clean cloth. Remove any excess juice, then buff the tabletop with a wad of newspaper.

Cut the mess when cleaning a chandelier

To clean all the pendants and bangles and bits on a crystal chandelier, do you have to go to the trouble of taking it apart? Not if you use this relatively easy method and don't mind standing on a ladder. First, make sure the ladder is secure and that your shoes have good, gripping soles. Second, flip out the tray at the top of the ladder and set a small bowl of diluted rubbing alcohol on top (1 part alcohol to 3 parts water). Slip an old cotton glove over your hand, dip your fingers into the alcohol, and wipe the glass clean with your forefinger and thumb. Then soak a second cotton glove in fresh water and go over the same areas. Dry all of the parts of the chandelier with a clean, soft cotton cloth.

Cleanups for drippy candlesticks

You might have more than romantic memories to remind you of your candlelight dinner: a table full of wax-encrusted candlesticks. Gather up the candlesticks and head to the kitchen, where you have several cleaning options.

- Hold the candlesticks under running hot water and rub the wax off with a soft cloth. Wash them in hot soapy water until any wax residue is gone.

- If the candlesticks are glass, lay them in the microwave on a paper towel and run the oven at its lowest setting for 3 minutes. When you open the door, you'll find the wax on the towel, not the candlesticks.

- Pop candlesticks of any material into the freezer for a couple of hours. When you take them out you'll probably be able to lift the wax right off.

PEWTER TO BE PROUD OF

Pewter bowls and candlesticks are not only attractive but also easy to clean—you can usually restore the gentle sheen by simply wiping pewter pieces with a damp cloth. If smudges and smears remain, head for the fridge or fireplace. A rubdown with **cabbage leaves** or moistened wood ashes will make pewter look like new.

10 Ways to Clean with Lemons

1 Shine chrome with the inside of a lemon rind.

2 Remove beverage stains from marble by rubbing it with lemon juice.

3 Remove water spots from the metal parts of shower doors.

4 Mix lemon juice with borax to clean a toilet bowl.

5 Deodorize a smelly humidifier by pouring 3–4 teaspoons of lemon juice into the water.

6 Sweeten the smells coming from the fireplace by throwing a few lemon peels on the burning logs.

7 To keep ants, fleas, and cockroaches away, add the juice of 1 lemon to 1 gallon of mop water.

8 Rid garments of mildew by rubbing a paste of lemon juice and salt on the affected area.

9 To make white socks look really white again, throw them into a pot of boiling water with 2 lemon halves.

10 Soak delicate fabrics in lemon juice instead of bleach.

Clean fireplace doors

Fireplace doors covered with soot and carbon can spoil the cozy effect of a fire. But it's not hard to clean the glass. If the dirty side of the glass is easy to reach, leave the doors attached when cleaning. If you need to remove the doors, lay them on a soft towel to clean. (Most doors have spring-loaded clips at the top for easy removal.) Start by scraping away any built-up deposits with a razor blade. Then fill a gallon bucket with water, add 1 cup white vinegar and ½ teaspoon dishwashing liquid, and scrub with newspaper crumpled into a ball. Rinse well with a clean sponge or towel, dry the doors, and stand back and admire the view.

Mirror, mirror …

Your mirrors will show nary a streak if you wash them with equal parts water and white vinegar. But it's your technique that matters: Spray-cleaning a mirror can end with moisture seeping behind the glass and turning the silvering black. Instead, dip a clean sponge or wadded-up newspaper (sans colored ink) into the solution and clean the mirror. Wipe dry with a soft cloth, a paper towel, or more newspaper.

Cleaning monitors and TV screens

Less is more when cleaning a computer monitor or TV screen: Turn off the monitor, and then simply dust with a clean cloth, preferably an antistatic wipe. Wipe the screen with a clean cloth barely dampened with water, from top to bottom; if fingerprints and other marks remain, add a small amount of white vinegar to the cloth and wipe again. Liquid crystal display (LCD) laptop screens should be wiped very lightly, and only with a clean cloth (paper towels can scratch the sensitive surface). *Never* clean an LCD screen with commercial glass cleaners, which contain ammonia, acetone, ethyl alcohol, or other substances that can do serious damage.

Reduce tarnish with charcoal or rice

Although sooner or later you'll need to polish your silver pieces, you can make the task easier by keeping tarnish to a minimum. Protect you silver from tarnish causing moisture by placing a few charcoal briquettes or a small bowl of rice in the cabinet where you keep silver; both are super absorbent. Place a briquette inside a silver teapot or coffee pot to prevent moisture from building up.

Shine silver with banana peels

Is your grandmother's cherished silver tea set tarnished? Polish it with banana peels or toothpaste. Whichever you use, rinse the pieces well after wiping them clean and then buff them dry with a soft cloth.

- **Banana peels** Remove the banana (and eat it—it's packed with heart-healthy potassium), and gripping it, massage your silver with the inside of the peel. For tougher tarnishes, puree the peel in a blender, and massage in the paste. Remove with a soft cloth.

- **Toothpaste** Rub non-gel white toothpaste onto the tarnished pieces and work it in with a damp soft cloth.

Keep brass looking golden

For a tarnish-free shine, clean any brass item in one of these two ways: Sprinkle a slice of lemon with baking soda and rub it onto the brass. Or sprinkle salt onto a soft cloth dipped in white vinegar and rub the surface. Rinse the brass with a cloth dipped in warm water and then buff it dry. For some extra shine, rub just-cleaned brass with a little olive oil.

Ketchup makes brass shine

A good way to clean knickknacks, drawer pulls, and other pieces made of brass is to boil them in ketchup or hot sauce! Just put the items in a saucepan, cover with ketchup (more practical and economical than using Tabasco), and place the pan over high heat. Bring to a boil, then lower the heat and simmer until the brass shines like new. Rinse with warm water and dry with a soft cloth.

Chores Around the House

Use a ruler to clean your louvers

The slats in louvered doors and shutters attract dust in a flash, but cleaning them can be a real chore. Speed the task with fabric softener and a ruler. Wrap a fabric softener sheet (or a cloth sprayed with fabric softener) around a ruler and clean the louvers by running the makeshift tool over each slat. A bonus: Fabric softening agents repel dust, so you won't need to dust quite so often.

Baking soda freshens artificial flowers

While artificial blooms may last forever, they attract lots of dust. You can't use water on silk or crepe, so give the flowers a baking soda bath instead. Put at least a cup of baking soda in a large plastic bag, insert the flower heads, and close the top of the bag around the stems. Grasp the top of the bag tightly and shake it vigorously so the soda can absorb all the dust and grime. Remove the flowers, shake off the soda, and dust residue off the petals with a soft toothbrush or artist's paintbrush.

Stained marble tabletop?

Marble makes a beautiful countertop or tabletop, but this porous stone is a real stain magnet.

To remove a beverage stain, rub a paste of baking soda and equal parts water and lemon juice into the area, rinse with water, and wipe dry.

To remove other kinds of marble stains (including scuff marks on a marble floor), shake a good amount of salt over the area. Wet the salt with sour milk for as long as two days, checking periodically to see whether the salt–sour milk combo has done its job. When it has, mop up the salty little puddle with a sponge.

Scrub away soot

It's hard to keep a fireplace spotless, but these easy cleanups will make it look miles better.

- Clean the tiles or bricks around the fireplace with a scrub brush moistened with white vinegar.

- Rub soot marks off the hearth and surrounding tiles or bricks with an art-gum eraser.

- After removing ashes from the fireplace, set a plate of baking soda inside for a day to get rid of the sooty odor.

Vinegar for vases

It's hard to clean dirty, long-necked vases and bottles. Make the task easier by filling the vessel

FRESHENING A MATTRESS

To rid a mattress of urine or any other odors, sprinkle it liberally with **baking soda**, let sit for a day or two, and then vacuum well.

The Home Library

Who but the super-rich has a library in the house? Pretty much everyone. It doesn't have to be a wood-paneled room lined floor to ceiling with oak shelves; a library is merely a collection of books. And whether books are shelved in a room fit for a king or stacked haphazardly in a single pine bookcase, they must be cleaned. Keep your favorite hardcover tomes in best-selling shape and you'll have them forever. Here's how:

To dry a damp book, fan out the pages and sprinkle on cornstarch or talcum powder to soak up the moisture. Let sit for 5–6 hours and then brush off the white stuff.

To get rid of insects that reside in books, place an infested book in a plastic bag and pop it into the freezer for a day or two. No more bugs or larvae.

To freshen up a musty-smelling volume, pour some clean cat litter into a paper bag and keep the book in the bag for a week or so. Then remove the book and brush off any litter.

Mildewed pages? Wipe away the mold with a cloth barely moistened with a solution of 1 part white vinegar to 8 parts water. To dry, open the book to the affected pages and place it in the sun; let it sunbathe for no more than half an hour or the paper will fade and yellow.

Use a clean, soft paintbrush to dust one book at a time, brushing the covers and the outer edges of the pages. Do not dust a shelf of books with a feather duster, which will only redistribute most of the dust on the volumes.

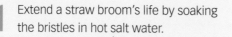

Household Superstar!
13 Reasons to Take Salt Seriously

1 Extend a straw broom's life by soaking the bristles in hot salt water.

2 Toss salt onto a log fire to prevent soot from building up in the chimney.

3 Keep windows frost-free by wiping with a sponge dipped in salt water.

4 Remove watermarks from wood tables with a paste of salt and water.

5 Spiff up wicker furniture by scrubbing with a stiff brush dipped in salt water.

6 Clean copper, bronze, brass, and pewter with a paste of salt and white vinegar.

7 Scrub away rust stains with salt mixed with turpentine.

8 Brighten cutting boards by rubbing with a damp cloth dipped in salt.

9 Refresh kitchen sponges by soaking them in salt water.

10 Pour salt into a washing machine overflowing with suds.

11 Add salt to the washing machine's rinse cycle to sharpen colors.

12 Make clothespins last longer by boiling them in salted water.

13 Sprinkle salt on an ironing board to clean an iron.

with warm water and an equal amount of vinegar. Add up to ¾ cup of uncooked rice and shake vigorously. (If cleaning a vase or a bottle without a lid, put a sheet of aluminum foil on the top, mold it to the sides, and grip the top tightly as you shake.) The rice acts as an abrasive that scrapes the glass clean.

Whiten piano keys
If you wonder how your piano keys got so yellow, don't despair: You can restore their whiteness a few simple ways. Use a soft cloth to rub the keys with lemon juice and salt or with a 50/50 mix of rubbing alcohol and water; or apply mayonnaise and gently scrub with a soft cloth or soft toothbrush.

Whichever method you choose, prevent seepage by holding a piece of cardboard between the keys as you work your way down the keyboard. Wipe off each key with a slightly damp cloth before moving on to the next one. Let the keys air-dry—and then sit down and take it away, maestro!

Shine up your ivory
Bring ivory pieces back to their former luster by rubbing them with a lemon wedge dipped in salt. Let the juice dry, then wipe the piece with a clean cloth. Finally, buff with a second cloth.

Dusting a ceiling fan
All you need for a dust-free ceiling fan cleanup is a ladder, an old cotton sock, and a bucket of soapy water. Stir 1 teaspoon dishwashing liquid into 1 gallon water. Dip the sock into the water and wring it out. Slip the sock over your hand, climb the ladder, and rub your stockinged hand over each blade. Take care to clean the blades on both sides—the heaviest dust layer is on the top. The dust will be transferred directly to the damp sock, not to the air. A breeze, no?

In the Bathroom

Keep showerheads unclogged

If you live in an area with hard water, you've probably noticed how mineral deposits can clog showerheads. No need to buy a new one—just use denture tablets or vinegar to unclog it.

- If you're able to remove the showerhead, dissolve 4–5 denture tablets in a bowl of water and put the head in to soak. Or let it soak overnight in white vinegar. (For extra cleaning action, heat the vinegar in the microwave first.)

- If the showerhead isn't removable, pour the denture tablet solution or vinegar into a plastic bag, tape or tie the bag to the fixture so the showerhead is completely immersed, and leave the bag in place for 1–2 hours.

To make sure the showerhead is fully unclogged, clean out the holes with a needle, piece of wire, or toothpick. Then wipe the head with a cloth dipped in vinegar.

Good-bye to grime and soap scum

Forget about those store-bought "miracle" products. Instead, stir 3 tablespoons baking soda and ½ cup household ammonia into 2 cups

Septic Systems and Bleach

While bleach is a must-have cleaner that can do everything from whiten laundry to kill off pesky mold, it has to be used carefully in homes with septic systems. To make sure that no bleach gets into your groundwater or septic tank when you're scrubbing your tile or sink, use a toothbrush, and be sure to wipe any excess off the surface material with a water-dampened cloth.

warm water. Once you've wiped the solution on and rinsed it off with a sponge or rag, bathroom surfaces will gleam!

Make glass shower doors sparkle

Glass shower doors are a convenient addition to any bathroom but can quickly cloud up with soap scum. For some heavy-duty cleaning, try:

- Shaving cream Squirt the foam on and wipe clean with a dry rag; the foam will leave a film that keeps the door from fogging and makes it harder for scum to stick.

KEEP CHROME SHINY

Chrome faucets and other bathroom fixtures get spotted in seconds, but you can shine them just as fast with **fabric softener sheets**. Keep some on hand in the bathroom and wipe off fixtures as needed. Rubbing alcohol, white vinegar, and the inside of a lemon rind will do a good job, too.

- **White vinegar** Keep a spray bottle filled with vinegar and a sponge by (or in) the shower so you can make washing down the surfaces part of your post-shower routine.

- **Baking soda-plus** Make a solution of ¼ cup dishwashing liquid, ¼ cup hydrogen peroxide, and ¼ cup baking soda. Then scrub it on the doors with a sponge—and, if you have time, all of the other shower surfaces as well.

- **Vegetable oil** Simply pour a little vegetable oil on a sponge or paper towel and scrub the doors, adding more oil as you go.

- **Furniture polish** Use a cloth to rub polish directly on doors, then wipe it off with a clean cloth. The polish will not only clean but will also leave a protective coating against soap scum buildup.

Mildew-free shower curtains

The moist environment of a bathroom is just made for mildew, so don't be surprised when it pops up on your shower curtain. You can keep it at bay for a while, at least, by soaking curtains and liners in salt water before hanging them. Once they're up and any mildew appears just …

- Add ½ cup borax and ½ cup vinegar to 2 cups water, pour onto the affected areas and let sit for 8–10 minutes. Then scrub with a sponge or cloth.

- Mix 2 tablespoons dishwashing liquid with 1 pint household bleach and spray the solution on the curtain.

- Make a paste of vinegar and salt and spread it on the mildewed area. Let dry for 1–2 hours and then clean it off with a damp cloth.

Lemony toilet cleaner

Make a paste of 2–3 parts borax and 1 part lemon juice (stir the juice in gradually until you have the right consistency) and apply it to a stained toilet bowl, rim included. Let sit for 1½–2 hours, and then scrub it off with a toilet brush. This treatment is especially effective for getting rid of the bowl ring that often appears at water level.

Clean that ceiling

You're probably so busy cleaning the fixtures and tiles in your bathroom that you don't even think about the ceiling. Look up, but prepare yourself what you might see—mildew, spotting, built-up grime. For an easy cleanup, fill a mop bucket with equal parts water and white vinegar. Then don goggles or other protective eyewear. Dip a long-handled sponge mop into the vinegar, squeeze it out, and reach up to clean one section of ceiling at a time. One more spic-and-span surface, one spiffier-looking bathroom.

Good riddance to grout grime

The grouting between bathroom tiles is a magnet for dirt and germs, and it's easy to miss these hard-to-reach crevices during regular cleaning. Every so often:

- Make a paste of 1 part borax, 2 parts baking soda, and 1–2 parts water and scrub it onto the grout with a toothbrush.

- Rub away grime with a new pencil eraser, well suited to reaching these narrow spaces.

- Scrub with a mouthwash containing a tooth-whitening agent.

- Soak a cotton ball in household bleach and set it on a spot of badly stained countertop grouting for a few hours; for walls, attach the cotton ball with duct tape.

Solutions for stubborn scum and water spots

Non-porcelain surfaces in the bathroom—including ceramic tiles around sinks and tubs and fiberglass and acrylic shower stalls—can become dulled by water spots and built-up scum just as easily as tubs and sinks. Tackle these heavily soiled surfaces with vigor and …

Toilet Cleaning Made Easy

Cleaning a toilet ranks somewhere around zero on the Pleasant Cleaning Tasks scale, but you have no choice but to tackle it. Here are a few ways to make the job easier and pocket the cost of specialty cleansers.

Chalky tablets Drop 2 antacid tablets or 1 denture tablet containing sodium bicarbonate into the bowl, let them dissolve for about 20 minutes, then scrub the bowl with a toilet brush. A vitamin C tablet will do the trick as well.

Mouthwash Grab a bottle of mouthwash from the medicine cabinet and pour ¼ cup into the bowl. After about half an hour, scrub the bowl with a toilet brush and flush.

Cola Empty a can of cola into the bowl and let sit for 30–60 minutes before scrubbing and flushing.

- 2 cups salt dissolved in 1 gallon hot water.

- ½ cup vinegar, 1 cup ammonia, and ¼ cup baking soda added to 1 gallon warm water.

Apply one of the solutions, let sit for about 15 minutes, then scrub off and rinse.

Brush away rust stains

To get rid of hard-water rust stains on commodes, tubs, and sinks, just squeeze a little toothpaste onto an old toothbrush and scrub away. Or scrub the stain with a paste of borax and lemon juice or a solution of equal parts turpentine and salt. Whichever method you choose, attack rust stains right away. The sooner you deal with them, the easier they are to remove.

Window Treatments

Gelatin for window curtains

Machine washable cotton drapes may emerge from the washer fresh as a daisy, but more often than not, they come out so wrinkled that you're in for a tough time at the ironing board. How to keep wrinkling to a minimum when washing cotton curtains? Dissolve 1 tablespoon plain gelatin in 1 cup boiling water and add to the final rinse cycle. The same trick restores shine to polished cotton curtains.

Use a blackboard eraser

You've washed your windows, and when you step back to admire your handiwork you spot those dreaded streaks. What's worse, you can't tell if they're on the inside or the outside of the pane. You'll have to reclean the panes on both sides, but with what? One of the best tools is a clean blackboard eraser, rubbed in a circular motion. To keep from guessing about which side of a window is streaked, try this trick next time: Use an up-and-down motion when cleaning and drying one side of the window and a back-and-forth motion on the other side. You'll now know which side to "erase."

Two old window-washing standbys

People have probably argued about the best ways to clean windows since glass was invented. Two formulations that never disappoint are 1) half a cup of ammonia in 2 gallons warm water or 2) a cup of white vinegar in 1 quart water. To remove isolated smudges and execute other quick cleanups, wipe windowpanes with a soft cloth dipped in white vinegar.

Dust window screens with a roller

It's nice to open a window to get a breath of fresh air, but the effect isn't nearly as pleasant when the screen is full of dust, pollen, and other airborne debris. For a quick cleanup, dig a brush-type hair roller out of the bathroom drawer and run it lightly over the screen. If the

STREAKING: READ ALL ABOUT IT!

One of the biggest window-washing challenges is to prevent streaking. For starters, wash your windows on a cloudy day, when they'll dry more slowly and leave fewer streaks. You'll also ward off streaking by using the right equipment, which needn't be costly or even commercial. Crumpled up, no-colored-ink newspaper is ideal for streak-free cleaning and drying. So is the packing paper used by professional movers—merely newsprint without ink.

last time you used a hair roller was around 1989 and you haven't happened upon a stray one under the sofa, dust the screen with a lint remover used for clothing.

Effervescent washer

One of the simplest and most effective glass window cleaners around is club soda, which dries without streaking. Just pour it into a spray bottle and spritz the windows, then dry with a cloth.

Solve the dirty windowsill problem

If you like fresh air and keep your windows open, even a window screen won't be able to keep out all the dust and soot that soils indoor sills. Outdoor sills fare even worse, of course, since theirs surfaces tend to trap dirt in pits and cracks. To make cleaning windowsills a breeze, wash them thoroughly, let dry, and spray the sills lightly with clear floor wax. Smoooooth …

Awesome awnings

A good spray with the garden hose every once in a while will help keep window awnings clean and free of debris, but they also need a thorough cleaning every few months. Scrub awnings made of canvas and most other materials with a brush dipped in warm water and mild detergent. If you're faced with stubborn stains or mildew, sprinkle baking soda onto a stain and let it sit for about 5 minutes before rinsing it off with the garden hose. Treat mildew with a solution of 1 part colorfast bleach and 3 parts water; just let it soak into the material for 3–4 minutes and then rinse.

Don't wash windows on a hot day!

It might be tempting to do your window washing on a warm day, but you'll wind up worse off than you were when you started. Why? Your window washing solution will dry on contact, leaving your windows streaky.

Buck Up and Clean the Blinds

Of all household chores, cleaning slatted blinds (vertical or horizontal) may be the most tedious—the reason it's so often neglected. Help is at hand. With these two techniques, you'll get rid of all that dust and dirt on your blinds with no trouble.

Clean with a glove All you need to wash blinds is a clean thick cotton glove (a gardening glove is ideal) and a small bowl of fabric softener. Pull on the glove, dip your fingers into the bowl, and simply slide your forefinger and middle finger along both sides of each slat. Fabric softener not only cleans hard surfaces but also slows dust buildup.

Clean with a kitchen spatula Wrap a cotton cloth around a spatula and secure it with a rubber band. Dip the spatula in either a 50/50 vinegar-water solution or rubbing alcohol and run your makeshift cleaning tool along the slats. Of course, you could also apply vinegar water or alcohol to the blinds with the gloved-hand technique. No more hidden blinds, no more self-reproach.

Always-new curtain rods for the green-conscious

Hate to clean and dust your curtain rods? So do we, so, we don't. Instead, for smaller windows, we head outside and find an appropriate length and width of fallen tree branch (that's key: it has to be on the ground when you find it)—generally 5 feet long and 3 inches in circumference for a 4-foot-wide window—and run it through the tops of our curtains or through curtain rings. If it starts to get dingy or dusty, simply look for another to replace it, remove the first one, and use it as kindling.

Routing Household Pests

Lure ants with sugar

Give ants what they want: sugar. Make a trap by adding 23 teaspoons sugar to 1 cup water, moisten a few paper towels or old kitchen sponges in the solution, and set them in spots where ants are seen. Leave the traps overnight and check them in the morning. If they're crawling with ants (almost a certainty), sweep the traps into an empty dustpan and dump a pot of hot water over them. Repeat the process until no ants are left to lure.

Repel ants with vinegar

If ants love sugar, it only makes sense that they hate vinegar. To get rid of these unwelcome pests, mix equal parts white vinegar and water in a spray bottle and squirt it on counters, windowsills, baseboards, and anywhere else ants show up.

Spiced-out silverfish

These wingless insects enjoy munching on, among other things, paper, glue, and starch. What they *don't* like? Herbs. Leave sachets or tea bags of dried lavender, mint, sage, or bay leaves in bathroom and kitchen cabinets, where silverfish typically congregate. Wiping down surfaces with lavender oil or a similarly potent herbal solution should also encourage silverfish to make tracks.

Lethal treat for cockroaches

Ingesting baking soda will kill roaches, but you'll need to make it palatable. Bait the pests by mixing baking soda with equal parts confectioners' sugar and sprinkling the mixture inside cabinets and other cockroach hidey-holes.

Minty mouse repellent

Whip up a quart of peppermint tea—not for your morning pleasure but to repel those mice you've heard scurrying about at night. Boil 2 cups water, turn off the heat and add 4–6 peppermint tea bags, and let the tea steep for 6–8 hours. Now stir in 2 teaspoons dishwashing liquid to make the super-strong solution stick to surfaces longer. Fill a spray bottle with the tea and coat baseboards and any areas where you suspect mice are entering.

Ground those flying insects

As much as you may enjoy the aromas of basil, oranges, and cloves, houseflies and other flying insects are repelled by them—one whiff and they'll wing their way elsewhere. So chase them off while treating yourself to some nice scents.

- Put dried basil in organza and muslin sachets (sold at craft and kitchenware stores). Hang the bags in the kitchen and anywhere else flies and other winged pests like to buzz around, and they'll quickly stop dropping by.

- Make a pomander—a whole orange stuck with cloves. Hang it from a light fixture or hook, and you'll enjoy pest-free air and a nice scent as well.

Trap mice with melted cheese

Mice are crafty at stealing a piece of cheese from a mousetrap. The trick is to make sure the trap will trip while mice are nibbling the treat. How to do it? Just set the cheese in the trap and heat it with a lit match so the cheese melts. Unable to spirit it away, mice will sample the melted cheese long enough for the trap to spring shut.

Everyday Laundry Tips

Outfox the sock bandit

Face it: The invisible sock bandit who hangs around washing machines and snatches one sock from a pair will never be apprehended, but here's a way to thwart him: Give each family member a mesh produce bag for stashing soiled socks. Then, on washday, tie the bags closed and toss them into the washer and dryer. The sneaky thief will leave empty-handed, and you'll have to replace socks only when they wear out.

Freshen a laundry hamper

Hampers are handy for keeping dirty laundry in one place, but they can get a little ripe when packed with soiled clothes. Two ways to prevent hamper smells:

- Cut the foot off a pair of old panty hose, fill it with baking soda, knot it, and toss this makeshift odor eater into the hamper. Replace the baking soda every month or so.
- Keep a box of baking soda next to the hamper and sprinkle some on soiled clothes as you throw them in the washer, where the soda will freshen and soften the load.

Whiter whites

Do your white T-shirts tend toward gray? White socks look dirty no matter how many times they're washed? Try one of these tried and true methods for making whites stay white.

- Soak in a solution of 1 gallon water and 1 cup baking soda.
- Soak in hot water in which you've dissolved 5 aspirin tablets (325 milligrams each).

make your own
Fabric Softener

There's no need to spend money on commercial fabric softeners when you probably have all the ingredients you need to make your own. See for yourself with this simple recipe.

Lickety-Split Fabric Softener

You can also use this solution to make a fabric softener sheet to toss in the dryer. Just dilute with water, dip in a washcloth and wring it out, and add the washcloth to your load of wet clothes.

> 2 cups white vinegar
> 2 cups baking soda
> 4 cups water

1. Combine ingredients in a gallon-size pail or pot and stir to dissolve the baking soda.
2. Pour the solution into a plastic bottle with a lid. (An old liquid detergent bottle is ideal.)
3. To use, add ¼ cup softener to the washer's final rinse cycle.

- Add 1 cup of white vinegar to the washing machine's rinse cycle.

Blacker blacks, darker darks

While faded and distressed-looking garments are the rage for some age groups, you may prefer not to look as if the last time you went clothes-shopping was 1998. Herewith, some tips for keeping black and dark-colored wardrobe items looking like new.

Add **coffee** to your rinse cycles to keep dark clothes dark!

- For blacks, add 2 cups brewed coffee or tea to the rinse cycle.

- For dark colors like navy blue or plum, add 1 cup table salt to the rinse cycle.

- For denim that will be slow to fade, soak jeans in salt water or a 50/50 solution of water and white vinegar before the first wash. Turn the jeans inside out before putting them in the machine and turn the temperature setting to cold.

Two starch substitutes

No need to run out to the store to buy starch to stiffen your shirt collars or restore body to shapeless clothing. Make your own by pouring 2 cups water into a jar and adding 2 tablespoons cornstarch. Screw the jar lid on tightly and shake well. Now pour the solution into a spray bottle for use when ironing.

If your permanent press items are looking a bit shapeless, don't use starch when ironing.

Instead, add a cup of powdered milk to the final rinse cycle of the wash. Got milk? Got shape.

Boil yellowed cottons

With time, white cotton and linen tend to turn yellow—hardly the fresh, crisp look for which cotton is famous. Let sodium come to the rescue by mixing ¼ cup salt and ¼ cup baking soda with 1 gallon water in a large cooking pot. Add the yellowed items and boil for 1 hour.

Brightening rugs and curtains

If cotton rugs or cotton curtains have faded, simply add ⅓ cup salt to your laundry detergent to brighten the colors. If a rug is too large for the machine washing, scrub it well with a clean rag dipped in salt water.

Banish odors

Know that "new" smell of dye or chemicals that comes with just-bought sheets or shirts? Have a teenager who thinks nothing of leaving sweaty clothes in a locker or gym bag for weeks on end? Worse, ever have a run-in with a skunk? Grab two old deodorizer standbys. First, add ½ cup baking soda to 1 gallon water and presoak any smelly washable items for about 2 hours. Then, as you machine-wash them, add ½ cup white vinegar to the rinse cycle.

An improv drying rack

Running a dryer bumps up your electric bill, so if you're thrifty, you'll want to air-dry any items you can. But don't think you need a sunny day or even a clothesline or store-bought drying rack. Just suspend an old (clean) refrigerator shelf or oven rack from a beam in your garage or basement and hook wet clothes on coat hangers onto the rack. Smart move!

Listerine in your washing machine

Add half a cup of mouthwash to your empty washing machine and run it through a cycle to disinfect it simply with a household product that virtually everyone has in their bathroom.

Dry sweaters with panty hose

Don't pin sweaters directly to your drying line; instead, run an old pair of panty hose through one sleeve, through the neck, and out the other sleeve, and clothes pin the hose to the line.

Keeping Your Iron Clean

You're pressing your nicest 100 percent cotton white blouse or shirt in preparation for dinner with your boss when—oh no!—the iron leaves a black streak on the collar. Sound familiar? You can say good-bye to marred garments by cleaning your iron regularly. Try one of these methods to rid the soleplate of burned starch and other debris:

- Lay several sheets of wax paper on the ironing board, turn the iron on low and the steam off, and run the iron back and forth over the wax paper several times.

- Fill the iron with white vinegar, turn the heat on high, switch on the steam, and let the iron spew for about 5 minutes. Empty the iron and refill it with cool water. Shake the iron gently, drain it, and wipe the soleplate with a clean cloth.

- Unclog steam vents by poking them with a cotton swab dipped in a solution of equal parts water and white vinegar. A toothpick will unclog smaller vents.

Clean your dryer vent ... from the outside

Stuffed-up dryer vents can, in worst case scenarios, cause fires, but most of us never think of examining the vent from the outside, on a regular basis. To do so, carefully lift up the vent flap and clean it out ... assuming that it's not inhabited by any of the following creatures: pigeons, skunks, fox kits, snakes (yuck), field mice, or racoons (this is a favorite passageway into a warm house).

   If you do have visitors, call your local animal control.

The Science of Removing Stains

When you attack stains with ordinary household staples, you transform yourself into a domestic mad scientist (no lab coat required). With the right formula you can remove almost any kind of stain from clothing, and there's no reason not to experiment with ingredients that "do no harm"—in alphabetical order, baking soda, cornstarch, flour, lemon juice, liquid detergent, a raw potato, shampoo, and white vinegar. Follow stain treatments with a regular wash. (To treat garments without machine washing, see "Saving Stained Clothing," pages 197-98.)

Blood	As quickly as possible, soak a bloodstained item of clothing in a pot of cold salt water. After 3–4 hours, rub the stain with liquid detergent and launder.
Coffee	Presoak the stain in a solution of 1 quart water, 1 tablespoon white vinegar, and 1 teaspoon laundry detergent.
Grass	Either soak grass stains in full-strength white vinegar or brush non-gel, non-whitening toothpaste directly on the stain.
Gravy	Cover the stain with baking soda, cornstarch, flour, or salt, all of which soak up grease. After brushing the substance off, pour liquid laundry detergent and hot water directly onto the stain.
Ink	Pour salt on an ink stain that's still wet, gently dab with a wet paper towel, and then brush off the salt; repeat as necessary.
Mud	Rub the stain with a peeled slice of raw potato, and then soak the garment in cold water for at least 15 minutes.
Mustard	Stir 1 tablespoon white vinegar and ½ teaspoon liquid laundry detergent into 1 quart warm water. Sponge the solution on the stain and let air-dry. Before washing the garment, apply liquid detergent directly to the spot.
Ring around the collar	Rub shampoo directly onto the stain with your finger or a toothbrush. Let sit for 25–30 minutes before washing the shirt. (Make sure the shampoo you use contains ammonium lauryl sulfate, an ingredient that cuts through oil.)

Special Care for Special Items

Fluff fluffy stuff with a sneaker
When drying a feather-filled item—whether a pillow, duvet, or parka—toss a sneaker into the dryer, too (the less smelly, the better). The soft-soled shoe will make a bit of a racket, but it will fluff up the item nicely as it bounces around.

Speed-dry a wet blanket
Make a soggy blanket fresh from the washing machine look warm and welcoming again in no time. First, put two large towels in the dryer and let them heat for 20 minutes. Now throw in the blanket and let the towels soak up the moisture. Take the blanket out when it's still damp and drape it over the backs of two chairs (ideally, lawn chairs out in the sun) or two parallel clotheslines to air-dry.

Prevent panty hose runs
Runs in a pair of panty hose can ruin the look of the sharpest outfit, so take preventive action when you bring them home from the store. Wash new panty hose, let them dry, and then soak for 3 hours in a solution of 1 gallon water and 2 cups salt.

Salt your new jeans
Nothing's more comfortable than a pair of jeans, but it can take a little time before the stiffness wears off. Hasten the process by throwing a new pair of jeans into the washing machine with ½ cup salt. They'll feel softer the first time you pull them on.

New life for soiled whites
It's a sad day when a favorite white shirt or blouse just can't be seen in public anymore—yellow stains, a dreary cast, and seemingly permanent ring around the collar. But all is not lost. Perk up the garment (and yourself) by working a paste of vinegar and baking soda directly onto stained and soiled areas, then hang the garment outside in the sun for a couple of hours. If the collar remains soiled, pour a capful of 3 percent hydrogen peroxide along the ring. Now wash in hot water as you normally would and make room in the closet for your old friend.

Kettle-clean your felt hat
To deep clean your wool felt hat, fill a teakettle with water, place it on the stove, and bring it to a boil. Carefully hold the hat above the steam, rotating it as necessary. Brush with a dry toothbrush, and let dry.

Wash silk in hair shampoo
Use a protein-based hair shampoo and cool water to hand-wash silk; the protein will feed the protein in the silk, giving it body, and making it last longer.

Chapter Four

Winning the War on Clutter

Some people keep their living quarters so orderly that it's almost scary. Others seem congenitally incapable of controlling clutter, and their houses look as if Hurricane Bruno just blew through.

From all appearances, a talent for organizing is like music or athletics or math: You've either got it, or you don't, and if you're reading this, you know who you are!

Many of the simple solutions in this chapter may work so well that keeping your house orderly will not only be easy, but fun, too. Clutter-controlling hints also give you creative ways to use things you already have, like cardboard boxes, shoe boxes, and plastic containers. Other hints call for common items that aren't normally used for storage, but which work perfectly, like a suitcase, a stockpot, and even a pair of panty hose. It's a well-known fact that orderly surroundings have a positive psychological effect on the psyche. So applying the advice found in this chapter might not only help you dig out from under the mess, but boost your spirits, too!

Corral your shoes in a *laundry basket!*

Smart Storage Strategies

How to clean out a drawer

Thought you knew how? Guess again! To organize a drawer in the most efficient manner, have a plastic trash bag and three shoe boxes or similarly sized containers at the ready. Dump the contents of the drawer onto the bed or floor and start sorting the bits and pieces, distributing them like this:

- Put anything you *want to throw away* in the trash bag.
- Place anything you *want to store* elsewhere in the first box.
- Stash anything *worth giving to charity* in the second box.
- Save any *candidates for a garage sale* in the third box.

  Now stash everything that's left over back in the drawer. Plan your trip to the dump, the storage facility, your favorite charity, and your upcoming garage sale.

No cheese, please

The next time you order pizza to go at the pizza parlor, chat up the cashier and ask if you could have an extra box. Pizza boxes make excellent containers for everything from road maps to souvenir newspapers to children's artwork.

CD storage

Your CD rack is filled, and you've taken to stacking new CDs beside it on the floor. Time to put that empty shoe box to good use! Sort your CDs and put the ones you rarely listen to in the box; label each box according to genre of music and return it to its former place (probably on a closet shelf). Stack other shoe boxes on top as your CD collection grows.

Special storage for special stuff

Turn shoe or hat boxes into a keepsake box for each member of the family. Covering the boxes in different-colored contact paper will distinguish them from one another and make them more durable as well. You could also let your child use tempera paint to paint his or her box. The boxes will ensure that all medals, ribbons, special greeting cards, and any other paraphernalia worth keeping doesn't get lost in the shuffle.

THE HOME ORGANIZER'S DREAM BOX

Wine and liquor boxes have 12 compartments, each about a foot tall and just begging to hold rolled-up posters, holiday decorations sorted by type, and whatever other flotsam and jetsam you want to keep in order. The boxes are always easy to come by, since wine and liquor store personnel are more than happy for you take a few off their hands.

The Small Container Hall of Fame

Some common items found in the average home have achieved such status among organized homemakers that we hereby induct them into the Small Container Hall of Fame. Buy an indelible marker and a roll of first aid tape, and label, label, label! When the contents change, relabel.

Cigar box
Hard to find, but when you do, they're worth their weight in gold. Look for them at tag and rummage sales.

Berry basket
This small, ventilated plastic basket from the supermarket is good for storing anything that needs a little air, like kitchen sponges and soap pads.

Coffee can
It's roomy and has a lid. Who could ask for more? Just keep the contents dry.

Film canister Soon to be extinct, but not yet. Hoard film canisters and use them to hold rings and earrings, small change for tolls, fishing flies, and garden seeds.

Hanging shoe bag
Perhaps the best all-purpose holder known to man and woman. Hang it on a closet door, in a bathroom, in a home office, or in a child's room and start stuffing the roomy pockets.

Baby wipes container
Sturdy and stackable, this rectangular plastic receptacle is ideal for small office supplies, sewing paraphernalia, small tools, and cookie cutters.

Ice cube tray
The plastic ice cube tray has two more compartments than the egg carton but no lid—which make it the perfect drawer divider for itsy-bitsy odds and ends. Fill it with small office necessities or rings and earrings, put it away, and you're good to go.

Egg carton
Twelve small compartments and an attached lid make this lightweight container the choice for buttons, washers, tacks, paperclips, pushpins, and more.

Newspaper Clipping Preservative

The acidic nature of newsprint means that newspaper clippings will not only yellow but will also eventually disintegrate. To save articles reporting your golf trophy, your grandson's acceptance to Harvard, or your wife's distinguished service award, give the clippings a Milk of Magnesia bath. Though "milk of magnesia" is a common term for magnesium hydroxide, $Mg(OH)_2$, it is trademarked as an over-the-counter antacid and laxative.

$Mg(OH)_2$ Clipping Saver

Before soaking a clipping, make sure the ink won't run by adding a drop to a tiny area of print, preferably outside the margins of the article you want to preserve.

1 Milk of Magnesia Tablet
1 liter club soda
1 large nonaluminum bowl
Shallow glass pan

1. Combine the tablet and club soda in a bowl and let sit overnight.

2. Pour a ¼-inch layer of the soda mix into the pan and submerge the clipping for 60–90 seconds.

3. Lay the clipping on a double layer of paper towels, and then cover with another double layer and press gently to absorb the water.

4. Remove towels and air-dry the clipping on a wire rack or screen.

Storing gift-wrapping paper

Save long, cardboard mailing tubes and use them to store leftover wrapping paper. The tubes will make use of the air space in the corner of a storage closet. You could also attach a plastic bag filled with gift cards and spools of ribbon to a tube with a metal binder clamp or a clothespin. Tape the tubes together with masking tape, and group by occasion or holiday.

Jot it down

You reorganized your drawers and closets last spring, and you can't remember where you stashed the measuring tape or the heating pad. Prevent wasting time hunting things down by recording their new locations in a notebook labeled "Where It's At" (or, if you're a stickler for grammar, "Where It Is"). Better still, use your computer and save the list on your hard drive so you won't have to hunt down your notebook!

Curtail junk mail

A combo of three things in your household will slow the flow of junk mail that adds to clutter: 1) a pen or computer; 2) paper; and 3) a postal stamp. Write and ask the American Direct Marketing Association (DMA) to remove your name and address from their mailing lists. *Their* address? Direct Marketing Association, Mail Preference Service, P. O. Box 643, Carmel, NY 10512 (www.the-dma.org). Don't expect a quick fix, however; it takes a few months for the DMA to dam the flood of mail. Or if you live in Canada, contact the Canadian Direct Marketing Association at Concorde Gate, Suite 607, Don Mills, ON M3C 3N6 (www.the-cma.org).

Organized Entryways and Living Areas

Here's your hat (and your keys)

A hat rack in the foyer is the handiest place to park jackets, scarves, dog leashes, keys, and—oh yes!—hats. If you're a woodworker with an artistic bent, you could turn the right fallen tree limb into a sculptural rack that works equally well as a functional item and decorative feature.

A hanger rack from scratch

Turn a straightened coat hanger and clothespins into a hanger rack on the back of an entryway closet door. Do the same on the back of a kitchen cupboard door to hold extra dish towels.

1. Measure the door and cut a piece of wire that will leave 2–3 inches of space at each end.

2. Mount a screw eye in the center, then another at each end. Run the hanger wire through the screw eyes and bend both ends around the outer eyes with pliers.

3. Now clip clothespins to the wire and use them to hold mittens, caps, and any other small items of clothing.

Shoe catcher

Devote a plastic laundry basket not to your wash, but to wet shoes. Place it just inside the mudroom door as a catchall for sneakers, galoshes, and anything muddy. (A large, shallow basket is more eye pleasing, but plastic is the utilitarian choice because it's so much easier to clean.) To speed the drying of wet shoes, use two items that normally belong in the kitchen: a cookie sheet and a cooler rack. Place the cookie sheet near the mudroom door, set the rack on top, and you have a wet shoe catcher that allows for better air circulation.

Clear the way

If access to your garage is through the laundry room, you don't want to dodge clutter each time you pass through, especially if the space is tight. One way to keep the coast clear is to mount two plastic milk crates side-by-side on the wall above the washer. Use them to hold your detergent and other laundry supplies, and they'll not only stay out of the way but will be right at hand when you need them.

Impromptu umbrella holder

If you have a tall cylindrical garbage bin that's seen its day, think twice about retiring it. A coat of paint or a layer of contact paper will turn it into an umbrella stand for your entryway. The real article can cost a pretty penny, but your recycled stand will do just as well. Note: If the can is metal, spray the interior with clear lacquer to prevent rust.

Household Superstar!
27 Things to Store in Panty Hose

Only 27 things? What *can't* you store in panty hose? (Basically, liquids, grains, flour, and anything that won't fit.) Among the items to stash in a panty hose leg or foot are these, listed in orderly fashion—i.e., alphabetically.

1 Apples

2 Badminton shuttlecocks

3 Colored pencils

4 Curling irons

5 Dog toys

6 Eagle Scout merit badge sash

7 Flower seed packets

8 Golf balls

9 GPS trackers

10 Hair clips

11 Instant oatmeal

12 Jellybeans

13 Kazoos

14 Lightbulbs

15 Mothballs

16 Narcissus bulbs

17 Oreos

18 Ping-pong balls

19 Q-tips

20 Ribbons

21 Take-out menus

22 Undies

23 Vampire teeth

24 Walkie-talkies

25 X-ray eyeglasses

26 Yo-yos

27 Zip discs

Feng shui this!

According to the principles of the ancient Chinese art of feng shui (pronounced *fung schway*), placing furniture and objects to align with magnetic north optimizes energy flow, or chi, and brings the home environment into harmony (or something like that). If you want to give feng shui a whirl, rearrange your furniture accordingly to see if it makes a difference in your sense of orderliness and well-being. Stranger things have happened.

That mountain of magazines

It just keeps mounting, doesn't it? To reduce clutter without giving up the articles, invest in a craft knife to slice out the pages you want and then save them in a "To Read" file. A craft knife will not only give you a cleaner cut but also will do the job three times faster than scissors.

Storing tablecloths

A tablecloth folded like a sheet is a tablecloth that will have to be ironed. Keep tablecloths crease-free by hanging them over a towel rod mounted on the inside of a storage closet door. If the rod isn't round, slice paper towel tubes lengthwise and fit them over the rod to minimize wrinkling.

Take care with collectibles

The best storage compartments for tender antiques are polyethylene plastic containers, acid-free cardboard boxes, and enameled metal storage cabinets. But if a lack of space demands that you store collectibles in a wooden cabinet or drawers, take these measures to keep stamps, dolls, textiles, and metals (including coins) from being damaged by the sulfuric and acidic vapors given off by both unfinished and painted wood.

- Keep items out of contact with the wood by wrapping them in acid-free tissue paper or prewashed, unbleached cotton muslin.

Store guestroom blankets or pillows in an **antique suitcase!**

- Seal wood box interiors with at least two coasts of polyurethane varnish.
- Whether you collect comics or stamps, give them the right conditions: no excessive light, heat, moisture, or dust.

Double-duty furniture

Your great-great-grandfather's footlocker in the attic can do more than just gather dust. Topped with a runner, it makes a coffee table that's a conversation piece as well as a storage unit. Pack it with extra blankets or sheets or use it for board games, playing cards, and any sports equipment small enough to fit in.

A bookkeeper

A device to keep books from falling off open-ended shelves, that is. To secure the books, cut two wooden dowels to size and stain them to match the shelves. Screw two teacup hooks on each shelf end, pinching the hooks on the bottom shelf closed so they'll hold the dowels in place. Slide the dowels through the hooks, and you have two bars that will keep books in place on your airy but precarious shelves.

Mount a CD cabinet in an entryway

Get rid of that painting you never liked and replace it with this organizing marvel. Basically a bookcase divided into individual squares meant to hold 10 or so compact discs each, it's also a perfect way for family members to keep their keys and cell phones instantly "grab-able" first thing in the morning.

Kitty litter tubs for storage

Perfect for organizing everything from toys to infrequently-used linens, these uber-storage containers have more uses than we have room here! Wash them thoroughly, label them, and use them to store dishes, tools, small kitchen appliances, boxes of photos, cassette tapes, and much more.

In the Bedroom

Between the sheets

There's no room for the set of flannel sheets you were given for your birthday, so where can you keep them? Hide the two halves of the set side by side between the mattress and the box springs at the foot of the bed.

Three square feet of extra space

Doesn't sound like much, but it's enough to hold the towels or shoes that won't fit into your bulging linen closet or even your stack of weekly magazines that you insist you'll get around to reading some day. What is it? A suitcase. Going on a trip? Dump the contents in a cardboard box you store in a corner of the bedroom with a sheet thrown over it. Whether you're home or away, your stuff is still all in one place and out of sight. Be careful, however: Don't store things in a suitcase that smells of mold or mildew, which will do whatever you've stashed away no favors. Also be sure to wrap any glass or ceramic objects in bubble wrap to protect them when the suitcase is moved.

Two-level clothes rod

If the clothes rod in your bedroom closet is high up, suspend a second rod below it. Cut a second rod to the desired length, and then do the same with two vertical lengths of light but sturdy chain. Attach steel rings to both ends of the chains and hang the lower rod from the original.

Under-the-bed dresser drawer

Have an old dresser up in the attic? If you're smart, you're storing what you don't need in its drawers. But you can also bring one of its drawers right into your bedroom and keep it out of sight. Just attach casters to the bottom four corners for a rolling chest that's kept under the bed.

Homemade sock organizer

You may not be able to keep a sock from losing its mate, but you *can* bring order to the pairs you keep in a dresser drawer. To avoid rummaging through a big pile of socks to find what you want, cut shoe boxes in half and then position them so the open ends fit snugly against the front of the drawer. (Or, if you're handy with a bow saw or coping saw, cut two or three fiberboard dividers to the drawer depth.) Sort dress socks, casual socks, and athletic socks into the appropriate compartments, and you'll be able to zero in on what you're looking for in a jiff.

Door stops = hangers

When screwed into the back of a closet door, door stops with rubber tips make excellent hangers for shoes. Group the stops in pairs, setting them a few inches apart. Shoes hung, floor space cleared!

Swinging from the ceiling

A length of brightly colored plastic chain will keep the stuffed animals in a child's bedroom off the floor and out of the way. Hang the chain in a corner at the appropriate height, affixing the ends to both walls. To make it possible for your little one to hang up the toys, stitch a loop of hem binding to each one and use S-hooks to suspend the stuffed animals from the chain.

"The baseball corner"

That's what you'll call the corner shelf you make in Mikey's bedroom so he can keep all of

Hold the Gold *(and Silver and …)*

Keeping jewelry neat and accessible can be a challenge even for the most organized person. For every perfectly organized jewelry box, there are at least 10 that amount to a jumbled mess of necklaces, bracelets, rings, pins (ouch!), and mismatched earrings. Try these no-extra-cost storage ideas—gems in themselves!

Silverware box
If your grandmother's wooden silverware box is sitting empty in the attic, odds are the velvet-lined interior is in good enough shape to hold your jewelry. The velvet will slow silver jewelry from tarnishing, while the compartments will keep it in order, particularly necklaces, which can be held in place by the utensil dividers. Polish the exterior wood to a nice sheen, and keep it on your bureau as a showpiece.

Needlepoint canvas
Tiny squares of leftover needlepoint canvas are perfect for storing pierced earrings. Make them more secure by slipping the mesh into a plastic bag before storing them in your jewelry drawer.

Prescription pill containers
Don't throw these out when empty; the tinted brown plastic is just transparent enough to show the jewelry.

Egg cartons and ice cube trays
The compartments of egg cartons and ice cube trays are just the right size for keeping jewelry separated, organized, and visible. Especially great for keeping pairs of earrings together! Line cartons or trays side by side in a drawer.

Pierced earring holder
Clip a skirt hanger onto the waistband of an old pair of panty hose and you have an instant pierced earring holder. Just push the studs through the nylon and attach the backs. Hang from a closet rod. You'll be able to see your collection all at once, keep pairs of earrings from being separated, and have immediate access.

Herb or spice jars
Repurpose well-washed 1-ounce plastic or glass spice jars as jewelry holders. They're small, see-through, and perfect for keeping pairs of earrings together and storing rings, pins, and chain-link bracelets. Keep in your jewelry drawer or stash in a suitcase when traveling.

his baseball equipment in one place. Here's how to put it together.

1. Cut a 12-by-12-by-17-inch triangle from ¾-inch plywood.
2. Bore 1½-inch diameter holes for the baseballs.
3. Cut bat slots with a coping saw.
4. Nail the shelf to ½-by-2-inch cleats fastened to wall studs.

Now watch Mikey take pride in keeping everything together on his own special shelf.

Storing loose change

Instead of keeping loose change in a dish on your dresser, let resealable plastic kitchen bags be your organizers. Sort the change into separate plastic bags, putting a few coin rollers in with the appropriate coins. Then stack the bags in the corner of a drawer until you're ready to cash the coins in for bills. If you live in an area where coin-sorting machines are available, by all means use them (if you don't mind paying a small fee). Still, don't think you're a Luddite if you prefer to roll your own coins, which to some people is as meditative an exercise as washing dishes.

A pared-down "wallet"

When leaving for your morning walk or run, you usually take a few dollar bills along in case you decide to stop for a sports drink or newspaper on the way home. The easiest and most lightweight alternative to a wallet? A metal binder clip, which will firmly secure the bills (and your ID, if you like) to the waistband of your running shorts or sweats.

Jewelry within reach

Draping necklaces and bracelets from the hooks on a coat rack mounted on the wall next to your dressing table is a smart idea. For one thing, your baubles are right at hand. For another, they add a nice decorative touch to an expanse of bare wall.

Kitchen Storage Tips

Compartmentalize your cabinets

To keep your kitchen cabinets from becoming a jumble of boxes and bags and cans, gather some flat-bottomed rectangular baskets or small wooden or cardboard boxes—shoe boxes are usually ideal. Line up the containers on the shelves and reserve each for a different kind of food—one for sugar, syrup, and other sweet stuff, one for baking-related items like flour and baking soda, and so on. If you use boxes, you can paint them to blend with your kitchen's color scheme. Whether you spiff them up or not, label the containers with their contents so you don't confuse the sugar with the salt (yuck).

Organize spices by style of cuisine

Is your spice rack a mess? Can't find the cumin when you need it? Arrange them in a low-sided, unlidded box (old cigar boxes work great) by type of cuisine, and whenever you're cooking Italian food (or Mexican, German, French, Asian, Indian, Middle Eastern, or good old American), the appropriate spices will be together in one place. Cumin, oregano, cilantro, and red pepper? Sounds like Mexican. Tarragon, parsley, sorrel, bay? French. Label each box according to its nationality, and whenever you're in the mood for that style of cuisine, your spice hunting will be kept to a minimum.

New rack = less racket

Tired of having to take the pots and pans out of a cabinet to get to the cookie sheets on the bottom? (Bang, bang, bang!) Transfer a metal desk file organizer to the kitchen. This compartmentalized metal rack will allow you to store cookie sheets, jelly-roll pans, and thin wooden or acrylic cutting boards vertically. The upshot?

Label, Label, Label

Labeling devices should come with a warning: *Use with caution.* Some people are so enamored of hand-held label printers at first that they go on a labeling binge, labeling every shelf in the pantry and linen closet and toying with the idea of labeling the pets so nobody will confuse Fluffy with Fido.

Actually, compact label printers are a godsend for anyone whose constant refrain is, "If I only knew which box I put it that in.... " It's amazing how many boxes go unlabeled when people move. Then they have to sift through a stack of boxes to find the can opener—or go out and buy a new one. And it's not just boxes you should label, moving or not. Marking home videos, file folders, and any other objects that don't immediately reveal their contents will make your life much easier and also remind family members where to put things.

Sure, you can use your computer to print out sheets bearing the words Baby Books, Old CDs, San Francisco Souvenirs, and the like, and tape them to boxes. But it's faster to key in the letters on you labeler and then print out the self-sticking tag.

You'll be able to pluck flat items out of a crowded cabinet with ease.

Newspaper buffers for nonstick cookware

When you nest nonstick saucepans and pots one inside another, you're almost sure to scratch the delicate coating. To keep nonstick cookware scratch-free, simply tuck a newspaper sheet into each pot and nest them without worrying.

Protect your knives (and yourself) with a **paper towel tube!**

Rack 'em up

There's the pot, but where's the darned lid? Rummaging through a cluttered cabinet full of pots and pans can be an exercise in frustration. A solution to the problem is as near as your toolbox. Just mount an ordinary towel rack or two on the back of the cabinet door and slide the lids between rack and door. The knobs on the lids will keep them from falling through.

Keep your storage lids on

Ever find yourself faced with the perfect storage container for that batch of tomato sauce you made, but the container lid has made its way to who knows where? Keep all the lids organized—and together—by storing them inside the largest empty kitchen storage bin you have.

Protect fine china

When stacking fine china in the cabinet, keep dinner plates scratch free by alternating them with paper plates. For salad plates and saucers, use coffee filters for the same purpose. China teacups are best stored right-side up. If your cabinet won't accommodate all the cups, create an extra tier of cabinet space by setting a coated wire rack inside. Or, you ask, why not hang the cups from hooks attached to the bottom of the shelf above? Hooks are fine for everyday china, but hanging antique teacups means they'll be bearing their own weight—a bad idea if you want to give these heirlooms all of the tender loving care they deserve.

Let it slide

In some wooden kitchen cabinets, the drawers sit on wooden slides on the bottom rather than lubricated metal slides at the sides. Dirt easily accumulates on the slides and makes opening and closing drawers anything but smooth. To rectify the problem, clean wooden glides with soap and water. Then, when the slides are dry, rub candle wax on all wood-to-wood contact points. Friction-worn wooden slides can also be fixed right up with the insertion of one or two smooth-headed thumbtacks or upholstery tacks. Smooth sailing from here on out.

Multipurpose furniture

Have an old china cabinet lurking in the attic? Put it to use in the kitchen, if you have the room: instead of storing grandma's plates in it, turn it into storage for spices, measuring cups, and baking tools, or anything that otherwise clogs your cabinets.

Hats off to plates

Whether you keep inheriting piles of plates from well-meaning relatives, or you just can't resist them at tag sales and antique fairs, don't let them overrun your cupboards. Empty out those old hatboxes you have, and use them to store plates on top of each other, separated by pieces of soft cardboard or paper plates. Label the boxes and stow them in the attic or on a basement shelf.

Sheathe your kitchen knives

The razor-sharp knives you use for cooking can be dangerous, so never keep them loose in a drawer with other kitchen tools. If you don't have the countertop space for a butcher-block knife holder, fashion protective sheaths for your knives from empty paper towel tubes. To make a sheath, just flatten a tube, fold over one end and staple or tape it closed, then slide a knife in the other end. For small knives, use toilet paper tubes.

Keep small appliances in clear plastic containers

Kitchen counters a mess? Can't find the coffee grinder behind the electric pepper mill? Large, clear plastic storage containers are a great way to keep small tools used infrequently out of the way, but still in sight, on a garage, basement, or walk-in pantry shelf.

What's the Story?
The Arrival of Plastic

When did man-made plastic first appear? It made its debut at the 1862 Great International Exhibition in London, the work of British chemist Alexander Parkes, who named his cellulose-derived creation Parkesine—the first organic material able to retain its shape after being heated and molded. Six years later, an enterprising Albany, New York, printer named John Wesley Hyatt discovered that the solvent action of camphor on cellulose nitrate under heat and pressure created a clear and durable material—celluloid, which transformed photography and, in the early 20th century, movie film.

The first mass-marketed plastic, Bakelite, was introduced in 1907. The phenol-formaldehyde resin—perfected in Yonkers, New York, by Belgian-born Leo Hendrik Baekeland—was used to manufacture everything from telephone handsets to kitchenware to engine parts. Teflon made its first appearance in 1937, and nylon one year later. The arrival of polyester in 1942 would transform the manufacture of clothing, as anyone who donned a leisure suit or pink polyester pantsuit in the 1970s could attest.

Today's liquid crystal polymers and other new plastics in no way resemble Mr. Parkes's rudimentary invention. Little could he have dreamed that a century and a half later, flying machines would be as ubiquitous as horse-drawn carriages, and that one of those machine's bodies would be plastic: the Boeing 787 Dreamliner, made from the same reinforced plastic used for golf club shafts.

Repackage dried food in plastic

If your cabinet space is cramped (and whose isn't?) repackage dried food products. Food manufacturers seem to delight in filling containers only two-thirds (or even half) full—and as the food diminishes, the size of the box doesn't. Gain precious room by transferring most of your dry food to see-through plastic containers (and then label and date them!). Flat rectangular containers work best, since they're stackable and ideal for storing tea bags, dried beans, rice, pasta, and cereal.

Ready-made picnic totes

A six-pack container (the kind used for beer or cola) is ideal for carrying picnic supplies from the kitchen to the car to the blanket spread out in the meadow or park. Bind plastic utensils with a rubber band and put them in one compartment, then fill the other compartments with picnic paraphernalia such as rolled up napkins, salt and pepper shakers, squeeze bottles of ketchup or mustard or mayo, and a can of insect spray.

Smart idea for storing leftovers

If you have a label-making machine, here's an idea that may not have occurred to you. Store all of your leftovers on the same rack, and label the shelf so no one forgets where to put them. No machine? Cut a piece of paper to size, write "Leftovers" in indelible ink, and tape the label onto the rim of the rack with transparent tape. Designating a leftovers shelf and labeling it will make it much less likely the remains of the steamed broccoli you enjoyed in April won't be covered in mold in June.

A movable candy bin

When organizing your kitchen cabinets with the aid of baskets or boxes, keep a special one for candy. Either place the goodies bin on a low shelf that the kids can reach or on a high shelf where it's out of reach.

Three-ring recipes

A box will keep your recipe cards all in one place, but a three-ring binder will go it one better. Slip the cards into pocketed plastic photo holders made for ring binders. Arrange recipes by type and then tape a colored plastic file tab on the first page of each category: soups, chicken dishes, and so forth. Using a binder will make it easier to browse through your cards and choose the perfect recipe for the occasion.

Scan your recipes

If you're computer savvy, clear your clutter by scanning all of those yellowing recipes into computer files. Organize them into style of food, entree, desserts, holiday favorites, salads—the possibilities are endless. This will enable you to search for recipes with a couple of keystrokes!

DECANT BIG BAGS OF FLOUR

If large bags of flour, sugar, cereal, or pasta are on sale, don't worry about keeping them on your cabinet shelves; empty the bags into individual, supersize clear plastic **storage containers**, label them, and stack them on an out-of-the-way shelf in the basement.

The Clutter-Free Bathroom

Downsize your essentials

If the total of family members in your household equals three, do you really need 18 bath towels, 12 hand towels, and 10 washcloths? And how many bottles and tubes of cosmetics and ointments and painkillers crowd medicine cabinet shelves and vanity drawers? The first task for the clutter fighter is to get rid of what you don't need; the second is to look for ways to save space—and here are ways to do both.

- To free up shelf space, attach three or four towel rods on the back of the door and hang a week's supply of towels from the rods.

- Make two bathroom toolkits, and store one in a ready-to-go ziplock bag for quick packing. Include tweezers, nail clippers, scissors, Q-tips, and cotton balls.

Search out shelf space

If you have a window, a shelf supported by brackets of the same material will hold towels and supplies.

A 2-foot expanse of wall is room enough for two- or three-tiered shelving, good for holding supplies of any kind. Get more mileage out of it by attaching a board to the bottom and installing hooks for hanging wet towels.

Racks to the rescue

Wish you had more towel racks in your bathroom? Forgo time-consuming installation and simply stand a coat rack in the corner—ideal for hanging towels and bathrobes.

Lunch Box to First-Aid Kit

Your son Henry outgrew his superhero lunch box a long time ago and consigned it to the attic, but there's life in the colorful aluminum carrying case yet. It's just the right size to hold bandages, gauze, scissors, and tape on one side and a bottle of isopropyl alcohol and an antiseptic spray or ointment—plus the cotton balls used to apply them—on the other.

Keep the kit in a bathroom cabinet, and you'll be able to grab everything at once whenever you have to run out to the yard and treat little Henry Jr.'s cuts and scrapes.

When it comes to *storing* towels, a wine rack meant for countertops fits the bill. You'll want to put the rack, which will accommodate from five to 10 rolled-up towels, depending on the design—wherever it seems most practical— the floor, perhaps, or atop a cabinet. A bonus: Besides saving space, the rack brings an attractive architectural note to the bathroom.

Hang tiered baskets

Those tiered wire baskets made for decluttering the kitchen will come in handy in the bathroom as well—and the less room you have, the more you need to make use of the bathroom's air space. Hang a set of tiered baskets from the ceiling and then stash rolled hand towels in the largest basket and toiletries or what-have-you in the smaller ones.

An unused lunch box makes a perfect *first-aid kit!*

Toiletries to go

Here's a clever space-saving idea for large families with too few bathrooms: Turn small wicker baskets into toiletry caddies and keep one in each family member's bedroom. Everyone can then carry his or her toiletries to the bathroom as needed.

Paint each basket a different color and fill it with customized supplies—for Dad, his preferred toothpaste, shaving cream and razor, and other grooming supplies; for Mom, cosmetics, hair care products, and the like. Whatever you load into the baskets will help keep bathroom countertops clutter-free.

Move meds out

Removing your prescription and over-the-counter pharmaceuticals from a bathroom cabinet to the kitchen or bedroom will do more than save space in one of the home's smallest rooms. The warmth and humidity in bathrooms can degrade the stability and potency of some drugs, so put them in a lidded plastic container or shoebox and store them in a cool, dry place. You'll want to make sure the medicines are out of the reach of children, of course.

Mount a magnet

A magnetic knife holder mounted on the bathroom wall makes an ideal holder for small metal necessities like nail clippers, tweezers, and toenail scissors. No more searching for small stuff in a messy drawer or cabinet!

A hair fashions box

Present your favorite little girl with a compact, compartmentalized box with a clasp (a flat fishing tackle box is ideal), and then ask her to sort her hair accessories into the compartments by type. If she is so young she has difficulty opening the box, ask her to bring it to you whenever she likes. As she observes you taking items from the box and returning them to their proper places, she'll learn to keep her hair accessories and other belongings in order on her own.

In the Workshop and Garage

The magic of magnets

Given a magnet's powerful hold over metal, it's no wonder that so many home-repair folks feel a strong attraction to magnets. They come in handy for a multitude of tasks around the workshop—everything from organizing your workbench to cleaning up spills. Here are a half-dozen fantastic ways to put them to work for you.

- Fix a large round magnet to the wall next to your workspace (or suspend it from the ceiling, if necessary) to keep small metal parts and tools from getting lost in the middle of repair work.

- Before using steel wool, wrap a small bar magnet inside the pad to catch any loose steel strands or particles and keep them from messing up your work area.

- Place small round magnets inside jars or boxes of screws and brads to prevent or contain spillage if they're accidentally knocked over.

Neat Ways to Store Lumber

Keeping loose lumber around your workshop can be dangerous for you and damaging to the wood. But an old wooden ladder can straighten things out. Secure the ladder rail to a wall with wood brackets, and then use the spaces between the rungs to sort different lengths of lumber. You could also stand several pieces of lumber in an old golf bag or keep them bound together inside a pants leg cut from an old pair of jeans.

- Put a bar magnet inside a plastic sandwich bag to pick up spilled nails, nuts, or washers— or even to clean up metal filings. The objects will stick to the outside of the bag, which you can then turn inside out to contain them.

- Magnetize the head of a screwdriver by rubbing it several times with a small horseshoe magnet.

- Hot-glue several magnet strips inside your toolbox or workbench drawer to keep your favorite flat tools at the ready.

Childproof your power cords with a **key ring!**

Pull the plug on power tools

If you're unable to lock up your power tools or place them out of the reach of young children, you can still prevent curious youngsters from plugging them in. Simply slip an ordinary key ring through the hole on the power prongs.

Hang a power cord

Loose power cords can be hazardous around the workbench. Besides posing a danger underfoot, they take up precious space in your work area and can be a real pain to untangle. Keep them neat and out of the way by screwing a few large bicycle hooks into the ceiling joists above your workbench and threading the cords through the open loops. Finally, a way to keep that jungle of wires off the floor and out of your workspace!

Cords for clamps

Don't toss out those old bungee cords; wrapped around furniture, appliances, and other household items, they make excellent band clamps when you tackle repairs. Although the cords aren't adjustable, they can be combined to create almost any desired length or, in the case of long cords, shortened by multiple wrappings.

Keep supplies in the gutter

Who says gutters have to be outside? Not the savvy do-it-yourselfer. Mount a couple of vinyl rain gutters around your work area for an inexpensive yet sturdy way to store lengths of molding, lumber, PVC pipe, and dowels. Simply screw the mounting brackets into the wall studs and snap in the gutters. You could also use the bare gutter brackets to hold wire coils, extension cords, and hoses.

Make the cut

Here's a sharp idea: Remove the serrated cutting strip from a box of aluminum foil or plastic wrap, cut it in half with a metal cutter or shears, and tack or nail one of the sections to the least-used side of your workbench. Make sure the teeth are positioned slightly above the top of the surface. You'll never have to search again for a knife or scissors to cut a piece of tape, rope, or sandpaper.

A place for parts

Make your own parts bins out of recycled plastic milk jugs. Leave the caps on the jugs (seal them with epoxy, if needed), and cut off about ⅓ of the side panel with a utility knife or scissors. Fill the jugs with nails, screws, nuts, and other small parts, then place them on a small bookshelf or cabinet. You can also stand the jugs upright, of course, and the handles make for easy transport.

Prevent rust on tools

If your garage is damp and you store tools there, prevent rusting by lightly coating them with petroleum jelly or car wax. If you're storing tools you don't use often, spray them with a silicone lubricant and wrap them in aluminum foil. The next time you use the tools, just wipe them with a soft cloth.

Hammock in the garage?

Yes, but not for lazing about. Make use of the space above your car by stringing a hammock from screw eyes fastened to the garage walls' exposed joists. Presto! A sling for light but bulky items such rolled-up small rugs, basketballs, hockey and lacrosse sticks, and exercise mats.

Repurposing Has Its Rewards

A quick look through your home recycling bin can usually turn up a bunch of items that can significantly reduce the clutter around your workshop. Here are a few suggestions to get you started.

- Use empty prescription pill bottles, film canisters, glass jars, coffee cans, and the see-through plastic tops from CD spindles to hold nails, screws, and other fasteners.

- Turn an old ice cube tray or a muffin pan into an organizer for washers, tacks, brads, nuts, and bolts.

- Number the 12 compartments in an egg carton and use each cup to hold disassembled parts in the order they're removed.

- Use cardboard tubes from paper towels, gift-wrapping paper, and toilet paper rolls to neatly hold extension cords, ropes, and dowels.

- Mount a large block of recycled Styrofoam near your workbench to use as a "pincushion" for drill bits, screwdrivers, pens, punches, wrenches, and other tools.

- Glue a piece of cardboard onto the bottom of a building brick (the type with holes in it) and use the brick to hold files, drill bits, brushes, craft knives, and the like.

Your Home Office

The No. 1 home office storage space

Forget about fancy desk dividers or those costly built-in shelves; the most important home office storage space under your roof is the hard drive of your computer. Your Rolodex, appointment book, desk calendar, and business card holder (not to mention pictures of your children) that seem to travel about on your worktable will be immediately available in the most uncluttered way possible, if you digitize them.

Filing cabinet as conference table base

Well, a round conference table that can seat two or three. The space between the tabletop and the floor won't go to waste if you use a metal filing cabinet or an old bedside chest as a support. Use ¾-inch plywood for the top and bolt it to the top of the cabinet. Then cover with a tablecloth that almost reaches the floor. Store rarely-used files in the cabinets below, and you'll be crawling under the table only once in a blue moon.

A secret filing cabinet

No intrigue here—just a filing cabinet that looks like anything but. What is it? A straw rectangular basket with a lid, something more often found in a living area than a home office. A basket with dimensions of roughly 20-by-20-by-10 inches should accommodate around 30 files of average size or up to a dozen well-stuffed file folders. Placed under or beside your worktable, the basket is decorative as well as functional.

Invest in a small safe

Store deeds, birth certificates, insurance information, and passports in a fireproof safe that can be stowed on the top shelf of a closet. Out of sight, but not out of mind.

Door-top bookshelf

When you run out of space for books, put a shelf in the space above the door and below the ceiling. If you have a piece of lumber in the garage or storeroom, you have yourself a shelf whose only cost is the support brackets you buy at the home store. A coat of paint on a sawn-to-size board will keep it from looking like a makeshift shelf in a college dorm room.

Tips for Packing, Mailing, and Shipping

Some of those things you're trying to keep in order are mailed to you (hello, catalog shopping) and others are things you want to send—say a care package to you son at summer camp. Herewith a few tips for making things run smoothly when you pack and ship or prepare a letter for mailing.

Rustle up free packing material

Wadded-up newspaper is probably the first thing you reach for when packing something in a box, but you can also use several other items you most likely have on hand—like these:

- Plastic grocery bags
- Paper grocery bags
- Dry cleaning bags
- Paper strips from your shredder
- T-shirts bound for the dustbin

Store such stuff in paper bags in the basement or garage so they won't steal space in your closets or cabinets.

Pop some popcorn

Unbuttered air-popped popcorn makes excellent packing material because it's soft and light as a feather. It's also green—not because popcorn is now coming in colors (it isn't), but because its biodegradability makes it environmentally correct.

Towel fragile items

You've collected everything you need for your college-age daughter's care package, and it's time to pack up all the items you need. Instead of filling the box with packing peanuts, why not use something she can keep? That would be bath towels and, if she has kitchen facilities, dish towels. Wrapped several times around fragile items, towels provide protection and make a nice gift.

No-stick hands

Those infernal polystyrene packing peanuts cling to your hands when you unpack a shipment. To keep the peanuts from sticking, simply rub your hands with a fabric softener sheet.

Keep paper-shredder blades sharp

Cutting aluminum foil will sharpen your scissors, and the shiny stuff will do the same for the blades in your paper shredder. Lay a sheet of 8½-by-11-inch paper on two sheets of heavy-duty aluminum foil as a cutting guide, then snip away. Feed the sheets of foil through the shredder one at a time, and the blades with sharpen right up.

A good-looking bulletin board

A jungle of Post-it notes and envelopes and papers stuck to a bulletin board isn't the prettiest sight to behold. So make your easy-to-reach "filing system" more attractive by covering the board with felt and attaching ribbons to hold your stuff. Start by choosing felt in the color of your choice. Then cut it 4–5 inches larger than the board on all four sides, pull it taut over the board, and staple the overage to the back. Use upholstery tacks to secure ribbons to the board, pulling them as taught as possible so that paper slipped behind the ribbons won't fall through. You could crisscross the ribbons to create a diamond pattern over the whole board, or position them to look like latticework—as long as it works, the design is up to you.

A real vertical file

"Vertical file" is business slang for "wastebasket." But an actual vertical file borrowed from your child's toy box will keep mail, tickets, and papers of similar size from cluttering up your workspace. What is it? A Slinky. Set it on your worktable and slide stray papers in between the wires.

A business card album

A small photo album is ideal for keeping business cards in order. Simply slip a card or two in the protective plastic sleeves made for ring binders. With a ring binder to leaf through, your days of shuffling through a stack of cards for the one you seek are gone.

Office-in-a-closet

Tight on space but long on office need? Turn a spare coat closet into your workspace at home; if you're lucky enough to have a double closet, even better. Remove the doors, attach a thick plank of plywood from one inside wall to the other; use upper shelves to store less frequently used items such as a dictionary, extra stationery, your laptop. Slip a filing cabinet under the "desk," add a lamp, and you'll be good to go.

Keep documents in a scrapbook

Scrapbooks outfitted with plastic sleeves or pockets are ideal for keeping business contracts and other documents in order.

MISPLACED YOUR PENCIL SHARPENER?

In a pinch, sharpen a pencil with a **vegetable peeler**. This kitchen instrument beats a pocketknife when you have to rely on something other than your usual tool.

Storing Holiday Decorations

Tangle-free twinklers

What are the holidays without strings of lights, whether they illuminate trees, mantels, or yard displays? And what are fresh-out-of-storage cords of lights if not tangled? All you need to keep them orderly is an empty coffee can and its lid.

First, slice the plastic lid of the can with a sharp knife and insert one end of the light cord. Then wrap the cord of lights around the can, taping the end to the can to keep everything in place. Before putting on the lid, fill the can with extra bulbs and an extension cord. No tangles, no misplaced accessories!

Give fragile items top billing

Tree and mantel ornaments range from wooden toy drummers to delicate winged doves made of crystal—the latter and their ilk needing special care. If you pack fragile items with other ornaments, first wrap them in tissue and put them in a self-sealing plastic bag. When putting them in the storage box, be sure to place them on top of the other ornaments so they won't be damaged as you dig into the box next year.

Storing big stuff

The Santa on your lawn, complete with sleigh and reindeer, isn't inflatable. Rather, the components of the merry tableau are made of molded plastic that can't be squashed flat—and unless you have room to spare, they present a storage problem bigger than Santa's toy bag. Your first step toward smart storage is to save zippered garment bags, which should be large enough to hold one or two or the pieces—or more,

depending on their size. Then hang the bags from rafters in the attic or basement. You could also consider hanging a hammock between two rafters and heaving the bagged pieces into it.

Make bows easy to spot

Have an extra glass canister that you haven't found a use for?

If it's tall and has a lid, store self-sticking bows in the canister so that, come gift-wrapping time, you'll see what your choices are at a glance.

How to store candles

If stored in a hot place, candles tend to warp and curve—and a curving candle is good only for the person who enjoys candle making and melts down candles. Prevent the problem by choosing a storage spot that stays below 75°F for the year, even if that means the cellar or a closet. Wrap individual candles in tissue paper and lay them flat in a plastic container or a cardboard box—or, in the spirit of repurposing, paper-towel tubes or cylindrical potato chip cans.

New life for wrapping paper

Don't throw away wrapping paper and tissue that piles up as your family opens gifts. Instead, use it to keep the holiday ornaments you'll soon be storing from getting scratched or chipped, or donate it to a pet care center. Choose one or all of these three options:

- Wrap each ornament in leftover paper when placing in the storage box. If desired, store ornaments by type and Christmas tree balls by color. However you choose to store, label each box with the contents.

- Feed the wrapping paper into a shredder. Then use the paper ribbons as packing material to keep your ornaments in good shape.

- Donate shredded wrapping paper to a veterinary clinic. Many veterinarians use shredded paper as bedding for the animals in their care. Just call first to make sure the paper is wanted and needed.

Holiday spirit in a black plastic bag

Look at old clothing, furniture, appliances, electronic equipment, and odds and ends of any sort not as "just something to get rid of" but as items that would be welcomed by the less fortunate. Organizations or charitable groups will accept virtually anything that is still in good condition. Clothing can be donated to the clothes closet of a local house of worship or a charitable consignment store.

A cardboard box filled with gently worn shoes or a black plastic trash bag filled with towels and sheets that no longer match your color scheme becomes a vessel of hope, not of refuse bound for the city dump. Either deliver your goods to the charity in person or schedule a pickup. Your reward is less the tax deduction you can take for donated goods than the knowledge that someone in need will benefit from a "new" shirt, pair of shoes, sofa, or even the connection to the world at large, a computer.

GREETING CARD ART

If you enjoy tackling crafts projects with your kids or on your own, look at the **holiday cards** you receive as a wealth of raw material. Snipping images from the cards and using them to create collages or abstract compositions gives you artworks suitable for framing. Even better, it consolidates the wishes of friends and family into a memento that's both aesthetically pleasing and meaningful.

Garlanding Made Easy

The artificial garlands you draped on the staircase drew raves from friends and family last Christmas, but this year you're not sure which lengths of garland went where. There they sit in a large plastic box, and you foresee wasting your time by laying and re-laying them alongside the second-floor railing until they all come together as they should.

How to eliminate the guesswork? Take these three simple steps before putting the garlands away for storage.

1
Tag the lengths with their location, numbering them in order from the top railing to the newel post at the bottom.

2
Use twist-ties to mark the spots where the lengths were tied to the banister to make swags.

3
Label the storage box clearly ("Staircase Garland") so it won't be confused with any other garlands you might have used.

This 'n' That

Elevated basement storage

Storing furniture and other large items in the basement is risky because of the humid conditions. If you have no choice but to keep Grandma Lila's old cherrywood sideboard there for a while, safeguard it or any other vulnerable item from moisture by placing it on a wooden pallet and covering it with a large tarp.

If you're wondering where to find a free pallet, check with the nearest grocery store. An alternative platform is a 1-inch slab of plywood supported by cinder blocks.

Attic air-freshener

Your attic contains everything from hanging bags of clothes to old hats and gloves and scarves. So wouldn't it be nice if it didn't smell like an attic? Banish mustiness with the lava rocks used for barbecue grills. Just scoop rocks into four or five mesh bags and hang the bags from the attic's beams. Every few months, refresh the rocks by setting them outside in the sun for 4–6 hours. Lava rocks left out in the sun should absorb musty odors for years on end.

The wandering shower caddy

It doesn't take an Einstein to realize that a shower caddy needn't be confined to the bathroom. Use it anywhere inside the house to stock items of all sorts—laundry room supplies, gardening products and small tools, and so on. Just hang the caddy from a doorknob or from a sturdy hook or nail on the wall of the garage, basement, workshop, or garden shed.

TLC for anything framed

You should not only store framed photographs and artworks properly to extend their life but also label them as clearly as possible—the latter accomplished by taping a photograph of the framed piece to its wrapper (use a Polaroid or the printout of a digital shot). Wrapping paintings, framed prints, lithographs, and photographs takes some time, but pays off in the end. Wrap each piece in acid-free tissue paper and sandwich it between two layers of $\frac{1}{4}$-inch foam board cut a bit larger than the frame. Tape the corners and middle of the board, then wrap the package in brown paper. After taping the paper at every seam, attach the photograph of the piece within.

Bonus hint 1: Never wrap artwork of any kind in plastic, which can trap moisture and cause warping or the growth of mold.

Bonus hint 2: Wear cotton gloves when handling an oil painting. Touching the surface (back or front) will leave oils and salts from your hands—substances that can eventually crack or otherwise damage dried oil paint.

Two ways to hang twine

Say that you need to keep three balls of twine or string fairly handy—jute twine for bundling newspapers and flattened cardboard for recycling; nylon garden twine for tying plants to stakes; and colored string for gift-wrapping. How would you go about saving yourself from fishing for them in drawers or tool bin? Try these two tricks:

- Install three hooks on a wall or on the back of a door, spacing them 6–8 inches apart. Now slide a cord or ribbon (or a length of twine from the ball itself, for that matter) through each spool and knot it. Hang a ball of twine from each hook, and your twine is easily accessible.

- Use funnels instead of hooks. Choose funnels large enough to hold a ball of twine and nail the top rim of each to the wall. Put a ball of twine in each funnel and run the ends out of the spouts—and presto! A twine dispenser that works like a charm.

Bank on this one

Bank statements seem to accumulate faster than you can say "prime interest rate," especially when you're so busy you can't find the time to check them. A quick fix: Each time a statement arrives in the mail, scan it and save it as a file in your computer. The result? All the info you need, and no paper to take up space.

Free labels for your stuff

Some charities that send out promotional mailings include a small batch of personalized address labels in the packet. If they've gotten your name and address right, you can use the unsolicited gift to label personal items as well as envelopes. Paste the labels inside books, on the underside of staplers and other small pieces of office equipment, and on the back of your cell phone. With the aid of tape, you could even affix one of the labels to your umbrella or the inner cuffs of mittens or gloves.

What's the Story?
Science's Take on Tangling

When you put away last year's Christmas tree lights, you carefully looped the strings so they wouldn't get tangled. And here they are—one big mess. It's enough to tie a neatnik in knots.

Relax: Physics, not you, is to blame. In October 2007, experiments conducted at the University of California, San Diego, showed that strings basically tie themselves when agitated. Physics Professor Douglas Smith and research assistant Dorian Raymer wrote in the prestigious journal *Proceedings of the National Academy of Sciences* that they had developed a mathematical formula explaining why strings and cords knot so easily.

Their method? Shaking strings placed in boxes. The result? Roughly half of the shaken strings came out of the box knotted.

We'll spare you the particulars of knot theory (a mathematical branch of topology) and let a scientist encapsulate why strings of lights tangle themselves. During an interview aired on National Public Radio (NPR) in December 2007, Stanford University Professor Keith Devlin—known on NPR as The Math Guy—laid it out:

"[Smith and Raymer's] program gave them tremendous insight into how Christmas tree lights or iPod earphone cords ... get tangled up. What we know now is that roughly half of the times a knot forms, it begins to form within the first two or three seconds of shaking. So even if you've only taken that Christmas tree box up the stairs into the attic, the chances are high that you're going to tangle it."

See there? The tangling of strings of lights isn't always caused by haphazard storage habits but rather by forces beyond your control.

Chapter Five

Making Your Home *Sweet* Home

Okay, you're no Martha Stewart or Christopher Lowell. But honestly, who is (except, of course, for Martha or Christopher)? And for that matter, do we really need to be them?

When it comes to decorating, our list of helpful household items and intuitive but surprising tips includes almost everything in the house and will make you feel like you could easily teach Martha herself a thing or two. This chapter is about using what you already have to make the place you call home look, feel, and function to meet your needs, your style, and your budget. You'll find loads of practical ways to create fresh looks by reusing, refurbishing, and repurposing.

Ever thought of whitewashing or glazing wallpaper to give it a brighter feel or using a beat-up old ladder as a design feature? Ever throw away a piece of fabric or an old glass bottle just because you're not sure what to do with it? You're about to discover how easy it is to update all sorts of furnishings and accessories by using what you have on hand. So get inspired, get to work, and get ready to delight in being your own decorator.

Turn your living space
into a photo gallery with
a clothesline!

Changes Around the House

Looking for the best free decorator?

No problem! Just look in a mirror. This two-step trick will turn you into an interior decorator without costing a penny.

1. "Edit" a room by putting everything that *isn't* furniture out of sight. Remove personal items, linens (leave the curtains if it's a pain to take them down), pillows, throw rugs, lamps, artwork, electronics, books, and magazines.

2. Look at what's left. By getting down to the bones of a room, you'll gain a better perspective on what you have and whether it works for you.

Most likely, you'll decide to reposition or eliminate some furniture. Perhaps a fresh coat of paint or adapting your existing window treatments is all you need. Or it may have been all that "stuff" that was making an attractive room look dowdy or overcrowded. With the room stripped down to basics, you can envision the space and its contents anew, see fresh possibilities, and improve the room—and at no cost whatsoever.

Laundry basket as pillow nest

What can you do when all those fancy throw pillows get in the way? Convert an old wicker laundry basket into a pillow holder. If you have a plastic laundry basket, cover it with a sheet by setting the basket on it and folding the sides and corners into the basket itself (like you were wrapping a gift). Fill with pillows and no one will know that you didn't buy it at that fancy design shop.

New furniture from spare chairs

Nobody ever seems to have enough small tables, but many of us have too many chairs. If so, think about converting those extra chairs into something more useful. In most cases, straight-backed armless chairs with hard, flat seats are easiest to work with.

- Paint two chairs of different designs in the same color to make an attractive pair of bedside "tables."

- Refinish or paint a straight-backed chair that has arms and set it in the mudroom as a catchall for hats, bags, and umbrellas.

PUT TOGETHER A NO-FRILLS DESIGN KIT

Use the tried and true design-planning method that's easy, cheap, fun, and free of any sales pressure—a do-it-yourself design kit made with a **ruler,** a **pencil,** graph paper, a pencil, construction paper, and a tape measure.

That old woven basket will make a great place to store pillows!

- Make a coffee table substitute with two or three wooden chairs; they needn't match so long as the seats are approximately the same height. Saw off the back of each one at seat level and sand well; you may also need to trim off any corner protuberances that rise a bit above seat level. To guard against stains, paint the chairs with water-resistant enamel. When the paint dries, line up the little tables as a unique and practical coffee table.

Lay that sledgehammer down!

Renovating a kitchen brings out the beast in the homeowner, but don't destroy those cabinets yet. Instead, consider how you might reuse them in another part of the house. You could …

- Hang wall cabinets in the workroom or garden shed, removing the doors for open shelving.
- Put two single or one double wall cabinet (standard depth approximately 12 inches) in a kid's closet to hold toys and clothes or in a hall closet for storing seasonal gear.
- Add casters to a base cabinet to make a rolling cart for the laundry room.
- Make a study desk or worktable with a couple of base cabinets topped with a plain, smooth-surfaced old door.
- Stack two single or double top cabinets to make a nifty storage unit for sewing and craft supplies.

Create a strong focal point in any room

The focal point of a room is the first visual element to which the eye is immediately drawn. Rooms without an obvious focal point tend to look bland, disorganized, or incomplete, regardless of the quality of the furnishings. To add flair to a blah, unfocused room, the quick and inexpensive fix is to use items you already have. Decide on the logical focus of attention, and then go through your storage closets and attic for things you've tucked away or forgotten.

- Bright throw pillows or a quilt will add impact to a plain-Jane bed.

- Frame that beautiful silk scarf or lace shawl you haven't worn in years and hang it on the wall behind the bed.

- If your fireplace and mantel don't grab the eye, use leftover paint to set them off with a floor-to-ceiling background panel of a different color. Hang a large mirror or a display of eye-catching pottery plates above the mantel.

- Get rid of clutter to bring the eye to a focal point: Remember that less is more, so rotate collectibles instead of displaying all of your treasures all the time.

Shelving from odds and ends

Instead of spending big bucks on shelving, look around you: What about those wooden trays you never use? A shallow drawer from an old dresser or desk? Or the sturdy in-out boxes someone at the office was about to give the heave-ho? Maybe the decorated drawer fronts from a baby's old chest would make fun shelves for a growing youngster. The size and weight of a makeshift shelf will determine the kind of brackets and hardware you need when attaching it to a wall, so take your "shelf" to a good hardware store and ask for advice. If you

plan to load anything heavy on the shelf, like books, attach it to a wall stud or studs.

New uses for louvered shutters

Don't throw out those old louvered shutters until you've considered the possibilities. Hinge three or more shutters together so they'll fold accordion-style, to create handsome, practical screens for indoors and out. Long shutters make an attractive screen to separate sleeping and dressing areas in a bedroom or to shade a sunny area on a porch or patio. Secure a panel of hinged shutters to the wall behind a plain bed for a knockout headboard. Have a weird corner space calling out for something? Stand up a tall louvered screen to soften the angle.

Bonus idea: Metal or vinyl louvered shutters, laid flat over two sawhorses, make a great outdoor potting table for gardeners. Water and air go through the slats, making it easy to wash and dry pots and garden tools, water and drain houseplants, and hose away dirt and debris.

A Tiny Touch of Originality

Remember what refrigerators used to look like? Today they're likely to be covered with more magnets than a millipede has legs. While the fridge as magnetic bulletin board filled with notes, photos, take-out food menus, and you-name-it is a boon to busy folks, it will benefit greatly from the occasional decluttering. And why not use magnets that reflect *you,* not the taste of some anonymous designer? Make your own simply by hot gluing small magnets, sold at craft stores, to tiny souvenirs and found objects like small seashells; clip-on earrings (clips removed); lapel pins from museums; smooth, flat river rocks; or unusual buttons.

Color Your World

Save those leftover paints

Whenever the decorating bug bites, you'll be very glad you didn't toss out your half-empty paint cans. Hang on to them to create small "patch" tests during those redecorating binges. Better still, use them for:

- Patching nicks and scratches in existing wall paint
- Priming for new paint
- Redoing or touching up old furniture and accessories
- Painting a closet or pantry
- Painting the inside of a small cupboard
- Tinting other paints to create color washes
- Creating multicolor faux finishes
- Doing decorative stenciling
- Painting trim work on everything from furniture to picture frames

Transfer small amounts of leftover paints to wide-mouthed plastic storage containers, like clean mayonnaise or peanut butter jars. Label by color, type of paint, and manufacturer. Air and moisture are the enemies of stored paint, so be sure tops and lids seal tightly. Alkyd and oil-based paint will form their own protective skins in the containers. For latex (water-based) paint, lay a layer of plastic wrap atop the paint before putting the lid on. And always store leftover paints in a cool, dry place, away from direct sunlight.

Make that bookcase pop!

One of the simplest ways to add depth to a room is to paint or wallpaper the inside backs of built-in bookcases and display shelving—a great way

to use leftover decorating materials. If you paint, keep in mind that darker colors appear to recede, fooling the eye into seeing a deeper recess—hence

What's the Story?

The Famous Novelist Who "Invented" Interior Design

Modern interior design owes its origins to one of America's greatest fiction writers. Edith Wharton (1862-1937), born Edith Newbold Jones to a socially prominent New York family, went on to skewer her own class in *The House of Mirth*, her Pulitzer Prize–winning *The Age of Innocence*, and other widely read novels and story collections. But it was her first book, *The Decoration of Houses* (1897) that punctured the pretensions of upper-class Victorian decorating and set out many principles that guide interior design to this day.

Collaborating with architect Ogden Codman Jr., the well-traveled Mrs. Wharton brought her knowledge of French and Italian home decor to the mix, comparing European lightness, elegance, and comfort to the "exquisite discomfort" of the dreary, cold, overstuffed drawing rooms of New York's upper crust. Her book is credited with elevating interior decoration from lady's hobby to profession. Not the bestseller she hoped for, *The Decoration of Houses* did earn her first royalty check, sold steadily for many years, and is still studied today.

Age Furniture with Candles

Do you like the worn, "shabby chic" look that's all the rage but don't want to spend the (large) amounts of money that these pieces cost? Use a common household candle to reproduce the look on any wooden piece of furniture (new or old) that you plan to paint.

1

First, prime the piece with an under-color primer (as though the furniture had been painted this color previously) and allow the prime coat to dry thoroughly.

2

Rub a white candle along edges and corners, around knobs and pulls, randomly over chair arms—wherever the furniture finish would be worn away by frequent use. Be generous with the wax but brush away any flaky bits.

3

Now paint the piece with a coat of the main color, which won't adhere to the wax. If you need another coat of the top color—a possibility if you're painting a light color over a darker one—rub a little more wax over the exposed places.

4

When the piece is completely dry, just rub away the wax with a soft cotton cloth dipped in warm water.

a larger room. A solid or discreetly patterned wallpaper will achieve the same effect.

Spruce up trim with color

Before starting a large-scale "freshening" project, look up at your wall moldings and trim, and check your supply of leftover paints. In general, a single trim color is carried throughout the home to unify the spaces from room to room. But you could add color to, say, a child's room, family room, or game room by painting the trim in an accent color. (To maintain the visual flow with the rest of the house, keep doors and window frames in the overall trim color.)

Don't strip that wallpaper; glaze it!

If your wallpaper has fallen out of style but you dread the hideous job of stripping it, apply a glaze to soften colors and tone down patterns. Far less mess, much less time—and with luck, you already have the key ingredients: white latex interior paint, latex glazing liquid, water, and a small amount of colored latex for tinting the wash. This is a great two-person project— the application requires coordination but goes very quickly.

1. Mix 1 part white latex to 1 part white glaze Add water to thin. As you add the water, test the mix on a paper remnant or a small, out-of-the-way patch of wall. If the wash is too strong, add more water and test again. (Water can account for up to half of the finished product).

2. Once you're happy with the look, wash the mix over the paper with a lint-free cloth, using a swirling motion as if you were cleaning the wall. Work in sections and work fast, because glaze dries rapidly.

3. Use a brush to apply the glaze wash at corners and edges, tamping with a cloth to remove brush strokes. Then, step back and pat yourself on the back for having chosen such a clever and attractive solution.

Take an old ladder and …

Give it a new lease on life. It may be too wobbly to stand on, but an aged wooden ladder—with its many nicks, paint splatters, and worn-down rungs—has *character*.

- Prop it against an outside wall and use the rungs to display plants.

- Add some heavy-duty hooks and hang the ladder horizontally on a mudroom or porch wall to make a handy catchall for coats, hats, gloves, wet swimsuits and towels, and whatever else your family usually dumps on the floor.

- Suspend an old but still-sturdy ladder from the kitchen ceiling and equip it with metal S-hooks for a unique, cost-free pot rack. Point is, that ladder may not be ready for retirement yet—just a change of career.

Rainbow colors for outdoor furniture

Outside, you have five lawn chairs that have seen better days. Inside, you have five cans of leftover paint. Here's your chance to make good use of those paints you've been saving and to go a little crazy with color to boot. There's no rule that all outdoor furniture has to look the same, so be adventurous and go for the bold. As long as you prepare surfaces well by sanding and cleaning and follow manufacturers' instructions, you can use leftover interior paints on outdoor pieces and protect them with a polyurethane finish. Rusty metal furniture should be scraped as needed and primed with a rust-resistant undercoat. Thanks to modern technology, you can also spray paint faded plastic yard furniture.

Bright Ideas for Lamps and Lighting

Use a light-diffusing slipcover for a shade

Lamplight owes its beauty more to the lampshade than the bulb. To soften harsh light from a fabric or paper shade, try this gathered slipcover—especially easy for a round shade. Check your flame-retardent remnants and linen closet for a lightweight fabric in a pale-to-medium color or pattern, and rustle up some narrow ribbon to make the fabric gather.

1. Cut the material about twice as wide as the smaller circumference of the shade (longer for a shade with one very wide end) and about 2 inches longer than the top-to-bottom measurement. Piece the fabric if needed, perhaps alternating solid and patterned panels.

2. Seam together the short sides of the fabric. Fold over and stitch the top and bottom edges to make ½-inch pockets, leaving a small opening in each. Now take the ribbon and cut lengths twice as long as the shade's top and bottom circumferences and wrap one end of each length tightly with tape, like a shoelace tip.

3. Thread ribbon through the pockets, playing with the fabric so the gathers are evenly distributed. Tie off excess ribbon as little bows. To secure the cover, tack down top and bottom edges with thread or double-sided fabric tape. The finished shade's look will be as soft and pretty as the lamplight.

Caution: Halogen lights get very hot, so stick with heat-appropriate shades for those lamps.

Perk up your lampshades

Did you know you can spray paint a fabric shade for a snappier look? And you won't have to buy paint if you have some craft paint or leftover latex on hand.

- Using a ratio of 1 part paint to 10 parts water, mix enough to fill a regular-size plastic spray bottle. Be sure the lampshade is clean and free of dust. Protect the inside of the shade with paper secured by masking tape. Begin by spraying a light, even coat; let dry. Spray on more paint, drying between coats, until you have the intensity of color you want.

- Add design by using painter's tape to make vertical or diagonal stripes. Or cut shapes from a coated paper, attaching them to the unpainted shade with spray adhesive (follow instructions for a temporary bond). After spray painting, remove the cutouts once the paint is dry. For a soft, mottled effect, use the same paint formula and dab paint, a little at a time, directly onto the shade with a natural sea sponge. The fabric will diffuse the color, creating a light and airy look.

Silhouettes on the shade

Give extra interest to a plain paper or fabric lampshade with dark or black construction paper cutouts—also a fun way to decorate for special occasions. (Think leaf patterns for Thanksgiving, snowflake silhouettes for a winter holiday, hearts for Valentine's, jack-o-lanterns for Halloween, footballs for a Super Bowl party.) A medium-weight card stock works, too. Translucent white, cream, gold, beige, and pastel shades give the best effect. When cutting out the shapes, size them to the shade—not too large and not too small. Affix the shapes to the inside of the shade with double-sided tape, taking special care that paper doesn't touch, or lie too close to, the lightbulb. Now turn on the lamp and see how the silhouettes appear almost "embedded" in the light. Paper cutouts will begin to curl over time, but they're easy to remove and replace.

Sky's-the-limit lamp bases

Picture your beautiful ceramic flowerpot illuminating your living room. It's relatively simple to convert just about any non-fragile container, large or small, into a one-of-a-kind lamp base. Most containers need a hole drilled in the bottom or side for the cord. You can cannibalize an old lamp for no-cost parts, but if you lack experience with electrical wiring you should take your object of choice to a home store or electrical supplier for help. You might have to spend some money (store-bought lamp kits have almost everything you need)—but compared to a new lamp, you'll be shocked (no pun intended!) by how much you'll save when you create your own. Great lamp bases can be repurposed out of old:

Decorate a drab lampshade with a *paper silhouette.*

- Inexpensive vases
- Tag-sale pitchers
- Large coffee mugs
- Overturned ceramic mixing bowls
- Loving cup-style trophies
- Books that have been placed atop each other and glued together
- Antique wooden boxes
- Flower pots

Paint an old lamp base

Spark up an old or inexpensive wooden, metal, plastic, or even glass lamp base with a coat of paint. Use paint you already have, but check the info on the can to be sure the paint is suitable for the lamp base material. If you must buy paint, one spray can or one small can of enamel should be plenty for a pair of medium-sized lamps. (Glass requires special paint, available from craft suppliers, for a permanent finish.) Color and design are up to you. Anything goes, from an antique finish to a thoroughly modern industrial look.

Before painting, use flexible painter's tape to mask off the fittings and any areas that you want to keep paint-free, such as a metal base or trim. Also tape over the top of the socket to avoid getting paint on the contact points.

Bedazzle an ordinary chandelier

A plain chandelier can become a dazzler when hung with artful strands of crystals and beads. Go through what you have already—leftover glass beads and faux pearls from other craft and sewing projects, crystal baubles from an unused chandelier, beads from broken or no longer fashionable costume jewelry. Look for beads with sparkle. Though stringing with pliable wire will allow you to form shapes, dental floss and

The Stunning Side of Seam Binding

If you sew, you know that inexpensive rayon seam binding has a lovely, silky look and comes in many colors. But did you know it can also substitute for expensive ribbon in some decorating projects? For instance, rejuvenating an old lampshade by wrapping it entirely in silk satin or grosgrain ribbon can cost a small fortune. By using seam binding instead, you'll get the same elegant look. Generally available in ½-inch widths for about 40 cents per yard (less through discounters), seam binding will also work in woven ribbon projects, ribbon flowerets, and even some ribbon needlework. Give it a try. Here's a notion: Rummage through your sewing supplies for all unused bindings and fabric tapes and visualize them not as ho-hum sewing notions but as colorful trims, bows, piping, appliques … whatever strikes your inner decorator's fancy.

beading thread are just as strong as wire. String baubles and beads in interesting combinations, and then loop and swag them on your light fixture (turned off at the switch) until you have a look you like. Then turn on the light and appraise the dazzling results.

Paint a simple ceiling medallion

Plain, flush ceiling light fixtures are the Cinderellas of room lighting; they work so very hard, yet no one pays them any attention. But with a little leftover latex paint, some string, and a ladder, you can dress up an underwhelming ceiling light for the palace ball. The idea is to mimic a circular plaster medallion. On paper, work out an attractive design, such as concentric circles in different colors and shades.

Remember that you'll be painting upside down, so keep the design simple.

Tie a pencil to one end of the string, tape the other end to the center of the fixture, and mark off your outside circle. Use the string compass to mark other circles and semi-circles and a straightedge for lines. Evaluate your design from ground level before painting. If you're not confident of your painting abilities, use flexible painter's tape to outline sections of your medallion as you proceed. Wipe away any mistakes with a wet cloth. With some advance practice, you might add shading and highlighting to give your faux medallion a 3-D look.

Make dinner more intimate

Soft lamplight adds intimacy, and you can duplicate that romantic experience in your dining room, using a lamp and a table runner you already have, plus some masking or painter's tape. Lay the runner on your dining table and position the lamp. If the runner has a cutwork pattern, you may be able to slip the lamp cord through. Otherwise, cut a slit in the runner, just wide enough for the plug, at the point where the cord exits the lamp base. (You can also do this with a tablecloth you don't mind cutting.) Run the cord under the fabric and tape it to the table. Now tape the cord to the inside of a table leg and run it to nearest electrical outlet. To keep anyone from tripping, tape loose cord unobtrusively to the floor. Dim the room lights to get the full effect.

Beautiful botanical candles

Turn plain candles into boutique-worthy, botanical beauties, using the bounty of your garden and nonflammable household glue. Choose small, flat-faced flowers like violets, pansies, or nasturtiums, and press them for a few hours in a telephone book. Flatten ordinary lawn grass (unmowed), fern stems, plant leaves, and flower petals in the same way. Glue the natural material to the lower half of candles. Tip: If you're not going to use the candles immediately, dip them in paraffin melted in a double boiler. A thin coat of paraffin will protect the botanicals and preserve their colors.

ABRACADABRA!

Beeswax candles can cost a pretty penny. If you've got ordinary candles you haven't used, you can get the unique appearance of beeswax by wrapping your candles in **a sheet of beeswax**. Crafts suppliers sell very affordable sheets of beeswax (approximately 8-by-11 inches) in honeycombed or plain textures. With a sharp kitchen or craft knife, cut a rectangle equal to the circumference and height of your candle. Use a hairdryer to soften the beeswax just enough to make it pliable. Wrap the candle and press the beeswax edges together to close the seam.

Ordinary Things Worth Saving

Let's face it: you can't hang on to everything, no matter how devoted a problem solver you are. But there are some basic decorating tools and materials that are worth saving for new projects. Paints, fabric, and wallpaper remnants are obvious. After all, you chose the colors and patterns, so you'll probably like them in new applications. Here are some more prosaic leftovers that won't need to be bought again. Plus, they all have everyday household uses, so saving them means you can find them when you need them.

Special purpose glues and adhesive tapes

Paint solvents

Metal hooks and brackets of any size

Picture hangers

Grommet dies and hole punching tools

Metal hinges

Specialty cutting tools and scrapers

Cleaned paint brushes, rollers, and wooden stirrers

Drop cloths

Regular and heavy-duty metal staples

Upholstery tacks

Curtain rods, hooks, and rings

Metal hooks and brackets of any size

Sandpaper and steel wool

Measuring cups and spoons no longer used for cooking

Tea lights in a sandy bed

Want an economical way to transform any fairly large, shallow, flameproof container into an unexpected light show? Simple! From a treasured silver or wooden tray to a serving platter with gently sloped sides to a simple sheet pan—you're sure to have a suitable container around the house. Even the lid of a large popcorn tin will do. Line the container bottom with aluminum foil and add a smooth layer of clean sandbox or aquarium sand. No sand? Try table or rock salt or small dried legumes such as green and yellow split peas or black beans. Embed tea lights to the top of their sides. Use a small paint or makeup brush to sweep away any material on the candle itself.

Sparkling votive holders

A little glitter and clear-drying household glue will turn a humble votive candleholder into the shimmering, sparkling star of any candle display. Check first that both glitter and glue are not flammable. Brush the votive holder with glue and roll it in glitter. A really thorough coat of glue will produce a nearly opaque glitter covering; less glue, applied randomly, will give the look of a dusting of glitter. If you don't have any glitter, lightly brush on glue and roll the holder in granulated sugar, table salt, or kosher salt. You can't wash these votive holders, but when stored in plastic wrap they will keep their sparkle for quite some time.

Glassware candleholders

Got tons of candles but not enough candle holders? Look through your good, better, and best glassware, and even mundane items like jelly jars, canning jars, tumblers, and imprinted drinking glasses. A mix of pretty glasses with candles—different sizes, shapes, and colors—will make an intriguing arrangement on a table and mantel. Two or three stemmed crystal wine

Light Up That Mantel

During the holiday season, illuminated nativity scenes and menorahs and all kinds other religious or merely decorative lights take pride of place on fireplace mantels the world over. But why not light up a mantel at other times as well? Just forgo packing away your string of lights this year, and hang onto extra bulbs. Here are five ideas to get your imagination going—but first, some cautions: Be very careful that lights are never near water or flammable materials, and unplug lights whenever there's no responsible adult in the room, when you leave the house, or when you turn in for the evening. Use lights that don't heat up, and always check wiring for breaks and wear before using.

- Hide lights in an arrangement of silk flowers or a leafy artificial topiary.
- Feed a strand of lights loosely into a large colored glass bottle or jar.
- Arrange lights in polished silver or brass bowls and cups lined up across the mantel.
- Encircle the frame of a mantel mirror with lights taped just behind the frame edge.
- Fill a long, narrow metal tray with marbles or flat, Asian-style river rocks, and embed twinkle lights among them.

or water goblets can be sublime candleholders on a formal dining table. Float tea candles in cocktail glasses, filled about two-thirds with water. Pillar candles will rest easy inside flat-bottomed water glasses. For glassware with concave or convex bases, adhere pillars or tapers to the inside base with removable putty and pour in enough salt to support the candle. (Salt will catch drips and is easily disposed of.) For a really spectacular look, use a dripless candle and substitute metallic glitter or glass seed beads for the salt.

Decorating for a Party

Garden-fresh flower arrangements

Instead of spending money at the florist for your table arrangements, pick flowers and greenery from your own garden. No garden? Shop the floral section in your grocery for bargains on bunches of flowers that are several days old but still fresh looking. If you're lucky and live near a well-stocked farmers' market, go there first. Another idea: Fill in fresh floral arrangements with your own artificial flowers. In the tangle of blossoms and leaves, it's hard the see the difference between real and faux.

A pumpkin vase for autumn flowers

Move over, Martha! Remove the top of a medium-sized pumpkin and scrape out seeds and pulp, as you would for a jack-o-lantern. In the bottom, cut a hole slightly larger than an ordinary glass kitchen or canning jar that will fit comfortably inside the pumpkin. Fill the jar with water, and add your flowers. You can cut the pumpkin a day or two in advance if you have a cool, shaded place to store it (outside, if the weather is cooperative). Wrap the pumpkin inside and out with several layers of wet paper towels, rewetting the towels as needed.

Protect your holiday decorations from Fido

Are you worried about pulling out Grandma's priceless collection of Christmas vases from the attic, only to have your new puppy, kitten, or grandchild knock them over? Worry no more. Attach a drop of plumber's putty to the bottom surface of your treasures, display them as planned, and they'll stay *put* until the holiday is over.

Don't hide Grandma's silver!

Silver used to be just for special occasions, but there is no better way to add a splash of sparkle to any room than to stand up silver utensils in tall, clear glassware; for a rustic look, place that fancy ware in green antique mason jars (lid off, please), and arrange together on the mantle or wherever a bright light might shine down on Grandma's collection.

DRESS TABLES WITH NATURE'S BOUNTY

An autumn centerpiece of **leaves** at the height of their color is cost-free and beautiful. Add some of nature's dried bounty, like thistle and wild grasses, and light the table with earth-toned candles—exquisite. You can also use leaves as place cards; write names in metallic permanent marker. If you have clear glass charger plates, slip a perfect fall leaf under each charger when you set the table.

Fall arrangement from the wild

To make an eye-pleasing dried arrangement for a fall mantle, coffee table, or sideboard, fill a plain, tall glass vase or deep glass bowl with brown rice, dried beans, or bird seed—simple staples that will not only support your arrangement but also look surprisingly elegant. Or go on a hike and collect dried grasses, cattails, thistle, milkweed, and other long-stemmed flora.

Create a cost-free lightscape with glasses

Forget costly flowers! Instead, gather an interesting selection of drinking glasses, glass bottles, and decorative glass vases and bowls. Include cut glass pieces if you have any. Arrange glass items almost randomly on your dining table or buffet, and add ordinary white candles to some of the containers. Clear glass and crystal will create a wintry look; a mix of clear and colored glass will yield a jewel-like effect.

A hearts-and-flowers centerpiece

How to add heart to a Valentine's dining table without a lot of cost or effort? You'll need a handful of common household items, one of those little plastic sharpeners children keep in their pencil boxes, and thin bamboo skewers.

1. Cut two lengths of waxed paper 18–24 inches long. Place a larger piece of newspaper on your ironing board and then lay one sheet of waxed paper on top.

2. With a pencil sharpener, shave pink and red crayons and the scatter the shavings randomly over the surface of the waxed paper, making sure there aren't any clumps or hard pieces.

3. Lay the second sheet of waxed paper over the shavings-covered sheet, then place another piece of newspaper on top. Run an iron on a low-medium setting (no steam, please) over the newspaper until the crayon shavings are melted and the waxed paper sheets stick together completely.

4. After the paper has cooled, use a template to trace hearts in several sizes. Cut them out and attach a bamboo skewer to each heart with a couple drops of glue.

Add the hearts to your floral arrangement so that they appear to be sprouting upward. The hearts will be translucent in the light—candlelight, of course, for an intimate Valentine's dinner.

A creepy Halloween door wreath

Add some ghoulish fun to the mix when trick-or-treaters come to the door. Some of the essentials, including a magazine and spent flowers, are probably right at hand in your house or yard.

1. Tear pages from a magazine and crumple the paper to make something resembling a chrysanthemum bloom. The resemblance doesn't have to be close; you're going for an effect, not realism.

2. Using a glue gun, glue the "flowers" to cover the wreath form, then spray the wreath and flowers with black paint. So you won't saturate the paper, apply the paint in several layers, letting it dry between coats.

3. If you have some dead and dry garden leftovers, such as purple coneflowers, zinnias, or magnolia leaves, glue them into the wreath. To finish, tie 3 feet or more of wide red ribbon diagonally around the wreath and let the ends trail. Or tie a bow if you have extra ribbon.

4. Hang the wreath on your front door and wait for the arrival of small goblins armed with vampire teeth and paper bags.

Create a Seasonal Centerpiece
with Found Objects

One of the most expensive decorating items you can buy are seasonally correct, holiday-specific centerpieces sold at most florists, but there's no reason to spend the money if you have access to a mirror, a few wide-bottom candles, putty, and extra greenery from your garden. To make a stunning dining table centerpiece that you'll use year after year, holiday after holiday, you'll need these materials, some of which you probably already have:

> An inexpensive, beveled mirror, 2–3 feet long and 1 foot wide
>
> Platter "feet"
>
> 2–3 wide-bottom candles, depending on the length of the mirror
>
> Plumber's putty
>
> Holiday greenery and flowers

If your dining table is long enough, avail yourself of a mirror that's 3 feet long and 1 foot wide; the narrow size will enable guests to see each other and chat over dinner. Plumber's putty and feet can be purchased inexpensively at any hardware or home repair center.

1. Turn the mirror over, and glue the small, round platter feet at each corner. This will keep your centerpiece from sitting flush to the table.

2. Turn the mirror back over, and stand each candle on its surface, at equal distances from each other. If you're using a 3-foot long mirror, attach three candles, equidistance, starting with the middle candle.

3. Apply plumber's putty to the bottom of each candle, and secure it to the mirror by pressing firmly but carefully. Repeat with each candle.

4. Cover the mirror with seasonal decorations such as pine trimmings, roping, holiday decorations, and poinsettias. For Easter, nestle colored eggs among the trimmings.

5. At the end of the holiday, dispose of any fresh trimmings, carefully remove the candles, wipe the mirror with a solution of 50 percent water and 50 percent white vinegar, dry, and store safely until the next holiday.

Clever Cover-ups

Slipcover a headboard

Remember how Grandma would fold her best quilt or comforter over the foot of the bed so it wouldn't get mussed during the day? That's the inspiration for quick, cost-free, and very modern bedstead slipcovers—one at each end. Use fabric or a bed sheet you already have; only a few yards will bring a whole new look to a plain vanilla bed. Take the vertical and horizontal (between the end posts) measurements for the head and footboards, then double the vertical measurement of each board. (If the horizontal measurement is wider than your fabric, you'll have to seam two lengths together.) If you use a sheet, cut it down to size. Hem the edges and add fabric ties to both sides. This look can be as nostalgic as Grandma's bed or as sleek as a New York loft. Slipcovering is also a smart way to protect the finish on an antique or much-treasured bed and continue to use it as intended.

Window drapery to doorway curtain

Curtaining doorways is a very old way to keep heat in or out of interior spaces (think tent flaps). So if you have a set of long win-dow drapes you're not using, you've got ready-to-go door curtains. For a standard door, mount a curtain rod at or slightly above the door frame. Extend the rod six or more inches beyond the frame, making room to slide the curtain to one side so you can easily close and open the door. Then hang one drapery panel that's long enough to reach to the floor. (Standard door frames are approximately 7 feet tall, but measure yours just in case.) Metal or plastic curtain rings or clips make it easier to move the curtain along the rod. To prevent billowing on windy days you can sew weights such as metal hardware washers inside the hems.

Tile an old tabletop

A battered and bruised wooden coffee table or small side table can become a canvas for tiles, even for beginners. You'll need tiles (saved from a renovation project) or purchased from a tile or

10 Reasons to Grab the Tape When the Going Gets Tough

Here are 10 around-the-house decorating dilemmas that an adhesive tape can resolve in no time.

1 Fabric tape to mend broken seams in slip covers

2 Painter's tape to make even stripes while painting, without measuring

3 Painter's tape to mask edges of baseboards and door and window frames when painting

4 Brightly colored, waterproof electrician's tape to decorate and identify children's plastic toys and adult tools

5 Double-sided tape to secure throw rugs to the floor and seat cushions to chairs

6 Clear shipping tape and a permanent marker to label paint and solvent cans

7 Masking tape to wrap the metal portion of paint brush handles to catch drips

8 Nonslip tape to mend worn spots on the underside of rubber-backed bath mats

9 Double-sided acid-free scrapbooking tape to mount and frame precious art on paper

10 Adhesive-backed Velcro tape as a temporary closure on a cabinet door with a broken latch

home store (look for sales). Measure the tabletop to determine how many you need. If you're careful with your measurements and buy tiles of the right size, you can probably cover the entire top without making any tile cuts. Keep in mind that you must leave approximately ⅛ to ¼ inch of space between tiles for grouting.

- Sand the tabletop and clean off the dust. (If you want to refinish or paint your table, do so before sanding.) Then lay out the tiles on the tabletop in your pattern of choice and make any changes and adjustments. Affix the tiles with tiling adhesive or white glue. (If using glue, be sure it's dry before grouting.)

- Grout the tiles with commercial grout, which is available in many colors. As you work, wipe off excess grout with a damp sponge. To remove any remaining grout film, wash again with water after the grout has dried. And there you have it—a table that may as well be brand new.

A quick change for dining chairs

If the upholstered seats of your dining room chairs are removable—some lift out and others are attached only by screws underneath—you're in luck! You can make a quick, temporary change with some fabric and strong masking tape. Use what you have on hand: fabric remnants, a tablecloth or bed coverlet, large scarves, sheets or pillowcases. Mix and match colors and patterns if you like. Choose a medium-weight material, since heavy or highly textured fabrics won't always give a smooth, finished appearance. Remove the chair seat and use it as a template to cut a piece of material extending 3–4 inches beyond the edges. Then center the seat, top down, on the wrong side of the fabric. Drape the fabric over one side of the chair bottom and secure it with a piece of tape. Do the same on the other side, pulling the fabric taut. Repeat on the other two sides, and then tape all four folds all the way to the corners. Fold the fabric over each corner for a neat finish. Secure the cover with an extra layer of tape, replace the seat, and voila!

Rug on rug

You know the problem: wall-to-wall carpeting that's flattened, matted, and stained in a heavily trafficked area but otherwise in good condition. The solution? Scout your home for the perfect area rug to cover the trouble spot—a rug that could be in the next room or stashed away in the attic. If you have a carpet remnant that would look great but is too large, ask a local carpet dealer to cut it to size and bind the edges.

Covering the nicks

Did your beloved Aunt Betty accidentally ram into your treasured coffee table with her walker? Did your grandson motor his tricycle through the house and into the legs of that antique rolltop desk? Don't weep, and don't call a pro: If the nick is shallow, color it with a similar-hued indelible marker. If the nick is deep (but still superficial), soften a small amount of white candle wax and using a small butter spreader, massage it into the gash. Wait for it to harden, and then color it with the right-colored marker. Any deeper than that? Call for help.

Wallpapered storage boxes

Cardboard boxes—free from the grocery or liquor store or purchased from a business supply store—have to be America's favorite storage units. They're also ugly and not always easy to stash out of sight. So pretty them up with leftover wallpaper, preferably vinyl coated. Prepasted wallpaper can be cut to size,

Leaf It to You

Leaves make beautiful printing stamps for decorating fabric—and hey—they fall *free* from the trees! Even if you live in the most urban of cities, you can find leaves in parks, public gardens, and on your own potted plants sitting on your windowsill. Look for fresh, well-shaped leaves with prominent spines and veins.

- Flatten the leaves by pressing them for a day or two in a phone book weighted with something heavy, like more books.
- To use a leaf to stamp fabric, brush fabric paint evenly on its top side. Test the leaf stamp first on a fabric scrap, laying the leaf on the material and pushing—not rubbing—it down with your fingers.

Practice until you get the look you like, and then stamp fabric for a tea towel, a throw pillow, or whatever your heart desires. Leaf stamps won't last very long, but you can always gather more as they fall.

dampened, and pasted on in a relative blink. Unpasted paper can be stuck down with wallpaper paste, craft glue, or rubber cement. Arrayed on open shelves or neatly stacked under a desk or along a wall, revamped boxes look attractive, and their wallpaper covers are durable enough to take a good deal of wear.

Add Dash with Fabrics

Sewing box embellishment for pillows

To jazz up throw pillows and pillowcases, look through your sewing and craft supplies for interesting and unusual embellishments. Ribbons, lace, rickrack, buttons, beads, tassels, bits of fabric for appliqués, yarn, netting, old handkerchiefs and antimacassars, stencils, and decorative stamps for fabric painting—practically anything that won't break and will wash can perk up a plain throw pillow or pillowcase. Here are four simple, quick, and cost-free ideas:

- Tie on a satin or grosgrain ribbon. Two yards or less will wrap around a 12-by-12-inch pillow and let you tie a pretty bow. Tack under the bow and on the back of the pillow.

- Sew a band of lace or decorative trim around the hem of a pillowcase. Seam the trim to cover the seam line at the pillowcase opening.

- Sew a row of mismatched buttons in any direction—vertical, horizontal, or diagonal—on one side of a tailored throw pillow for an unexpectedly wry look.

- Sew pretty tassels to the corners of a throw pillow, or sew or glue tasseled fabric trim around the pillow edges.

Make a duvet cover with sheets

Sleeping under a down-filled duvet is blissful, but washing or dry cleaning it frequently is less than heavenly to your pocketbook. Instead of buying a pricey duvet cover, hunt up a couple of flat bed sheets that will fully cover your duvet. Pin the sheets together, right sides facing, and sew bottoms and sides together with a straight seam.

Turn the cover right side out and slip it over your duvet. The simplest closures are sewn-on ribbon or fabric tape ties, Velcro, or snaps.

Now you have a cost-free duvet cover that can be washed as often as you like; under normal conditions, your duvet will need washing or cleaning just once or twice a year.

Save a too-short curtain

Don't toss your old house curtains if they're too short for your new windows; just add a bottom panel. Search your fabrics and be ingenious. For one panel, measure the width of your curtain and add seam allowances. Now determine how much you need for the length you want; include seam and hem allowances. If your fabric is large enough, you're practically home. Remove stitching from the curtain hems and trim. Cut the extra fabric to your measurements. Seam, hem, and hang your "new" old curtain.

A plush bath towel shower curtain

If you enjoy the luxury of terry-cloth bath sheets, this is an idea for you. Two terry-cloth bath sheets are nearly the same size as a standard shower curtain (70–72 inches wide by 70–74 inches long). Use bath sheets you already have: white bath sheets will create a spa feeling; bright colors can add "pow" to a plain bathroom. Don't seam the towels; simply overlap the edges and sew together, stitching down the selvage. Add grommets near the top (grommet kits are available at fabric stores). The standard number of holes is 12. To determine spacing, measure the full width of the sewn curtain and subtract 4 inches to leave 2 inches free at each side. Now divide the remainder by 12.

Picture This...

Cheap art

Think outside the box and frame an interesting magazine cover, a child's painting, a piece of needlework, a collection of men's silk ties, coins, exotic stamps, a photo collage, a map, or postcards from your favorite vacation spot. An example: Save seed packets when you plant in the spring; open packets at the back to preserve the graphic fronts. You may already have some small frames; if not, you can purchase inexpensive 3-by-5 or 5-by-7-inch photo frames at discount stores. Cover the cardboard backing that comes with the frames in leftover wrapping paper or fabric, then attach the seed packets with double-sided tape. Now find just the right place to hang your new "botanical prints"— quick, easy, cost-free, and a pleasing memento of your summer garden.

Old frames in new colors

Use leftover paints to refurbish old picture frames for a cost-free way to highlight artwork and add splashes of color to your decor. Remove everything from the frame and clean it well; if the frame is ornate, use damp cotton swabs to

Cleaning Pictures under Glass

Picture frames and glass don't usually get filthy dirty, but they do collect dust, residue from heat sources, and fingerprints. Regular dusting and an occasional cleaning will keep them in good shape. To wash glass, dampen a cloth in a mild vinegar and water solution, wring almost dry, and wipe the glass. Don't spray liquid directly on the glass; it can easily seep under the frame and damage the mat or, worse, the artwork. Polish glass with a coffee filter or used dryer sheet; they're lint-free.

get into the nooks and crannies. Dry thoroughly, sand lightly if the frame is wood, and simply brush or spray with your color choice. You can give your frame an antique finish by sanding the dry paint back to the original finish and rubbing the whole frame with brown shoe polish, buffing well. Create a contemporary frame by painting it with high-gloss auto paint.

SHOE POLISH FOR AN ANTIQUE FINISH

Sand a new frame and rub on and buff off a thin coating of brown or reddish-brown **shoe polish** for an antique frame finish.

For added nostalgia in your home frame some **vintage seed packets.**

Individualizing picture mats

Aside from paintings on canvas, most graphic art is framed under a mat—a cardboard border with a quality paper veneer—that prevents the image from touching (and sticking to) the glass. Cutting mats the meticulous professional way isn't easy, but even a rank amateur can make attractive mats with glue and materials found around the house. Start with the cardboard mat that came with the frame; if the commercial border is just paper, use it as a template to cut a piece of cardboard. Choose something attractive to cover the cardboard. Consider the frame and the photo or artwork, and pick something that will complement both. It won't take much of any of the following to create an individualized mat:

- Remnant wallpaper
- Curtain or upholstery fabric
- Any leftover medium-weight fabric
- Fake leather, suede, or fur
- Wrapping paper or foil
- Parchment paper
- Résumé paper or card stock
- Origami paper
- Shelf or drawer lining paper
- Wide ribbon or lace
- Magazine or old book pages

Cut a piece of material slightly larger than the dimensions of the mat. Thinly coat the cardboard with glue and affix the material, smoothing to eliminate air pockets and wrinkles. When dry, cut away the material from the outside edges. Now turn the mat face down and cut excess material diagonally from each top corner to opposite bottom corner, taking care not to cut into the cardboard. Fold the flaps over, trim away all but about ½ inch, and glue the edges.

Whitewashing a gilt frame

When a new gold gilt or painted frame looks *too* new, tone it down with a wash of white. Dilute a small amount of leftover white interior paint—latex with water, alkyd or oil-based with turpentine or mineral spirits—to make a thin wash. Be sure the frame is clean of dust and grease. Use a clean cotton cloth to apply the wash, wiping away excess paint as you go. Let dry. One or two coats should be enough—you want to calm the flashiness of new gilt, not cover it up.

A CD case photo gallery

Here's a great decorating project for teenagers, who tend to take lots of photos and have tons of empty CD cases. Twelve or more clear transparent CD cases, adhered to the wall with poster putty or low-tack, double-sided tape, make a totally awesome gallery. Standard cases measure 5½ by 5 inches—just right for 3-by-5 photo prints and other feather-weight items. Pictures can be changed whenever the mood strikes, just by opening the case. Rad? You bet.

"Clothesline" photo displays

Create a modern photo display by using these everyday office supplies. Scrounge desk drawers for clear 8½-by-11-inch acrylic document sleeves and some metal binder clips. Mount your photos in the sleeves and nail both ends of a length of wire or rope to the wall, clothesline fashion, leaving a little slack. (If you have some thin computer cable you're not using, use it to give the display a high tech look.) Now clip the photo sleeves to the hanging line. Because it's so easy to change photos whenever you want, your display will never get old.

make your own
Air Freshener

Never buy a commercial air freshener again; make your own! Many people swear by homemade fresheners made with baking soda or vinegar, which act as deodorizers as well as adding a gentle scent.

Double Treat Room Spray

Both lemon and baking soda are traditional odor eaters, and this recipe couldn't be simpler.

- 1 teaspoon baking soda
- 1 tablespoon lemon juice
- 2 cups water

1. Combine the ingredients in a bowl and let the mixture fizz.

2. When fizzing subsides, stir well.

3. Pour the mixture into a spritzer (a spray bottle that produces a fine mist). Spray rooms that need freshening two or three times a day.

The Glue Gun:

Every Home Decorator's Best Friend

Whether you're new to repurposing items found around your home or you're a seasoned pro who sews your own drapes, you'll want to make sure you have an inexpensive glue gun in your home design arsenal. Available for around $10, a basic model will enable you to add your own personal touches to virtually every room in your house, from the bedroom to the bathroom and beyond.

Have some great linens or textiles kicking around that you don't want to get rid of? You don't have to. Use them, along with your glue gun, to add appliqués to drapes, wallpaper, shower curtains, bed coverings, headboards, and more. Be creative: Appliqués can mean far more than just cut pieces of cloth or textile. Poke around your sewing kit and dig up some older-looking buttons to create a fabulous design treatment.

Too many Christmas ornaments for your tree? Make a reusable holiday wreath by glue-gunning extra ornaments to a twig wreath form (available at craft shops); at the end of the holiday, simply store it for next year.

Create one-of-a-kind gift boxes with everything from plain cardboard shipping containers to dilapidated shoeboxes: cover with fabric, glue-gun in place, and dress up with buttons, bows, and trim. What does it cost? Virtually nothing.

Love that bargain lamp but hate the boring shade? Get to a trimming store, pick up some inexpensive fringe or seam edging, and glue gun it to the edging of the shade.

Happy Holidays Decor

Spotlight the tree

Forget those gnarly miles of tree lights and use a spotlight instead. If you have track lighting, position your tree so the track fixtures can bathe it in light. Or use the portable indoor uplight that's now highlighting a big houseplant. A gooseneck or swivel desk lamp will also work; locate it so the light strikes the tree but not people's eyes. Basically any light you can direct will bring out the beauty of your holiday tree, without all the fuss and bother.

Fragrant holiday window box

Use your winter garden as the palette from which to fill a detachable window box with aromatic pine and pinecones; spruce and cedar clippings; sprigs of boxwood, holly, or mistletoe; and clusters of red or white berries. Place it on an inside window ledge, mantle, or fireplace shelf, or even your holiday table—a picturesque way to bring the colors and fragrances of winter indoors for the holidays.

First, remove any soil and wash the box with baking soda or vinegar and water. Most fresh-cut winter greenery will last for a week or more if you mist it daily. If you plan to add water to the box, plug drain holes with clay or putty. Protect paint finishes and furniture from drips and condensation by cutting a disposable diaper to the size of the bottom of the box and laying it, plastic side down, under the box. (Just as for babies, check and change diapers as often as needed.)

Offbeat homemade gift-wrapping

Instead of buying expensive wrapping paper, look around the house for creative and eco-smart substitutes. Newspaper, paper bags, crepe paper, painter's masking paper, parchment paper, paper place mats, fabric napkins you don't use, comic book pages, the kids' construction and drawing paper, bubble wrap—the possibilities are endless. Use stamps, stencils, and stickers to embellish your wrap, and substitute brightly colored yarns, workshop twines and cords, fabric trims and bindings, torn strips of fabric, or an old fabric measuring tape, for store-bought bows.

Dried citrus ornaments

Those extra oranges and lemons in your fridge that may be past their prime can be transformed into warmly translucent tree ornaments. Cut fruit into ¼-inch slices, lay the slices flat on a stick-proof cookie sheet, and place in the oven on the lowest setting for several hours. Test for dryness by lightly touching the pulp; if it feels sticky, leave the slices in the oven a short while

Dyeing Easter Eggs
(with Mother Nature's Help)

In this chart, quantities are based on 1 quart of liquid. Amounts of dyeing ingredients are approximate; more dyestuff and longer dye baths produce the deepest colors. All boiled eggs should be stored in the refrigerator, and any that have soaked in hot or warm water for several hours should not be eaten.

Dye Source	Quantity	Color
Beet juice	half strength or more of the vinegar water	deep pink
Cranberry juice	full-strength	light pink
Paprika	3 tablespoons or more	brick red
Yellow onion skins	up to 4 packed cups	sienna
Turmeric	3 or more tablespoons	yellow-green
Brewed coffee	1 quart strong coffee plus water to cover	brown
Blueberries	up to 4 cups	lavender
Purple grape juice	half or more of the liquid	blue-gray
Red cabbage	4 or more cups, chopped (boil and then soak overnight)	robin's egg blue
Spinach or grass	up to 4 cups	green
Red wine	full strength or diluted with water only	deep purple

longer; it's important to remove the fruit before it begins to brown. Cool on a wire rack. Thread the dried fruit slices with ribbon or yarn and hang them where they'll catch the tree lights. Preserve dried fruit slices by a spraying them with a clear acrylic finish.

Easter eggs, naturally

Budding young chemists and kids with curiosity will really enjoy helping to make naturally colored Easter eggs with ingredients straight from the cupboard and fridge. This family project costs nothing, but the delight in learning is priceless.

1. Gently wash eggs with soapy water and dry.

2. Place a single layer of eggs in a non-metal pot with the dye source (see chart at left).

3. Add 2 tablespoons vinegar to 1 quart water. Bring to a boil, reduce to a simmer for 15–20 minutes, and remove pot from burner. If you like the color as it is, dab off excess dye with a paper towel and set the eggs on a rack to dry. To deepen the color, leave eggs in the pot until cool. To get even richer shades, put cool eggs in a bowl, strain the dye water, and pour it over the eggs. Store the submerged eggs in the fridge for a few hours or overnight.

Snow globes from empty jars

Make your own old-fashioned snow globe at home with clean, plain, glass kitchen jars and whatever small holiday items you have—dig out those little plastic Santas and reindeer and ceramic elves and angels that have taken up permanent residence in the bottom of your decorations box. (Don't use wood or metal items.) Any size glass jar will work, so long as the objects will fit inside and the lid fits tightly. Small and medium olive, pimiento, and baby

Divine Twine

Those beautiful filigreed balls sold in high-priced decorator boutiques can be yours for nothing when you make them yourself. All you need is a spool of household twine, white glue, water, and a balloon.

- For each ball, soak several feet of twine in a mixture of 1 part white glue to 1 part water. Then blow up and tie a small round balloon.

- Wrap the balloon with the saturated twine, wrapping randomly. When it suits your eye, clip the twine and set the balloon on top of a drinking glass. Allow the twine to dry for at least a day, or until the balloon begins to deflate.

- Time to pop the balloon and remove it. Spray the ball with gold, silver, or copper metallic paint. Dust with glitter for a holiday look, if you like. Then pile the finished balls in a shallow bowl and set it in a place of honor. Divine!

food jars are ideal for small globes. You may have to buy several items—waterproof epoxy glue, distilled water, white glitter, and glycerin (available from pharmacies)—but you'll need only small amounts.

1. Roughen the inside surface of the jar lid with sandpaper or steel wool and then glue on your object or objects with epoxy; let dry. Fill the jar almost to the top with distilled water and add a drop of glycerin.

2. Glycerin thickens the water so glitter will swirl; for larger jars, add a couple of drops. Now add a pinch or two of glitter.

3. Screw the jar lid on tightly, being careful not to dislodge glued-on object. Finally, turn the jar over and enjoy the snowstorm.

Chapter Six

Nature's Home Remedies

These days, we can't get enough of all things health-related, be they the tried and true traditional remedies for what ails you (think aspirin and Alka-Seltzer) or the stuff that your grandmother swore by: the witch hazel and Epsom salt, the chamomile tea and the castor oil, the hydrogen peroxide and the mustard plaster.

And while many of these health-giving remedies are valid, there is also wisdom in the proverb, "Moderation in all things."

That said, it really does pay to stock your medicine cabinet with home remedies. Homemade witch hazel is, for example, more effective than its commercial equivalent because it isn't distilled. The herb feverfew staves off migraines more effectively when you chew the fresh leaves instead of swallowing a capsule. A hair dryer may help stunt a cold better than a pill (really!). And oh, the uses our distant forebears found for salt and stinging nettle, cloves, and castor oil! Leafing through the pages that follow may encourage you to emulate those hardy souls. (But remember to consult your doctor before using all but the most benign remedies.)

Fighting Colds and Flu

Kick the chicken soup up a notch

When science proved that Grandma's chicken soup really does help fight colds, the luscious favorite secured its place in the pantheon of healing foods. Chicken soup works not only because steam rising from the bowl helps clear congestion, but also because anti-inflammatory compounds in the broth slow the movement of neutrophils, white blood cells that spur the formation of mucus in the lungs and nose. To punch up chicken soup's cold-fighting abilities even more, add two peeled and minced garlic cloves to the simmering soup. Garlic contains antiviral sulfur compounds, and it's also said to boost the immune system.

Fire up the hair dryer

Inhaling heated air can stunt a cold's severity when you feel one coming on. Studies show that warm air kills rhinoviruses working their way up the nose. In one test conducted in England, subjects who breathed warm air had half the symptoms of those who inhaled air at room temperature, so set your hair dryer to warm (not hot), hold it at least 18 inches from your face, and inhale the warm air for as long as you can—preferably 20 minutes or so but 2 or 3 minutes at the very least.

Sip (and gargle) echinacea tea

Echinacea purpurea, or purple coneflower, can indeed help prevent colds and relieve the symptoms of colds and influenza alike. It works by boosting levels of the body chemical properdin, which strengthens defense mechanisms against infections. Drinking 3 cups of echinacea tea a

Rudolph Syndrome

You'd think the reddening (and soreness) of the nostril rims that results from constant nose blowing would have a name. Up until now, it hasn't, so let's call it Rudolph Syndrome (RS), after Santa's red-snooted reindeer. How to remedy this unsightly, uncomfortable redness? Simply rub a little petroleum jelly or Chapstick on the rim of the nostrils, replenishing it as necessary. Ah, sweet relief.

day will guard against colds, but limit consumption to 7- to 8-week periods so as not to risk nausea, fevers, and other side effects. (Resume sipping after a couple of weeks, and hope a rhinovirus doesn't target you when echinacea is taking "time off.") You can also gargle echinacea tea up to three times a day to soothe a sore throat.

Increase chicken soup's cold-fighting properties with *garlic!*

Cool that fever

In a cold's first stages, you can help your body bring down fever by giving yourself a sponge bath every hour or so. Dip a natural sponge in tepid water, lightly wring it out, and use it to bathe your face, shoulders, chest, and extremities. If the fever persists, drink 1–2 cups ginger tea every few hours; the ginger will promote sweating, which is the body's way of cooling itself.

Fight coughs with thyme

Thyme is a natural expectorant, so brew a pot of thyme tea to fight that nagging cough. Just steep 2 tablespoons dried thyme leaves in 6 cups hot water for 10 minutes. Strain the liquid into

a teacup, sweeten with honey if desired, and sip a cupful two or three times a day.

Three simple sore throat gargles

Invade the kitchen cabinet rather than the medicine cabinet to cure your sore throat. Here's how:

- **Honey** Honey coats the throat and has mild antibacterial properties. Stir 1–3 teaspoons into 1 cup warm water and gargle two or three times a day.

- **Salt** Salt water has been used as a gargle for centuries because it works so well: It draws moisture from the mucous membranes (thereby diluting mucus) and helps cleanse the throat of phlegm. Dissolve ½ teaspoon salt in 1 cup warm water and gargle three or four times daily.

- **Peppermint** The menthol in peppermint helps open the nasal passages, especially when you gargle strong peppermint tea. Pour 1 cup boiling water over 3 peppermint tea bags and let steep for 4–5 minutes. Gargle with the cooled solution two or three times a day.

A fiery gulp

For a practical way to rid yourself of throat congestion, whisk 1 teaspoon honey into 8 ounces warm water. Now whisk in ½ teaspoon hot red pepper (or Tabasco) sauce. (If this is too spicy for you, experiment by adding a few drops at a time.) Drink the concoction slowly; follow it with a small ginger ale chaser, which will cool the burn.

Pass the peas to relieve a stuffy nose

Use a frozen bag of peas as a flexible, bendable, cold pack to set on the bridge of your nose or on your cheekbones to reduce swelling. Put them back in cold storage to refreeze, and repeat as necessary.

Swat the flu bug with elderberry

If you feel you've been bitten by the flu bug, drink 3–4 cups of elderberry tea daily or take 20–30 drops of elderberry tincture in a glass of water. In Europe, elderberry *(Sambucus nigra)* has a long history as an antiviral herb, and research bears it out. In one study, 9 out of 10 test group subjects who consumed elderberry saw flu symptoms subside in two days, while symptoms in the group that consumed no elderberry continued for six days.

Curiosity Corner
Red Magic

Over a century ago, one of the most common cold cures was bought by the yard: red flannel, which was associated with warmth and healing. Why red? Because of the superstition that the color red kept evil spirits at bay. Less metaphysically, flannel was said to "draw out" a cold when worn next to the skin.

Flannel came on the scene in the late nineteenth century, when a napped cotton called flannelette appeared in dry goods stores. While considered inferior to wool, this new fabric didn't itch the skin. Mothers tied red flannel scarves around their children's necks to relieve sore throats (in addition to keeping away the evil eye). Many men wore red flannel union suits under their clothing to protect themselves not only from colds and the flu but to prevent attacks of gout and rheumatism. For back pain, flannelette bands were worn around the waist. In time, the fabric that sealed in heat without itching came to be known simply as flannel. Had it not come along, many a lumberjack, alternative band member, and flannel pajama-wearer would, in a manner of speaking, be left out in the cold.

Easing Asthma, Bronchitis, and Allergies

Inhale eucalyptus vapors

If you're lucky enough to have access to dried *Eucalyptus globulus*, just boil crumbled leaves and let them steep for 4–5 hours; strain out the leaf pieces before heating the liquid for inhalation. (Alternatively, add 5–10 drops commercial eucalyptus oil to the steaming water.) Place the bowl at the edge of a table, sit down, bend your head over the bowl, and put the towel over your head to form a tent. Breathe the vapors for about 10 minutes, taking care not to get too close to the steam. Lungs all better, plus a refreshing facial!

Bronchitis double dose

The head-clearing pungency of freshly grated horseradish paired with the acidic aroma of lemon helps dissolve mucus in the sinuses and bronchial tubes. To make a piquant cough medicine, grate a peeled horseradish root into a bowl (or cheat and use prepared horseradish) and transfer 1 cup grated horseradish to a small bowl. Add ⅓ cup lemon juice and stir well.

Dose yourself with ½ teaspoon of the mixture at a time, taking it two or three times a day. The expectorant action should set you coughing after each dose, ridding your lungs of mucus.

Loosen mucus with mullein

Mullein *(Verbascum thapsus)*, a longtime folk remedy for respiratory ailments, contains saponins that loosen phlegm and promote expectoration. It also contains gelatinous mucilage that tones and soothes the mucous membranes. To make mullein tea, steep 2 teaspoons dried mullein leaves in just-boiled water for 10 minutes. Herbalists advise drinking the tea up to three times a day to ease bronchial distress.

Elecampane the expectorant

Buy elecampane tea or liquid extract, sweeten the tea with honey, and drink 1–2 cups a day to stimulate the lungs' natural "housecleaning" mechanism. The active principle in elecampane *(Inula helenium)* is alantolactone, a proven

FIGHT ASTHMA WITH FISH

Omega 3, the fatty acids found in **sardines**, tuna, salmon, mackerel, sardines, and other oily fish, works much like a class of drugs called leukotriene inhibitors, which disable bodily compounds that contribute to inflammation of the airways.

expectorant with roots back to New World settlers, who used elecampane to treat the symptoms of asthma, whooping cough, pneumonia, and tuberculosis.

Chamomile's two faces

For an allergy-fighting tea, pour 1 cup boiling water over 2–3 teaspoons minced flower heads of German chamomile, steep for 10 minutes, strain, and drink three to four times daily. A caveat: while chamomile is a traditional hay fever fighter, it actually aggravates symptoms in anyone allergic to ragweed, a chamomile cousin. For everyone else, the azulene content in chamomile has antiallergenic properties that have led doctors worldwide to prescribe chamomile preparations for respiratory tract infections and allergies.

Use bleach to quell sniffles

If you have a sudden case of the sniffles that won't go away and you don't have allergies (or a cold), you may (unbenownst to you!) be living with mold. If you spot it in your bathroom, kill it instantly with a 50/50 mixture of household bleach and water. Spray it directly onto the offensive spots and let it sit. The mold will be stopped in its tracks within minutes, along with (hopefully) your runny nose!

Nettle and hay fever

If you have access to fresh stinging nettle (it's a common garden weed), wear gloves when harvesting and washing the leaves (the plant's not called stinging nettle for nothing). Add 4 ounces of the leaf to 6 cups of boiling water. Lower

make your own
Nasal Spray

Here's a homemade spray that will flush allergens from nasal passages. The isosmotic solution parallels the concentration of salt found in the body, making the spray mild but effective.

Salt Water Sniffle-Stopper

This spray works best at room temperature. Discard any unused solution after two days or it may become contaminated.

   1 quart water
   1 tablespoon chamomile tea
   2 teaspoons salt

1. Place water in a medium saucepan, add tea and salt, and bring to a low simmer.

2. Stir until salt is dissolved, then let cool to room temperature.

3. Pour solution into an empty nose spray bottle. Spray twice in each nostril as needed, holding the other nostril closed each time.

heat and simmer until the water turns green, then strain through a fine sieve into a large teapot. During hay fever season, drink a cup of nettle tea in the morning and one in the evening, sweetening it with honey if you like. Studies have yet to definitively confirm the efficacy of stinging nettle *(Urtica dioica)* for treating hay fever, but legions of people swear by nettle's powers to ease runny noses and watery eyes.

What Does That Mean?

You probably already know the meaning of many of the words in this list, not all of which apply only to herbal remedies. But when it comes to self-treatment, having a fuller grasp of the terminology becomes all the more important. Here's a great place to start:

Active principle A plant chemical proven to have a medical effect.

Antiseptic A substance that prevents or stops the growth of microorganisms that cause infection.

Astringent A substance that draws together the soft tissues, such as skin or mucous membranes.

Decoction A drink or liquid extract made by boiling plant bark, roots, berries, or seeds in water.

Diuretic A substance that increases the flow of urine.

Emollient A substance that softens and soothes the skin and mucous membranes.

Essential oil A plant oil that vaporizes readily and is often obtained by steam distillation; used interchangeably with *volatile oil*.

Expectorant A substance that loosens and helps to expel phlegm.

Infusion A preparation in which flowers, leaves, or stems are steeped in water that is not boiling.

Liquid extract Concentrated infusion made by soaking an herb in distilled water, grain alcohol, or glycerin for a long period.

Mucous membrane Lining of a body passage, such as the throat, that protects itself with secretions of mucus.

Photosensitivity Sensitivity to sunlight, resulting in rash or burning sensation, brought on by ingestion or application of certain substances.

Plaster Gauze or cloth in which medicine has been wrapped. A plaster is applied to the skin.

Poultice An herbal preparation that is usually applied directly to the affected area to relieve pain or swelling.

Purgative A very strong laxative.

Tannins Astringent and bitter compounds found in the seeds and skins of grapes, which slow oxidation and aging.

Tincture An herbal liquid extract that generally involves macerating the herb in alcohol.

Volatile oil A plant oil that vaporizes readily and is often obtained by steam distillation; used interchangeably with *essential oil*.

Wash A liquid herbal medicine preparation for external use.

No-Drugs Headache Relief

The herb feverfew (*Tanacetum parthenium*), whose medicinal applications were recorded as early as 78 AD by the Greek physician Discorides, was used to treat everything from joint pain to melancholy—and yes, fever. Flash forward to the 1970s, when clinical trials in London showed the herb to be an effective treatment for migraines.

The active principles in feverfew leaves and flowers, called parthenolides, inhibit the body's release of serotonin, prostaglandins, and histamines into the bloodstream, all of which can inflame tissue and trigger (and worsen) migraine headaches. The herb, which modern herbalists also recommend for colds, indigestion, and diarrhea, is sold in capsules and as liquid extract. Feverfew is also the perfect candidate for your own physic garden (page 167), especially because freshly plucked leaves are said to be more effective than processed feverfew. To help prevent migraines, chew two or three freshly picked feverfew leaves after breakfast and dinner each day, swallowing only the juice. (Take note: Some people develop canker sores and other mouth irritations after chewing feverfew—so stop chewing fresh leaves at the first sign of oral irritation.) Another unprocessed option is an infusion made from feverfew flowers and leaves.

Running hot and cold

To cure a tension headache (caused by contractions in the head and neck, and brought on by—among other things—stress, anxiety, and lack of sleep) without painkilling drugs, dip a washcloth in hot water, wring it out, and fold it into compress. Now place it on your forehead or the back of your neck to relax tight muscles. To ease a vascular headache (including migraine and cluster headaches, and stemming from the contraction and expansion of blood vessels in a particular area of the head), follow the same procedure, but using cold water, which constricts the blood vessels and reduces blood flow, taking the pressure off a hurting head.

A cup o' Joe makes the headache go

A clinical trial in Illinois found that caffeine, which reduces the swelling of blood vessels, can reduce both the intensity and frequency of headaches. Subjects in one group were given caffeine alone, and 58 percent reported complete relief. Subjects in the other group were given caffeine in combination with ibuprofen, and 70 percent saw symptoms disappear.

Sinus headache self-massage

Use your middle fingers to massage the points of the face just opposite your nostrils—that is, at the level of the tip of your nose. Massage with clockwise circles for 2 or 3 minutes.

To sooth a throbbing headache, soak your feet—in water and **mustard!**

Head-to-toe headache remedy

Blood drawn to the lower body will reduce pressure in the blood vessels of the head, and what's lower than your feet? To help soothe a throbbing vascular headache, soak your feet in a small tub filled with hot water mixed with mustard powder. After a half hour or so, hotfoot it to the nearest towel, dry your feet, and feel better!

Sip ginger tea

When it comes to treating headaches, ginger works especially well for migraines. Make a tea by pouring 3 cups water over 2 tablespoons freshly grated ginger. Let steep 4–5 minutes, then strain through a small sieve into a teacup. Ginger tea bags are also available, but the tea lacks the punch of fresh gingerroot tea.

WEAR A HEADBAND

Tie a **scarf, necktie, or bandana** tightly around your forehead to reduce the flow of blood to your scalp, and in turn, to throbbing, swollen blood vessels.

Eyes, Ears, and Mouth

Eye can see clearly now

Carrots, celery, kale, and parsley: Taken together, all contribute to the trouble-free operation of the optic system. Either juice the veggies for an eye-friendly beverage or puree to make a cold soup. The ideal proportions? Two parts carrots, 2 parts kale, 1 part celery, 1 part parsley. For best results, consume 2 cups of juice or soup a day. Vary the mix by incorporating spinach, endive, collards, tomatoes, and melons. Bon appétit!

Tea for two

Two puffy eyes, that is. Take two wet tea bags, place them on tired or swollen eyes, and lie down for 15–20 minutes as the tea soothes and refreshes. Green tea is ideal for these mini-compresses, but black tea and herbal teas work well, too. An added benefit: some herbalists claim that tea-bag compresses speed the healing of a black eye.

Let's 'ear it for mullein and garlic!

Paired with garlic, mullein *(Verbascum thapsus)* makes soothing earache drops you can keep on hand in the refrigerator. In a sterilized jar, combine 1 crushed clove garlic with 2 tablespoons dried or fresh mullein flower (minced if fresh), and ½ cup olive oil. Screw the lid on tightly and shake to blend. Store in a cool, dark place, shaking the jar daily. After two weeks, strain the oil into another jar and store it in the fridge. To treat an earache, bring the oil to room temperature or hold the jar under warm running water. With a sterile eyedropper, add 2–3 drops to the ear, then gently massage the ear to help the oil move through the ear canal.

Bubble away ear trouble

Dropping 3 percent hydrogen peroxide into the ear makes earwax easier to extract and will hasten the healing of an earache. Fill a sterile eyedropper with peroxide, lie on your side, and squeeze the liquid into the affected ear until it feels full. Let the peroxide bubble away for 3–5 minutes, then press a washcloth or folded paper towel against the ear and turn over to let it drain. Rinse the ear by repeating the process with water. Dry, then work softened earwax out of the ear with a cotton swab. Do not use hydrogen peroxide in your ear if you suspect that you have a perforated eardrum.

Homemade breath freshener

The makings for a super-duper, anti-bad–breath mouthwash is living right there in your spice rack. To make a mouthwash, pour 2 cups water into a saucepan and add 1 tablespoon cardamom seeds and 1 tablespoon whole cloves. If you like, add a few mint leaves and a little sugar to improve the taste (mint is a proven halitosis fighter). Bring to a boil, remove from heat, and let steep for 3–4 hours. Strain the solution into a bottle and gargle as needed. Cardamom is jam-packed with antiseptic qualities that kill the bacteria responsible for bad breath. Cloves, which have a long history as a breath freshener, are also antibacterial.

Brown stains on teeth?

If your teeth advertise your fondness for coffee, tea, or cigarettes, supplement your whitening toothpaste with a folk treatment: Add a dash of baking soda to your favorite whitening toothpaste and brush away.

Saltwater rinse for toothaches

Swishing warm salt water in the mouth can relieve toothache pain for the short term. Salt draws out some of the fluids from swollen gums as it soothes. How strong a solution to use? Two to 3 teaspoons salt in 8 ounces warm water.

Lips chapped?

Can't find that tube of lip balm you just bought? Try a benign oil of any sort instead. Soothe cracked, dry lips with a drop of olive, corn, safflower, or canola oil. Vegetable shortening and the trusty multitasker known as petroleum jelly also work well.

Ears ringing?

You may be suffering from tinnitus. Taking 120 milligrams of gingko extract (like Ginkgold and Ginkai) a day may reduce your symptoms, because it dilates your blood vessels. (But don't take it if you're also taking prescription anticoagulants, like Coumadin, or about to undergo surgery. And, as always, get your doctor's approval.)

Don't dry those baby blues

Dry eyes is so common that over-the-counter remedies for this ailment abound. What are the causes? Everything from pollution and smoke to age. The cure? Leave the packaged remedies at the drugstore, and eat a banana instead. Bananas are rich in potassium, which helps to control the balance of sodium and the release of fluid in your cells.

Clove Oil to the Rescue!

It's Saturday, the dentist's office is closed, and your sore tooth has gotten so bad you're entertaining thoughts of fishing your wrench out of the toolbox and pulling the offender out on the spot. But wait! You can ease the pain temporarily and save your sanity. The secret? Oil of clove, which you can either purchase or make at home. (Couldn't-be-easier recipe: Pour 1 cup vegetable oil over ¼ cup whole cloves and let sit overnight).

Put a few drops of clove oil on a cotton ball, place the ball on your sore tooth, and bite down. Keep your jaw shut tight for 3–4 minutes as the oil numbs the pain and kills bacteria. Now remove the cotton ball and make a mouthwash from 6 ounces water, ¼ teaspoon salt, and 6–8 drops clove oil. Swish the solution around in your mouth for about 30 seconds to kill still more bacteria, and rinse. Bear in mind that undiluted clove oil inside the mouth can cause burning, tissue or nerve damage, and pain. In large doses, clove oil taken orally can cause vomiting, sore throat, seizure, difficulty breathing, kidney failure, or liver damage. Clove oil shouldn't be applied to broken skin. Children, pregnant or nursing women, and people with diabetes, kidney, or liver disease or bleeding disorders should avoid taking clove oil.

Help lower blood pressure with bananas

Slice a 'naner into your breakfast cereal in the morning for Mother Nature's potassium-laden gift to those of us with high blood pressure. Check with your doctor first, as always.

Soothe Back, Joint, and Muscle Pain

Tin can massage

A cold, unopened 12-ounce beverage can makes a great back massager, whether it's filled with cola or club soda or beer. To loosen muscle tissue and spur blood flow to the area, stand against the wall with the can on its side wedged between your back and the wall. Then move from side to side to make the can roll. This impromptu massager does an especially good job of relaxing the rhomboids next to the shoulder blades and the lats lower down the back.

A back support for drivers

To make a lower back support to use in the car when you drive, fold a medium-size bath towel lengthwise, then roll it up; the roll should be about 1 foot long. Now cut the leg of an old pair of panty hose to size and slip the towel inside. In the car, tuck the makeshift cushion between the small of your back and the car seat, and you'll ride in comfort and with back-friendly posture.

Plast from the past

To give this favorite old pain remedy a shot, combine powdered mustard seed and all-purpose flour in a bowl (1 part mustard seed to 2 parts flour) and slowly stir in water to make a paste. Spread the mixture on one side of a 12-by-12-inch square of cheesecloth and fold. Now place the plaster on the ache, securing it with a bandage or slipping it under a tight T-shirt. Leave the plaster in place for no more than 20–30 minutes at a time. If any skin irritation occurs, remove it immediately.

More curry = less arthritis pain

Turmeric, one of the principal spices in curry powder, is as medicinal as it is culinary. The compound in turmeric called curcumin has been shown in clinical trials to reduce swelling associated with arthritis. If you find curries too spicy, use powdered turmeric as a seasoning, sprinkling it over meats, eggs, and dark green leafy vegetables like spinach.

Eat and drink ginger

Incorporating ginger into your diet will bring at least some relief from rheumatoid arthritis and osteoarthritis pains. For best results, take ½ teaspoon of powdered ginger or 6 teaspoons of fresh ginger once a day, whether in food or tea.

Painful leg cramp relievers

Standing barefoot on a cold floor decreases blood flow and could help relax tightened leg muscles, so if you're hit with these painful leg cramps in the middle of night, get out of bed and stand on a cold floor.

Quinine for cramping

To prevent cramps, make tonic water part of those 8 ounces of water we're told to drink eight times a day. (Just leave out the gin!) Quinine, from the bark of the South American cinchona tree, is the only drug actually proved effective for leg cramps, but serious side effects, including irregular heartbeat, put quinine on the prescription only list. What you *can* buy, and in any grocery store, is tonic water—called so because it's flavored with beneficial quinine.

Calming Gastrointestinal Distress

Stomach soothers

Got indigestion? Nausea? An ordinary tummy ache? Certain herb leaves, flowers, and seeds have traditionally been used to remedy gastrointestinal problems. Among them, in alphabetical order, are angelica, anise, caraway seed, chamomile, cinnamon, fennel seed, ginger, marjoram, oregano, and peppermint. And all can be used to make an herbal infusion or herbal tea.

Tummy taming turmeric

To alleviate stomach cramps, add a teaspoon of this very mild, flavorless, bright red powdered herb to an 8-ounce glass of water, or simply sprinkle it over whatever you're eating. Turmeric is an ancient Indian and Middle Eastern remedy for treating colicky babies and is a recognized antispasmodic.

Juniper as a gastrointestinal tract calmative

To make an infusion of this traditional digestive aid, stir 2 tablespoons oil of juniper into 2 cups boiling water. Once it's cool, drink small portions over the course of 24 hours.

Live in the Windy City?

To help keep flatulence under control, try one of these herbal teas or infusions.

- **Caraway seed** Pour 1 cup boiling water over 1–2 teaspoons freshly crushed caraway seeds. Steep 10–15 minutes, then strain. Drink a cupful two to four times a day between meals.

- **Fennel seed** Follow the directions for caraway seed tea, substituting fennel, then drink before or after meals.

- **Dried peppermint leaf** Pour 1 cup just-boiled water over 1 tablespoon dried peppermint, infuse for 10–15 minutes, and strain. Drink a warm cup of tea three or four times a day.

- **Dill seed** For a mild dill seed infusion, pour 1 cup just-boiled water over 1 teaspoon ground dill seeds and let sit for 10–15 minutes. Strain, then drink before or after meals.

- **Anise seed** Follow the directions for infusing dill seed, substituting anise for dill seed. (Caution: Some people may be allergic to anise.)

Go for the ginger

Sip a cup of virtually miraculous ginger tea after meals to help keep your digestive system in good working order. Gingerroot, which could be called the queen of digestive herbs, has been used for thousands of years to treat indigestion and diarrhea. Research over the past quarter century has shown that two compounds in ginger—gingerols and shogaols—also work on the inner ear and central nervous system as well as the gastrointestinal tract, helping to reduce nausea and dizziness.

What's the Story?
Castor Oil: Our Ancestors' Cure-All

Well into the twentieth century, a bottle of castor oil could be found in virtually every doctor's office, hospital, and home. It was used primarily as a laxative and stomachache cure but also to treat colds and skin problems.

Children in particular were subjected to the foul-tasting oil, which was given at the first hint of a sniffle, cough, or cramp. Many adults took it once a week as a purgative believed to "clean out the system." The oil was also used to induce labor and help a mother recover after childbirth.

Castor oil is extracted from the seeds of the castor bean plant (*Ricinus communis*)—the source of ricin, a deadly poison. But do not fear! The oil is denatured and made safe to use when it is extracted through cold compression and undergoes steam treatment. The venerable product is still on the market, so why not literally hold your nose and give it a try?

Sip cider vinegar

Stir 2 teaspoons cider vinegar into 8 ounces water and enjoy your "vinegar cocktail" up to three times a day for improved digestion and to fend off an impending stomachache. Apple cider vinegar, unlike white vinegar, contains malic acid, which helps to adjust the stomach's pH (the balance of alkalinity and acidity).

Treat diarrhea with berries

Simmer 1–2 tablespoons astringent blackberries, bilberries, or blueberries or their dried leaves in 1½ cups water for 10 minutes, then strain, for diarrhea relief. Drink 1 cup of this diarrhea-fighting tonic several times a day, preparing it fresh each time. Some herbalists recommend drinking 1 shot glass (2 tablespoons) every 4 hours.

Old-timey constipation cure

Your grandmother loved it for a reason: One of the primary uses for castor oil is as a laxative; taking 1–2 teaspoons on an empty stomach will give results in about 8 hours. Castor oil works because a component in the oil breaks down into a substance that stimulates the large and small intestines. Note: This is not recommended for repeated use, as it impairs absorption of nutrients.

Grease the skids with blackstrap molasses

This most refined molasses also contains lots of calcium, magnesium, potassium, and iron, in addition to easing constipation. Of course, it's essentially concentrated cane sugar so you'll want to brush your teeth after swallowing so you don't make your dentist rich. How much to take? One tablespoon before going to bed.

Grow a Physic Garden

Physic (or *physick*) was the name given to gardens of healing plants grown by physicians and monks in ancient times and by home gardeners well into the nineteenth century. Why not plant your own with some of the herbs shown here? By investing a little sweat and the cost of seeds, you'll have the makings of infusions, teas, and balms. Just choose a sunny spot with rich soil for your garden. Perennial plants will grow from season to season, while annuals must be reseeded or transplanted.

Basil
Annual. Harvest the young leaves of what's called "the king of herbs" as needed. Uses: Flatulence, lack of appetite, cuts, and scrapes.

Chamomile, German
Annual. Use the flower heads for infusions and salves. Uses: Indigestion, anxiety, skin inflammations.

Feverfew
Perennial. Use leaves and flowers for teas; chew leaves to ease headache pain. Uses: Headaches (including migraines), arthritis, skin conditions.

Lemon balm
Perennial. A relative of mint, lemon balm is a versatile medicinal herb. Uses: Anxiety, insomnia, wounds, herpes, insect bites, flatulence, upset stomach.

Parsley, Italian
Biennial. Like its curly cousin *P. crispum,* this herb is loaded with nutrients. Uses: Flatulence, bad breath.

Sage
Perennial. Sage's genus name, *Salvia,* means "to heal," reflecting its early use as a medicinal, not culinary, herb. Uses: Mouth and throat inflammations.

St. John's wort
Perennial. The glossy leaves and yellow flowers are this herb's active parts. Uses: Mild to moderate depression. (Talk to your doctor first.)

Thyme
Perennial. The active principle in thyme, thymol, is a strong antiseptic. Uses: Coughs, congestion, indigestion, gas.

Plumbing Problems?

The little red infection fighter

To prevent urinary tract infections (UTIs), drink 12 ounces to 4½ cups of no-sugar-added cranberry juice each day. Capsules of dried cranberry powder are also available—but in some brands, six capsules are the equivalent of only 2½ ounces of juice. Medical researchers learned as early as the 1840s that the hippuric acid in cranberries inhibits the growth of *E. coli* bacteria, the most common cause of UTI. The acid also keeps *E. coli* from adhering to the urinary tract walls and from spreading from the bladder to the kidneys.

Eat your parsley to ease your pain

Mince parsley leaves (Italian or curly), add 1 teaspoon to 1 cup boiling water and let steep 3–5 minutes. Strain, then drink up to 3 cups of tea a day. Because a volatile oil in the leaves and roots of parsley has diuretic properties, parsley tea is useful for treating mild bladder problems, reducing urinary tract inflammation, and even facilitating the passage of small kidney stones. Caution: Anyone with chronic kidney disease should consult a doctor before using parsley, and excessive ingestion of the herb can cause the skin to be photosensitive.

A cup o' corn silk

To make tea, place this natural diuretic in a teapot and add boiling water (¼ cup washed corn silk to 1 cup water). Let steep for 5–6 minutes, then strain into a teacup and drink up to 3 cups a day. Corn silk tea bags are also available. This natural remedy has been shown in tests to have anti-inflammatory properties that fight UTIs; it's also a traditional folk remedy for cystitis, urethritis, and prostatitis.

What's the Story?
Does "Natural" Mean "Safe"?

Not always. Even plain water can be lethal if you drink too much of it. (A water overdose actually dilutes the salt in the body and leads to a condition called hyponatremia.)

Take heed of the age-old advice to practice "moderation in all things" and follow these general guidelines:

- Always ask your physician or pharmacist about any possible interactions with prescription medications, and only use natural or herbal remedies under the advice and supervision of a physician.
- Never use herbal remedies when pregnant or nursing.
- If you aren't growing your own herbs, buy only from reputable sources, preferably at a store with reliable sales staff.
- Never exceed the recommended dosage.
- Discontinue use if you notice any negative side effects.
- Store products in a cool, dry place out of the reach of children.
- Do not use commercial products after one year from date of purchase.

Gotta love lovage

To ease the discomfort associated with a mild inflammation of the urinary tract, make lovage tea by pour 1 cup boiling water over 1 teaspoon minced dried lovage root, which is a member of the carrot family but tastes more like celery. Steep 10 minutes, then strain and drink. A note of caution: It should be avoided by anyone with chronic kidney problems.

Drink to kidney health!

(But do it with fruit juice, please, not booze.) Making sure you drink one or two 8-ounce glasses of fruit juice (especially cranberry juice, lemonade, or orange juice) a day will contribute to overall kidney health. That's because the ascorbic and citric acids in fruit juices acidify the urine and have an antiseptic effect on the kidneys. Just don't overdo it—a good rule to follow in any case, but especially when ingesting anything acidic.

Praise the weed and pass the teapot!

The dandelion isn't just any old weed: it has a long history as a medicinal, and its benefits are related to the kidneys in at least two ways. First, dandelion reduces fluid retention resulting from kidney disorders. Second, dandelion may be able to speed the passing of a small kidney stone. If you feel the pain that signals movement of a stone, drink as much dandelion tea as you can. A strong diuretic, dandelion stimulates blood circulation through the kidneys, increasing urine output and helping to flush out the stone. Dandelion tea bags are easily available, but you can also make your own. Wash dandelion leaves and root thoroughly and then chop finely. Add 3 tablespoons to 2 cups water, boil for 3 minutes, and let sit for 10–12 minutes before straining.

Dandelion tea may hasten the passing of kidney stones!

Foot Care

Beat athlete's foot

To put athlete's foot on the run, make a foot-bath with 1 tablespoon salt dissolved in 6 quarts warm water. Soak the affected foot for 10 minutes to help kill the fungus. To make the solution still more antifungal, add 1–2 tablespoons tea tree oil.

Fight toenail fungus

If you think you can't control a fungus without prescription drugs, think again—for the short term, at least. Mix equal parts warm water, vinegar (white or cider), and mouthwash, with a tablespoon of powdered cinnamon. Soak, dry feet, and then sprinkle with cornstarch. There's no guarantee the fungus won't return, but at least you can keep it in check without expensive drugs.

Got stinky feet?

Strong black tea will not only kill odor-causing bacteria but will close pores and help keep your feet less sweaty. Simmer 3 black tea bags in 2 cups water for 15 minutes, then dilute the tea with 2 quarts water. Once it's nice and cool, pour tea into a plastic tub (hold the milk and sugar), and soak those ripe dogs for 30 minutes. No more stinky feet.

Salty dogs

While Epsom salt—named for the English town where it was first mined commercially—has long been used to soothe dry, sore feet, ordinary table salt will do in a pinch. Pour 2 gallons warm water into a plastic tub, add 1 cup table salt, and stir with your hand to dissolve. Soak your feet in the solution for at least 20 minutes,

Kitchen-Cupboard Odor Eater

Take shoes (warm and airless), sweat (secreted by the eccrine glands on the soles of your feet), and poor hygiene (neglecting to scrub your feet when you shower) and you have a recipe for funky feet. Whether your stocking feet are only mildly odoriferous or smelly enough to fell a crowd at 40 paces, turn to the kitchen cupboard to help control the odor.

What to take off the shelf? Baking soda and cornstarch. Mix the powders 50/50 and sprinkle the mixture on your feet before you put on your socks. Baking soda helps neutralize the skin acids that harbor odor-causing bacteria, while cornstarch absorbs sweat. Sprinkling some of the powder into your shoes will also help to neutralize odors.

then rub them vigorously with a towel to slough off dead skin cells.

Terrific tired tootsie trick

If your feet are tired and aching, scatter a few pencils on the floor and pick them up…with your toes. This little workout rejuvenates and invigorates your dogs as much as a quick foot massage.

Cool that hot foot with peppermint

Give hot feet the chill-down by soaking them in iced peppermint tea for 10 minutes. All pepped up, they'll be ready to take you on a three-mile jog or an hourlong power walk.

Healing Cuts, Bruises, and Other Skin Problems

Treat a cut with garlic

To treat a cut or abrasion, gently wash the wound with soapy, warm water and pat it dry with a clean, soft cloth. Then bruise a peeled clove of garlic and press it against the cut for 5–10 minutes, securing it with a bandage if you like. Garlic contains allicin, which has been shown to inhibit the growth of several kinds of bacteria and protect against infection. (Fresh garlic is an irritant, so never leave garlic in any form—infused, minced, or whole—on the skin for more than 20 minutes at a time. Remove it immediately if it irritates the skin.)

Black pepper stops bleeding

Shaking a good amount of black pepper onto a bleeding cut will stop the blood flow pronto. Why? Because the pepper constricts the blood vessels. Many people who've tried this remedy claim that a wound treated with black pepper heals with less scarring.

Lessen bruising with an onion

Immediately press the cut end of a raw onion on a superficial bruise and keep it in place for 15 minutes. Why? Because the allicin in onions (the compound that makes your eyes water) stimulates the lymphatic flow in the body, helping to flush away excess blood in the just-injured tissue that creates the discoloration we call a bruise.

Aloe Straight from the Leaf

Commercial aloe vera lotions and creams are a dime a dozen, but an aloe treatment is yours for free if you have access to an aloe vera plant. Better still, fresh gel is generally more effective than store-bought lotions, which often contain more non-aloe emollients than aloe.

To get the real stuff, go straight to the leaf itself. Plants will keep well indoors, in a cool, sunny spot.

1. Cut off a 3-inch section of fleshy aloe leaf, slice open the inner portion, and scrape out the mucilaginous gel with a spoon, stopping short of the rind.
2. Apply the gel to the skin two or three times a day, washing the skin between applications to make it more receptive to glucomannan and aloe's other anti-inflammatory substances.

Be careful not to get aloe gel on your clothes, since it can leave a yellow stain.

Soothe sunburn with green tea

Just add 3 green tea bags to 1 quart just-boiled water, remove the pan from the heat, and let steep for 2–3 hours. Use a cotton ball or very soft cloth to dab the sunburned area with the cooled tea, and let the cooling tannins do their work.

Conquer the (creeping) cooties with alder bark

To get rid of lice, simmer 2 tablespoons chipped alder bark in 2 quarts white vinegar, then let cool before straining into a container with a lid. Using a cotton ball, apply to the scalp or other affected areas four times daily. Do *not* ingest the mixture, and be aware that alder bark may temporarily color the skin.

Chamomile salve

Melt ½ cup petroleum jelly in a double boiler and stir in 1 tablespoon chamomile flowers. Heat for 2 hours or until the flowers are crisp. Tightly fit a jelly bag atop a glass jar and squeeze the hot mixture through. Once the salve cools, apply to a mild skin rash up to four times a day. Choose the more efficacious German chamomile *(Matricaria recutita)* over Roman, or English, chamomile *(Chamaemelum nobile)*.

Double-duty paste for bee stings

A baking soda–vinegar paste applied to a bee sting immediately after removing the stinger will get some alkaline and acidic action going (use 2 parts baking soda to 1 part vinegar). When the paste dries, wipe it off with a clean, damp cloth.

Papaya milk for stings

Forget about milking a papaya after that painful bee or wasp sting. Instead, use commercial meat tenderizer, which contains papain. Moisten a teaspoonful of tenderizer with a little water and rub it onto the sting as quickly as possible; papain's protein-digesting properties help break down the venom.

Oatmeal and panty hose to cure hives

Cut a panty-hose leg off at the knee and put these four ingredients into the foot: ½ cup rolled oats; ½ cup dry powdered milk; and ¼ cup each dried chamomile flowers and lavender. Knot the nylon bag closed and hold it under warm (not hot) running water as you fill your bathtub. Submerge the bag and let the water cool. (Hot water makes hives worse, not better). Soak for half an hour, and every 5 minutes or so, hold the bag over the rash and squeeze to release the soothing stuff inside.

Douse skin rashes with witch hazel

The bark and leaves of the witch hazel plant contain high proportions of naturally astringent tannins and an aromatic oil—the perfect recipe for soothing itchy skin rashes.

Pimple pastes

Applied to pimples, quick 'n' easy homemade pastes will make pimples disappear quickly. Try these three.

- **Baking soda** Moisten ¼ teaspoon baking soda with a few drops of water and dab it onto pimples. Leave it for 5 minutes, then wipe it off with a washcloth dipped in cool water.

- **Oatmeal** Use some of your morning oatmeal as a pimple-fighter. Dab the cooked, cooled oatmeal onto broken-out skin, cover with a warm-water washcloth compress, and let sit for 15 minutes. Repeat daily until the pimples are gone.

- **Cornstarch and lemon juice** Make a paste with 1 teaspoon cornstarch and 1 teaspoon lemon juice. Apply to pimples and let sit for 4–5 minutes before gently washing your face with cool water.

Witch Hazel from Your Garden

If you have a witch hazel bush (*Hamamelis virginiana*) in your yard and it's at least 3 feet tall, you can prepare your own witch hazel astringent for treating skin irritations, cuts, and scrapes. Going the homemade route has two advantages: It puts you in touch with a time when self-sufficiency was a way of life, and your homemade astringent is more effective than witch hazel products that have undergone steam distillation and lost most of their tannins.

Because the leaves have to dry, it takes about a week to make witch hazel. Snip leaves at the stem base and rinse them well. To harvest bark, lop off a branch and scrape off the bark. Place the leaves and bark on paper towel–lined trays and store them in a dark place at 70–90°F for seven days.

While witch hazel can be prepared in a number of ways, the easiest is to use a blender. Blend the dried plant matter for 1–2 minutes, then combine it with water (1 tablespoon plant matter to 1 cup water). Pour into a saucepan, bring to a boil, and simmer for 20 minutes. Remove from heat and let steep for 2 hours. Strain through cheesecloth or a fine sieve into sterilized jars and use as needed. Good job!

Lifeguards never had zits!

The white zinc oxide cream slathered over the noses of lifeguards as a sunscreen is also an effective acne fighter. Dab a little zinc oxide cream or ointment before bed and it will not only help dry up pimples but is also said to prevent scarring.

Wards off vampires, too!

Rubbing a freshly cut clove of raw garlic on a pimple will help dry it up and make it disappear.

Just treat pimples right before going to bed, since garlic doesn't have to be on your breath to make those around you wrinkle their noses.

Kitchen-cupboard eczema salve

A white creamy substance good for soothing eczema comes not from the medicine cabinet but the kitchen cupboard: vegetable shortening. Coat the affected area with shortening, cover with plastic wrap, and secure the wrap with surgical tape. Leave it on for 2–4 hours at a time, if possible, repeating daily until the rash calms down.

Two ways to stop shingles from itching

Shingles, or *herpes zoster*, is caused by the varicella-zoster virus—the same virus that causes chicken pox. (It isn't as contagious as chicken pox but can be passed on to anyone who's susceptible.) The rash consists of small, crusting blisters that itch like the dickens, and both of these home remedies can bring relief:

- **Aloe gel** Apply gel to affected area to calm the itch

- **Nail polish remover and aspirin** Pour 3 tablespoons nail polish remover into a small cup, add two crushed aspirin, and stir until the aspirin dissolves. Use a

cotton ball to apply the solution to shingles blisters, and let it air-dry for hours-long relief.

Cure warts with a "garlic press"

Slice a fresh peeled garlic clove, place it on the wart, and bind it with a gauze bandage. Leave the garlic in place as long you're able to, and repeat the process morning and night. Because of its general antiviral activity, garlic has been said to cure warts even when other methods have failed.

Rosewater for chapped skin

To make a lotion for chapped skin (and a fragrant one, at that) mix ½ cup rosewater with ¼ cup glycerin and rub it into the skin as needed. This essential cupboard companion is as popular as ever in Asia and the Middle East, where it is used both to flavor food and in rituals. Find it in pharmacies and health food stores.

T(r)opical wart remover

Make several shallow cuts in an unripe green papaya, and collect the sap that it releases. When it congeals, mix it with water to make a thin paste. Before applying the paste, protect the skin surrounding the wart by swabbing on

ALOE FOR BLISTERS

Speed blister healing by rubbing it with gel from an **aloe vera** leaf. Slice open a leaf and use a spoon to scrape out the gel (see "Aloe Straight from the Leaf," page 171). Dab it on the blister, cover with a bandage, then reapply and rebandage once a day.

a thin layer of petroleum jelly (papain, the enzyme in papaya, is an irritant so powerful that it's an ingredient in meat tenderizers). Using a cotton swab, carefully apply the paste to a wart morning and night until it breaks down and disappears. Papain breaks down proteins in dead tissue, making it a wart remover of long standing.

Turmeric treats ringworm

If you have a bottle of the Indian spice turmeric in your kitchen cabinet, you have an antiviral powder that has been used in Asia as a ringworm remedy for centuries. In a small bowl, mix enough of the powdered root to make a paste. Apply the paste to the affected area with a cotton swab, cover it with a bandage, and leave it on for 20–60 minutes. Repeat three or four times a day. Note: Turmeric may irritate sensitive skin, so test it first on clear skin; if redness develops, try another treatment.

Seal in moisture with vegetable shortening

Dry skin and rashes alike benefit from a soak with a wet washcloth for several minutes, then a gentle rubdown with vegetable shortening. Cover the affected area and leave it on for 1–2 hours. Wipe the shortening off with a clean soft cloth and repeat the treatment as needed.

Relieve swimmer's itch

Protect yourself from swimmer's itch in freshwater lakes by spreading petroleum jelly on skin not covered by a swimsuit.

1,001 Ways to Remove Warts

We're not promising to run down all of the folk remedies tried over the ages to remove warts, since that would be one those lists that supposedly stretches all the way around the equator. Suffice to say that untold numbers of methods have been recorded. People washed warts in rainwater pooled in tree stumps. They pressed raw potatoes, banana peels, and any number of saps and oils on warts. They also believed in the Theory of Transference—the notion that an ailment could be transferred from the patient to a tree, animal, or object. Blood was drawn from a wart, placed on a grain of corn, and fed to a chicken. Warts could be "sold" to a folk healer called a wart charmer.

Surprising as it is, many of the most far-fetched wart remedies have been documented as successful. Some medical researchers now believe the body may be able to rid itself of warts through the power of hypnotic suggestion. Case in point: One physician who had no success in treating a man with multiple warts put the patient in an X-ray room and told him he was going to zap him with radiation. In fact, the doctor ran the X-ray machine without delivering any rays—and the man's warts fell off the next day.

Aiding Sleeplessness and Anxiety

A tryptophan snack before bed

Serotonin is a brain chemical that helps you sleep, and tryptophan is an amino acid the body uses to make serotonin. Two tryptophan-rich foods are turkey and bananas, your tickets to drowsy dreamland.

Drink passionflower tea

Despite its name, passionflower won't make your honeymoon all the more memorable. In fact, it will put you to sleep. Infuse 3 passionflower tea bags in 3 cups just-boiled water for 30–60 minutes and sip a cup half an hour before going to bed. Sweet dreams! (FYI, the "passion" in the name refers to the Crucifixion of Christ, not lust.) Alkaloids in the flower can help allay both insomnia and anxiety, conditions that often go hand in hand.

Calming Epsom salt bath

To calm yourself, pour 2 cups Epsom salt into a tub full of warm water, and soak to your heart's content. Epsom salt (magnesium sulfate) not only cleans and tones the skin but also may lower blood pressure—just what you need after a day so awful that your anxiety level is sky high.

Make a hops pillow

Hops pillows were popular sleep aids in days of yore, and it's easy to make a modern version. Take a zippered throw pillow or chair cushion cover and stuff it full of dried hops (available at natural product stores, online, and perhaps at the nearest brewery). If you like, throw in a handful of dried lavender, also a sedative herb, to sweeten the smell. When you retire for the night, put the pillow near enough to you head that you'll be able to breathe in the aroma. To keep the hops active, you'll need to dampen them with grain alcohol every three or four weeks.

Try St. John's Wort

A cup of St. John's wort tea can safely be drunk up to three times a day to allay mild depression, nervousness, and insomnia; capsules and liquid extracts are also available. Be aware, though, that some people using the herb have experienced delayed photosensitivity—an abnormal reaction to sunlight that usually results in a skin rash. This best-selling herb is Germany's leading antidepressant, outselling even Prozac. Studies show that hypericin and other compounds in St. John's wort act in tandem to prevent the enzyme monoamine oxidase (MAO) from breaking down serotonin, dopamine, and other amines that elevate mood and emotions. Check with your doctor before use.

Tomato paste snore stopper

If your bed mate's snoring is cutting into your sleep time, help is in the pantry. Put a small can (4–5 ounces) of tomato paste in the pocket of a cotton T-shirt and secure it closed with a safety pin. Have the snorer put the shirt on backward before going to sleep, and it will keep him (or her) from rolling over into prime snoring position: on the back.

Give yourself a soak

There's a reason why in-the-know parents give their babies warm baths before bedtime or nap-time: warm water is a natural relaxant. So fill the tub, turn the lights down low, soak for a few minutes, and crawl into a freshly made bed for no-lose snooze.

Pre-sleep sip

Chamomile, which is known to have sedating qualities, is an ideal sleep inducer. If you can get good quality tea bags, they'll do perfectly; if you can grow fresh chamomile in a small pot on a windowsill, all the better. Snip them about an inch below the flower, tie a few of them together with kitchen string, and steep them in a mug of hot water. Delicious!

White noise as sleep therapy

Studies have long proven that white noise—defined as noise that combines sounds of all different frequences so that they virtually cancel each other out—is an effective, completely non-narcotic, safe, and peaceful sleep aid. Where to get it? You can buy white noise machines, or even less expensively, CDs and tapes. Load them into your bedroom CD player, turn the lights down, climb into bed, and remember to set the alarm!

Keep your cool!

The term "warm and cozy" doesn't always translate to the right conditions for falling asleep; resist the urge to keep the heat up, and instead, lower your bedroom's thermostat to 65–70°F, and if possible, open the window a crack for good ventilation. Sleep experts maintain that cooler bedroom temperatures result in a sounder, better snooze.

Household Superstar!
8 Ways Petroleum Jelly Is Kind to Your Body

While petroleum jelly is usually thought of as a moisturizer, it was developed as a salve to heal and protect cuts and abrasions—and it's more versatile than you might think. Here are eight ways to use it:

1. Prevent chafing of back skin subjected to a backpack's straps and upper thighs clothed in denim by rubbing petroleum jelly on the vulnerable areas.

2. Rub petroleum jelly on dry, scaly patches of psoriasis to lubricate them and lessen itching.

3. To keep a crusted cold sore from bleeding, coat it with petroleum jelly applied with a cotton swab, not your fingers.

4. Spread a thick layer of petroleum jelly on an infested scalp, and when you wipe it off, the lice should go with it.

5. Dab a hemorrhoid with petroleum jelly, which is contained in many over-the-counter hemorrhoid treatments.

6. A layer of petroleum jelly on a small wound keeps moisture in and bacteria out.

7. Dab petroleum jelly under your nose to trap some of the pollen spores making their way toward your nostrils.

8. Rub petroleum jelly on the insides of your nostrils to moisten the mucous membranes and make nosebleeds less likely.

Caring for Baby

Diaper rash soothers

The exposure of a baby's skin to urine and poop cause diaper rash, especially when diaper changes are delayed. Soap can irritate the skin even more if it contains alcohol—and though most commercial baby wipes are alcohol-free, so are three cost-free diaper rash soothers in your cabinets:

- **"Toasted" cornstarch** Although moisture-absorbing cornstarch can be used straight from the box, it works better when dried in the oven. Just spread it on a cookie sheet and dry it in a 150°F oven for 10 minutes. Let cool before using.

- **Honey** The sugar in honey absorbs water, denying infection-causing bacteria the moisture they need to survive. Ask your doctor before using honey on children under 12 months of age; if ingested, honey can cause botulism.

- **Petroleum jelly** Wiping petroleum jelly on the rash gives Baby's skin a protective coating so the rash can heal.

A spicy baby powder substitute

The spice fenugreek has been shown to soothe diaper rash. Either apply it directly to the skin, like baby powder, or mix it with a little water to form a paste to apply sparingly to irritated areas.

Prevent diaper rash with salt and zinc

Stir 1 tablespoon salt into 4 cups boiling water and let the solution cool to room temperature. Wipe it onto your baby's bottom, then gently dab it dry. Now apply a zinc oxide lotion to create a barrier against wetness.

Easiest rash preventive of all?

Air! The less time a baby's bottom is covered by a diaper, the less she risks suffering diaper rash. At nap time, just place an unfastened diaper under your child or put the baby on towels placed over a waterproof sheet.

A rash remedy from the garden

Calendula, a marigold cousin, has long been used to treat skin rashes, so keep a homemade wash in the nursery to soothe Baby's skin.

Cut the flower heads from a calendula plant and let them dry. Pick the petals off over a bowl and put 1 heaping tablespoon petals into a bowl. Pour 3 cups just-boiled water over the petals, let steep for 1 hour, then strain into a bottle. Apply to the baby's bottom or other red or itchy areas up to four times a day.

Chamomile for congestion?

If your baby is 6 months or older and is stuffy, try easing her congestion with weak chamomile tea—weak meaning 1 chamomile tea bag steeped in 2 cups hot water for no more than 3 minutes. Put the lukewarm tea in her baby bottle and let her sip on it two or three times a day. Check with your pediatrician first; chamomile can trigger allergic reactions in some people.

Soothe heat rash with a baking soda bath

Heat rash can make babies miserable, and here's a way to help "take the red out": Add baking soda to Baby's lukewarm bathwater—2 teaspoons to each gallon of water. Then let Baby air-dry instead of wiping him with a towel. You can also gently press the rash with a cool, wet washcloth several times a day.

Two herbal teas for colic

Much to Baby's distress, the periodic intestinal spasms known as colic start at about 3–4 weeks of age and usually don't end until two or three months later. One colic fighter is the volatile oil in fennel seed, shown to expel gas and relieve cramps and flatulence in the process. Another is peppermint leaf, which calms the intestinal tract and stimulates the bile flow that aids digestion.

To make a fennel tea, pour 1 cup boiling water over 1 teaspoon crushed fennel seeds. For peppermint tea, pour 1 cup boiling water over 1 tablespoon crushed leaves. Let either tea steep for 5 minutes, then strain. Cool tea before giving to Baby.

A caution: Give peppermint tea to babies with care. The menthol in peppermint can cause a choking sensation, so start with a single sip and discontinue use if the child chokes or seems to find the tea disagreeable.

Stopping Baby's nosebleed

Your fingers, a facial tissue or soft washcloth, and patience are all the equipment you need to stop a small child's nosebleed. Seat the baby on your lap and lean him slightly forward. Now, with the tissue or washcloth in hand, gently pinch his nostrils shut. Apply constant (though gentle) pressure for 10 minutes, making sure you don't release pressure to check and see whether the bleeding has ceased.

How to keep Baby still all this time? Watch a favorite video or, if you can handle it, leaf through a picture book to hold his attention.

Sore throat for Snookums?

If your baby's old enough to be eating solids, warm beverages like tea or broth can be soothing. (No honey in the tea, please, since honey may contain spores that could grow in the baby's immature digestive tract.) Cool apple juice is another sore throat soother for the little one.

Dr. McFolk's Medicine Bag

Homemade hydration aid

Sports drinks are full of electrolytes—the salts that need replenishing after the body sweats—and are almost essential for keeping athletes and runners hydrated. You can make your own for next to nothing. Dissolve 1 teaspoon salt and 4 teaspoons sugar in 1 quart water, and you have a drink that isn't colored or adorned with a fancy label but that will nonetheless maintain your electrolyte balance and keep you hydrated.

Milk thistle for liver health

Our forebears used the weed milk thistle to "clean the liver," and they were on to something. Silymarin, a substance contained in the seeds, prevents toxins from penetrating the liver and stimulates the regeneration of liver cells—the reason milk thistle has been used in the treatment of hepatitis, cirrhosis, and jaundice.

If you think you can just harvest milk thistle weed and use the seeds to make a therapeutic tea, think again. Teas are ineffective because the active principles in milk thistle seeds aren't water-soluble. Instead, try milk thistle capsules and liquid extracts, making sure they contain 200–400 milligrams of silymarin.

Peanut butter for hiccups

Believe it or not, peanut butter may take care of those annoying hiccups. It's not the peanut butter per se that works but what it takes to swallow it. Eat 1 heaping teaspoon of peanut butter (plain or crunchy) and take your own sweet time swallowing it. As you chew and use

---

Curiosity Corner
"Like Things for Like Things"

Since the Middle Ages, one of the "laws" of folk medicine was based on the principle *similia similibus*—"like things for like things." When it came to medicinal plants, those whose characteristics match the body's organs were believed to have a curative effect, a belief that in time came to be called the Doctrine of Signatures and that eventually was proved utterly false.

As late as the nineteenth century, liverwort (*Hepatica* ssp.)—so named because its leaves are the shape of the liver—was used to treat liver ailments. Plants with red sap were applied to bleeding wounds, and the fuzzy burrs of the burdock plant were said to cure baldness. The Doctrine of Signatures was rooted in the belief of an inherent affinity, or sympathy, between living things and the forces of the universe—hence the reason it was often referred to as "sympathetic magic."

your tongue to clean the gooey treat off the roof of your mouth and your teeth, your breathing patterns are interrupted and may result in halted hiccups.

Oil and vinegar remedies

Grab some oil and vinegar from the kitchen cabinet when you need relief in a pinch. You can do a lot more than dress a salad with these staples.

- Vinegar takes the pain out of a bee or jellyfish sting. Scrape the stinger off with a credit card, and then pour undiluted vinegar directly on the sting.

- White vinegar dries up a cold sore when rubbed on the sore 3–4 times a day.

- White and cider vinegar take the burn out of sunburn. They also take the itch out of poison ivy rashes and insect bites.

- Olive oil is a good stand-in for shaving cream. Your skin will enjoy a nice moisturizing treatment as you wield your razor.

- Soaking in a bath to which you've added ½ cup olive oil and 2 cups baking soda will stop skin from itching and will soften it as well.

- Add 2–3 drops warm (not hot) olive oil to the ear to soften earwax. Drain your ear after 5 minutes. Do not do this if there's a chance you have a perforated eardrum.

Fight herpes with lemon balm tea

Lemon balm's volatile oil contains two substances that fight herpes simplex type 1 virus (HSV1), which usually affects the lips, mouth, and face, and HSV2, or genital herpes—the reason the herb is widely used in European over-the-counter herpes products. To make an infusion, pour 1 cup just-boiled water over 2–3 teaspoons minced lemon balm and let steep 10–12 minutes before straining into a jar. Soak a cotton ball in the solution and apply it to herpes blisters several times a day.

Remove splinters with an onion

Here's a pain-free (if rather smelly) way to get a splinter out of a finger or foot. Place a ¼-inch slice of onion over the splinter and wrap a bandage around the affected area to keep the onion in place. Leave the onion poultice on overnight, and by morning the skin should have shrunk and allowed the splinter to work itself out.

Cider vinegar tea for fatigue

Vinegar perks up a recipe, and it may perk you up, too. Every morning before breakfast, whisk together 1 cup warm water, 2 tablespoons apple cider vinegar, and 1 teaspoon honey. Sip the tea slowly until you've downed the last drop, and within a week you may find yourself feeling more energized.

Treat thrush with goldenseal

Thrush, or candidiasis—an infection of the mucous membranes of the mouth, vagina, or digestive tract—is made evident by a whitish, "furry" tongue. The dried root of goldenseal (*Hydrastis canadensis*) has a long history as a thrush treatment, and clinical trials have confirmed its efficacy. To treat thrush, make goldenseal tea by pouring 1 cup boiling water over 2 teaspoons powdered root; steep for 5–10 minutes. Let cool before using as a gargle or douche, or drink as a hot tea.

Chapter Seven

You're Looking Good

Every woman knows about fashion and grooming glitches: the runs in hosiery, the broken heels, the smeared makeup. The classic snafus for guys? Ketchup on khaki pants, no hair gel, gray ring around the collar. And for both sexes? The bad hair day, the broken zipper, the clothes as wrinkled as the face of Methuselah (who supposedly died at age 969). What, oh what, to do?

Just leaf through the next 23 pages for more than a hundred creative solutions to the often maddening grooming and clothing problems that plague us all, using items you most likely already have! Here, you'll learn how to recycle old garments and make them look brand new; make very cool jewelry from old-fashioned typewriter keys; whip up homemade skin treatments that will leave you glowing; revitalize your hair with beer and avocado; and even remove lipstick smears with bread! What's more, making your own grooming products is simple, environmentally friendly, and inexpensive. If our ancestors did it, why can't we?

Keep your straw hat
looking sharp with
hairspray!

Homespun Skin Care

Tape out that furrow

Is that furrow in your brow starting to become your own personal petite Grand Canyon? Smooth it out by putting tape on your brow overnight, every night for a month. Before going to sleep, rub moisturizer on the wrinkle and wipe off any excess. Now smooth the furrow with your fingers, hold it taut, and secure a piece of tape across the spot. Some folks recommend ouchless surgical tape, while other make do with any sticky tape. (Just make sure it extends beyond the moisturized area or it may not hold through the night.) Taping works by retraining the face muscles to relax—and, unlike Botox or plastic surgery, costs only pennies.

Look younger (and sweeter!)

Discourage wrinkling by applying a facial mask made of honey once a week, like Cleopatra did. Honey has properties that soften and hydrate skin and help it retain moisture, plus antioxidants and various compounds that can soothe irritations and inflammations. To make a honey mask, warm the honey. While it's heating, press a warm washcloth to your face to open the pores. Carefully spread the honey around the face, keeping it away from your eyes. Relax for 15 minutes and then rinse the mask off, using cold water in the final rinse to close the pores. Though your skin may not *look* like a baby's, it should feel almost as soft.

Soak in a hot tea bath

If a spot of tea in the afternoon is a calming break, a hot green tea bath in the evening after a tough day is a little touch of heaven. Place 2 tablespoons dried green tea leaves in the toe of an old nylon stocking, then bunch it up and close with a twist tie. Toss the bundle into a hot bath or tie it with string over the faucet opening so the water will run through. While you're enjoying the hot soak, the antioxidants of the tea will go to work, smoothing, soothing, and calming you both outside and in.

Chocolate body wrap

Love chocolate so much that you could bathe in it? Here's your chance. Just warm ½ cup of honey in a microwave or the top of a double boiler. Then stir in 1½ cups of unsweetened cocoa until it dissolves. If the mixture cools, reheat it, but don't let it get hot. Now spread the mudlike paste evenly over your body.

Here comes the good part: Wrap your legs, arms, and torso in plastic wrap to seal in the paste and sit tight (or lie down) for 20 minutes.

TURN A SOCK INTO A WASHCLOTH

Got yet **another mateless athletic sock**? (You're not the only one.) At bath time, simply turn it inside out (terry cloth on the outside), fit it over your hand like a mitten, and use it as an exfoliating scrubber.

Skin-sational Facts

Most of us take our skin for granted, but it is in fact the body's largest organ. Moreover, it grows faster than any other organ and continually replenishes itself. It's waterproof, flexible, generates all the hairs on the body, and can repair itself. And if you think that's amazing, read on.

• The average-size person's skin weighs about 9 pounds, or about 16 percent of body weight.

• An average-size person's skin would cover an area of about 17–21 square feet if laid out.

• Your skin has approximately 45 miles of nerves and more nerve endings than any other part of the body.

• The entire top layer of dead skin cells sloughs off and is replaced every month, yet we barely notice it.

• In the average person's lifetime, about 40 pounds of dead skin cells are shed and replaced.

• Within 1 square inch of skin are approximately 65 hairs, 100 oil glands, 650 sweat glands, 1,500 nerve receptors, and countless blood vessels.

• The average person has 5 million hairs on the body, with only about 100,000 growing on the scalp.

That done, peel off the wrap and wash away the paste in a warm shower or bath. Your skin should feel silky smooth, thanks to the hydrating and revitalizing antioxidants in cocoa and honey. And all without a single calorie!

Stomach medicine for a facial?

Strange but true: Over-the-counter stomachache medicines containing salicylic acid, like Pepto-Bismol, are beneficial to the skin. How so? Salicylic acid helps to slough off the top layer of dead skin cells and bring new healthy skin cells to the surface. Squash a few cotton balls together in your fingers, pour on some of the pink goo, and apply it to your face, taking care to stay clear of the eyes. Let it dry for about 15 minutes, then rinse and pat dry. Your skin will not only stomach this facial but will thank you!

Condition your legs

For a smooth leg shave without traditional shaving cream or gel, just substitute hair conditioner or an all-in-one shampoo-conditioner, both of which contain ingredients that soften, smooth, and moisturize hair. They'll do the same for hair and skin on your legs, underarms, and, for men, the face.

A summertime citrus body splash

Squeeze the juice from a lime, filter out the pulp, and pour the juice into a spray bottle. Add ½ cup rubbing alcohol and 3 teaspoons lemon or orange extract. Screw the lid on the bottle and shake well. Give yourself a spritz for a great way to cool down in the summer. Store the spray in the refrigerator with an identification label so no one will think it's safe to consume.

Prolong the scent

Add hours to the scent of your perfume by first dabbing a tiny bit of petroleum jelly on your wrists, neck, ear lobes, and anywhere else you apply the fragrance.

Three Ways to Slough It Off,
NATURALLY!

Many people use facials, masks, scrubs, and other methods to speed the natural process of shedding dead skin cells, called exfoliation. Sloughing off dead cells with exfoliants exposes new, plumper, cleaner, smoother cells that lie just underneath the skin's surface. Exfoliating also stimulates blood circulation, which brings a healthy glow to skin. There are lots of commercial products out there that exfoliate and stimulate skin renewal, and spas and salons charge a good bit of money for one session. You'll save a pocketful by sloughing off skin with items from your pantry and refrigerator. Just gently massage the exfoliants shown here into the skin, using circular motions. (When applying an exfoliating facial or mask, avoid the area around the eyes.) After rinsing and patting your skin dry, apply some moisturizer and feel renewed—literally!

1
Strawberry Scrub
Mash 5 or 6 strawberries, then mix in 1 tablespoon ground almonds and enough yogurt (about 2 tablespoons) for the mixture to be pasty enough to apply.

2
Oatmeal Ouster
Blend together 2 heaping teaspoons finely ground uncooked oatmeal with 1 teaspoon baking soda. Stir water in slowly until you have a spreadable paste.

3
Ginger Snapper
Blend together equal amounts of freshly minced ginger and brown sugar, then add vanilla extract or sweet almond oil to make an energizing body scrub. Ginger contains valuable antioxidants and is known to stimulate circulation.

The Eyes Have It

Bottoms up!

Models and performers have long held the secret to reducing puffiness and wrinkles no matter how late they were up the night before, and it's *not* an expensive eye cream. What is it? Hemorrhoid cream, which tightens puffy areas and wrinkles. If the odor of the cream is too strong, mix a bit of your moisturizer into it before applying. And do be careful not to get any of the cream into your eyes; after all, it's designed to be used much farther south.

Spoon 'em for energy

The next time your peepers need pepping, take two metal teaspoons from the kitchen drawer and hold them under very cold running water for a few minutes. Then lie down and place the bowls of the spoons over your eyelids for 30–60 seconds. The sharp cold of the metal will revive tired eyes and may boost your energy level at the same time.

Teething rings for tired eyes

Was the baby crying all night, leaving you with tired eyes? No problem. While baby naps, put two of his teething rings in the freezer until they're ice cold, stretch out on the sofa, and place the rings on your closed eyelids for about 10 minutes. The cold will not only reduce eye puffiness but invigorate you, too.

Lighten dark circles

For many people, tiredness causes dark circles under the eyes—"raccoon eyes" that add years to the appearance of men and women alike. If you can't catch up on your rest, place slices of ripe avocado under each eye or apply a paste

of ground almonds and milk to lighten the dark shadows.

Cool as a cucumber

When your eyes are all red and puffy (you party animal, you), cut a couple of slices of cold cucumber, lie down, and put a slice over each eye for 30 minutes. Once you're up, your eyes will be brighter and your body refreshed.

De-puff with tea

Caffinated tea—which contains natural tannins—is a mild diuretic and long-used by grandmothers and runway models alike for reducing eye puffiness. Soak two tea bags in warm water, and then chill the bags for a few minutes in the refrigerator. Place one tea bag on each eye for 5 minutes, and your peepers will be fresh as a daisy.

Makeup Tips

Firming up mushy lipstick
Purse sitting in the sun for too long? Instead of waiting for the air conditioning to firm up your softened lipstick, pop it into the fridge for a fast five-minute fix.

Emergency lip color
You can't decide if the new dress you're trying on is flattering to your face, and without extra color on your lips it's even harder to tell. So you dig into your handbag, and surprise! You've left both your lipstick and lip pencil at home. But you *do* have a brown eyeliner pencil. Press the eyeliner into service on your lips, and you may find that it looks fantastic!

A cheesy solution
Are you out of cotton balls and makeup remover pads and don't like to use tissues because of the residue they leave on your skin? Cut a few squares of cheesecloth for wiping off makeup. They're soft, porous, and absorbent. Use a bigger swatch as a covering for mushy facials so you don't drip goop on the floor or yourself; pat the cloth very gently over the mixture, just until it adheres.

A Surprising Cologne Corrective

Ever accidentally douse yourself with just a little *too* much cologne? (Haven't we all?)

If soap and water won't correct the problem, head to the liquor cabinet and grab a bottle of vodka. Dab a little on the places you applied the cologne or perfume, and the nearly odorless spirit will knock out the scent in short order.

No eye shadow applicator?
No problem. Use a cotton swab in its place: it's softer, the tip can be used to smudge and soften eye liner, and the best part? Toss it when you're done.

Makeup mistake?
If you go overboard with the mascara or sustain a smudge elsewhere during your makeup routine, just wipe off the slipup with a cotton swab dipped in petroleum jelly. Then start over with a lighter hand.

HOMEMADE LIP GLOSS

To make your own lip gloss, scoop the last bit of lipstick from the tube and blend it with a little **petroleum jelly.** Put the mix into an empty lip gloss pot, and voila!—it's ready to use. For a firmer gloss, refrigerate the mixture for an hour.

Home Hair Care

Instant dry shampoo

No time to wash your hair or are you caring for someone who can't step into a shower or bath? A dry shampoo will do the job. Take 1 tablespoon of cornmeal or cornstarch, and sprinkle the powder into the hair; massage it in section by section, and comb out any tangles. Brush well to remove all the powder, stopping often to shake out the brush. The powder absorbs dirt and excess oil, leaving hair clean and shiny.

Two-ingredient revitalizing conditioner

Give drab hair new life with this luscious conditioner—made with only two ingredients: take half of a ripe avocado, scoop out the fruit, and mash until smooth. Slowly stir in ¼ cup coconut milk; the mixture should look like a thick gel, so add more milk as needed. Work all of the mixture into your hair, then comb smooth. Wait 10–15 minutes before rinsing thoroughly. Your hair should feel thicker and look richer. (For an extra treat, use the other half of the avocado to whip up a little guacamole!)

Leave it to vinegar

Your hair has lost its luster, so you switched shampoos; that helped for a while, but now your hair has returned to dullsville. The reason? Buildup of the residue left by shampoo and other products. Vinegar will safely remove the residue and restore your hair's natural acidic pH balance, leaving it shinier, smoother, and easier to manage. Just mix 2–3 tablespoons apple cider vinegar with 1–2 cups of water in a jar. Then shampoo your hair as usual and rinse. Shake the vinegar solution and use it as a final rinse. Any vinegar smell will disappear as soon as your hair dries.

Run out of hair mousse?

You've shaken the can of mousse and turned it upside down, but not a drop comes out. Don't panic. Try a little shaving cream mixed with a drop of rubbing alcohol to keep your hair in place and moisturize at the same time.

SUPER (BOWL) HAIR

If you have a **six-pack of beer** left over from your Super Bowl party, use a little to make a hops shampoo that gives your hair body, shine, and volume. In an enamel-lined saucepan set over medium heat, bring ¾ cup beer to a boil, then simmer briskly until it reduces to ¼ cup. Cool, then mix with 1 cup of your regular shampoo. Transfer it to a jar with a lid and shake before using.

make your own
Hair Rinse

Herbal formulations have been used on hair for thousands of years, so something must be working. The bergamot in this herbal rinse helps control itching and dandruff, while the rosemary (used as a fragrance in soaps and perfumes) provides the nice scent.

Herbal Rinse and Shine

If the lid of the jar you use to steep the herbs is metal, place plastic wrap or wax paper between the lid and the jar to prevent the vinegar from corroding it.

  ¼ cup dried rosemary leaves
  ¼ cup dried bergamot
  2 cups cider vinegar
  2–3 cups warm water

1. Place the herbs in a heatproof, thick glass jar, such as one used for preserves.

2. Heat the vinegar until very hot but not boiling, then pour it over the herbs. Cool, then cover tightly.

3. Keep the jar in a warm spot for a week, shaking it once a day.

4. Line a funnel with cheesecloth and place the funnel over a jar. Strain the rinse into the jar and screw on the lid.

5. When ready to use, mix ⅓ cup of the rinse with 2 or 3 cups of warm water. Then pour over hair once or twice as a rinse.

Got mousse but out of gel?

Raid the pantry! Mix up a batch of flavorless Knox gelatin and you may never go back to the salon variety: dissolve ½ to 1 teaspoon unflavored gelatin in 1 cup warm water and refrigerate. Super hold, super price!

All set for gel but no hair spray?

No problem. Chop up 1 lemon and add it to a pan filled with 2 cups of water. Boil until reduced by half. Cool, strain, and pour into a spray bottle; add 1 ounce of rubbing alcohol. Stored in the refrigerator, the spray will keep for 3–4 weeks; unrefrigerated, it will last for 2 weeks.

Tame hairline frizzies

The hardest place to control frizzies is the area around your hairline. To show the frizzies who's boss, saturate an old toothbrush with hairspray and brush them back where they belong. Hold them in place with your fingers until the hairspray dries.

Panty hose scrunchies

Got long hair and can't find a scrunchie? Dig into that drawer with "emergency" panty hose—those with runs you've been saving to wear under slacks. Just cut the length you need, and you're ready to run for miles. Black and colored hose will look the most fashionable, but flesh tones will do in a pinch. Panty hose have the added advantage of not bruising or breaking your hair, as elastic sometimes does.

Eyeball those roots

If you're of a certain age, you may color your hair, and your white roots seem to peek out faster than a race car on the Indianapolis Motor Speedway. Here's a quick fix. Apply your mascara to the roots with an old toothbrush, blending it in as you go. This trick works best with dark hair—so what do you do if you're a blonde? Try beige or taupe eye shadow as temporary camouflage.

A sage decision for brunettes

Applied to brown or black hair, sage will darken gray hairs. Put ¼ cup dried sage into a bowl and pour 2 cups boiling water over it. Let the mixture steep for 3 hours or overnight before straining it into a bottle or jar. Shampoo your hair as usual, rinse, and then apply the sage tea to gray hairs one area at a time, dabbing it on with a cotton ball or a wad of cheesecloth. Air-dry or use a hair dryer, but *do not* rinse. You'll probably need to repeat the process once a week until you get the color you want.

Spike it with petroleum jelly

Feeling a bit funky (or, perhaps, punky) and want a new way to style your short hairdo? Use a drop or two of petroleum jelly to spike your locks into place. The bonus? When you wash it out, your hair will be softer and shinier!

Shelve the dye for darker locks

Leave chemical dyes on the shelf (where they belong!) and color your dark hair the way the ancients did: with rosemary! Pour a pint of boiling water over a cup of fresh chopped rosemary leaves, allow it to stand until cold, then bottle it and rinse hair after washing. Goodbye gray!

Household Superstar!

6 Quick Beauty Fixes with Lemon

Considering its size, the vitamin C powerhouse we know as the lemon provides an astonishing number of beauty benefits, six of which are listed below. (One word of caution: Lemons can cause skin to be extra-sensitive to sunlight, so don't expose yourself to the sun for too long after a skin treatment.)

1 Exfoliate dead skin and bring new skin to the surface by washing skin with lemon juice mixed with a little sugar.

2 Smooth wrinkles by boiling 1 cup milk, 2 teaspoons lemon juice, and 1 tablespoon brandy. Cool the mixture to room temperature, apply, and let dry before wiping it off.

3 Lighten age spots by dabbing them with lemon juice and rinsing off after 15 minutes. Repeat once later in the day.

4 Mix the juice from 1 lemon with ¼ cup olive oil or sweet almond oil for a facial that both exfoliates and moisturizes.

5 Fight dandruff with a daily scalp massage with 2 tablespoons lemon. Rinse with water and follow with a rinse of 1 cup water mixed with 1 teaspoon lemon juice.

6 Whiten and clean fingernails by soaking them in 1 cup lukewarm water and the juice of ½ lemon for 5 minutes, then rub the inside of the lemon rind against the nails.

Home Nail Salon

Why spend money at fancy nail salons when you can achieve the same look in the privacy of your own home? Here's how!

Cleaning nails

Soak dirty nails for 5 minutes in a bowl of water in which two denture tablets have been dissolved. While this method may seem odd, it stands to reason because teeth and nails are made of the same substance— keratin.

Caring for cuticles

Why waste money buying pricey, specialized cuticle creams? Instead, reach for the olive oil, sweet almond oil, baby oil, vegetable shortening, or even lip balm. Taking good care of cuticles will also discourage hangnails—a sign that both your nails and cuticles are too dry. As you massage oil into your cuticles, go ahead and oil the whole nail. No splits, no breaks, and less chance of an annoying hangnail.

Instant polish touch-up

Got a chip? Not on your shoulder, but on a polished toenail? If you're in a place where you can't repair it properly, dig into your purse and grab a lip pencil or lipstick and add color to the chipped spot. It won't hold for long, but it ought to get you through lunch or dinner or a movie. And you can always reapply your temporary fix in the ladies' room.

Freeze-dry your wet nails

You're late for your friend's wedding, but your nails are still too wet with polish to risk opening the car door. Quick! Open the freezer and stick your hands in. Your nails will be dry in a jiffy, and you can get on your way to the service.

Duds, Rags, Threads

Put a stop to static cling

Lack of humidity in the air is the main cause of static electricity in your clothes. Men have to worry only about trouser legs clinging to the skin, while women wearing panty hose experience the problem much more often. Try one of these methods to keep clothes static-free.

- **Spritz with hairspray** Spray a little hairspray along the underside of trousers or skirts. Or spray a paper towel and wipe the hairspray on the inside of the fabric.

- **Dampen with water** Wet a paper towel or your hand with water and run it along the exterior of panty hose and the interior of a skirt or pair of slacks. Or you could use a spray bottle to mist the inside of the clothing.

- **Separate with a coat hanger** Move a hanger up and down between the inside of clothes and panty hose or a slip.

The incredible shrinking waistband

It's not that unusual to find an elastic waistband has shrunk or expanded when you're putting on pants, shorts, or a skirt you haven't worn for months. Try this quick fix: open the waistband on the inside of the garment. Cut the elastic inside the band and insert a piece of taut elastic from the waist of an old pair of panty hose or a section of a stretchy headband. Attach the insert to one side of the cut elastic with a safety pin. Stretch the insert to the fit you want and safety-pin it to the other side of the original elastic. Cut off any excess for a flatter appearance and then smooth down the waistband with your fingers. You can cover any telltale bulge with a sweater, T-shirt, overblouse, or jacket.

Glue your bustin' buttons on

Buttons on new clothes will stay put longer if you dab the threads atop the buttons with white, clear-drying glue. Use a cotton swab to apply it neatly.

BLOWIN' IN THE WIND

Prevent skirts from flare-ups on windy days by sewing two or three small **mailbox keys or pennies** into the hem as weights. Wedding dress seamstresses use this trick to keep bridal veil hems hanging properly, choosing weights that can't easily be seen through gossamer fabrics—among them, the flat glass beads used in flower arrangements and fish bowls.

Iron-free wrinkle solution

Lay your wrinkled shirt on a flat surface (a countertop or dresser top will do). Hold a hair dryer a few inches above the shirt and aim the hot air at the wrinkle while smoothing it out with your other hand. After a few minutes the wrinkle should either be less noticeable or gone.

Serve musty clothes a cocktail

What do you do when you pull out an outfit to wear but are hit with a musty odor? Pour a little unflavored vodka into a spray bottle and lightly mist the outfit. The alcohol kills the odorous bacteria without adding an unwanted smell of its own.

Appliqués save the day

When a garment is beyond repair because of holes or stains, don't automatically shop for a new one. Consider hiding the damage with appliqués. They not only hide problem areas but also provide a decorative look. Most appliqués are iron-on these days, so you won't even need to sew.

Rid sweaters of pills

Pilling can ruin an otherwise perfect sweater. Use a razor or an electric shaver to cut the fuzzy pills off, taking care not to make a hole in the weave. Other handy de-pilling tools are an emery board, a pumice stone, and the rough side of a piece of Velcro. With any of these, rub lightly in one direction until the pills disengage.

Keep the zip in zippers

Stuck zipper? Take a closer look at the teeth. If they show lint or dirt between them, brush the teeth with dry toothbrush bristles, then rub them lightly with the stub of a beeswax candle. The zipper should now glide smoothly on its waxed track. If a zipper has *too* much zip and comes undone on its own (usually at the most embarrassing moments), use a cotton swab to coat the teeth with hairspray after you've donned the garment and zipped the zipper. Hairspray will hold both sides of the zipper together just enough to keep them from coming apart.

What's the Story?

It's a Cinch!

Nineteenth-century women were famous for their hourglass figures and for fainting—and one wonders whether they realized the two were related. Ladies owed their curvaceous figures to tight-fitting corsets that cinched in the waist and enhanced the bosom. The corsets were heavy and stiff, reinforced as they were with wood, whalebone, or steel ribs.

Once a woman was laced in, her posture was admirably erect. And no wonder: She couldn't bend! Worse, women often had trouble breathing. Corsets restricted normal movement of the diaphragm, the muscle below the lungs. When a diaphragm moves down, it allows the lungs to expand and take in fresh oxygen; when it moves up, the lungs contract and exhale carbon dioxide. In other words, the breath was actually being squeezed out of these figure eight, corseted ladies. Not surprisingly, as corsets disappeared, so did the smelling salts used to revive a person who fainted.

Putting Clothes Away

Perfume your lingerie

You've just dabbed the last drop of your favorite perfume on your wrist, and you're sorry you don't have anymore. But you can still enjoy its fragrance if you put the empty bottle in your lingerie drawer. The scent will waft up each time you open the drawer and will perfume your underclothes as well.

Eliminate pants creases with bubble wrap

How many times have you pulled on a pair of slacks only to take them off because unsightly coat hanger creases make them unwearable? Wrap the hanger bar in a layer of bubble wrap with the smooth side facing out (secure the wrap with duct tape). Other coverings that work just as well are strips of quilt batting or soft foam sheets used as filler in packing boxes.

Hang spaghetti straps securely

If your spaghetti strap tops and dresses are forever slipping off wire hangers, you've got lots of company. The easiest way to secure them is simply to clip both straps to the hanger with clothespins.

Stay-put scarves

A neat way to store scarves so that each is within easy reach is to attach a few shower curtain rings to a coat hanger's bottom bar, thread a scarf though each one, and then hang them on the closet rod—much easier than rummaging through a pile of scarves in your drawer to find the one you want.

Cedar scent

Cedar blocks have long been used as an alternative to strong-smelling camphor to keep moths from setting up shop in your clothes. If your cedar has lost its woodsy fragrance, don't spend money to replace it. Just use sandpaper or an emery board to rough up the wood and release the scent.

Moths also shy away from the scent of dried bay leaves, dried lavender, dried orange peel, cloves, and whole peppercorns. The feet of old panty hose make inconspicuous sachets for your closet or drawer.

DOUBLE YOUR HANGING SPACE

No need to redesign your closet or buy fancy hangers to increase your hanging space. Just slip a sturdy **shower curtain ring** over the necks of your hangers and hook a second hanger onto them. Presto! A hanger that takes twice the clothes.

Holey Hosiery!

What? In a book like this we're actually talking about *wearing* panty hose instead of using it as an emergency fan belt or dog leash!? Yes indeed. And these four hints about the hosiery itself have to do with keeping it in good condition.

1

Prevent runs
You'll get a lot more wear from panty hose if you first soak them for 30 minutes in a solution of ½ cup of salt dissolved in 1 quart of water. Rinse and drip dry. When you don't have time for pre-treating, soak the panty hose in salt water after use and then wash. Either way, the salt strengthens nylon fibers, making them less likely to tear.

2

Lengthen the life
Dampen a pair of panty hose and place them in a sealable plastic bag in the freezer. Remove the frozen hose, then defrost (not in the microwave please) and drip dry. Freezing the fibers hardens them, and your panty hose will last through many more wearings.

3

Soften to avoid runs
Rinsing panty hose with a drop or two of fabric softener in the water is a good anti-run tactic. The fabric softener makes the nylon mesh more stretchable and less prone to runs caused by tautness. To dry, roll the hose in a towel instead of ringing them out and hanging them.

4

Nip runs in the bud
If you don't have clear nail polish to stop a run in its tracks, rub a small amount of liquid soap along the run's top, bottom, and sides. The soap hardens into a barrier as it dries, preventing the run from continuing on its path. Rubbing a bar of wet soap over the run also works.

Saving Stained Clothing

Wash out makeup spills with baking soda

If you've spilled foundation makeup on your blouse, go to the kitchen and grab a box of trusty baking soda. Sprinkle the powder onto the stain until it's completely covered and press it gently into the fabric. Wet a nailbrush or a toothbrush and lightly brush the spot. If any makeup remains, repeat the process until all traces have disappeared.

Lipstick smear remover 1: petroleum jelly

Dabbing petroleum jelly on lipstick marks before washing a garment is a removal method used by stain specialists. If it's good enough for pros, let's hope it's good enough for you.

Lipstick smear remover 2: bread

Tear out the doughy center of the bread and knead it into a ball, then blot the smear repeatedly with the dough until the stain lifts from the fabric. Now wash the garment. The dough ball is also safe to use on lipstick marks on no-wash woolen clothing.

Soak out tomato sauce stains

It's a brave soul who eats spaghetti while wearing a white shirt without a big napkin tucked into his collar. (Even Emily Post says it's the sensible thing to do.) For an effective tomato sauce spot eradicator, combine ½ cup 3 percent hydrogen peroxide and 3 cups water in a dishpan, pot, or clean sink. Soak the stain in the solution for 30 minutes before laundering.

Shaving cream tomato sauce remover

Grab a can of non-gel shaving cream and spray it onto the stain, rub it in gently, and let dry before washing.

Foundation shaker

Blot up foundation makeup marks on washable fabrics with fresh white bread kneaded into a ball. The bread treatment should also erase pencil marks on woolen and washable clothing. Resist the temptation to use the pencil's eraser to rub out the marks, which in most cases will only make them look worse.

Milk an ink stain

To get rid of that nasty ink blotch on your shirt, put 2–3 tablespoons cornstarch into a bowl, and then stir in whole milk until you have a thick paste. Cover the stain with the paste and let it sit for 3–4 hours. Then brush off the paste and wash the shirt. Another paste to try is 2 tablespoons cream of tartar mixed with 2 tablespoons lemon juice.

Remove red wine stains

The wine tasted terrific last night, but the few drops on your slacks don't look all that great this morning. Club soda is a common antidote for red wine stains, but if that doesn't work, try one of these treatments:

- **Borax** Dissolve 1 tablespoon borax in 2 cups warm water. Submerge the stained part of the garment in the solution and soak for 1 minute, then toss the item in the washer.

- **Dishwashing liquid and vinegar** Dilute your favorite dishwashing liquid, and gently scrub it into the stain; rinse gently with water, then apply a drop of white vinegar. Pat dry, and rinse again with water.

- **Salt and boiling water** Pour a generous amount of salt on a still-wet stain and see if the salt turns pink as it soaks up the wine. If it doesn't, pour boiling water over the salt. In either case, wash the stained garment ASAP.

- **Baking soda** Heap baking soda on the stain and let sit for an hour or more to absorb the stain. Then shake off the baking soda and launder the garment.

Prevent perspiration stains

Spread baby powder or talcum powder along the collar and underarms of soiled clothing, and press gently with a warm iron. The powder should absorb the sweat and make it easier for the rest to come out in the wash.

Pop out bloodstains

You're nearing the end of a charity bike-a-thon when your front wheel hits a pothole, sending you and your bike clattering to the ground. Fortunately, all that's hurt is your pride and your bleeding elbow. You remember that a friend who knows about such things told you to soak bloodstains overnight in cola (yes, soda pop). You try it, and lo and behold, she was right!

---

make your own
Stain Remover

Vinegar, baking soda, and ammonia—a mighty trio beefed up even more by the addition of liquid castile soap. Even Lady Macbeth would've killed for this homemade cleanser, made for stains that have already dried.

Out-Darned-Spot Spray

Treat grease, coffee, fruit juice, and other common stains with this spray, shaking it well before using. Liquid castile soap is sold in natural products stores and some supermarkets.

½ cup white vinegar
⅓ cup clear household ammonia
¼ cup baking soda
2 tablespoons liquid castile soap
1½ quarts water

1. Combine all ingredients in a half-gallon container and stir well. Pour into a 16-ounce spray bottle.

2. Spray the solution onto a stain and let it set for 3–5 minutes.

3. Rub the stain gently with a soft cloth and then wash the garment as soon as possible.

A toast to club soda

The most successful way to get rid of stains is to treat them before they dry and become set in the fabric. If you're at a restaurant or a friend's home and food or drink drops onto your clothes, ask right away for a glass of club soda and a lint-free kitchen towel. Repair to the restroom with the soda and apply as much as you can. Wait 1 minute, then blot the stain gently with the towel.

Quick Fixes and Mends

Salvage discolored whites

Don't toss those drab and dingy whites just yet: dissolve 1 teaspoon cream of tartar in cold water in a clean plastic washtub or sink and soak the garment for a few hours before washing. (This is also a great way to restore old handkerchiefs.) To whiten yellowed clothes, soak the items overnight in a solution of ½ cup white vinegar and 6 cups warm water before washing.

Restore crispness to lace

If you have a lace scarf or shawl that's gone limp, wash it as you normally would and then dip it in a solution of 2 gallons warm water and 1 cup Epsom salt. The salt will cling to the fibers and add body.

No-snag, soapy thread

Anyone who's been sewing on a button when the thread tangles or knots knows how frustrating it is to have to start over when you can't free things up. To prevent frustration and time lost, run the thread lightly over a bar of soap before you begin sewing. The waxy coating will make thread easier to untangle and unknot.

Rethread a drawstring

Did the drawstring come out of your hoodie or favorite PJs? Attach a safety pin to one end of the string and use the closed pin to push the string back into place.

Use marbles to help mend gloves

Drop a marble into the fingertip of a glove that needs mending so you'll have a stretched, smooth surface on which to sew. Mend the toes

Undo a Scorch (Fast!)

It's your anniversary, and your first gift to your wife is to do the ironing before she awakens. Won't she be surprised! You bet, but not so much by your generous act as by the scorch on her pale blue blouse. Who knew the iron heated up so quickly?

Lucky for you, scorch marks don't have to be permanent. Here are four techniques to try:

- **For white cottons** Take a cotton cloth dampened with 3 percent hydrogen peroxide and dab at the scorch until it's gone.

- **For colored cottons** Wet a lint-free cloth with 3 percent hydrogen peroxide or white vinegar and lay it over the scorch. Press with the iron on low.

- **For all washable cottons** Cut an onion in half, rub it on the scorch, soak overnight in cold water, and then wash.

- **For woolens** Dampen the scorch with water and dab cornstarch onto it. Let sit for 20–30 minutes and brush off.

and heels of socks in the same way, using a tennis ball or billiard ball.

Sewing kit in a film canister

Your button falls off your blouse while you're en route to a potluck supper, but you're prepared. You have everything you need in a plastic film canister in your purse—a few shirt buttons, a set of sewing needles still stuck in their cardboard holder (don't want to get stuck!), thread, and different-size safety pins.

Especially for Guys

Hardworking hand lotion

Even if you take really good care of your finger-nails, hands with rough, dry skin take you down a notch on the "good grooming" scale. To take care of the problem as you sleep, whip up a thin paste by mixing together 2 table-spoons avocado oil, 1 tablespoon honey, and 2 teaspoons glycerin. Now stir in 1½ cups fine-ly ground rolled oats or almonds until you have the right consistency. "Wash" your hands and fingers in the paste, then slip on a pair of latex or cotton gloves before going to bed.

Skin pepper-upper

Diluted vinegar will not only tone your skin but help protect it from infections—and it's simple to make a vinegar-peppermint concentrate you can keep with your toiletries. Place 1 teaspoon dried peppermint (or 1 tablespoon fresh) in a sterilized bottle with a cap, then pour in ⅓ cup apple cider vinegar. Screw the cap on tight and set aside for 10 days.

Strain the mint-scented vinegar into a second sterilized bottle. To use, dilute 1 tablespoon of the scented vinegar with ½ cup boiled or dis-tilled water and splash it all over your face to pep up the skin.

Homemade aloe face mask

Men are no longer strangers to facials (in urban areas, at least), but you don't need to head off to a salon. Prepare a skin-friendly, moisturizing mask at home with an aloe vera leaf, an egg yolk, honey, and powdered milk. Start by slicing the aloe leaf open lengthwise and scraping 1 teaspoon gel into a small bowl. Beat in 1 egg yolk and 1 teaspoon warm (not hot) honey with a spoon, then stir in enough powdered milk to make a thin but spreadable paste.

Use your fingers to spread the paste from hairline to chin, steering clear of the area around your eyes. Leave the mask on for 20–30 minutes, then remove it with your fingers and a wet washcloth. Follow your facial with a splash or two of skin toner.

Experiment with aftershave

For a good-smelling antiseptic aftershave, play around with apple cider vinegar and the likes of orange flower water, witch hazel, and essential oils like bergamot and neroli. Experiment with different proportions until you find the formu-lation you like best, then store it in a sterilized bottle with a lid.

Double-duty scent for drawers

Drawers in a chest-of-drawers, that is—not your boxer shorts. Keeping a bundle of cedar shavings or pine needles in a drawer full of T-shirts, sweaters, or any other garments will not only give a nice, masculine scent to your clothes but also will keep moths and other insect pests at bay. (Oh, which reminds us: dried bay leaves are an excellent choice, too.) Just place a handful of the material in the cen-ter of a handkerchief, bunch the four corners together, and knot the bundle before tucking it into a drawer.

Keeping Shoes Shipshape

Bubble wrap for good form

You don't need expensive shoe trees to keep your shoes in good form: use bubble wrap. Cut two pieces small enough to roll up and fit into your shoes and boots. When packing a suitcase for a trip, remove the bubble wrap and stuff panty hose or socks inside the shoes to retain their shape and free up space in the suitcase. Now wrap the bubble wrap around the shoes so they won't dirty your clean clothes. True double duty!

Serving spoon shoehorn

Cinderella's stepsisters struggled to fit their feet into the glass slipper, but you needn't struggle if you find yourself without a shoehorn. Take an oblong-shaped serving spoon from the kitchen and place your heel into the bowl of the spoon as you work your foot into the shoe.

Instant shoeshine

You don't need to spend money on special shoe polish to get the shine you want on leather shoes. Just put a few drops of baby oil, olive oil, or even castor oil on the dull-looking leather and buff with a soft cloth. You'll not only have shiny shoes again, but softer ones, too. These oils lubricate the leather, softening stiff spots and creases. They also work on patent leather and leather boots, jackets, handbags, belts, and briefcases.

High-heeled wrinkles

They're the smart high-heel shoes you splurged on, and they still look as good as new—except for the ugly scrunched-up leather along the heel. Fix them yourself with a hair dryer and leather glue. Put your hair dryer on the warm setting and direct the air to the heel. The warmth will soften both the remaining original glue and the leather, allowing you to smooth the leather out from top to bottom. Glue down any loose edges, and you're ready for more high stepping!

Cover up spots with a marker

If your dark shoes are scuffed and you have no time to polish, pick a permanent marker that's a close match to the shoe color and "mark the spot."

Sock it to your shoes

Perhaps the worst thing about giving your bedroom a new coat of paint is the drips that splatter on your shoes, despite your best efforts to do the job neatly. A simple solution is to slip a pair of old socks over your shoes as protection. Then save the newly colorful socks for your next paint job.

Plain Janes to Fancy Janes

If you have a pair of plain Mary Janes, slip-on ballet shoes, or plain heels, why not dress them up with a pair of big clip on costume earrings that you don't wear anymore? The extra color or glitter may be just the touch of glamour you want for that New Year's Eve party.

Handbags and Hats

Polish leather with a potato

Rub a cut potato across the surface of your dull leather handbag, give it a buff with a clean, soft cloth, and it'll look good as new.

Steam your suede

To clean stains and spots on a suede purse, first lightly rub the spots with fine-grained sandpaper or an emery board. Then hold the purse 6 inches away from a teakettle or pan with steaming water until the stain gets a little warm, making sure the steam doesn't saturate the bag. Brush with a suede brush or toothbrush, repeating the brushing once the suede is dry.

A space-saving handbag rack

If you've recently replaced a tall wooden stepladder, use the old one to store purses in your closet—especially helpful if you're short of shelf space. To make the ladder prettier, cover the steps with adhesive shelf paper or glue on decorative fabric swatches.

A new hat resizer

You've found the perfect hat at a yard sale, the type that's worn with the brim low on the forehead, but it's just a little too big for you. Go ahead and buy it anyway, then wear a sweatband under the hat to fill in the extra space. If the sweatband is too thick and makes the hat too tight, try a stretchy, thinner headband (surely one will work). Just remember to take the band and the hat off at the same time or you'll reveal your little secret.

About Those Lost Keys

You're not losing it when you lose your keys in your purse, and you are not alone. Who doesn't lose her keys in a handbag now and then? A simple solution to the problem: Attach a key line. Measure your purse from the bottom to the base of one of the handles and then add 4 to 6 inches. Now cut a piece of dental floss, fishing line, or a thin corded ribbon to that length. Thread your keys onto the line and knot the end. Place this end into your purse and wrap the other end around the base of the handle, knotting it tightly. Now, whenever you need your keys, just pull out the line. You won't have to fish for them anymore!

Restore shine to straw hats

Over time, straw hats lose their crisp, shiny look. You can spruce up yours in time for the rodeo or Easter Parade by spraying it with a light coating of hairspray and letting it dry. Be sure to spray in a well-ventilated area or outside.

Stuff hats to save their shape

Ever notice that the brims of hats in hat shops don't ever touch the shelves? Milliners know that brims resting on shelves will flatten out, so they overstuff the crowns with tissue paper to let the hats rest on the paper instead. If you don't have leftover tissue paper, use bubble wrap, dry-cleaning plastic, plastic grocery bags, old socks or panty hose, or a discarded sweater as stuffing.

Your Jewelry

Buttons for your wrist

If you're the type who likes to make your own bracelets and necklaces, alternating beads with some spare buttons you've got stashed away will make an unusual accessory. String buttons and beads of different colors and sizes onto two strands of dental floss, fishing line, or heavy-duty thread. Then experiment with a variety of combinations until you've fashioned a piece of jewelry worthy of a chic boutique.

Magnetic brooch holder

When it comes to silk blouses, dresses, or jackets, the last thing you want is to poke tiny holes in the smooth, expensive fabric with a pin. Instead, use magnets to attach the brooch. Remove the shaft of the brooch and attach one magnet to the back with super-glue. Make sure the glue dries completely before wearing the brooch. Place it in the desired location on the garment, holding it with one hand. With your other hand, place the opposing magnet behind both fabric and brooch. The magnets will lock the brooch in place, and you're ready for a no-pinholes night on the town.

Buttons for your toes

Don't think that adding a bit of glam to your plain pumps isn't jewelry ... it is! Rummage through your button collection for two that are oversized and interesting; glue gun them to the vamp of your (formerly) boring shoes, and give them a new life!

Wristwatch earring holder

If you've ever left your pierced earrings in a hotel room or had one mysteriously disappear from the nightstand never to be seen again, keep

Men's Jewelry, Then and Now

Some etiquette arbiters advise that a man should never wear more than a wedding ring and a watch, but these days they're crying in the wilderness. That's not to say understatement didn't have its heyday, which ran from the late 18th century to the 1970s—the decade famous for open shirts showing a chestful of medallions and chains. Little did the swingin' sideburned dudes of the '70s realize that they were bringing things full circle, in a way: Men of a certain rank were loaded down with jewelry until Louis XVI lost his head in 1793 and bedizenment went out of style.

Prehistoric humans adorned their bodies with beads and feathers, regardless of sex. Thousands of years later, King Tut's mummy was covered with so many amulets, pendants, bracelets, earrings, and other pieces of jewelry that the young pharaoh surely couldn't have borne the weight of them in life. In ancient Rome, jewelry was used to an extent never seen before, and the gold ring—once reserved for dignitaries—gradually appeared on the fingers of men of lower social rank and even soldiers. Men's jewelry flourished in Europe during the Renaissance among the upper crust, and portraits of King Henry VIII of England show his garments and hat brim studded with jewels.

Flash forward to the early 20th century, when men's jewelry was no longer associated with rank. Still, the common man's adornment was generally limited to a pocket watch and a ring. Only later did the love beads of the hippie era, the medallions of the disco days, and the bling of the hip-hop age bring flash to a man's wardrobe that rivaled (or outshone) that of early kings.

Organize your everyday jewelry by tacking it to a **bulletin board!**

them safe and secure with another accessory: your wristwatch. After taking off your earrings, insert them into the holes of a leather or plastic watchband or between the links of an expandable metal band. You can now rest assured they'll still be there in the morning. No wristwatch? It's a cinch to use the holes of a belt as a temporary earring holder.

Unstick a stuck ring

Your one and only has just proposed marriage, and you want to slip on the engagement ring. But at this moment of a lifetime, you can't get your old ring off your finger! What to do? Fetch some mayonnaise and slather it on your finger. Romantic? No way. Necessary? Yes, in a (literal) pinch. Make a fist to help the mayo seep under the band of gold or silver. The ring should now slide off easily. Wash your hands and then mentally rehearse the funny family story you'll share with your grandchildren.

Bulletin board jewelry "box"

Tired of having to dump out all your precious jewels to find that one necklace you really want to wear today? Take a lesson from gradeschoolers, and buy an inexpensive bulletin board and some colorful push pins; paint the board your favorite color, and then hang each necklace and each ring to keep them from getting scratched and to keep them organized.

Fix those necklace knots with powder

It takes a lot of patience to untangle a knot in a necklace chain. How to complete the task in no time? Sprinkle the knot with talcum or baby powder, cornstarch, or vegetable oil and use a straight pin or two to pry the knot apart. The powder and oil lubricate the links, helping them to slide and separate more easily. Afterward, wash the untangled chain with a mild detergent, rinse, and pat dry.

Mind Your Specs

Protect eyeglasses from hair dye

Whether you're highlighting your hair at home or having it colored at a beauty parlor, it's possible that a little dye can drip onto the sidepieces of your glasses. To protect sidepieces, simply wrap them with plastic wrap until your new color "do" is done.

Got a screw loose?

The tiny screws holding your eyeglass frames together don't ever seem to stay tight for long, especially when the specs are reading glasses. One way to keep things tight is to dab the threads with a little clear nail polish when replacing a screw, then coat the screw heads once they're in place.

Tip: Don't spend money buying one of those extra-tiny eyeglass screwdrivers. A toothpick or the eraser end of a pencil will work just as well. To use the eraser, turn the pencil upside down, press the eraser against the screw, and turn.

Seeing is believing

Eyeglass cleaner is expensive these days, but some folks know that two common household products will clean and polish lenses just as well—try club soda or rubbing alcohol, the latter used either full strength or diluted with equal parts water. Keep your cleanser in a handy spray bottle and use a soft lint-free cloth to dry the lenses.

Clearing up foggy specs

Having your glasses fog up is no fun. It happens in cold weather when you go from outside to inside, when steam billows up from a pot of boiling water, or even when you're eating very spicy food. As a preventive, clean your specs with white foamy shaving cream, which will leave an invisible coating on the lenses that keeps water drops from sticking.

Shaving cream is also a fantastic cleaner for eyeglasses. If you've accidentally spritzed hairspray on your glasses and can't get the sticky stuff off, a dab of the white stuff on each lens will clean it right up.

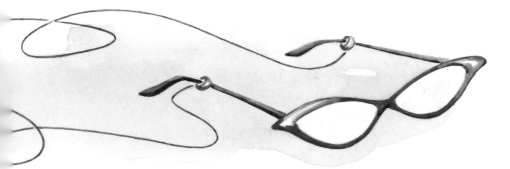

Chapter Eight

Smart Ideas for Parents & Kids

Imagine this novel idea: parents today can pamper their children without buying them every electronic gizmo under the sun or the latest hot toy to hit the market. Likewise, they don't have to break the bank to keep kids happy, healthy, and clean. Is this truth, or is it fiction?

We're happy to say that it's true, and this chapter is chock-full of great ways to provide for your children's needs, teach them interesting and important things in fun ways, and keep them engaged and entertained ... all without having to take out a loan. Where do we even begin when it comes to the fun of sculpting with salt dough that you make from scratch (instead of its store-bought counterpart)? Best of all, you'll find simple suggestions for keeping children safe, secure, and happy, and keeping their stuff organized at little or no cost.

Store tiny toys in an empty *milk jug!*

Bath Time!

Baby in a laundry basket

When your baby can sit by herself but is still too wobbly for a regular tub bath, a plastic laundry basket—the kind with perforations in the sides—is a great solution. Set the laundry basket in the tub, add a few inches of water, and put your little one in this "bathtub playpen." Be sure the holes in the laundry basket are large enough not to catch your baby's fingers or toes and that all plastic edges are smooth and safe. And follow the number one safety rule: Never leave a baby or small child unattended when she is in or near water.

Infant seat in the tub

Need an extra pair of hands when bathing baby? Your plastic infant seat will make bath time safer and less stressful for everyone concerned. Remove the seat pad, buckle, and straps, and then line the seat with a soft towel folded to fit. To prevent slipping and sliding, lay another towel on the bottom of the bathtub and set the seat on the towel. Then put your baby in his place, and run just enough water into the tub for the bath. The infant seat supports your little one and lets you use both hands to easily bathe him.

Petroleum jelly = no tears

Babies can't stand getting anything in their eyes at bath time, be it shampoo or water. Whether you have no-tears shampoo on hand or have to make do with a bar of mild soap, dab a drop of petroleum jelly across your child's eyebrows, gently wiping off any residue with a soft cloth or tissue. The jelly will deflect water and shampoo from the eyes and keep baby happy and comfortable.

make your own
Kiddie Bubble Bath

Who can resist the appeal of a warm, frothy bubble bath? Not many adults and not even the grubbiest, most bath-averse child. Show a kid a bathtub piled high with bubbles, like whipped cream on a sundae, and you're likely to convert a diehard bath-hater into a happy bather. The trouble is, bubble bath liquid can be costly if used frequently. So why not make your own with this easy recipe?

No-Tears Bubble Formula

Though regular shampoo will work in this recipe, using a no-tears shampoo will eliminate the risk of irritating children's eyes. Add a mere capful or two to running water—more for more bubbles.

> ½ cup no-tears shampoo
>   (clear or light in color)
> ¾ cup water
> ¼ teaspoon salt
> Food coloring (optional)

1. Gently mix shampoo and water in a bowl or a 2-cup measuring cup with a pour spout.

2. Add salt and stir until the mixture is slightly thickened. (This takes a minute or so.)

3. If you want to color the solution, add a drop of food coloring and stir. Continue adding drops and stirring until you have the desired color.

4. Pour mixture into a clean bottle.

To make bath time
pain free, pull on some
knee pads!

Cotton gloves and slippery babies

A wriggling infant in a soapy bath can feel as slippery as a wet banana peel, but you can get a grip by wearing a pair of cotton gloves.

Padded knees

Anyone who has bathed a grandchild knows how tough kneeling on the cold hard floor can be. Remedy? Athletic knee pads!

Soap in a sock

Here's a good use for the mismatched socks your washing machine *didn't* eat. Fill a sock with soap fragments or a small bar and tightly tie the sock closed. Kids like to wash with sock-soap because it won't fly out of their hands.

Reusing novelty bottles

Tear-free shampoos and liquid bubble bath in colorful molded plastic bottles are popular gifts for youngsters, but they're expensive everyday products. If your child enjoys shampoo or bubble bath from a bottle shaped like a duck or a frog, save the bottle and refill it with less costly bath products. Your child will have his bath toy, you'll save money, and you'll do the environment a favor by reusing plastic.

Bath-time help from the kitchen

Set a kitchen timer to go off when it's time for a bath—and also time for a bath to end. For youngsters who are inclined to delay, setting the timer to buzz five minutes before bath time is an early warning system. If your child likes to stay in the bath until he gets pruny, the buzzer will remind him to get a move on. Using a timer can help children acquire a better sense of the time required for a specific task. Timers may also be useful when older siblings are competing for time in the bathroom.

Stop itching with baking soda

Adding half of a regular-sized box of baking soda to your child's bath will help relieve the itching caused by bug bites, poison ivy, heat rashes, sunburn, and even chicken pox. Allow the child to have a good soak and then gently pat her dry with a clean, soft towel.

Splashy Bath Toys

Personalized floaty toys

Teaching your little one to recognize letters or to spell her name? Get personal by picking up some inexpensive floating craft foam at your local craft shop. Available in bright colors, they can be cut to resemble every letter of the alphabet, making them perfect for bath-time learning! F-A-B!

Playthings from the kitchen cupboard

Many of the best bath-time toys are likely to be found in your kitchen. Plastic food containers like margarine/butter tubs, measuring spoons, large cooking spoons, funnels, colanders, cups, milk cartons—if it floats, pours, stirs, or drips, it will inspire your child's imagination. Plastic lids become floating platforms. Funnels create waterfalls. Plastic mesh berry baskets will create masses of bubbles in soapy water. (It's best to avoid wooden and metal items; wood will splinter and can mildew, and metal rusts.) Simple, sturdy plastic items are safe and easy to clean; just wipe down plastic bath toys routinely with a water and baking soda solution or run them through the dishwasher.

Go fish with a kitchen strainer

A small plastic vegetable strainer lets toddlers scoop up sponges or shapes cut from craft foam and promotes hand-eye coordination, too. An aquarium net also works. (Thoroughly wash and disinfect a used net first.) Help your toddler drop her "catch" into a plastic container, and count the items together when he tires of fishing in the tub.

Cleaning Rubber Ducky

Molded plastic toys, such as a child's floating ducky, often have small holes that allow water to seep inside. Contaminated by sloughed-off skin cells and waste matter in the bath, this trapped water can breed unhealthy bacteria, so clean after each use. Here's how:

Squeeze the toy to remove as much bath water as possible. Then submerge it in a mild bleach solution (1 part household bleach to 15 parts water) and squeeze it to suck in the bleach solution. Shake the toy and then let it sit for 10 minutes before squeezing out the cleaning solution. In a separate container filled with clean water, rinse the toy using the same procedure and dry the now-safe toy for the next bath.

Commander of the fleet!

Save those wax-coated milk, cream, and half-and-half containers, snip the spout off, close the top with duct tape, and paint the little admiral's fleet in her color of choice, using water-insoluble paint. Add a name, numbers to the sides, and a Popsicle stick mast, and a no-cost bath-time armada is hers!

Throw in the sponge

Raid your kitchen drawers and storage cabinets for plain kitchen and utility sponges of all sizes and colors and cut them into different shapes. Your little one can play stacking games with floating circles, triangles, stars, crescent moons, leaves, keyholes, doughnuts, and whatever else your (and his) inventive mind can come up with.

Note: Before turning the playthings over to your child for the first time, disinfect used sponges by either 1) soaking them in a mild chlorine bleach solution and rinsing well or 2) wetting them and then microwaving on high for 1–2 minutes. *After* the bath, start a good habit by having your toddler help wipe the tub with a designated "clean-up" sponge.

Produce-bag storage

Turn a large-size, plastic mesh produce bag from the supermarket into a storage bag for bath toys. (Avoid string bags made of natural materials, which can become moldy and harbor germs.) If a plastic mesh bag has a paper label, soak it off in warm water. If the bag's drawstring isn't strong, replace it; a length of plastic-coated clothesline, knotted tightly, works well. Be sure to remove any metal staples or plastic tags. After your child's bath, put bath toys into the bag and rinse them under running water. Then hang the bag from a faucet handle or shower head so the toys can drip-dry.

Mesh produce bags are perfect for wet toys.

Simple Solutions from the Kitchen

Homemade bubbles

The ingredients for a homemade substitute for bubble-blowing liquid are right at you kitchen sink—dishwashing liquid and water. Pour 1 ounce dishwashing liquid into a clean 2-cup measure and fill with tap water (1 part dishwashing liquid to 15 parts water), then mix gently. This bubble solution performs best when left to sit overnight before use. Hard water will yield poor results, so test your tap water by making a small batch of solution. If you can't get bubbles, switch to distilled water.

Making salt sculptures

Why buy that colorful sculpting dough when you and junior can make your own from regular pantry staples? Here's how: mix 1 cup of salt together with 1 cup of flour. Using your fist, make a deep indent in the mixture, and pour in ¾ cup of water. To add color, simply use some nontoxic watercolor paint or food coloring. Knead well and shape into a ball. Roll out, and hand the little one some blunt-edged cookie cutters to cut out shapes, mold into sculptures, or make into holiday ornaments. Store in an airtight container, for tomorrow is another day!

Make slime with Metamucil

That nasty, gunky green favorite of kids everywhere is only a kitchen cabinet away and can save you at least 10 bucks worth of store-bought, kid-friendly YUCK. To make it, combine 1 teaspoon of Metamucil or psyllium husks (available at pharmacies everywhere) with 1¼ cups of water in a lidded jar, and shake vigorously for 3 minutes. Pour into a microwavable container, and add a few drops of hideous green food coloring. Microwave on high for 3 minutes; stop the process if the slime starts to ooze out the top of the container. Let rest for 3 minutes, and microwave for another 5 minutes. Remove carefully, and let cool for an hour. Store in an airtight container.

Kitchen cabinet toy box

Most babies know that the kitchen is where the real action is—it's full of shiny things, interesting sounds, yummy smells, and, oh yes, food. It's always important to childproof your kitchen, to install safety latches and plugs, and to make sure that anything even remotely dangerous is out of reach. Once done, you can designate one lower cabinet to be baby's kitchen toy box and stock it with a few specific items that your little one

can play with: smaller pots and lids, a few plastic containers, a wooden spoon, a sturdy set of measuring spoons, and nesting metal measuring cups.

Shake, rattle, and roll!

Some metal and plastic food cans, like containers for coffee and stacked potato chips, come with plastic lids. Turn them into fun noisemakers by cleaning and drying an empty can, making absolutely sure that all sharp edges have been removed or filed down, and tossing in a small amount of dry pasta, cereal, hard candy, dried beans, or rice. Secure the plastic lid with duct tape, testing the noisemaker to be certain the top won't come off. A quieter alternative? Put crunchy cereal in a cardboard oatmeal box and secure the top with tape. When rolled on the floor, this homemade rattler makes a neat swooshing sound.

Milk jug to toy caddy

Too many tiny toys underfoot? No problem. You can bring some order to the tiny toy invasion by making a simple toy carrier from an empty gallon milk jug or household bleach container with a handle. With scissors or a utility knife, carefully cut a large opening out of the top third of the bottle, leaving the handle area and the plastic cap intact. Cover the cut edge with duct or masking tape (while the cut edge could be filed or sanded smooth, taping gives extra protection). Let your child decorate the carrier with permanent markers and then fill it with small toys. Arguing siblings can keep their treasures in separate carriers and perhaps avoid the usual arguments.

Invisible lemon juice "ink"

If your child has a taste for the mysterious, teach him the secret of invisible writing. All that's required is a small bowl of lemon juice, a

make your own
It's the Bomb!

Nothing makes kids happier at bath time than splashing around and creating some good, clean fun. Bath bombs, those expensive balls found in spa shops, are a literal blast to toss into the tub, but pricey. Here's how to make your own from scratch:

All-Natural Baking Soda Bath

2 teaspoons baking soda
   (sodium bicarbonate)
1 teaspoon corn starch
1 teaspoon citric acid
20 drops glycerine
   (available at pharmacies)
Food coloring or liquid watercolor paints
   (optional)
Fragrance (optional)

1. Mix baking soda, corn starch, and citric acid in a medium bowl.

2. Add the glycerine, 3–4 drops of food coloring, and a few drops of fragrance (if desired).

3. Combine well until the mixture becomes crumbly.

4. Form and pack the mixture into golf ball-sized balls (or smaller), and set aside to dry, and harden overnight.

5. Place the child and baking soda bath bomb in the tub, and watch the fun!

cotton swab, and a piece of paper. Dip the swab in the juice and write on the paper. When the paper is dry, there will be no sign of the lemon juice "ink." Now hold the paper near to, but not touching, a hot lightbulb, moving the paper slowly over the heat. Magically, the writing will turn brown and legible. A trick worthy of the wizards of Hogwarts!

All-Time Favorite Play and Craft Recipes

You've probably run across some or all of the following recipes at one time or another, but they're not always easy to track down when you need them. All are basic to children's play and crafts—and luckily, all are easy to make.

Finger Paint

Keep containers of finger paint safely away from eager little hands. Finger painting is one of the kid activities that beg for supervision.

> ½ cup cornstarch
> 2 cups cold water
> Food coloring

1. Combine cornstarch and water in a saucepan and place over high heat.

2. Bring the mixture to a boil and cook until thickened, stirring constantly.

3. Remove from heat and cool to room temperature.

4. Divide mixture among containers and stir several drops of food coloring into each.

Storage. Pour the finger paint into small plastic containers with snap-on lids and store it at room temperature.

Craft Paste

This white paste is used for craft projects and making papier-mâché.

> 1 quart water
> ¼ cup salt
> 1½ cups white flour

1. Bring water to boil in a medium saucepan.

2. Remove from heat and stir in salt.

3. Add flour a little at a time, stirring constantly. Continue to add flour and stir until mixture is the consistency of thick gravy.

4. Cool to room temperature before using.

Storage. Store the paste in an airtight container in the fridge. It may keep as long as five days, but throw away immediately if it becomes moldy or has a bad smell.

Play Clay

Two kitchen staples—baking soda and cornstarch—are the basis of this easy-to-make clay.

> 2 cups baking soda
> 1 cup cornstarch
> 1¼ cups cold water
> Food coloring (optional)

1. In a medium-size saucepan, mix together baking soda and cornstarch.

2. Add water and stir. Add food coloring to the water, if desired.

3. Set over medium heat and stir continuously for 10 to 15 minutes. Do not overcook. Mixture should have the consistency of mashed potatoes.

4. Transfer the cooked mixture to a plate and cover with a damp cloth to cool to room temperature.

Storage. Between uses, store play clay in a self-sealing plastic bag or an airtight container. It keeps in the fridge for up to a week.

Hardening. Harden clay objects by air-drying overnight on a wire rack. Or place them on a cookie sheet in a preheated 350°F oven; then turn off heat and keep objects in the oven until it's cold. To microwave, place objects on a paper towel and microwave at medium power for 30 seconds. Turn objects over and heat for another 30 seconds, repeating as necessary until objects are hard and dry.

An egg carton game

Here's a fun activity that can help preschoolers master their counting and sorting skills. With a marker, write the numbers 1 through 12 in the egg sections. Then provide edibles such as shaped cereal, raisins, or nuts and have the child put the right amount in each numbered section. You can play a similar sorting game by having him separate different shapes and colors of cereal, dry pasta, or dried beans.

Alternatively, give the child a bowl of raw fruit and vegetable pieces—sliced carrots and apples, peas, grapes, mandarin orange segments, cherry tomatoes, broccoli, button mushrooms—whatever you have on hand. Then have him sort the food into the egg sections by type.

Food coloring to brighten snow-day play

After they've pelted one another with snowballs, kids can get antsy for more entertainment on a snow day, so try this: fill several plastic squirt bottles—ketchup and mustard bottles are ideal—with water and add a few drops of food coloring to each. Kids can "draw" designs on the snow with the colored water.

A carrier for precious papers

School children sometimes have important papers to take to school—like that world map your daughter has been working on for weeks for her geography class, or that book report your son keyboarded all by himself. Tubes from rolls of paper towels or standard-size plastic wrap, foil, or waxed paper are just the right size for 8½-by-11-inch and 11-by-14-inch sheets of paper. For larger projects, save longer tubes from wrapping or craft paper or oversized aluminum foil. Be careful not to cram too much into a cardboard tube or papers could be difficult to extract.

Household Superstar!
11 Things Kids Can Do with a Round Oatmeal Container

1 Store pencils, crayons, and rulers

2 Make sand-castle towers at the beach

3 Fill with small plastic toy soldiers

4 Fill with dried beans, seal with lid, turn on music, and use as a shaker

5 Seal with lid, turn on music, and use as a drum

6 Store secret jewelry

7 Have Mom cut a slice in the middle of lid, seal, and use as a not-quite piggy bank

8 Store favorite hand-me-down CDs and DVDs

9 Seal with lid, turn over, use as a stool

10 Fill with barrettes, scrunchies, and other hair accessories

11 Make a time capsule: have Junior write a small essay or draw a picture, add personal items, seal with lid, bury in yard, unearth next year!

Bubbles, Bubbles, Everywhere

Kids love bubbles. Big bubbles. Little bubbles. Clouds of bubbles. And your house is full of items that can make bubbles of all shapes and sizes. Many bubble-ologists swear by a simple blower made of two sheets of plain typing paper. Here's how to make what is prized for its humongous bubbles:

1

Stack the sheets and roll into a cone lengthwise, with the tip at the corner of the pages; the diameter at the large end of the cone should be about 1¼–1½ inches;

2

Tape the cone with masking tape starting about 2 inches above the large end (it's vital that the tape and bubble solution don't touch). Trim the small end of the cone to about ½ inch in diameter.

Try a straw!

3

To make the flat, smooth-rimmed opening essential for bubble blowing, trim the large end at a point where all layers of paper are overlapping. Cut off any rough spots on the bottom rim, testing for smoothness by running your finger over it; then test it for evenness by making sure the cone will stand upright on a smooth surface.

4

Dip the large end in bubble solution and blow slowly to make bubbles. Experts advise leaving the cone in the mix for 30 seconds the first time it's used; after that, a 2- or 3-second dip will do.

We used a metal coat hanger!

Plastic berry baskets work as well!

Playful Pantry Crafts

Glitter from salt

Bring some glitter and glitz to your little ones' projects, without the expense of buying the commercial stuff. Mix 1 tablespoon liquid watercolor with ¼ cup table salt or rock salt, then shake the salt and coloring in a plastic bag to distribute the color evenly. Spread the mixture on paper towels on a flat microwaveable plate and microwave on high for 2 minutes. Cool and break up any clumps with your fingers, then store in a dry, airtight container.

Play-dough hair with a garlic press

To make hair for play-dough figures, roll up a small ball of play dough, put it in a garlic press, and slowly press out the strands. Use a small paintbrush to dab a little water on the spot where a strand will be attached; then press the piece in place with a toothpick or the pointed end of a small-size knitting needle.

Pasta art

Even little kids can make beautiful abstract designs with this project that's old as the hills: poke around in your pantry for stray, half-empty boxes of dried pasta (we know they're in there!). Make different shapes and sizes by breaking up long strands of spaghetti and lasagna, add elbows or ziti, and color as desired with non-toxic food coloring. When dry, the possibilities are endless:

- Make a personal treasure chest by covering the top and sides of a shoe or cigar box with the pasta, using craft glue.
- Draw designs on folded construction paper or card stock and glue on pasta for a personal holiday or birthday card.

A Kitchen Christmas Tree

A star-shaped cookie cutter as a tree topper this Christmas? Yes, if you want to do something different and have a kitchen-themed tree. Decorating a holiday tree with kitchen items from your own cabinets and drawers can be a wonderful family project, especially when everyone enjoys cooking together. Almost anything but the kitchen sink can be used as ornaments—and herewith enough ideas to almost fill Old Saint Nick's toy bag:

- Your children's baby cups and spoons
- Cookie cutters attached with red ribbons
- Old salt and pepper shakers filled with silver and gold glitter
- Stainless steel spoons, attached with shiny ribbon to add sparkle
- Vintage tea strainers
- Vintage napkin rings
- Colorful pot holders
- Salt clay ornaments (see page 212)

To add pizzazz, string cranberries and popcorn or miniature marshmallows around the tree, and tuck colorful cloth or paper napkins into the branches. Finally, and most important, have fun creating a fond memory for everyone.

- String together colored elbows or any tubular pasta to make necklaces, bracelets, or anklets.
- Glue pasta shapes to barrettes, hairpins, and even belt buckles!

Paper Towel Tube Constructions

Paper towel tubes make super toy and craft materials and are usually stronger than toilet tissue rolls, so don't throw them out. Here are six kid-pleasing ideas that require little more than tubes, tape, glue, and scissors:

1

Make a fort by taping cardboard rolls together vertically to form a square and leaving an opening on one side to serve as a door. The size of the fort will depend on the number of tubes you have.

2

Fashion a log cabin by taping tubes together horizontally and taping ends together to form a square. Cut a door, then add a roof made of flat cardboard. Leave the roof unattached so that children can remove it and set their toy figures inside the cabin.

3

Make Easter egg holders by cutting cardboard tubes crosswise into 1½- to 2-inch-wide sections. Children can decorate the sections with poster paints or washable markers and then set their Easter eggs on the pretty rings. Use the same basic technique to let the kids create their own decorative napkin rings.

4

For sandbox play, supply toddlers and preschoolers with a selection of tubes cut in different lengths. They can stick tubes in the sand and build whatever they imagine.

5

Create a safe magic wand for a toddler by taping or gluing a construction paper star to one end of a cardboard tube.

6

Make music with a simple flute. Use a pencil to punch four holes about an inch apart in a cardboard tube. Secure wax paper to one end of the tube with a rubber band. A child can make music by humming into the open end of the flute.

Around the House

New use for an old aquarium

An old aquarium or fishbowl can be transformed into a fascinating 3-D decoration for a child's room—and your child can pick the theme and do much of the work. Start by cleaning and disinfecting the tank or bowl. Then paint the inside of the glass with a diluted mixture of water and water-soluble craft paint to create the look of ocean water, blue sky, billowy clouds, rainbows, green fields, or even abstract designs. The paint should be thin enough to see through, so test it for transparency and thin with more water as needed. On the bottom of the tank, spread a fairly thick layer (2 inches or more) of sandbox sand or fish bowl pebbles. Now let your child choose what goes inside.

Quick clean-ups

By their very nature, kids and dirt go hand-in-hand. Here are some easy ideas to keep your home clean using basic household supplies:

- **Plastic or painted wooden toys** Clean these with a paste made of 2 parts baking soda to 1 part dishwashing liquid. Apply with a soft cloth. Use a toothbrush to work the paste into small spaces. If the dirt is really stubborn, leave the paste on for a while. Remove it with a damp cloth or sponge.

- **Outdoor toys and kiddie vehicles** Rub with full-strength white vinegar, applied with a cloth. Remove residue with a damp cloth or sponge, or hose it off and dry with a clean cloth or towel.

- **Stuffed toys** Clean these unwashables by putting them in a plastic or paper bag, adding half or more of an 8-ounce box of baking soda, and shaking the bag for 30 seconds or so. When the toy looks and smells clean, remove baking soda residue by either vacuuming the toy with your machine's drapery attachment or shaking the toy in the open air, brushing off any residue with your fingers.

- **Crayon marks on washable wallpaper** Try warming the marks with a hair dryer. Give it a minute, then wipe the marks away with a damp cloth. Another idea is to apply a coat of rubber cement to the

BELLS ON THEIR TOES

Want to keep track of your little bundle of energy as she zips around the house? Poke around in your Christmas supplies, and tightly attach those **tiny bells** to each sneaker; not only will you know whether they're in the laundry room or racing around the den, they'll make music as they do it. Note: Bells should be attached only for children over the age of 3.

Household Superstar!
7 Kid-Friendly Uses for Tape

Tape is indispensable nowadays, especially in households with children. And the variety of tapes available, including easy-release painter's tape, make it simpler than ever to find the right tape for just about every need. Here are a few quick tape solutions for today's busy parents and active kids.

1 Use masking tape to secure disposable diapers when the sticky tabs fail.

2 Wrap the midsection of new crayons and chalk pieces with transparent tape to help keep them from breaking.

3 Wrap transparent tape tightly around the ends of string and ribbons to make stringing objects easier.

4 Attach address labels to children's pencils, pens, crayon boxes, and other school supplies with transparent tape or clear shipping tape.

5 "Laminate" library cards, bus passes, lunch tickets, and other paper take-alongs with clear shipping tape. Apply to both sides; then trim tape at the edge of card. Scanners are able to read bar codes through clear tape.

6 Can't find a bandage? Substitute a piece of gauze or tissue secured with transparent tape.

7 In a pinch, use masking or transparent tape as a temporary safety cover for electric outlets and switches.

marks, let it dry, and then gently roll off the rubbery glue.

- **Vomit or urine on a rug** First, wipe up what you can. Pour baking soda on the affected area, pat it in with a paper towel, and let it dry completely before vacuuming up the residue. Baking soda will clean, sanitize, and deodorize the spot. Use the same method to clean a wet mattress.

Dry a baby's cap on a balloon
Machine drying a baby's bonnet or cap, even on the delicate cycle, often leaves it looking wrinkled, limp, and less than adorable. Just inflate a balloon to the approximate size of the child's head, tie it securely, and attach it to a smooth surface with tape (away from baby's reach). Slip the washed and still-damp cap or bonnet over the balloon. With your hands, lightly smooth out wrinkles and gently shape the cap and brim. "Press" ribbons and ties by running them through your fingers and laying them out straight.

When the cap is dry, just pop the balloon and discard it. A few touchups with a warm iron will have the cap looking as good as new.

Secure sewing with dental floss
Tired of lost or dangling buttons on your kids' coats and jackets? Substitute dental floss for sewing thread to get a strong, longer-lasting hold. Also use dental floss when replacing buttons, eyes, and ears and stitching ripped seams in stuffed toys.

Tape your troubles away
Toy boxes, paperback book spines, and coloring books falling apart? Use clear shipping tape to reinforce corners, spines, and edges of books, game boards, and game and toy boxes.

Safety, Health, and Hygiene Hints

Cover dangerous corners with shoulder pads

A great way to safeguard new walkers and runners is with old shoulder pads—remember those? Cut open the long straight side and slip the pad over a corner so the inner padding encases the edges. Adjust as needed, and then tape the pad securely in place. Hiding these pads under an attractive cloth will not only please the eye but also stop curious youngsters from disturbing the pads.

Colorful bandages

Your little one just fell down and scraped his elbow/knee/fill-in-the-blank, and you're trying to console him, to no avail. Distract the little guy from his pain by having him color his own bandage while you gently clean the wound with a dab of soapy water and first-aid cream. While you're busy, make him busy: Give him a few plain bandages and a rainbow of nontoxic, water-based markers, and let his imagination run wild. He'll wear his bandage as a work of art!

Freeze stuffed toys for allergic kids

Forestall sniffles in allergic kids by giving their stuffed toys the deep freeze for three to five hours, once a week. Slip the toy into a freezer bag, stow it amidst the frozen peas and ice cubes, and any dust mites will be killed.

Bathtub appliqués = safe jammies

You can replace worn slip-preventive soles on an infant or toddler's footed pajamas with foot-shaped pieces or stripes cut from non-slip bathtub appliqués. Remove any loose bits from the old soles and sew on the new appliqués. Parents who don't sew can use fabric glue.

Two tip-to-toe uses for fabric softener sheets

If your child's sneakers smell like something died inside, stuff each shoe with a fabric softener sheet every night to lessen the odor. At the other end of the body, you can solve a flyaway hair problem by rubbing your child's hair with a dryer sheet to control static.

Ouchless Bandage Removal

Ouch! In the old days, parents were advised to rip bandages off of a child, causing many a boy or girl to do almost anything to postpone the inevitable. A quick rip didn't reduce the pain but merely got everything over with quicker.

A kinder, gentler, and generally pain-free approach is to carefully but thoroughly rub baby oil or dishwashing liquid along the edges and over the top of the bandage. Use enough to penetrate and lubricate the adhesive (but not the gauze), then slowly lift the bandage off, rubbing on a bit more oil or dishwashing liquid if you hit a sticking point. Your children will thank you, if only with an expression of relief.

In the Great Outdoors

Painting stones

Decorating medium-sized rocks with smooth surfaces is a longtime favorite kid's craft. Let their imaginations run wild when they find stones in different shapes. Wash them to remove dirt, grease, and any mossy patches, and then let the stones dry completely in the sun. Using poster or craft paints, youngsters can paint the tops and sides of the rocks however they like. When the paint is dry, seal the surface with several coats of spray-on, nontoxic, clear acrylic varnish, drying between coats. (Avoid brush-on varnishes because brushing is likely to smear the paint.) A sufficiently large stone would make a homey doorstop, while small stones could decorate a kitchen windowsill or serve as paperweights on a desk.

Cleaning outdoor equipment with vinegar

A simple, inexpensive solution of 1 part white vinegar to 1 part water makes a reliable cleaner for outdoor play equipment, kiddie cars, and bikes. For tough dirt, wipe with the vinegar solution; then rub the spot with baking soda on a damp rag or sponge and rinse. It's smart to wash swing seats and chains or ropes frequently. You can also use the vinegar solution to clean children's car seats.

Autumn leaf paintings for Junior Picasso

Nature offers us one of the most versatile and kid-friendly paintbrushes in fallen leaves. For a lovely way to spend an autumn afternoon with a child, take them on a walk in a park and ask them to collect leaves of various shapes and sizes. Bring them home, and using an old toothbrush,

Lessons from the Garden

Think about this, fellow do-it-yourselfer: Teaching young children to garden can become a lesson in the joys of thrift and creative thinking. The child who decides to use a seen-its-day hockey stick as a stake for tomatoes, an old sneaker as a planter for kitchen herbs, or tape and a ballpoint pen to straighten a bent flower stem is a child who will learn to love the challenge of solving problems in imaginative ways—a budding member of the eminent DIY fraternity.

Equip your child with a small spade and bucket to begin, and let him get his hands in the dirt. Help him to plant a mix of flowers and vegetable seeds that will produce easy-to-tend compact plants, and let him learn by trial and error. Serve as an example by using as many ordinary household items in the garden as you can, and he'll soon follow your lead. Also be sure to let him help you compost kitchen waste and autumn leaves for the garden so he'll learn to think "outside the plot."

At the end of the growing season, leave plantings in place so your child can observe what happens in his garden in the fall and winter. Over the years, your child's plot can grow in size, and he can do more of the work on his own—hopefully as a full-fledged apprentice in the art of self-sufficiency.

gently remove any dust or dirt from their surfaces. Mix up a small batch of nontoxic finger paints (page 214) spread the table with a few pieces of newspaper, and top them with sheets of favorite, light-colored construction paper. Roll

*Make a delicious homemade bird feeder with pinecones and **peanut butter**!*

up your little one's sleeves, and using her index finger as a paint brush, have her paint one surface of each leaf; immediately press them down onto the paper, paint-side down. Count to 20 (another good lesson!), and remove the leaf by its stem. Instant (and free) art!

Pinecone bird feeders

The kinds of bird feeders you and your children can make from available materials are many, and this one is especially easy and fun. All you'll need: pinecones, sugarless peanut butter (the amount varies depending on the number and size of cones used), and all-purpose birdseed. Using a plastic knife, spread peanut butter over the cone, pushing it into the nooks and crevices. Now spread a layer of birdseed on a cookie sheet or a pie pan. Roll the cone in the birdseed, making sure it's covered, and gently shake off any excess. Tightly tie a length of string or yarn around the top or bottom of the cone, and hang it from a tree branch, fence, gatepost, balcony railing, or a secure plant hanger. How could any bird resist such a tempting feeder?

Organizing athletic equipment

Parents of young athletes are all too familiar with a house overflowing with a jumble of baseball bats, hockey sticks, tennis rackets, golf clubs, balls of every size and shape, sweatshirts, shoes, and stuff you can't even identify. Even one member of the junior varsity can create a major mess. Here are three suggestions for digging out of it.

- Put a tall plastic or metal garbage can in the garage or on the back porch to hold long items like bats, sticks, extra golf clubs, and volleyball posts. Weight the bottom of the can with bricks or heavy stones so it won't tip over.

- Install a pegboard and hooks (you may already have one in a work area) for hanging rackets, hats, gloves, protective padding, swim goggles and caps, wet clothes, and shoes.

- Designate one large laundry basket for athletic clothing—and do yourself a favor and lay down rules about who is to wash what, and when.

Chapter Nine

Pointers for Pet Lovers

Do you ever feel like Fluffy or Fido is the only one who really understands you? Do you ever find yourself talking to your fish or confiding in your parrot? If so, don't worry: you're definitely not alone!

Today, you can visit a canine bakery and buy cookies that a human would positively drool over—and you'll be paying that gourmet price for them. Or you can follow the recipe for Arlo and Scamp's Favorite Cookies in this chapter, using just a few simple and inexpensive ingredients to make your own delicious doggy delicacies. Likewise, you can buy your kitty a toy that costs as much as dinner for two at a fancy restaurant, or for a fraction of the cost you can recycle a belt to make a cat-sized collar, fashion a new pet bed by covering a pillow with fabric to match your décor, and turn an empty pill bottle into a rattling toy.

Read on, fellow animal-lovers, for great ideas on how to keep your pets well fed, clean, healthy, and happy, and your wallet full.

Instead of your slippers,
puppies should teeth on
frozen bagels!

Feeding Fido

Go bananas!

Add about a third of a soft banana to 1½ cups dry food. Slice it, mash it, and stir it into the pellets. Not only does it add variety and a bit of healthy sweetness (which pooches all seem to love), but a bit of banana also will settle your dog's stomach.

Healthy snacks

If you're on a diet, you know all about carrying around those petite peeled carrots to quell your appetite during snack time. The good news is that dogs generally love them, too. They're crunchy, sweet, and healthy enough to make them a regular part of Fido's diet in place of a biscuit.

Yogurt containers as doggie travel totes

Save those plastic yogurt containers with fitted lids; when you're taking Sparky along on a trip, they're the perfect size for your dog's favorite small treats. Though most dogs don't like to eat during travel, you can reward Sparky for his good behavior once you arrive at your destination.

Put the jerk back in the food

Is your faithful friend feeling finicky? Try this safe trick: put a stick of beef jerky in a new bag of dry dog food and reseal it for 24 hours. The scent will make the dry food more tempting to your canine, be he a purebred or a mutt.

Hydrogen peroxide for an upset stomach

If your dog has eaten something she shouldn't have (chocolate candy, echinacea, etc.) induce vomiting by forcing her to swallow 1–2 tablespoons of hydrogen peroxide mixed with a ¼ teaspoon of sugar. This medicine-cabinet staple will make her barf up anything that's bad for her in a hurry.

Pills for your pooch

No reason to wrestle your friend to the ground to try and get him to take a pill; this is what spray cheese is for. Avail yourself of a can, encase the medicine in a thick cloak of cheese, and it'll go down the hatch in a matter of seconds. (For a natural version, spread the offending pill with a heavy layer of peanut butter.)

Foods to Never, Ever Give Your Dog

Chocolate, which contains theobromine, a substance that is poisonous to dogs.

Onions, garlic, and other onion family members (leeks, shallots, scallions), whose ingredient thiosulfate can destroy your pet's red blood cells.

Add sweetness and flavor to dry dog food with a **banana!**

make your own

Gourmet Dog Biscuits

You can buy pricey dog biscuits in the grocery store and even pricier bakery-made dog biscuits at pet specialty shops. But if you like to bake, it does not cost much to create your own delicious treats. This vegetarian recipe comes from an upstate New York dog owner and is named for her two cockapoos.

Arlo and Scamp's Favorite Cookies

These wholesome treats smell so good coming out of the oven that you'll be tempted to sample one for yourself. (And you may!)

2 cups whole-wheat flour
1 tablespoon baking powder
1 cup natural peanut butter
1 cup skim milk

1. Preheat oven to 375°F.

2. Combine flour and baking powder in one bowl. In another bowl, whisk together peanut butter and milk.

3. Combine wet and dry ingredients and mix until a dough forms. Place the dough on a lightly floured surface and knead until the dough is pliant (about 5 minutes).

4. Roll dough to ¼-inch thickness, then use a dog bone–shaped cookie cutter to cut out shapes.

5. Place cutouts on a greased cookie sheet and bake for 20 minutes or until lightly browned. Cool the cookies on a wire rack and store in an airtight container.

Keeping Fido Groomed

File Scruffy's nails with sandpaper

Most dogs don't like having their nails filed, but doing so will keep their nails in generally good condition and keep them from splitting in colder weather. To ease your dog's stress about the big, mean, evil, nail-filing machine used by groomers, cut a half-dollar-sized round of 120-grit sandpaper, wrap it around your index finger, and *gently* go to it, stopping frequently to praise the little guy and reinforce his behavior with a favorite treat.

Tube socks for post-shampoo itchiness

Many dogs are skin-sensitive to shampoos, leaving them scratching and irritated after their bath (which they didn't want in the first place, in case you weren't sure). Keep any larger dog from scratching his neck and face by putting his back feet in cotton tube socks, and pulling them up as far as you can; if you have a smaller dog (with shorter legs), try a pair of cotton baby socks.

Use olive oil on matted hair

Loosen your dog's matted hair by rubbing a little olive oil into the knot. Then gently comb through the matted area with a wire brush until the brush teeth glide smoothly through Lucy's coat.

Oil away tar

Remove tar from your dog's foot pads by gently rubbing them with mineral oil or petroleum jelly. Then wash away the residue with a mild solution of soapy water. To help keep tar pickup to a minimum on your dog-walking expeditions, very carefully trim the hair that grows between your doggie's toes.

Dab off teary residue with baby oil

Some dogs' tear ducts create a residue that collects in the hair below the corner of the eye. This may stain the hair of light-colored dogs, and despite numerous products sold to "whiten" it, veterinarians say there is little you can do—so it's best not to fret. Still, you should remove it. Pour a little baby oil onto a cotton ball and gently work it into the area to loosen the residue and make it easier to dab off. You could also use a mild face-freshening astringent, in which case take care to keep it out of your dog's eyes.

Vinegar ear cleaner

All flop-ear dogs—especially water dogs like Labs and Retrievers—should have their ears gently cleaned at least once a week to prevent waxy buildup and infections (which result in both pain and odor). Mix 1 part white vinegar to 1 part water; dip a cotton ball into the mixture, and carefully wipe out your dog's ears, *without* inserting the cotton ball into the ear canal. Use a separate cotton ball for each ear to avoid cross contamination in case of infection.

Prevent dog hair clogs with a scrubber

At bath time, you can keep your dog's hair from clogging the tub drain if you place a nylon pot scrubber or a snipped-off section of kitchen sponge over the drain. This porous barrier will collect hair, which you can easily remove and discard.

Playtime for Pooch

Buying toys for your dog is a nice gesture, but it can get expensive. Fido may have great taste, but he'll be just as happy with homemade games, like these:

Blue jean baby

Tiny puppy teeth *should* chew—but not on your furniture, the cat, slippers, or fancy high heels or loafers. How to remedy this? Make sure your pup has plenty of toys to call her own. Make inexpensive, sturdy toys out of old denim jeans. Cut a double layer of denim into a square, stitch together on three sides, stuff with a few old tennis balls (not panty hose, which she can choke on if she tears the toy apart), and stitch up the fourth.

Softballs for small dogs

If your furry friend is tiny, he will have a blast chasing around an inanimate object larger than he is; an old softball is just the ticket to occupy his attention for hours.

Chase the flashlight

What could be more fun for a frisky dog than chasing a flashlight beam in a large, darkened room? Make sure not to shine the light in the little guy's eyes, and move the furniture to avoid the crashing that generally follows the careening.

Soda bottle toss

Punch two holes in the cap of an empty plastic soda bottle. Thread a thick string through the cap and knot it, then screw the cap back on tightly. Now toss the bottle toward your pup and draw it back. He'll enjoy chasing the elusive toy for hours, if you're willing to play along.

Walking the Dog

Panty hose leash
Your dog will appreciate the elasticity of a leash made from an old pair of panty hose. The idea is to knot it along every 4 or 5 inches and create a handle at the end by looping the hose and knotting it.

Cool wet T-shirt
Hot enough for you? Yes, and for your pooch, too! If you're walking him on a warm day, dampen a large (or small, depending on the dog's size) children's cotton T-shirt with cool water, wring it dry, and fit it over Buster's head, pushing his two front paws through the sleeves. Tie a knot on the side to take up the slack, making sure the shirt fits comfortably—neither too tight nor too loose. (Check it periodically to make sure it stays that way.) If the shirt dries out after a while, spritz it with water.

Glow-in-the-dark collar
Even a few regularly spaced strips of reflective tape along your dog's (or cat's) collar will help drivers see them if they happen to be out at night or at dusk.

Plastic bag pooper-scooper
Never throw away those plastic grocery store bags. They make prefect pooper-scoopers, and they're *free*. Just stick your hand into the bag, pick up the poop with your amply gloved hand, and turn the bag inside out before tying it off and disposing of it.

Cardboard cleanup tool
Cut a section from an empty cereal or cracker box to use as a disposable pooper-scooper whenever you walk your dog. Slide it under the pile of poop and put both the pile and your scooper directly into a plastic grocery bag. Tie the whole thing up, and it's ready to throw in the trash.

Soothe paws with petroleum jelly
Extreme temperatures can damage a dog's paws during a walk. Hot sidewalks, freezing paths, and road salts may irritate his foot pads and lead to cracking. To soothe Rex's feet and help initiate healing, rub a little petroleum jelly onto his paws. If Rex is a yard dog, no worries. If he's a house dog, be sure to wipe any excess petroleum jelly off his paws so that he won't track it onto carpeting or upholstery.

OLD BELT = TEMPORARY LEASH

Your dog's leash has been lost or stolen? **An old belt** will serve as a substitute until you can go to the pet center to buy a new one. Buckle the belt onto your dog's collar and use duct tape to create a handle at the other end. (Twist the tape into a "rope," loop it, and attach it to the end of the belt with several more layers of tape).

Cats and Their Litter Boxes

Foil litter box odors!

Once odor penetrates the bottom of a litter box, it's almost impossible to remove completely—a reason to whip up this easy-to-make aluminum foil odor barrier. Cut a piece of cardboard box to size, cover it with heavy-duty aluminum foil, and secure the foil to the cardboard with masking tape. When changing the kitty litter, don't toss out your homemade liner; instead, swab the foil with a wet sponge soaked in a solution of 2 parts vinegar to 1 part baking soda. If you treat the liner gently, you should be able to get at least three or four uses out of it.

Slice lemon, neutralize odor

Let's face it: There's nothing pleasant about eau de litter box—and here's a way to control odor in the area where the box sits. Place half a lemon, cut side up, on a saucer and set it on the floor a few inches from the box. (A scientist could explain to you why the smell of lemon in the air neutralizes unpleasant odors, but suffice to say that lemon gives baking soda a run for the money when it comes to odor control.) For tough odors, place several lemon halves on a paper plate or try a combo of orange, lemon, and lime halves.

Three ways to sweeten a litter box

If you're buying scented litter or the kind that neutralizes litter box odors, you're probably spending a lot every week on this kitty essential. Here are four suggestions that will help you achieve the same result at less expense:

- Add ⅓ cup baking soda to regular litter and mix well
- Sprinkle ⅓ cup baby powder onto the litter to keep it fresh
- Stir a handful of dried parsley or other aromatic dried herb into the litter.

No-cost litter box cleaners

Instead of using name-brand or off-brand cleaning products, choose one of these kitchen pantry or under-the-sink items to keep a litter box fresh as a daisy. After removing litter and liner, clean the box weekly with:

- Vinegar
- Household ammonia
- Lemon oil
- A solution of 1 part household bleach to 10 parts water

Finish the job by rinsing the litter box with plain water. Then wipe it dry with a clean cloth before refilling it.

A doormat for cats

To keep your cat from tracking dusty paw prints on the floor when she leaves her litter box, place a carpet remnant or an old place mat on the side of the box where Precious makes her exit.

Cats at Play

It never matters how expensive the toys are that you bring home for your little fluffball; they take pleasure in the extraordinary everyday objects that are found in every home. Case in point: aluminum foil. Simply ball up a piece, toss it, and watch your furry friend go skittering around the house after it. Other "free" toys include: plastic cap guards from bottled water jugs; empty wooden thread spools; old golf balls; plastic bottle tops; empty corrugated cardboard boxes; empty shoeboxes; empty plastic buckets (cleaned, please); and heavy gauge wire, with one end held in place by closing it in a door or drawer, and the other end looped, with a feather or some thread attached to it.

Rattlin' good fun

Use plastic medicine bottles or old film canisters to make toys for cats. Fill the vessel with coins, paper clips, or buttons—any small items that will rattle when shaken. Roll the toy out on the floor and watch as your kitty delights in batting it around.

Sock it to 'em

Clean an old sock, stuff the toe-end with some catnip, and tie it off tightly. Dangle the tempting toy from a string, and you've got a game going with your cat. Alternatively, tie the filled sock to a doorknob and let Kitty bat it about on his own. A sock isn't the only thing to use: You could also stuff a baby bootie with catnip or cut off the sleeve of a worn-out blouse or shirt and turn it into a catnip holder.

"You're pulling my leg!"

That's the name of the game you'll play with your cat when you stuff a leg of old panty hose, and a feline-human tug of war ensues. Cut off one panty hose leg and fill the toe with catnip. Knot the hose above the filled area and make several more knots along the length of the leg. A catnip-free version of the toy uses old rags or wadded-up panty hose as stuffing; in this case, you'll want to engage your cat in a game of "chase the snake" as you wiggle the toy around on the floor.

Watching your own Wild Kingdom

Have an active bird feeder and a video camera? You've got the makings for hours of unbridled entertainment for your little indoor hunter. Video the birds in action, pop in the DVD or tape where your kitten can see the television, turn it on, and watch the fun unfold. Marlin Perkins never had it so good!

Food and Drink for Pets

Healthful stir-ins

When cooking, save the rich liquid from steamed, oil-free vegetables and the drippings from meat and stir a spoonful or two into your pet's food bowl, adding a little warm water to thin the juices if necessary. If your cooking session doesn't coincide with pet-feeding time, put the juices in a jar and store in the fridge for later use. Heat the stir-ins in the microwave to warm, not hot, before sharing them with Sadie.

Panty hose Kitty's brush

For easy brush cleanup, slip a small piece of panty hose over the head of the brush *before* grooming. Make sure the bristles poke through. Once grooming is done, remove the panty hose, which should be laden with cat fur, and discard.

A mouse pad for Tomcat's bowl

When you replace your computer mouse pad, use the old one as a place mat for your pet's food bowl. It's perfect for keeping it from skidding and for catching spills.

Ant-proof your pet's food

When you feed dogs or cats outdoors, keep ants out of the food bowl with this neat trick: Set your pet's bowl in the center of a baking pan filled with water.

Mineral oil = fewer hairballs

Just add 1 teaspoon mineral oil or petroleum jelly to your cat's daily feedings to help ease hairballs through the digestive tract. (Note: Vegetable oils and other oils won't work because your cat will absorb and digest them.) To get a jump on hairballs, give your cat a good brushing every day.

---

make your own
Cat Treats

Rolled oats are the basis of these cookies made just for cats. They're more healthful than their commercial equivalents because they contain nary a trace of preservatives and artificial ingredients—well, if you make your own stock, that is. Even if you use canned broth or stock cubes, your treats may be more "natural" than the store-bought equivalent.

Miss Kitty's Oatmeal Cookies

Note that your cookies can be chicken-, beef-, or tuna-flavored. If you choose tuna, you could substitute the liquid in a can of water-packed tuna instead of oil; if the liquid doesn't amount to half a cup, just thin it with tap water.

    1½ cups rolled oats
    ¼ cup vegetable oil
    ½ cup all-purpose flour
    ½ cup chicken broth, beef broth, or oil
    or water from canned tuna

1. Preheat oven to 350°F.

2. Mix all ingredients into a dough.

3. Dust your hands with flour and shape dough into ½-inch thick round cookies. Set the cookies on a greased baking sheet.

4. Bake 30 minutes or until the cookies are lightly browned, then cool for 30 minutes on a cookie rack. Once cool, break them into bite-sized pieces for your little friend.

Keeping Pets Bright-Eyed and Bushy-Tailed

A kitchen staple bed freshener

Between washings of your pet's bedding, sprinkle it with baking soda and let it sit for about an hour. Shake off the baking soda outdoors, then vacuum off the rest.

Quick 'n' simple panty hose pet bed

Stuff the seat of a pair of old panty hose with soft material that your pet will happily sink into—cotton balls, chicken feathers, orphan socks, store-bought pillow stuffing (synthetic or all-natural), or even wadded-up panty hose. Just knot the legs and snip off the excess hose. To smarten up the bed, cover it with an attractive pillowcase and stitch the case closed.

Shrink an old sweater for Sweetums

To keep your dog warm during cold-weather walks, provide her with a sweater by shrinking one of your old round-necked or v-neck, pullover woolen ones to pooch-size. (Use a child's sweater if your dog is small.) First, measure the sweater against your dog; if it's at least three times too big, you've got a winner. Toss it into the washing machine with ¼ cup mild detergent and set the

What's the Story?
Old Wives' Tail

Have you heard that adding tomato juice, apple cider vinegar, or baking soda to a dog's diet will neutralize the acidity in dog urine? The urine that kills your grass? Well, that turns out to be a spurious piece of folklore. Adding any of these ingredients to your dog's diet won't prevent dog pee from killing grass—and anyway, it's not the acidity that does the damage but rather the high concentration of nitrogen in dog urine.

What's worse, following this discredited advice may be quite harmful. According to the Web site for the University of Wisconsin's Cooperative Extension Service, "Veterinarians warn that feeding pH-altering supplements such as tomato juice, vinegar, or baking soda [to dogs] could result in urinary tract diseases, bladder infections, crystals, and bladder stones." Read all about it at http://polk.uwex .edu/hort/lawnanddogs.html.

water temperature to hot; set the machine for a large wash, even though the load consists of a single sweater. After removing the sweater, press it between two towels to squeeze out as much water as possible. While the sweater is damp, it's time for a fitting. Reshape the sweater so that the neck is wide enough to fit easily over your doggie's head. (If it doesn't, cut a slit and bind the edges with seam binding to prevent fraying). The arms of the sweater should fit over the dog's two

front legs, and the body of the sweater should reach about halfway down her back. Lay the sweater on a drying rack and let it dry in a well-ventilated room. Now let Sweetums strut her stuff in her new winter outfit—which didn't cost a cent.

Recycle a belt as a collar

Save a few dollars by making a pet collar from a small leather belt. (A grosgrain belt is suitable for smaller, lightweight pets, but only if it has a binding along its length). Cut the belt to the desired length for your little dog or cat or rabbit. Place the new collar on a block of wood and poke holes in it with an awl, then buckle it around your pet's neck to make sure it fits comfortably.

Shoe bag pet-stuff organizer

A hanging shoe bag placed inside a closet door or in your laundry room can help you get a handle on all your pet stuff. Use the pockets for storing toys, treats, cloths—even your pet's vital health statistics, including the vet's name and number. With everything in one place, you'll have an easier time locating what you need whenever you need it.

Polish makes pretty (easy to find)

Glow-in-the-dark pet-safe nail polish dabbed onto your cat or dog's collar—and on his claws or toenails—will make your pet easier to spot when he's out after dark. Available at pet stores.

Keep basic info handy

Place all important papers having to do with your pet in a small lidded box (a cigar box is ideal) so you can easily grab it if you have to run to the vet's office in an emergency. Likewise, a pet sitter will be able to easily find everything in one place if he needs to.

Don't throw away that old comb!

Use it as a belly scratcher for your dog or cat. Your fingernails will do the job, too, but pets seem to love the feel of a fine-toothed comb digging into their fur.

Skin and Coat Care

Eggs make coats shine

A weekly scrambled egg added to your cat or dog's food helps keep her coat shiny, and it's a healthy treat your pet will love. Raw eggs are off limits, of course, because they could be contaminated with salmonella.

Unsticking something sticky

That sticky something in your pet's fur could be pine sap, mud, or something unmentionable. Before you get out the scissors and cut away the icky patch, leaving your dog or cat with a bald spot, try this: Mix 1 teaspoon mild shampoo or liquid dish detergent with ¼ to ½ cup warm water and whisk it well. Wearing rubber gloves, apply some of the solution to your pet's sticky spot, rubbing it in with your fingers. Then comb the spot with a wire-toothed brush. Once you've removed the sticky stuff, wash away any soapy residue with fresh warm water.

De-skunk your pet with vinegar

Many people have heard of using tomato juice to rid a pet's coat of skunk odor, but here's a less expensive and neater way to remove the scent: Deodorize your pet with a bath of 50/50 white vinegar and warm water. Keep rinsing and washing until all odor is gone. Your pet is a water-wary cat, you say? Consult cat care guides or browse the Internet for ways to bathe a cat, which involve enlisting a helper, using a hand-held shower nozzle, staying patient and calm, and reassuring Missy repeatedly that everything's going to be okay.

An under-the-sink itch stopper

Dry skin isn't a problem for humans alone. If you notice your dog or cat scratching more than usual, gently rub a little Murphy's Oil Soap into his coat.

Mouthwash for skin problems

You may think mouthwashes are for oral hygiene only. But they're also a good all-around disinfectant for your dog or cat (and for *you*, for that matter). Use one of the stronger mouthwash brands as an astringent on your pet's skin to disinfect wounds, clean cuts and scrapes, and cool down boils and other hot spots. Just moisten a cotton ball with mouthwash and dab it on the affected area to help a banged-up dog or cat heal more quickly.

REVITALIZE DRY HAIR WITH TEA

If your pet's coat is looking a little less than lustrous, shampoo Fluffy or Fido as you usually do, then complete the wash by rinsing the coat with a quart of **warm unsweetened tea.**

Chasing Away Fleas

Mix your own repellants

Homemade flea repellents are easy to mix and bottle, so why not give them a try?

Use them to spritz your dog or cat *almost* all over, especially under the "armpits," behind the ears, and around the head, taking care to shield the eyes. When you spray at the base of the tail, avoid spraying the pet's genitals. Herewith, two quick and easy recipes:

- **Lemon Lash-Out** Cut 2 lemons into small pieces, toss the pieces into a saucepan holding 1 quart water, and boil the pieces for 1 hour. Remove the pan from the heat and let the mixture stand overnight. Strain the lemony liquid into a spray bottle and spritz your pet as directed above.

- **Vinegar Vamooser** Repel fleas with a solution made from 10 parts water to 1 part white vinegar. Pour it into a spray bottle and spray your pet as directed above.

Pine scent in the doghouse

A pile of fresh pine needles placed underneath your doggie's bed will discourage fleas.

Draw a line in the salt

Pour table salt around all the crevices of the doghouse to keep fleas out of your dog's cozy abode.

Cedar deterrents

Add cedar chips or cedar sawdust to the stuffing for you pet's pillow or bedding. If your dog has a doghouse, hang or nail a cedar block inside. The odor of cedar repels fleas as well as other nuisance insects, including moths.

Scent flea collars with essential oils

Store-bought flea collars often carry an unpleasant odor, and you may hesitate to put a chemical-laden collar so close to your pet's skin. Fit your pet with a natural, pleasant-smelling flea collar instead. Rub a few drops of essential oil of tea tree, citronella, lavender, eucalyptus, or scented geranium into an ordinary webbed or rope collar or a doggy bandana, and then refresh the oil weekly.

Kill eggs with salt, too

This flea killer takes a little time to work its magic. Sprinkle salt on your carpets to kill flea eggs; let it sit for a day, then vacuum. Repeat the process a few days later to make sure you haven't missed any flea eggs. Each time you vacuum the salt, be sure to tie up and discard the vacuum cleaner bag.

A Systemic Flea Repellent

Who says fleas can be repelled only with topical treatments? Not your vet. He or she probably knows that brewer's yeast works as a systemic flea repellent when your pet ingests it. If you use the powdered form, sprinkle 1 teaspoon into your cat or small dog's food daily (a 50-pound dog will need a tablespoon).

That this treatment is systemic doesn't mean you can't use brewer's yeast topically as well; just rub it directly into your pet's fur. But take note: Some animals develop a skin allergy after eating or being rubbed with yeast. If your pet is one of them, discontinue use of this repellent immediately.

Pet-Related Housecleaning

Prevent chewing with oil of cloves

Puppies do chew—even on the legs of tables and chairs. Discourage chewing by dabbing the most attractive spots (your shoes, a cardboard box, and anything wooden your pup can get his teeth around) with oil of cloves. The bitter odor and taste are a deterrent to nibbling.

Frozen teething bagels

Not just for teething human babies, this traditional method for soothing painful gums is perfect for pups, too; freeze a few baby bagels until they're rock solid and ice cold. Let the little one chew on those to ease his painful choppers. When the bagel gets mushy, take it away before he eats it, and replace with a dog toy.

Odor-eating vinegar

Accidents do happen, especially with new pets.

Eliminate that unpleasant urine smell from carpeting with a 50/50 solution of white vinegar and warm water. Pour it onto the affected area so that it soaks through to the padding, then allow it sit for half an hour. Wash the affected area with cool water until the vinegar is rinsed out, then pat the carpet dry with towels. Cover with a ½-inch-thick layer of dry, clean white rags, towels, or paper towels, weight them down with heavy objects (bricks, paperweights, door stops, and the like) and let the absorbent material sit for several hours to soak up the moisture.

Clear the air with coffee beans

Some pet owners have found they can remove pet odors from a room by heating a cupful of freshly ground coffee beans in a cast iron skillet over low heat. As soon as the scent is released, remove the pan to the smelly room and set it on a trivet. By the time the ground beans are cool, much of the pet odor should have dissipated.

Away with pet hair!

It's embarrassing when guests don't want to sit on your sofa because they don't enjoy "wearing" your pet's coat on their clothing. Here are some ways to remove dog and cat hair from your furniture and clothing—and preventing pet hair from getting there in the first place.

- Lightly mist your hair-covered garment with water, then put it in the dryer with a damp towel and a fabric softener sheet. Dry on the air cycle for a few minutes.

Cats Gotta Scratch

So your cat has ripped one side of that new (and not exactly cheap) chair to shreds? While you're having it reupholstered, make him a simple and inexpensive scratching post by stapling or gluing a carpet remnant to a log or a section of 2-by-4 board. Attach the post vertically to a ½-inch thick section of plywood by hammering nails though the bottom of the plywood and into the log or board.

If you saved the leftover sections of carpet last time your den was carpeted, your new scratching post should cost nothing. If you don't have any carpet remnants, pick one up at the local home supply or hardware store.

Keep Fido off the furniture with a *shower curtain!*

- Gently rub upholstered furniture and your clothing with a slightly damp kitchen sponge to remove pet hair.

- Wrap your hand with masking tape or duct tape, sticky side out. Run both your palm and the back of your hand over furniture or your clothing to collect pet hair.

- Slip a rubber glove onto your hand and rub your fingers back and forth over your upholstered furniture until pet hair balls up and you can lift it off.

Kill carpet odor with baking soda

If a musty smell has infiltrated the carpet, as often happens with recently cleaned pet urine spots, use baking soda to neutralize the odor. Once the carpet has thoroughly dried, sweeten the area by working ⅛ to ¼ cup of baking soda into the carpet pile. Wait 15 minutes before vacuuming it up.

- Cover a sponge, a blackboard eraser, or your hand with a fabric softener sheet and rub away pet hair.

- Try vacuuming your pet, using the brush attachment on your vacuum. If she doesn't mind the noise, make this a weekly task that will collect loose hairs before they start flying around the house. If your pet doesn't like being vacuumed, try holding the vacuum brush about 2 inches away from her fur.

Foil as a noisy deterrent

Noise deters pets from jumping on furniture. To train cats to stay off upholstered couches and chairs, top the cushions with aluminum foil.

If cats jump onto the furniture, the crunching sound of foil under their paws will send them scurrying in a hurry.

Recycle a shower curtain liner

Covering your furniture with an old shower curtain is likely to keep pets at arm's length. It isn't comfortable to lie on, and the crunchy plastic makes an unpleasant noise when your pet climbs onto it.

If You Own a Horse...

Make a tube sock snood

Rather than buying a tail bag, or snood, make one from a tube sock—a thrifty way to protect your horse's tail on your way to a show. Here's how:

1. On each side of the sock cuff, cut a strip that will remain attached to the sock—each one about 3 inches in length and 1 inch wide.

2. Braid your horse's tail, and slip the tube sock over it.

3. Interlace one of the loose sock strips with the top of the braid, then tie the second sock strip to the first one, knotting it tightly.

Bleach it away

Rain rot is a common skin infection affecting horses. Mix 1 part household bleach to 10 parts water, and pour the solution into a spray bottle. Use it to clear up the affected area. Just be sure not to spray near the horse's eyes.

Shine her up

After hosing off your horse, sponge on a solution of white vinegar and water (1 part vinegar to 10 parts water). This simple mixture will remove soap residue, repel flies, and shine the coat.

Alternatives to store-bought hoof dressing

Keeping your horse's hooves in good condition is essential to his well-being. While many products are found on the market, here are three dressings you already have at home:

- Vegetable shortening
- Aerosol cooking spray
- WD-40

In winter, it's important to apply dressing to the hooves to prevent "snowballing." This occurs when snow freezes in a hoof and makes it hard for a galloping horse to place it flat on the ground, often leading to sprains. Just remember that any of these dressings may make the hoof and shoe slippery, so be sure not to apply too much in winter or apply too frequently.

Freeze factor

Smear petroleum jelly inside your horse's water bucket in winter before filling it with water. When it ices over, you'll find it much easier to slide out the ice as it coasts along a coat of slippery gel.

Fight those flies!

Keep flies away from your horse's eyes by dabbing a little petroleum jelly around each eye. During the summer, smear zinc oxide ointment in and around Angel's ears to repel flies.

Shine up your saddle

Clean and polish your horse's chrome bits, buckles, and straps with toothpaste. This handy and inexpensive polish works wonders on a saddle's shiny parts.

Flies and gnats

These pesky creatures are notoriously annoying when it comes to horses. Help your friend Flicka keep her cool by shading her eyes and giving her a spritz of bath oil spray.

Saddle smarts

When you take apart your saddle for cleaning, it's easy to forget which stirrup strap is left and which is right. Take two empty toilet paper tubes and mark one *Left,* one *Right.* As you remove each strap, lace the strap through the correct paper tube and buckle it.

Hair gel keeps manes tidy

Forget fancy grooming techniques and tools; if hair gel works for you, it'll work for your horse, too. Use a dollop to make braiding easy and to keep stray hairs from popping out of place on show day.

Spray stalls with vinegar to keep nibbles at bay

To keep stalls from being chewed on by nickering nags, mix a spray that's half white vinegar, half water; horses hate the taste of anything tart, so they'll leave the real estate alone.

make your own
Hoof Dressing

A horse's hooves can easily become dry and cracked, especially in dry climates. This simple homemade hoof dressing, made from equal parts lard and pine tar, will work as well as any store-bought product to keep Stardust's hooves in good shape. Pine tar is available at farm supply stores and online.

Pine Tar Hoof Soother

This concoction has a thick consistency in warm weather and hardens to a paste in the winter, when you may have to microwave it to make it easy to apply.

> 1 pound lard
> 1 pound pine tar

1. Put lard in a large microwave-safe container and microwave on low power until the lard melts.

2. Add pine tar and stir with a large wooden spoon until the dressing is well mixed.

3. Apply the dressing to your horse's hooves with a soft 2½-inch-wide paintbrush.

Rabbits, Hamsters, and Other Creatures

Give rabbits plenty of paper

Rabbits are burrowers, and a pet bunny with something to burrow into will be a happy camper. Offer Bunny shredded newspaper, balled-up phone book pages, or other similar paper, placing it in the bottom of his cage so he can dig away.

Cardboard hidey-hole for Bunny

Rabbits enjoy the comfort of a "cave." Remove the lid from a cardboard box and cut out a door shape. Turn the box upside down in the rabbit cage and your pet will use it as a cozy hideaway. Choose a shoebox or a larger cardboard box, depending on your pet's size.

A roll to gnaw on

It seems almost all animal pets—dogs, cats, rabbits, chinchillas, mice, gerbils, guinea pigs, hamsters, ferrets, and the like—enjoy gnawing on an empty paper towel or toilet tissue roll. So do some birds, like cockatiels, so put some rolls aside for your furry or feathery charges. They also like to gnaw on cardboard tissue boxes. Just make sure to remove the thin plastic liner attached to a tissue box's dispensing slot.

Let hamsters branch out

Hamsters like fresh branches to climb on and gnaw. Choose small willow or fruit wood branches. Make sure they're pesticide-free.

Coconut gerbil house

Gerbils and other rodents are active creatures and like to stay occupied. A coconut shell suspended from the top of the cage makes a great climb-in, climb-out toy. First, clean the shell well, removing all coconut meat. Then use a jigsaw to cut an opening in the shell, filing down the rough edges. Boil the shell in water for 10 minutes and let it air dry. Insert an eye hook into the shell so that when you suspend it from the cage ceiling, the opening will be on the side (not pointing downward). Hang the shell low enough for your pet to reach.

Nibble, nibble, nibble

Sure, your pet rodents enjoy those expensive chew toys. But you can provide just as much munching pleasure for free. Besides all those empty cardboard rolls and small cardboard boxes, give your nibblers small blocks of wood left over from woodworking projects. Do not, however, give them any treated wood.

"SO WHERE'S THE HINT FOR MY FERRET?"

Right here. **Ping-Pong balls** and tennis balls make great toys for ferrets, and guinea pigs will find them rather amusing as well. Ferrets and guinea pigs understand that not every toy has to be a chew toy.

Turtles, Snakes, and Other Reptiles

Save your turtle's gravel

Don't throw away the gravel or aggregate in your turtle's bowl every time you clean it. Dump the gravel, aggregate, and any other bowl materials into a colander. Place the colander over a bucket and pour pitchers full of water over the contents until the gravel is clean. Next, pour household bleach over everything. Finally, run water over the colander contents until the bleach smell dissipates.

Your pet snake is lost?

It happens, but don't panic. Here are two good ways to find your missing pet:

- Place foil or crinkly plastic packing material around the room in potential hiding places, so you can hear the snake moving around.

- Sprinkle some flour on the floor in areas where you suspect your pet might be hiding.

Bring the outdoors in for a pet lizard

Your pet lizard will enjoy having fresh small tree branches in his cage. Lizards like to climb and hang out on the branches you can collect from your yard.

Lazin' lizards!

Caged lizards like to relax, so make your pet a little hammock. String a section of old pillowcase or a bandana between two corners of the cage, and you'll soon see your lizard resting comfortably in her new piece of furniture.

A reptile cage catchall

Keep the area around a reptile's cage neat by placing an old shower curtain liner or plastic tablecloth beneath the cage. When it's time to straighten up, bundle up the plastic liner, brush sand or crumbs or any other bits of detritus into the trash, and then wipe the liner with a sponge before returning it to its original spot.

Curiosity Corner
Girl Turtle or Boy Turtle?

Want to give your pet turtle a gender-appropriate name? Finding the answer to the question of female vs. male is easier than you might think. Just turn the turtle over and examine its undershell—which, by the way, is called the plastron.

If the plastron is convex (curved outward), the turtle is female; if it's concave (curved inward), the turtle is male.

Because the curves are slight, you may have to hold the turtle horizontally before your eyes to determine which way the undershell curves.

Creatures of the (Not So) Deep

Tape fish food dispensers

Some fish food containers have big open tops; others have way too many large holes—and both can lead to overfeeding your aquarium or goldfish-bowl fish. Cover half of the container mouth with masking tape to better control the dispersal of fish flakes.

Panty hose tank cleaners

Save an old pair of panty hose for yet another household use! Once you've removed the fish, the water, and any ornaments from an aquarium tank, you can turn panty hose into a cleaning tool in two ways: 1) Fit a leg over your arm so you have the foot over your fingers, like a mitten. 2) Ball the panty hose up and use it as you would a sponge. No matter which method you choose, make a simple vinegar and water solution (1 part white vinegar to 1 part water) and use panty hose to wipe down the sides and bottom of the tank.

Put aquarium water to good use

When you change the water in your tank, don't pour it down the drain! It's excellent for hatching brine shrimp (the favorite food of sea horses, if you keep a sea horse or two in your aquarium), and it makes an excellent fertilizer for houseplants and outdoor ornamentals alike. The nutrients in the water make flowering plants and vegetables thrive like few other fertilizers. And don't be put off by the smell—it will dissipate about an hour after you water your plants.

Pep up Goldie with salt

Treat your goldfish to a swim in the ocean. Well, a *simulated* ocean. Stir 1 teaspoon marine salt into 1 quart room-temperature water and pour it into a wide-mouthed container. Let Goldie swim for about 15 minutes in this slightly salty mix and then return her to her bowl. The saltwater will put a little pep in her step. (Caution: Do not use table salt because the pH is too high.)

Tasty treats for hermit crabs

Enhance your hermit crab's diet by adding bits of any of the following to its food dish. The list is long, so take a deep breath and jump in: mango, papaya, coconut, apples, applesauce, bananas, grapes, pineapple, strawberries, melons, carrots, spinach, leafy green lettuces (not iceberg), broccoli, grass, leaves, strips of bark from deciduous trees (no conifers), unsalted nuts, raisins, unsalted crackers, unsweetened cereals, and plain rice cakes. A wide-ranging crustacean menu indeed!

Eggshells for hermits

Hermit crabs need a lot of calcium, a mineral available in various forms in pet stores. To provide calcium to your pet crawler for free, boil an egg, dry and crush the shell, and add it to your crab's regular food once a week.

Our Fine Feathered Friends

Lights-out drapes

An attractive small tablecloth or a pillowcase or scarf can become a nighttime cover for your bird's cage. Covering the cage will help your bird relax.

Natural decor for Tweety

Clip a small tree branch for your cockatiel's cage. He'll be able to climb and reclimb and also will peck it to sharpen his beak.

Clean house with vinegar

A 50/50 mixture of white vinegar turns a birdcage into a sparkling clean home and does a good job of cleaning plastic bird toys. After wiping on the mixture, rinse with fresh tap water and then dry the cage with a clean cloth.

Paper bag fun for Polly

Open a brown paper bag and set it on a table or other surface. Your bird will enjoy peeking in and out.

Let your bird play peck-the-spools

Make a hanging toy for your bird's cage by stringing wooden spools on a leather cord and tying it diagonally near the top of the cage. Your bird will enjoy pecking at it and making the spools sway back and forth.

Use your imagination!

It's easy to keep a bird occupied. While pet stores sell a ton of toys for caged birds, you can easily entertain your pet with items you have around the house. Milk jugs, mop heads, and

Baubles for Birdie

Make use of old jewelry to occupy your pet bird. Suspend an old bracelet, necklace, or ring from the top of the cage—Patty the parakeet doesn't give a hoot what's in fashion as long as she has something shiny to play with. Just be sure not to use anything with gems or parts that your bird could pry off and swallow. For safety's sake, place the item on the outside of the cage so your bird can peck at it but can't pull it into the cage.

whisk brooms are good toys for birds that like to pluck feathers.

- Plastic bottle caps
- Plastic milk jugs, with the top cut off and the edges frayed with scissors
- Wads of newspaper
- Shredded computer paper
- A natural-bristle whisk broom
- Wireless clothespins
- Small wooden balls

A fun (or frustrating?) toy

Add a new dimension to a clear plastic beverage bottle by putting beads, plastic clothespins, or other brightly colored objects inside and recapping the bottle. Your bird will spend hours on end trying to figure out how he can get to the objects inside.

Chapter Ten

Tips for Travelers

Vacations have always been our chance to relax, to unwind, to learn, and to have fun. But in a time when flights are canceled at the drop of a hat and highway traffic can slow to a snail's pace, you may find yourself worrying more about controlling your rocketing blood pressure than the relaxation that used to be synonymous with the word "vacation."

That said, there are plenty of things you can do to make your trip run more smoothly. Ordinary transparent tape and plastic bags take up no space in your suitcase but go a long way toward solving and preventing problems. Then there's panty hose, which help keep your clothes wrinkle free and your bags organized. Whether you're setting off on a camping trip or a big-city adventure, put on your traveling duds and browse the information-packed pages to come.

For safety, cover your luggage zippers with *duct tape!*

Practical Packing

Take tape along for the ride

Throw a roll of tape into your suitcase and see how useful it is when you're on the road. Use transparent tape to:

- Reseal the caps of any liquids you open, like shampoo and hair gel
- Make emergency repairs on torn hems
- Fix torn maps
- Tape postcards and other mementoes into your travel journal
- Tape together earrings, cufflinks, or any other tiny items that might go astray
- Remove lint from dark clothes
- Tape driving directions to the dashboard for quick reference
- Tape stray buttons to their respective garments for repair upon returning to your hotel room

Save those newspaper bags!

The long plastic bags your morning newspaper comes in offer protection in your suitcase as well—and they're just the right shape for shoes and hairbrushes. To keep dirt or hair from marring your other belongings, slip shoes and brushes in, one to a bag.

Pack jewelry in hose toes

It can be hard to handle jewelry when you're on the move; small items can easily get lost in your suitcase, and necklaces and other dangly jewelry tend to become tangled up and snag clothing. Old pairs of panty hose provide an easy solution. Just cut out the feet, place a single piece of jewelry in each one, and tie off the little bags with twist ties. Your jewels and bangles will be readily at hand and in good condition when you need them.

Make a suitcase divider

Take a tip from smugglers: the old false-bottom suitcase trick. You'll keep packed items separated and be spared the annoyance of digging through layers of clothing to get to your toothbrush. Just take some sturdy cardboard and cut out a piece that matches the width and length of

CHUCK IN SOME CLOTHESPINS

Clothespins—the lightweight, plastic clip-on type—don't take up much room in a bag, and they earn their freight. Use clothespins to hang up the socks and dainties you wash out in the bathroom sink, clip together maps and other documents, and draw draperies tightly for privacy and to keep out light.

your suitcase interior—and voila: You have a portable divider. Put items you aren't going to need until later on the bottom of the suitcase, lay the cardboard on top, and place toiletries, a change of clothing, and the other items you'll use right away on the cardboard. Or place shoes and other heavy items on the bottom, then put lighter clothing on top to make it less likely to wrinkle.

Tote some tubes

Before hitting the road, save a few toilet-paper tubes, and then put them to work when you pack for a trip. Here are three ways empty rolls will come in handy:

- Stuff one or two tubes with socks and use them as shoetrees to keep leather shoes from becoming crunched and creased.

- Wrap necklaces and chains around a tube to prevent tangling.

- Tape small pieces of delicate jewelry inside a tube for protection.

A bit o' baking soda

You already know that baking soda keeps your fridge smelling fresh—and it can do the same for the contents of your suitcase. There's no need to tote a whole box, though. Just fill a pill bottle or film canister with baking soda and poke a few small holes in the top. A little might spill out in the course of your travels, but baking soda is unlikely to harm anything in your bag. (To keep any spillage contained, tuck the container into one of the open sleeves found in the interior of most suitcases.) Baking soda does more than just help control odor. While on the road, you can dip into your stash to do anything from soaking your tired feet to cleaning a thermos. Caution: Baking soda may arouse suspicion when traveling by plane, so make sure to remove prior to checking in for your flight.

Smooth out wrinkles

When it comes to packing clothing, rolling beats folding. Why? Because rolled clothes are less likely to wrinkle—and they take up less room in

12 Amazing Uses for Plastic Bags

You can hardly have enough self-sealing plastic bags with you when on a road trip or wilderness vacation. Bags of various sizes allow you to:

1 Carry guidebooks and other sightseeing gear in the rain

2 Make an instant rain bonnet

3 Wear as a rain poncho (you'll need a large-size trash bag for this)

4 Wrap your feet to keep them dry

5 Store dirty laundry

6 Store cotton balls and other toiletry items

7 Organize clothing in a suitcase

8 Store liquids that might spill

9 Collect trash

10 Save leftovers

11 Carry MP3 players and other electronic portables

12 Carry crayons, pencils, and other kids items

the suitcase to boot. They wrinkle even less if you roll them in:

- **Plastic dry-cleaning bags** Your dry cleaner returns your clothing in sheer plastic bags because plastic prevents fabric from rubbing against fabric and creating tiny creases. You, too, can minimize creases by wrapping garments in the bags and rolling them up.

- **Panty-hose legs** Simply cut off the legs of a pair of panty hose and slip a rolled garment into each one. If you leave the panty-hose foot sections on, use these pouches as secure compartments for cameras, MP3 players, and other valuables; with a piece of clothing stuffed into a hose leg, there's no way such items are going to fall out and play hide-and-seek in your bag.

Roll up your tie

A creased tie really puts some wrinkles in the smooth business look—but here's a way to ensure ties are wrinkle free every time you pull one from the suitcase. First, lay the tie out full length. Beginning with the narrow end, roll it into a coil. Take a sock and gently stuff the rolled-up tie inside. If you're the forgetful type, pin a note to the sock so that when you're rummage through your suitcase for your tie you won't think you accidentally left it behind.

Pack a lunch box

Not with sandwiches but with toiletries and other items that might spill or leak when jostled. Stashing cosmetics and toiletry items in such a compact, sturdy, and separate case will also make it easier to get your hands on them. Of course, the lunch box will come in handy when it comes time to pack some snacks and beverages to take along on a picnic or day of sightseeing.

Instant Travel Totes

A plastic-bag filing system

Various sizes of self-sealing plastic bags provide an easy way to stay organized when you're on the move—small sandwich bags for receipts and large freezer bags for pamphlets, brochures, maps, and other memorabilia you collect along the way. The more bags you bring, the more organized you'll be. For instance, you might want to use separate bags for each place visited; for each type of receipt (restaurants, hotels, shops); or for each day of your trip.

Pack trash bags

Common sense alert: You can fill up trash bags with dirty laundry when you travel. Heavy-duty bags are especially handy because you can just toss them over your shoulder and head out to a laundromat. On a picnic or car trip, the trash bag will come in handy for—you guessed it—trash. And if you don't fancy yourself a fashionista, you can even cut a couple of slits for your arms and one for your head and don a trash bag as an improvised raincoat. (Just hope you don't run into anyone you know from back home!)

Note: If you forget to pack trash bags, the plastic laundry bags you'll find in many hotels will serve the same purposes (except for the raincoat).

A handy coin holder

Don't discard torn panty hose, which can come in handy as a coin holder when you're on the move. To keep all those coins you get as change from cluttering the bottom of your purse or weighing down your pockets, tuck them into the foot of a pair of old panty hose, tie the top in a loose knot, and store this money bag in your suitcase. You won't have to lug around a lot of extra coinage, and since the loose change will all be in one place, you can easily dip into your coin reserves as needed.

Little moneybags

Foreign currency can flummox even the worldliest traveler, considering how long it takes to start feeling comfortable with unfamiliar coins and bills. For easier sorting, stash bills and coins of various denominations in self-sealing plastic bags—a different bag for each denomination. When it comes time to pay for something, you won't have to sort through a pile of confusing currency.

The case for taking a pillowcase

Nothing adds a homey touch to strange quarters like laying your weary head on one of your own pillowcases. This nice touch of home takes up little room in your suitcase, and it can do double duty as:

- **A protector** To keep knitted garments like sweaters from snagging on other items in you suitcase, slip them into a pillowcase.

- **A laundry bag** When the pillowcase becomes soiled, stash your dirty clothes in it. Clothing will be less prone to mold and mildew when kept in a pillowcase than it will in a plastic bag, and you can just empty the case and throw it into the wash when you come upon a laundromat.

Picnic-in-a-Bag

Traveling overseas can be costly, but one of the best (and most delicious) ways to be both clever *and* tastefully frugal whether you're in Boston or Brighton is to pack yourself a picnic in a bag. Tuck a few self-sealing plastic bags into your pocket, purse, or backpack, and visit a local bread bakery, a cheese shop, and a meat shop; then, head to a park or courtyard, and enjoy your feast in the out-of-doors. Use your imagination, and fill a bag or two with any combination of the following:

Hard cheese:
Cheddar, Parmesan, swiss, gruyere, and Gouda are all cheeses that travel well. If you're in a foreign country, ask for advice from the cheese monger. Stay away from ultrasoft cheeses that may not survive a long walk to a picnic area or park.

Bread:
Baguettes, rolls, or thick slices of fresh bread are ideal for out-of-doors picnicking, and local bakers will often lend their advice on great places to enjoy your meal.

Meats:
Cured meats—smoked turkey and smoked ham, for example—will withstand not being refrigerated for up to 2 hours and are delicious accompaniments to hard cheeses.

Remember to carry a bottle opener, a small picnic knife, a napkin, and something to sit on (other than the ground), and enjoy your out-of-doors feast more than the priciest restaurant meal. When you're done, put your trash in another sealable plastic bag, and go on your way.

Handy Helpers

Three ways duct tape eases life on the road

Like to read in bed but need some light on the subject? Tape a small flashlight to the wall above your pillow (but not on wallpaper). Want to come and go without the door locking behind you every time you step out? Place a small strip of tape across the bolt. Prefer to sleep past sunrise? Tape the draperies shut to keep out the light.

Put toilet-paper tubes to good use

You'll find some nifty uses for toilet paper tubes in a hotel room—so save a few empty tubes at home to take on your trip. Or, in the hotel, you could stash empty tubes before the chambermaid has a chance to discard them. Read on for some ways to use them.

- If your laptop computer power cord is unruly or takes up too much desk space on your worktable, loop the cord in a loose coil and stuff it into the tube to keep it contained.

- Pamphlets, small prints, and other fragile paper mementoes almost never make it back home without a crease or two—so roll them carefully and insert them into the tube for safekeeping. For larger papers, you might need to tape two tubes together or bring along a tube from a roll of paper towels.

- Mosquitoes are annoying roommates. If they appear unexpectedly and you're unprepared with spray or other

Household Superstar!
11 Duct-Tape Favors for Travelers and Campers

When you run up against a problem while driving down the highway, hiking, or camping, a roll of duct tape can bail you out in a flash. Here are 11 ways you could make use of the shiny silvery stuff.

1. Tape your pants tightly around the ankles to keep ticks and other bugs off your legs.

2. Tape your pants tightly around the ankles to keep cloth from getting caught in bike pedals.

3. Twist tape into a "rope" to use as a clothesline or to lash things together.

4. Twist it into an emergency shoelace.

5. Repair a rip in a tent.

6. Tape a flashlight to a wall or tree.

7. Reseal bags of potato chips and other road food.

8. Trap flies by cutting the tape into strips and laying them out, sticky side up.

9. Tape up purchases wrapped in newspaper or bubble wrap.

10. Patch a hole in a canoe, inner tube, or air mattress.

11. Tape curtains shut to keep out light and prying eyes.

A beanbag will steady your camera as well as a fancy tripod.

repellants, make your own "flypaper." Just wrap some adhesive tape around the tube, sticky side out, and set it upright on a flat surface.

Buffer sore bums

Long car rides can take their toll on your rear end and lower back. So why not turn bubble wrap into a comfy seat cushion? Just place a long double layer of bubble wrap, bubble side out, against the back and bottom of your car seat. Your body will conform comfortably to this cushy padding. And consider this: If you do some shopping along the way and come across a fragile item you just can't resist buying, you'll have some packing material right at hand!

Aromatherapy at 35,000 feet

We all know how stressful air travel can be, so why not bring along some sniffable relaxants? Before you leave home, drip some lavender oil or clary sage oil onto cotton balls. (Herbalists have long prescribed both as calmatives.) Pack the cotton balls in a small, self-sealing plastic bag or pill bottle and take them out for a good whiff when you want to unwind or doze off. You might also want to dab a dose of these oils onto your skin as you would perfume to make sure you'll arrive at your destination smelling fresh.

Cap your camera

When shooting a picture in the wet, slip a disposable shower cap over the body of your camera so that the lens pokes out of the cap opening. You'll be able to press any buttons you need to, thanks to the thinness of the plastic.

A beanbag camera steadier

If you want to shoot pictures from a speeding car, a train, or a boat, you'll find it almost impossible to keep your camera steady. The answer? A makeshift beanbag. Just pop into a supermarket and buy some dried beans or rice, pour them into the foot of a panty-hose leg, tie it closed, and rest your camera on the beanbag to keep it from vibrating as you snap your picture.

Quick Fixes on the Road

Hole in the sole?

Make a temporary sole-hole fix with duct tape; the backing is waterproof, so your repair might hold up through a couple of downpours. If a broken shoelace is slowing you down, cut off a strip of tape that's about as long as your lace, roll it tightly (lengthwise) with the sticky side in, and thread your new "lace" through the holes.

Tape a broken car hose

You can use duct tape to fix gas-powered loco-motion, too: Tear off a strip to make a quick repair on your car's broken water hose—but don't rely on your handiwork to get you any farther than the nearest garage.

Damp umbrella holders

Hate toting around a wet umbrella? Make sure you always have a plastic grocery bag with you; simply stuff the closed umbrella in the bag, roll it tightly like a sausage, and stow it in your purse or pocket.

Plastic bag galoshes

Rain can really dampen your enthusiasm for walking or hiking—but you needn't let bad weather get in the way of your fun. Before pulling on your boots, wrap each foot in a plastic bag. Your feet will stay warm and dry all day, and you can put your wet footwear in one of the bags when it's time to pack and move on.

Wick water from wet shoes

To speed air-drying, stuff water-soaked shoes and boots with crumpled newspaper, which will wick out the moisture. Speed the drying even more by placing the shoes or boots on their

Duct-Tape Fixes at the Tumbledown Inn

It's midnight. A severe ice storm has forced you into an unintended overnight stay in a motel. And the only one with a vacancy looks like it might fall down around your ears. Duct tape to the rescue!

Broken window? Tape a broken pane of glass to keep out the breeze or a ripped screen to keep out mosquitoes.

Cracked toilet seat? Skittish about sitting on it? Wrap the break for the sake of comfort and safety.

Torn shower curtain? Tape up a rip in a shower curtain with duct tape. Or use the tape to repair a torn shower-curtain eyelet that won't keep a curtain ring in place. Just fold a piece of tape and slip it over the eyelet, cut a hole through the tape, and place the ring through it.

sides, turning them over from time to time, and replacing the newspaper as it becomes damp.

Freshen car air

The air in your car is getting a bit stale, and those little cardboard pine trees that hang from the rear-view mirror aren't what you have in mind as a solution. The trick is to plan ahead and bring a plastic bag filled with cotton balls soaked in pure vanilla extract, tea tree oil, or eucalyptus oil. Take out a couple, put them in the car's ashtray or cup holder, and enjoy a natural scent that's subtler than that of over-perfumed or synthetic commercial air fresheners.

Safety Measures for Travelers

An improvised money belt

You can save some of the green stuff you stash in a money belt by making your own out of a pair of panty hose. Put your money, passport, and other valuables into the foot of the hose and tie the top around your waist. Your makeshift (and free) accessory will be concealed by your clothing.

Point your shoes toward the emergency exit

When you check into a hotel, take a few minutes to study the fire-exit diagrams posted on the inside of your door. Then place your shoes by the door before you retire for the night, pointing them in the direction of the emergency exit in your corridor. This way, if an alarm goes off in your hotel room and you wake up and smell smoke, you won't panic trying to remember which way to turn to escape.

Seal luggage latches

When you check your bags on a flight these days, you'll probably be told to leave them unlocked in case security decides to inspect them. You then proceed to visualize your luggage being tossed about and the latches popping open—and your belongings suddenly vulnerable to thieves. Allay your concerns by covering the latches of your suitcase with just enough duct tape to fit over the fastenings. Security will then be able to inspect the bag by peeling back the tape, and they'll more than likely retape the fasteners once they're done. Use tape that matches the color of your suitcase so that your quick fix won't be obvious to watchful wrongdoers.

Thwart pickpockets

A simple safety pin can make your wallet a lot more secure. Put your wallet in a pocket of your trousers or your jacket and close the opening with a safety pin in such a way that you can still squeeze the wallet out—but just barely. The pin is sure to thwart an unsuspecting thief who tries to pickpocket you, since you'll doubtlessly notice the tug.

A fine-toothed wallet protector

If you're a man, a wallet and a comb are two items you're likely to carry at all times. But did you know you could use them in tandem to prevent pickpockets from nabbing your wallet? Place your comb in the fold of your wallet so the teeth extend beyond the open edge; then double-loop a rubber band around the wallet through the comb teeth. When you put the wallet in your pants pocket or the breast pocket of your jacket, the teeth will catch on the fabric when moved. The upshot? When a thief tries to slip the wallet from your pocket, the comb will act as both a barrier and an alarm.

Hidey-Holes
to Outwit Thieves

Burglars break into buildings, but garden-variety thieves look for loot anywhere they can find it—like your suitcase, whether it's en route to the cargo hold of a plane or perched on the luggage rack in your hotel room. One way to protect your valuables from theft is to conceal them in unexpected places. Three safe carriers for expensive items are:

1
An empty film canister
The size and shape of these containers make them especially convenient for rings and earrings.

2
A tampon box
Leave some of these products in the top part of the box and stash valuables at the bottom.

3
A tennis ball
Make a slit along one of the seams and put jewelry and other small valuables inside the ball.

Traveling with Kids

Keep baby essentials organized

Pack a separate self-sealing bag with the essentials little Zack or Zoe will need each day—a set of clothing, a change of clothing, and some disposable diapers. If you have more than one child in tow, prepare a separate bag for each of the little ones. The payoff? You won't have to dig through suitcases to put outfits together when dressing the troops every morning.

Save that empty dishwashing liquid bottle!

If you've traveled with kids before, you know the sorts of messes they can create. Prepare yourself for the inevitable by saving an empty (but unrinsed) bottle of dishwashing liquid. Fill the bottle with water before you set out, and tuck it away in a leak-proof, self-sealing plastic bag, along with some paper towels or washcloths. Use this cleaning kit to wipe faces after snacks, wash hands after bathroom stops, and clean up spills and smudges in the car and hotel room.

A petite plastic tote

Young travelers will like keeping their small personal items—coins or gum—in a tote they make

themselves. All you need is an empty film canister or pill bottle and a key ring with a plastic spring-lock clip that attaches to belts or backpacks (the clips are sold in hardware stores and locksmith shops). Help a young craftsperson cut two holes near the top of the canister to accommodate the metal ring, then let her choose beads and ribbons and glue them on for extra pizzazz.

Map fun for little navigators

One way to keep kids busy on a car trip—and teach them about geography as well—is to help them follow your route on a map. While planning the trip, cut out and color photocopy the portion of a map that corresponds to your route for each day of travel. Attach the segments to a clipboard, give the kids some washable markers, and have them chart your course and check off towns and landmarks as you go. Who knows? If you need directions, you might be able to get some help from the back seat.

Double duty for fruit and veggie bags

Apples, onions, and other fruits and vegetables often come in mesh bags. Once the kids have eaten their way through these healthy staples, stash the bag for a day of outdoor fun. Mesh bags are ideal for carting toys to the beach or anyplace else where gear is likely to become sandy and dirty. At the end of the day, just stick the playthings in the empty bag and rinse the whole kit and caboodle out under the hose. If you can't get your hands on a mesh bag, take a plastic bag and punch holes in it—just enough holes to allow the water to run out.

Bag it

Family car trips can be a wonderful experience—and even more so when you're equipped with a good supply of self-sealing plastic bags in various sizes. Use them to:

- Store crayons, pencils, and other items that can easily go astray.

- Stash trash that collects en route (tape a bag to the back of one of the front seats so it's handy, and kids get accustomed to using it).

- Save leftovers when the kids refuse to eat.

- Serve snacks you can pull out when the crew starts whining, "I'm hungry."

- Sock away soiled garments until you have a chance to launder them.

Backseat snack tray

Little appetites always seem to get bigger on car trips. This fun way to dish up snacks may be eggs-actly what you need to keep the kids satisfied. Thoroughly wash an empty Styrofoam egg carton with warm soapy water. After it dries, fill each compartment with a different treat—cheese cubes in one, breakfast cereal in another, M&Ms in another. When the gang in the back seat chimes in with a chorus of "I'm hungry," pass the carton around.

Delicious pre-trip prep

A great way to prepare your young travelers for the sights, smells, and tastes they'll experience on your family excursion is to have a living room picnic with foods that are indigenous to your destination. While your intrepid kids are eating, take the opportunity to educate them on the history of the location, its geography, and other interesting facts that they'll retain once they get where they're going!

Crafty Diversions

"Mine!" "No, *mine!*" scream the kids from the backseat when they're not robotically asking, "Are we there yet?" Junior road warriors inevitably get bored and restless, but less so if you keep those little hands busy with a travel activity kit they help create. Before leaving home, have your kids decorate a paper bag or shoebox of a size that won't take up too much space in the car or on a plane, then pack it with materials for activities kids can do on the move. Use your imagination, but consider bringing along:

- Coloring books and crayons
- A blank book for writing
- Stickers
- Colored pipe cleaners
- Plastic safety scissors
- Colored construction paper
- Transparent tape
- Roll-on glue or glue sticks

Spray-bottle play

On a hot summer's day, a simple spray bottle can be a godsend for young travelers—and their parents, too. Recycle a couple of spray bottles from the laundry or cleaning closet, clean them well, fill them with water, and keep them on hand. Use them to:

- Spritz the kids for a cool-down while sitting on a beach, hiking, or hitting the hot city sidewalks. Turn the spray in your direction, too.

- Dress the kids in their swimsuits and set them loose in a park or other public outdoor spot with a couple of spray bottles. Drenching one another with parental approval might be the highlight of your children's trip.

Outdoor Survival

Scrounge around for old film canisters

If you still use a film camera, horde your film canisters for use when hiking or camping out. These convenient, waterproof containers with their snap-on, leakproof lids are great for storing matches, small batteries, or other small items that could leave you high and dry or in danger if they become wet and unusable. If you've made the switch to a digital camera and don't have easy access to film canisters, use old pill bottles instead.

Zap sap with butter

Sticky tree sap is one of the more harmless hazards you'll encounter in the wild, but that hardly means it isn't really annoying to find sap on your skin. To get rid of it, just open your cooler, take out some butter or margarine, rub a little into the sap wherever it happens to be, and wash the area with soap and water. This gentle treatment will not only be easy on your skin but has another application for campers: It will waterproof tent canvas and other outdoor equipment fabrics.

The Compass on Your Wrist

A compass is the standard tool for guiding your way in the wild, but you don't always have one at hand. And that's a bit of a pain when you want to find your way out of the wilderness before a bear or bobcat finds *you*. Luckily, your wristwatch and the sun can come to your rescue, so hope to high heaven it's not cloudy, and then use them to get your bearings. Here's how:

1. Point your watch so that the hour hand faces the direction of the sun.

2. Find the midpoint of the smallest section on the watch face between the hour hand and 12 o'clock—and you've found due south.

An example: If it's four o'clock, due south is midway between the four and the 12, at the two; if it's 10 o'clock, due south is midway between the 10 and the 12, at the 11.

When daylight savings time is in effect, add an hour. So, if it's four o'clock, point the five at the sun, and you'll see that the midpoint between the two and the three points due south.

A nifty tin-can fire starter

It's cheaper and more eco-friendly to start a campfire without lighter fluid. Instead, try building a fire with this homespun, fluidless charcoal starter.

Cut both ends off an old one-gallon can. Punch several holes near the bottom of the can, then punch two holes near the top and insert a length of coat hanger wire through them to form a handle. When it comes time to start a fire, set the can in the fire pit, place a piece of crumpled newspaper in the bottom, and lay briquettes on top of the newspaper. Light the paper through the holes punched at the bottom. When the briquettes are glowing, lift the can away with the wire handle—which will be hot as blazes, so be sure to wear gloves or use tongs when grabbing it.

Tin-can candleholder

Don't curse the darkness. Instead, make a reflective candleholder. When opening a large can of cat food or tuna, be sure to keep the lid partially attached. Once Felix has made meals of the contents, wash out the can and bend back the lid so it faces straight up. Put a candle inside and then place the can so the lid blocks the wind. The candle will burn steadily—and seem all the brighter because the lid will reflect the light.

Great (cotton) balls o' fire

Nothing's more frustrating than trying to start a fire when the wood is damp and won't ignite, so here's a trick to warm an outdoor enthusiast's heart. Pack a dozen or so cotton balls heavily saturated with petroleum jelly in a plastic bag. When a fire just won't get going, place several of the balls among the paper scraps and kindling and light them. Then get those marshmallows ready, since the petroleum jelly usually burns long enough to get even the most reluctant campfire blazing.

Repurpose breath-mint tins

Once you've finished your breath mints, save the tin for your next outdoor outing. A tin with a tight lid is great weatherproof carryall for:

- Fishing hooks and artificial flies
- Matches
- Aspirin
- Packets of sugar and artificial sweeteners
- Safety pins
- Loose change and keys you don't want to carry in your pockets while fishing, hiking, or doing other outdoor activities.

Floss it in the wild

Your dentist will applaud you for flossing when you're roughing it, and floss is useful for many other purposes around the campground as well. Such as:

- **Hanging stuff** Floss is so strong you can use it to hang a small lantern, shaving mirror, and other gear from a branch.

- **Repairing canvas gear** Floss is slender enough to thread through the eye of a needle, yet sturdy enough to hold canvas in place, making it ideal for mending tents, backpacks, and tarps.

- **Cutting and slicing food** Hold a piece of floss taut and slice your way through cheese, cake, and other soft foods.

What's the Story?
Mr. Nelson's Backpack

In the spring of 1920, Lloyd Nelson, inventor of the modern backpack, set off to explore the Alaska wilderness for oil. After an Indian lent him a sealskin pouch stretched across willow sticks strapped to the back, Nelson decided his fortune might lie instead in designing a pack that could be carried over the shoulders for support and comfort. Soon he was sitting in his basement in Bremerton, Washington, sewing together canvas packs and mounting them on wooden boards.

Before too long, forest rangers and Boy Scouts were toting what was then known as Trapper Nelson's Indian Pack Boards. In the 1960s backpacks began showing up in college bookstores, where they were an instant and enduring hit with students setting off to explore the world.

Shampoo to the rescue

Though shampoo may seem like a luxury item when camping, it's well worth putting some into a small plastic container you can easily fit into a backpack or bag. Not only will you keep your locks squeaky clean, but you can also use shampoo to:

- Lubricate a tent zipper
- Remove sap and other sticky stuff from your hands
- Stand in for shaving cream when you decide to get rid of wild-man stubble.

Vinegar at your campsite

Vinegar adds some zest to your campsite meals, of course, but it also:

- **Repels gnats and mosquitoes** Just dab some white vinegar on your exposed skin.

- **Traps flies and mosquitoes** Pour some apple cider vinegar into a container and place it on the picnic table, in the camp kitchen, or anywhere else these pests tend to congregate.

- **Helps kill bacteria in water** Add a few drops of apple cider vinegar to your water bottle or canteen.

Wave bye to beach sand

You'll probably come home from a day at the beach with an unwanted souvenir: plenty of sand in the car, in your shoes, on your clothes, and even around the house. Leave the sand where it belongs—on the beach—by bringing along a plastic bag you've partially filled with baby powder. When you're ready to call it a day, dip your feet and hands into the soft white stuff, and then dust more powder over the rest of your body. When you brush the baby powder off, the sand will go with it.

The Many Merits of a Walking Stick

The humble piece of gear known as the walking stick is easy to come by and needn't cost you a penny. It can also make you feel like, oh, the lord of the manor moseying about his estate or one of those stalwarts who hike the entirety of the Appalachian Trail.

How to obtain one? Just find a suitable piece of wood that's not too heavy, easy to hold on to, and, so that it won't be unwieldy, no taller than you are—a broomstick, a fallen branch, a dowel, or a piece of thick molding. If you want to get fancy, carve convenient hand grips in the stick and sand the wood down and varnish it. Or visit your local vintage shop and walk away in style.

Among the stick's many merits are these:

A stick helps you keep your balance when you're out walking, especially when you cross streams and rocky terrain.

It reduces stress on your knees, legs, hips, and back as you climb uphill.

It's a handy poking-stick for checking crevices, ledges, tall grass, and underbrush for snakes and other creepy-crawly creatures.

The stick needn't sit idle when you aren't walking. You can use it to lean against when you want to stop and enjoy the scenery; as a pole to hold up a tent or tarp; and as a prop to keep a heavy backpack from falling over when you set it down.

Creature Comforts in the Wild

Take a drop cloth along

Been spending your spare time painting the house and doing other messy home repairs? Finally getting a chance to go camping? Well, leave the work behind but do bring some of the painter's drop cloths you used to protect floors and furniture. Choose one that more or less matches the dimensions of your tent floor and pitch the tent on top of it. The drop cloth will prevent dampness from seeping in and keep the tent cleaner in the bargain.

You might want to bring another drop cloth (a new plastic one—they're cheap!) to use as a tablecloth; campsite tables are often covered with pitch, sap, bird droppings, and other unappetizing debris.

Pill-bottle salt and pepper shakers

No need to eat bland food just because you're roughing it. Pour salt, pepper, and any other spices you like into separate small screw-cap pill bottles and label them with an indelible marker—preferably on a piece of masking tape so you'll be able to reuse them. Because these containers are airtight, moisture won't cause the contents to dampen and congeal. For a taste of the comfort of home, take two lids from another set of pill bottles and punch small holes in them with an ice pick. When you set the camp table, put one of the holey lids on the salt and the other on the pepper, and then shake away to suit your taste. Be sure to replace the solid caps at the end of the meal to keep moisture at bay.

Staying Clean in the Wild

The great outdoors smells great, but *you* won't smell so good after a few days of roughing it. Here are some ways to clean up in comfort:

Wash up with sun-warmed water Fill a large plastic bottle with water and leave it in the sun; after a few hours you'll have warm water for a soothing sponge bath.

Bathe in a wading pool For a bit of luxury, pack a small inflatable wading pool. Find a sunny spot, inflate the pool, fill it with water, wait a while for the sun to do its job, then step into your warm bath.

Shower with a holey bucket Poke sieve-like holes in the bottom of a plastic bucket, then stack it inside a larger (and solid) plastic bucket. When it's time for a shower, hang the bucket with the holes from a branch and fill the bucket without holes with warm water. Stand beneath the hanging bucket, pour warm water into it, and enjoy the brief sensation of warm water rushing over you.

Save those plastic bottles!

Before you pitch plastic bottles into the recycling bin, consider the ways you can put them to good use on camping trips and picnics. When you're in the great outdoors, you can use a plastic bottle to:

- **Make a bowl** Cut off the bottom portion to make a bowl of any depth you want;

you might want to sandpaper the edges to make them less rough.

- **Dispose of liquids** Pack out used cooking oils and other liquid trash.

- **Create an ice pack** Fill a bottle with water, freeze it, and use it to keep a cooler cold. Or put it in a backpack to keep food cool on a day hike.

- **Serve as a makeshift latrine** Keep it just outside the tent so you don't have to wander into the woods in the dark. (This works at least for the males in the family.)

And those plastic tubs, too!

Dig into your plastic butter or yogurt container supply the next time you go hiking or camping for many practical outdoor uses. Plastic containers make it easy to:

- **Snare stingers** To keep bees and wasps from invading your outdoor meals, fill a container with water, add a little sugar, poke a hole in the lid, and place this sweet trap off to one side of your dining area. The pests will fly in but won't be able to fly out.

- **Feed Fido** Fill a container with kibbles so the dog's dinner is ready when he's hungry, and use a second container for water.

- **Block ants** Fill four plastic containers with water and put one under each leg of a table. Ants won't be able to get through your makeshift moat and crawl up the table legs to ruin your picnic.

Freshen sleeping bags with soap

Sleeping bags tend to become a bit musty after a couple of uses, but you can freshen a bag by putting a bar of soap or a fabric softener sheet inside. Do it after you crawl out of the sleeping bag each morning, then zip the bag shut. The next time you slip in, remove the bag freshener and put it aside to use again, then drift off into sweet-smelling dreams.

Bubble-wrap mattress

Pack a 6-foot length of bubble wrap and lay it under your bag before you crawl in. Those air pockets are not only soft, they'll also protect your sleeping bag from dampness.

Hula-hoop privacy protector

Maybe it's happened to you—you head out to get away from it all with a group of like-minded outdoor enthusiasts, only to find yourself in a crowd and yearning for a little privacy. If you have a hula hoop, some rope or twine, an old shower curtain or table cloth, and a few large metal binder clips, bring them along—to build your own portable cubicle that's great for changing, washing up, even showering under a bucket (see "Staying Clean in the Wild," on page 264). Suspend the hula hoop from a branch with the rope or twine. Drape the shower curtain or tablecloth over the hula hoop, fastening the material on the hoop with binder clips or any other fasteners you might have. While your creation probably won't be a thing of beauty, you'll welcome the chance to disappear inside it whenever modesty is in order.

A bug-shooing hanky

Fabric softener sheets aren't as cool-looking as a lot of outdoor gear, but you'll be glad to have some along when mosquitoes start swarming around the campsite. Just pin or tie one to your clothing to keep the pests away.

Foil dampness and grime

For a little extra campsite comfort, take some aluminum foil from the kitchen when packing your gear. Here are three ways to use it:

- Wrap your matches in aluminum foil to protect them from moisture.

- Lay a large piece of foil under your sleeping bag to prevent dampness from seeping in.

What's the Story?

The Amazing Swiss Army Knife

It's hard to imagine a piece of travel gear handier than a Swiss Army Knife. Depending on the style, this pocket-sized gadget might contain, in addition to a couple of blades, a ballpoint pen, bottle opener, file, magnifying glass, nail file, pliers, saw, scissors, toothpick, tweezers, and often lots more. Some recent models are even equipped with USB flash drives, digital clocks, and laser pointers.

The first Swiss Army Knife was introduced to the Swiss Army in 1891 and was a relatively simple implement: a pocket knife with a wooden handle that contained a blade, a screwdriver, a can opener, and a punch; an improved version with an extra blade, a corkscrew, and a special spring mechanism appeared in 1896. In Switzerland, the device was known as Offiziersmesser (officer's knife)—too much for U.S. soldiers to pronounce when they became familiar with the knife during World War II and dubbed it "the Swiss Army Knife."

By the way, there are two Swiss Army Knives: the Genuine Swiss Army Knife and the Original Swiss Army Knife. That's because the Swiss government once allowed two companies—Wenger and Victorinox—to produce them. In 2005, Victorinox acquired Wenger, and a year later produced a knife with 85 devices and 110 functions: The Giant, a nearly 9-inch-wide collector's item that costs around $1,200.

- Wad some foil into a ball to use as a scouring pad. Foil is great for scraping off barbecue-grill grime and blackened residue from the bottom of pans you set over an open fire.

Traveler's Rx

Balloon therapy

Balloons lift your spirits, and they can be good for the body, too. Pack a durable, uninflated balloon in your traveling medicine kit and use it to make a cold or hot pack to soothe a sprain or muscle soreness. Just fill the balloon with very cold water or very hot water and lay it over the afflicted area. If you have a freezer and want to go all out, make an ice pack by freezing a water-filled balloon.

Chest rub for barking dogs

If a day of sightseeing leaves you with pleasant memories but sore feet, rub a little medicated chest rub on your feet before going to bed (put on a pair of socks to keep the rub from marring the sheets). Your feet will feel like new in the morning.

Presoaked bug repellents

You never know when bug spray might come in handy, but cans and bottles can take up a lot of room in your portable medicine kit. Here's a way to leave those bulky containers behind: Before leaving home, soak cotton balls in repellant and store them in a self-sealing plastic bag. When pests make an appearance, just pull out a cotton ball and dab some of the defensive liquid on your skin.

Pill-bottle toothbrush protector

Ever opened your travel kit to find your toothbrush soaked in shaving cream? An easy and tidy way to keep up with dental hygiene on the road is to make a toothbrush holder kit out of an old plastic prescription drug bottle. Cut a slit in the lid and slide the lid over the handle of

Baking Soda: Don't Leave Home Without It!

You might not devote much time to thinking about the marvels of baking soda, but throw a plastic container into your suitcase and you'll be surprised at how often you reach for it. Use baking soda to:

Treat burns Add 1 tablespoon baking soda to 1 cup cold water, dip a cloth in the solution, and lay the wet cloth on the burned area until it no longer feels hot.

Take the itch out of poison ivy Apply a paste made from 3 teaspoons baking soda and 1 teaspoon water to the rash.

Take the sting out of a bee sting Apply a paste made from 1 teaspoon baking soda and 1 teaspoon of water and let it dry.

Brush your teeth and gargle Dip a wet toothbrush in a small amount and brush as you normally would. Finish your dental hygiene routine by mixing 1 teaspoon of baking soda with ½ cup water and then gargling the solution.

Soothe sore feet Fill a receptacle—say, a tub, wastepaper basket, or large ice bucket—with about a quart of warm water, add 1 tablespoon baking soda, and soak your tired tootsies until the water cools.

your toothbrush; then replace the lid so the bristles of the toothbrush are inside the container, where they'll remain clean.

Chapter Eleven

Hints for Home Gardeners

The typical family throws out a surprisingly large amount of food. But what's unfit for you to eat may very well be the perfect food for your plants! It turns out that many kitchen staples can either be composted into the perfect plant food or can be fed to plants as is.

And that's just the start. Your cupboards are *filled* with natural, nontoxic gardening aids, from bananas and bath soap to peanut butter and pine needles. Not only will using them save you time and money, but you'll officially join the ranks of "green" gardeners who switch away from factory-made, often-toxic fertilizers, pesticides, and weed killers.

Gardening creatively with what you already own is a rewarding endeavor—a money-saving, eco-friendly approach to one of our favorite hobbies. So whatever color your thumb is, get out in the yard and get growing!

Start your garden by growing seeds in *paper cups!*

269

Starting Seeds, Rooting Cuttings

Make seed holes with chopsticks

Instead of buying a dibbler—the wooden garden tool used to poke seed holes in the soil—why not use a chopstick or pencil? Same holes, no cash outlay. A third choice: A full-size folding nail clipper, the blunt arm of which you can poke into the soil and twist. Later, when it comes time to transplant seedlings, use the same arm of the file to work a seedling and its root ball from the seed flat.

No dibbling (or watering) required

An alternative to dibbling holes into the soil of a seed flat is to wet the soil, lay the seeds on the surface, and then cover the seeds with another thin layer of soil. Shrink-wrap the flat with plastic wrap, and your job is done. Condensation on the wrap will drip down to keep the seeds moist until germination.

Spice jars as seed sowers

When sowing seeds directly into a garden plot, put them in an empty dried herb or spice jar—the kind with a perforated plastic top. Then shake them over the bed or along a row. This improvised sower works best for medium-sized seeds.

Sowing tiny seeds

Seeds of impatiens, lobelia, carrots, lettuce, and a few other flowers and vegetables are so miniscule that they're difficult to sow evenly. To remedy the problem and make seedlings easier to thin out once they sprout, combine the seeds with grainy foodstuffs like semolina, couscous, grits, or dried herbs, all of which will put some space between diminutive seeds.

Keep It Clean

Dirty gardening equipment can carry molds, plant diseases, even bugs. So don't underestimate the need to sanitize clippers and pots when rooting or otherwise propagating plants. Guard against plant disease with this two-step washing:

1. Scrub any pre-used propagation equipment with a brush dipped in mild dishwashing liquid.
2. Fill a big galvanized washtub or your bathtub with a solution of 1 part household bleach to 9 parts water. Then submerge containers or tools for about 5 minutes.

Once they're completely dry, your germ-free, spore-free implements are ready for their respective jobs.

Easy-free-sey plant markers

To label your seeds flat by flat so you won't risk confusing, say, your Better Boy tomatoes with your Early Girls, turn empty yogurt cups, bleach jugs, or other white plastic containers into plant markers. Cut strips from the plastic, trim the ends to a point, and use an indelible felt-tip marker to write the plant name (variety included) on each. Stick the strips into the flats as soon as you plant seeds so you'll know which plant is which from the start.

Transport cuttings to a friend's house in a sliced potato.!

Paper cup seed starters

Small paper drinking cups—the kind dispensed at water coolers—make excellent seed starters. They're the right size, you can easily poke a drainage hole in the bottom, and they're easily cut apart when it comes time to plant your seedlings. Note that we specify *paper* cups: Plastic-foam cups might sit in your local landfill until your great-great-grandchildren have come and gone.

Dry-cleaning bag humidifier

To provide the humidity needed to root a flat of cuttings, lay a dry cleaning bag over the cuttings, making sure it doesn't touch the plants. (Ice cream sticks or pencils can serve as "tent poles.") Clip the bag to the rim of the flat with clothespins or small metal clamps.

Root rose cuttings under glass

An easy way to root a cutting from your favorite rosebush is to snip off a 4–6-inch piece of stem and plant it in good soil, whether in the garden or a pot. Then cover it with a large fruit jar to create a mini-greenhouse.

Willow tea rooting preparation

Soaking six or eight willow twigs in water gives you a solution of indolebutyric acid (IBA), a natural plant-rooting hormone. Start by snipping the twigs from a willow (any species will do), then split them with a few hammer blows. Cut the twigs into 3-inch pieces and steep them in a pail filled with 4–5 inches of water for 24 hours. Use the tea either to water just-planted cuttings or as an overnight soaker for cuttings.

A rolling seed flat

Turn a child's wagon into a seed flat on wheels. Poke holes in the wagon bottom with a screw-hole punch and hammer, then fill the wagon with peat pots or expandable peat pellets, labeling them as you go.

Potatoes as transporters

If you need to take cuttings to another town, use a potato as a carrier. Slice a large potato in half crosswise, poke three 1-inch deep holes in each cut side with a chopstick or pencil, and insert the cuttings, which will stay moist for 3–4 hours.

Caring for Trees and Shrubs

Papery protection for young trees

If you've put out tree seedlings that look a bit spindly, wrap the trunks in newspaper pages to protect them from the elements. Secure this newsprint sleeve with double-knotted dental floss or twine.

Lichens: Love 'em or hate 'em?

Lichens are the ruffled, funguslike organisms that grow on stones, brick walls, and tree trunks. Many gardeners love the natural look lichens lend to trees—but if you don't count yourself among them, here's a simple way to make lichens disappear: Scrub them with a stiff brush dipped in a solution of 2 tablespoons household bleach and 1 quart water. Just make sure none of the runoff comes into contact with your garden plants.

A warm sleeve for tree rose grafts

Tree roses, also called standard roses, are really just regular rosebushes grafted onto long rootstock trunks. To protect the graft over the winter, cut the sleeve off an old sweater or sweatshirt. Prune back the bush's top growth in late fall so you'll be able to slip the sleeve over the branches and around the graft scar. Stuff the sleeve with dry leaves, peat moss, or straw for insulation, then tie a plastic bag over it for protection from snow and ice. When you remove the sleeve come spring, your tree rose will grow more vigorously.

Speed rose-blooming with foil

In late May or early June, place sheets of aluminum foil on the ground beneath your rosebushes and anchor the foil with stones. Sunlight reflecting off the foil will quicken blooming, whether your roses are hybrid teas, floribundas, or climbers.

Feed bananas to roses

Most gardeners know that banana peels make a good fertilizer for tomatoes, peppers, and their solanaceous cousins, but roses love them too. Chop banana peels (three max) into small pieces

SOAP YOUR SAW

When trimming tree branches or shrubbery with a garden saw, run the blade through a bar of **antibacterial soap**. The soap will not only give the blade more glide but will help reduce a branch's wound-threatening bacterium population as well.

and dig them into the soil beneath a rosebush. The peels provide 3.25 percent phosphorus and more than 10 times that amount of potassium, spurring sturdier stems and prettier blooms.

A grassy boost for azaleas

After mowing your lawn, lay some of the grass clippings out to dry. Then spread a thin layer of clippings around the base of azalea plants. As the grass decays it leaches nitrogen into the soil, supplementing regular feedings. Many gardeners find this "something extra" speeds the growth of azaleas and darkens the leaves. Be careful, though: Piling grass clippings too thickly may make them slimy and, in turn, expose the plant's stems to disease.

Cola and tea for gardenias

Occasionally watering a gardenia bush with your favorite cola will increase the acidity of the soil, while the sugar will feed microorganisms and help organic matter to break down. And tea? Place tea bags around the base of a gardenia and cover them with mulch. Whenever you water the plant, the ascorbic acid, manganese, and potassium present in tea leaves will trickle down to the shrub's hungry roots.

Sappy post-job cleanup

Taking saw or shear to tree branches usually leaves stubborn sap on the tool. Use a clean cloth to rub any of the following substances onto the blade(s), and say "so long" to sap:

- Nail polish remover
- Baby oil
- Aerosol cooking spray
- Suntan oil
- Peanut butter
- Vegetable shortening

Lubricate pruning shears

Rubbing petroleum jelly or spraying WD-40 on the pivot joint of your shears will have you snipping away at shrubs so smoothly you'll feel like a pruning pro.

Growing Annuals, Perennials, and Bulbs

A seed-starting secret

You've just sown flower seeds in a planting bed and are pleased with the spacing and soil coverage. But did you know that one extra step will warm the soil and speed germination, keep the earth moist, and thwart birds foraging for seeds? It will—and all it takes is spreading a layer of clear plastic wrap over the seeded area. Anchor the plastic with rocks and remove it as soon as the seeds sprout.

A salt flowers crave

Epsom salt is magnesium sulfate—which, as a supplement to your plants' regular feedings, will deepen the color of blooms and help fight disease. Every three or four weeks, scratch 1 teaspoon Epsom salt into the soil around an annual or perennial's stem and water well. Alternatively, dissolve 1 tablespoon Epsom salt in 1 gallon water. Every two weeks or so, pour some of the solution into a spray bottle and spritz the leaves of your flowers.

Prop up tall perennials

Peonies, delphiniums, and gladiolus are among the tall perennials that generally need support. A wooden stake is the usual answer, but a less obtrusive option is an old lampshade frame. Place the metal frame, narrow side down, amid seedlings when they're about 6 inches tall, working the frame into the soil to a depth of about half an inch. As the seedlings grow, tie them loosely to the top of the frame with twist ties. The leaves will obscure the frame as the blooms above stand tall.

Bromeliads like fruit

To encourage a potted bromeliad's rosette of leaves to sprout its pretty flower, place the plant in a plastic dry cleaning bag with a ripening banana or three or four ripe apples. The ethylene wafting from the fruit will stimulate flower production.

Splints for bent stems

If any of your flower stems are bent, pick one of these common items to use as a splint: For thin stems, a toothpick or cotton swab; for thicker stems, a drinking straw, pencil, ballpoint pen, or ice cream stick. Affix splints to stems with transparent tape, but not too tightly.

Ties for stakes

Panty hose "ropes" have long been used to tie snapdragons, hollyhocks, tomatoes, and other tall flowers and viney vegetables to stakes (they're soft and pliable), but panty hose is hardly the only household item that will serve the purpose. Try these ties:

- Gift-wrapping ribbon left over from birthday parties
- Broken cassette tapes
- Plastic interlocking trash bag ties
- Dental floss (tape size)
- Velcro strips
- Fabric strips cut from old sheets
- Yarn from your knitting basket

Dry Flowers with Cat Litter

All you need to dry those roses, cornflowers, or peonies you're so proud of is cat litter, a microwave oven, and a deep microwave-safe bowl. How to? Read on.

Drying flower heads

Pick the flowers when they're dry (no dew or raindrops) and snip off the flower heads. Pour 4–5 cups litter into the bowl and scoop out space for one or two flowers at most. Nestle the flowers into the litter and gently spoon on more until they're covered. Microwave on high for 2 minutes and then let the litter cool completely—not so much because it's hot to the touch but because the drying continues at this point. Once you remove the dried flower head(s), blow off any dust or brush it away with a small paintbrush.

Drying long-stemmed flowers

To dry snapdragons, statice, or other long-stemmed flowers for dried arrangements, pour cat litter into an airtight container large enough to accommodate the stems. Arrange the flowers on top so that there's a little space between them, then cap the container. After 7–10 days, your flowers should be dried and ready to display.

Flowerdome

Get creative and use an old umbrella—stripped of both its handle and fabric—as a frame for a flowering climber or vine. In your spot of choice, drive a 5-foot metal pipe wide enough to accommodate the handle into the ground about a foot deep, then slide the umbrella stem inside. Plant seedlings of morning glory, trumpet creeper, or any other thin-stemmed flowering vine next to the pipe. Over the next few weeks a unique garden focal point will take shape.

Scrape some soap

If your garden gloves have gone missing but you need to work in the soil of your flower beds post haste, just scrape your fingernails over a bar of soap beforehand. The dirt will come out from under your nails more easily when you scrub your hands.

Bag bulbs to prevent rot

Brown paper grocery bags filled with sawdust or peat moss are the easy answer to winter storage of tender crocus, tulip, daffodil, iris, and other bulbs and rhizomes. Put a 2-inch layer of sawdust or peat in the bottom of the bag, and then arrange bulbs of the same type on top, making sure they don't touch. Continue layering the bulbs and organic material until the bag is about three-quarters full. Clip the bag closed with clothespins or metal clamps, and use a marker to label each bag with the name of the bulbs therein.

Plastic bulb protectors

To keep rodents from nibbling on newly transplanted bulbs, seal bulbs off in wide-top plastic containers. Before planting, punch drainage holes in the bottom and sides of a large plastic jug or carton (think laundry bleach with the top cut off or economy-size yogurt), bury it in the soil up to the open top, and fill it with soil and humus. Plant two or three small bulbs in the container or one or two larger bulbs.

Old plastic storage boxes are more space efficient—and who knows what kinds of potential bulb protectors you might find if you go rummaging through your basement or attic?

Flavor food with scented geraniums

Scented geraniums (*Pelargonium* cultivars) have edible leaves that release a fragrance when rubbed. Among the varieties to grow in pots (or in warmer climes, flower beds) are those with the aroma of rose, lemon, apple, apricot, mint, cinnamon, ginger, or nutmeg. Foods benefiting from the addition of finely chopped scented geranium leaves include fruit compotes, cookies, cakes, and poached pears.

Flowers You Can Eat

Eating flowers is nothing new. In fact, it dates from the days of the Roman Empire and ebbed in popularity only after the Victorian age. Edible flowers are enjoying a revival, and you can join the trend by putting some of the cut flowers from your garden not only in a vase but also on serving platters and dinner plates.

A warning: *Never* use flowers that have been sprayed with pesticide of any sort. Also avoid such toxic plants as azaleas, bleeding hearts, crocuses, chrysanthemums, daffodils, hydrangeas, lilies-of-the-valley, oleanders, rhododendrons, and sweet peas.

Bee balm These red flowers, said to taste like oregano with a hint of mint, are most often used in fruit dishes and leafy green salads.

Calendulas The golden-orange calendula, a marigold cousin, resembles saffron in taste. Sprinkle petals on pasta and rice dishes.

Dandelions Dandelion flowers should be eaten only when very young and just-picked; try the honeylike petals as a garnish for rice dishes. The leaves are a great addition to salads, but be aware that dandelions grown in a flower bed are tastier than those that pop up on the lawn.

Johnny-jump-ups The mild wintergreen flavor of these flowers is a refreshing complement to salads and soft cheeses.

Nasturtiums Nasturtium blossoms have a sweet-and-spicy taste reminiscent of watercress, and the leaves add a peppery tang to salads.

Sage blossoms Sage flowers have a subtler taste than the sage-leaf kitchen herb and add a nice touch to bean, corn, and mushroom dishes.

Roses Use larger petals to sprinkle on desserts or salads, smaller petals as a garnish. Rose petals are also used to make syrups and jellies.

Squash blossoms Fried squash blossoms are an Italian specialty beloved the world over. A typical recipe calls for dipping the blossoms in beaten egg white, then in bread crumbs and grated Parmesan cheese before frying.

Houseplant Hint-o-Rama

Free houseplants!

Every time you eat an avocado, save the pit and grow a houseplant. Just scrub the pit clean and insert three sturdy toothpicks into it just above the base. Fill a drinking glass with water and set the toothpicked pit on the rim. Change the water often and top it off as necessary.

After several weeks, the pit will sprout a shoot and roots, at which point you can pot your fledgling houseplant. Keep the pot in a sunny window and pinch off appropriate new shoots to make the plant bushier. Pinching off the shoot of the central stem after the stem grows about 6 inches tall will result in an even fuller plant.

Coffee filter soil guard

When potting plants in flowerpots, put a small coffee filter in the bottom of the pot first, then add drainage material and soil. This way, excess water will leak out of the drainage hole while the soil stays put.

Cleaning fuzzy or corrugated leaves

Smooth-leaved houseplants can be cleaned by wiping with a damp paper towel, but fuzzy or corrugated leaves require special care.

- **Brush dust away** An effective way to clean African violets, bertolonias, and other fuzzy-leaved houseplants is with a soft-bristled toothbrush, a paintbrush, or a pipe cleaner. Brush gently from the base of each leaf toward the tip.

- **Breeze dust away** Dust plants with corrugated leaves, like peperomias, with a hairdryer. Set the appliance on cool or low and blow air on every leaf.

The cloth glove trick

Wearing an old cloth glove lets you clean houseplant leaves in half the time. Just run each leaf through your gloved fingers from bottom to top, and presto! You've dusted both sides.

Go one size larger

To prevent houseplants from becoming root-bound (and dying quickly), replant them in a container larger than the one they originally come in. Add extra dirt, and your plants will grow faster and live twice as long.

A when-to-water pencil gauge

Houseplant manuals tell you to water whenever the soil dries out, but determining dryness is easier said than done. Not so with a pencil. Push a pencil deeply into the soil and then pull it out. If bits of dirt cling to the bare wood point, the soil is still moist. If the pencil comes up clean, it's time to water your houseplant.

Water with ice cubes

Place ice cubes atop the soil of potted plants, making sure they don't touch the stem. The ice will melt slowly, releasing water gradually and evenly into the soil.

Pot within pot

Use a stockpot, Dutch oven, or large saucepan to water cacti and succulents. Just pour a few inches of water into the pot, put in the houseplant, and leave it there until no more air bubbles come to the water's surface. Drain the plant well before putting it on a saucer. Other houseplants that benefit from the pot-in-a-pot method include anthuriums and grassy-leaved sweet flag (*Acorus gramineus*).

Going Away for Awhile?

When you leave home for a few days, you needn't ask a neighbor to water your houseplants. Try one of these three methods.

1

Plastic bottle/Paper towel waterer

Slice the bottom off a 2-liter plastic soda bottle and stuff three paper towels into it up to the neck. Turn the bottle upside down and stick the neck into the soil of a houseplant you've just watered. For support, insert a chopstick alongside the bottle and fit two rubber bands around the items. Right before you leave home, fill the bottle with water, which will trickle through the towels and into the soil for about a week.

2

Plastic bag greenhouse

A large plastic bag can become a greenhouse for small houseplants like African violets. Water the plant well and let it drain. Spread a layer of peat moss on the bottom of the bag, then place the plant on top (the peat will absorb excess moisture). Tie the bag loosely with a twist tie, leaving a small gap for ventilation. When the bagged plant is placed in indirect light, the soil will stay moist for two weeks.

3

Bath towel soaker

Dampen a plush bath towel and spread it out in a sink or bathtub near a sunny window. Turn on the cold water tap just enough so that water drips slowly onto the towel. Arrange houseplants (sans saucers) on the towel, making sure the drain holes and towel are in contact. Leave the tap on while you're away, and the moisture in the towel will be drawn up by the plants' roots.

Smart Tricks for Better Vegetables

Sun boxes for veggie seedlings

When you're starting vegetables indoors near a normally sunny south-facing window but the early spring sun won't cooperate, maximize the rays with aluminum foil–lined sun boxes. Cut out one side of a cardboard box and line the three inner "walls" with foil. When you face the boxes toward the outside, sunlight will reflect back on your vegetable seedlings. Plants will not only catch more sun, but their stems will grow straight rather than bending toward the light.

Foil pesky cutworms

Before setting out a tomato, pepper, or eggplant seedling, wrap each stem with a 4-inch-square collar of aluminum foil, leaving it loose enough to allow the stem to grow as it expands. Plant the seedlings with 2 inches of foil above the soil and 2 inches below so that cutworms won't be able to penetrate the shiny armor.

Nighttime warmers

If you wake up to the weatherman's prediction of an unseasonably cold night, get outdoors as early as possible and flank your vegetable plants with something that will absorb the heat of the sun all day and radiate it at night. That "something" could be large, flat stones or those terra cotta tiles left over from your bathroom renovation. Another solution is to bend wire coat hangers into wickets, secure them over the plants, and drape them with black plastic trash bags for the night.

Safeguard your ears (of corn) with mineral oil

Are corn earworms and black beetles targeting your ripening ears of corn? Protect the ears by squirting mineral oil at the base of the silk, using a medicine dropper. Repeat the process every few days as the plant grows. The right timing is essential: Apply the oil only after the silks have begun to dry and turn brown; if you start earlier, less pollination will occur and the kernels won't develop properly.

What about those pesky birds looking for a fresh meal? Keep them from pecking ripening corn by enclosing the ears in paper bags and tying the bags closed with twine.

Secure trellis-grown melons with panty hose

If you grow your melons on a trellis, a sling made from panty hose will keep growing melons from falling to the ground. Cut off a hose leg, slip it over a melon, and tie the hose to the trellis.

Keep root vegetables straight with pipe

To prevent horseradish and heirloom varieties of carrots and parsnips from forking or getting bent out of shape, grow them in PVC pipe sections placed vertically in the ground and filled with rich soil and humus. When you harvest the roots in the fall, you'll be surprised how straight and thick they've grown.

Prevent melon rot with tile

Cantaloupes, honeydews, and other melons will eventually rot if they grow heavy enough to rest on the soil and are left to sit there. If you slip a large travertine tile or slate roof tile under a melon, the tile will absorb heat during the day and keep the melon cozy on cool evenings. No tiles on hand? Substitute a panel cut from a cardboard box.

Hang a bag of mothballs

Mothball haters include rodents and insects (duh!), so consider putting some of the smelly orbs in your vegetable garden. Just don't let them touch the soil, or the toxic chemicals mothballs contain (usually naphthalene or dichlorobenzene) could contaminate it. (If you think you can simply place mothballs on lids, tiles, or other flat surfaces to keep them off the ground, think again. In no time at all, wind and garden invaders will knock them off.) For safety's sake, put a few mothballs in small mesh bags and hang them from a cornstalk or a beanpole trellis.

Grow onions through newspaper

Here's some headline news: One of the easiest ways to grow healthy onions is through newspaper mulch. Why? Because onion stalks cast a very slim shadow at best, letting in the sunlight that will sprout weed seeds. A lights-out mat of newspapers will stop sprouters short.

In early spring, wet the soil of the onion patch. Then spread three or four sections of newspapers over the area, hosing down each one. With one or two fingers, punch holes about 5–6 inches apart through the wet mat and place an onion set within each. Firm moist soil around the sets and cover the mat with shredded leaves and grass clippings. Weeds won't stand a chance as your onions grow and thrive.

Household Superstar!
10 Garden Uses for Panty Hose

Among the many places panty hose have been used around the house are the yard and garden—with the following a mere selection.

1 Slip panty hose "caps" over unpicked produce to thwart birds, squirrels, and insects.

2 Tie plant stems and vines to stakes with panty hose, using a figure-eight loop.

3 Tie climbing roses to a trellis with panty hose—white hose for a white trellis, neutral-colored hose for natural wood.

4 Use panty hose as bags to hold human hair clippings or soap slivers, which when tied to stakes around the garden plot may repel deer.

5 Keep coiled garden hose from coming loose by tying it with panty hose.

6 Cover a watering can spout with panty hose when watering delicate flowers.

7 Store bulbs in panty hose in winter—different varieties in different legs, labeled.

8 Prevent soil loss in patio plants by laying a piece of panty hose over the drainage holes of pots.

9 Use as a tea bag for manure tea.

10 Use to strain liquid fertilizer (including manure tea), pesticide, or fungicide into a sprayer.

Keep your seedlings warm with *aluminum foil.*

A tire tower for potatoes

Increase your potato yield by growing potatoes in a stack of tires. Fill a tire with soil and plant two whole or halved seed potatoes about 2 inches deep. Once the potatoes have sprouted 6–10 inches of foliage, place a second tire atop the first and fill with more soil, leaving 3–4 inches of foliage exposed.

Repeat the process again, and your three-tire tower will triple your potato crop. Potatoes sprout on the underground stems—and the taller the stems, the greater the number of tasty tubers.

Two sprays for pumpkins

Ward off fungus diseases in the pumpkin patch by spraying each pumpkin with this homemade mix: 1 teaspoon baking soda and ½ teaspoon corn oil stirred into 1 quart water.

Fungus diseases aside, some gardeners claim they can enrich a pumpkin's color with a different spray: aerosol whipped cream, applied around the base of each plant every three weeks.

Grow your own luffas

The luffa, or loofah, gourd (*Luffa cylindrica*) is a purely practical choice for gardeners: It's grown primarily for its dried pulp, which we know as the exfoliating beauty sponge of the same name. Just plant and cultivate luffas as directed on the seed packet—though if you live in a climate zone with a growing season shorter than seven months you'll need to start seeds indoors.

When a gourd lightens in weight and its skin begins to brown, peel it. Wet it thoroughly and squeeze out the seeds with both hands, then set the gourd on a rack to dry for two to four weeks, or until hard. (Placing gourds near a heating vent will speed the process.) Use a sharp knife to slice the dried luffa crosswise into rounds, and *ta-dah!*—homegrown skin scrubbers for the whole family.

Tomato-Tending Tips

Fertilize with banana peels

Grow stronger tomato plants by placing three or four banana peels in the bottom of each planting hole. (Note: No need to eat all the bananas at once! Freeze peels in freezer bags until you have enough to work with.) When you plant a tomato seedling, top the peels in the hole with a mixture of dry leaves, manure, and soil. Banana peels act as a kind of time-release fertilizer, leaching potassium and trace minerals into the soil.

A corny hot-climate moisturizer

Save corncobs and shucks to help tomatoes thrive in arid climates. Place 4–5 inches of corn waste at the bottom of each planting hole and cover with a layer of cow manure. Then refill the hole with soil as you plant the seedling, taking care not to mix the three layers. The spongy corn waste will conserve moisture for the roots on hot, dry days.

Tin foil root-cooler

On really hot days, lay sheets of aluminum foil around the base of your tomato plants, shiny side up, and anchor them with a few stones. The foil will reflect the sun's rays upward, reduce soil temperature by about 10 percent, and help keep the tomatoes' root zones from drying out.

An ornamental yet practical support

If you grow tidy determinate tomato plants, which grow only so big and then stop, consider painting a stepladder in bright colors and using it as an ornamental A-frame trellis. Plant one seedling 3–4 inches from each leg, then tie the

What's the Story?
The Tomato: Fruit or Vegetable?

You're probably aware that the tomato is technically a fruit, which botanists define as the reproductive body of a seed plant, usually having edible sweet pulp. (Actually, it's a berry, but we're not about to bore you with a botany lecture.) Yet for all intents and purposes, the tomato is a vegetable because of the way it's used: as a savory side dish, in green salads, and as a base for the red sauces bequeathed to the world by the Italians.

Indeed, in 1893 the United States Supreme Court declared the tomato a vegetable. Why? Because U.S. tomato growers claimed they were being hurt by a flood of tomatoes imported from Mexico and Cuba, and at the time fruits were not subject to tariffs. Vegetables *were* taxed, and the Court ruled that because the tomato is eaten with the main part of a meal rather than with dessert, it should legally be classified as a vegetable. With imported tomatoes now taxed, the U.S. tomato industry flourished as growers planted thousands of acres more of everyone's favorite fruit, um, we mean berry … oh yes, *vegetable*.

stems loosely to the ladder as they grow. As the plants mature, they'll be supported by the ladder's brackets and slats, and no ripening tomatoes will have to rest on the soil and risk rotting.

"Just a spoonful of sugar ... " makes what? Your tomatoes sweeter.

When your tomato fruits start to show color, add a spoonful of sugar to your watering can—especially when you've found a variety you like but that seems a bit too acidic. (That old-time tomato taste we all long for results from an optimum balance of acidity and sweetness.) Your tomatoes will not only be sweeter but juicier.

Prevent blossom end rot with Epsom salt

The bane of many a tomato grower, fruit-spoiling blossom end rot is often caused by a calcium deficiency. Stop the disease before it starts with this simple addition to your tomato bed: ½ cup Epsom salt poured into the bottom of each planting hole. Cover the salt with a thin layer of soil before putting in your seedlings.

Epsom salt is magnesium sulfate, which aids the transport of calcium to the tops of tomato plants and the fruit. As a bonus, Epsom salt helps the plants absorb phosphorus and sulfur.

Grow rooftop tomatoes in hay

Live in an urban apartment and have no place to grow tomatoes? If building regulations permit, haul a bale of hay up to the roof and you have a nitrogen-rich medium that heats up like a compost pile. (Plenty of big-city garden centers sell hay, especially in the fall.) Starting in very early spring, give the bale a daily hosing to activate the heating process. Once the bale decays into fertile compost (usually seven to eight weeks), it's cool enough for planting. Stand two stakes in the bale and nestle a tomato seedling into the hay next to each one. A daily watering will keep the plants growing well for the rest of the season.

PAINT YOUR SMALL TOOLS

To make small tools easier to spot when you're working in the tomato patch, **paint their handles** bright colors—say, fluorescent orange. This way, you won't waste time searching for the trowel you left under the sprawling Golden Jubilee tomato plant two rows away.

Secrets for Fruit Growers

Rake-it-up pine tree mulch

Money doesn't grow on trees. But if you're a blueberry grower, free mulch does—if you have pine trees in your yard. Naturally acidic pine needles will not only leach the acid blueberries crave into the soil but also will help protect the plants' shallow roots. Just rake up needles and spread them beneath the blueberry plants to a height of about 2 inches.

Aluminum peck-peck prevention

If you grow productive fruit trees and enjoy making fruit pies for friends and neighbors, don't throw away those aluminum pie plates! Use them to scare away blackbirds, starlings, and other fruit-loving birds. Poke a hole in the rim of each plate, thread a 2-foot piece of dental floss or string through the hole, and triple-knot it tightly. Hang a couple of plates on the branches of each fruit tree, and that's it. Shiny reflective objects swinging in the wind are more effective bird repellents than stationary plastic owls and scarecrows.

Toss thread, thwart birds

You don't always have to buy netting at the garden center to protect ripening cherries and other tree fruit from birds. Just buy two or three spools of black thread. Stand beside the tree, grab the loose end of the thread, and toss the spool over the tree to a helper. (If you're thinking this activity would be great for kids, you're right.) Continue tossing the spool back and forth until it is empty. The invisible thread won't seal birds off from the tree, but once they hit it a time or two they'll look for their ripe fruit lunch elsewhere.

The Value of Netting

Serious fruit growers will almost certainly need netting if they're to keep tree fruits and berries safe from birds, squirrels, and other pests. Available at garden centers and home stores, netting is usually made of nylon or polypropylene and comes in various dimensions and assorted mesh sizes, from about 1/8 inch to 2 inches.

Is there an around-the-house alternative to store-bought netting? Not really, unless you want to sew lots and lots of fishnet T-shirts or supermarket onion bags together. Or maybe you're in possession of a racy "peek-a-boo" mesh shower curtain, which at least is large enough to cover a couple of raspberry bushes.

Ant stick-ups

Ants won't be able to climb your fruit trees and have their way with ripe fruit if you wrap the trunks with one of these stick-'em-fast materials:

- Contact paper, folded in half with sticky-side out
- Two-sided transparent tape, wrapped around the trunk in a 3-inch-deep band
- Sheets of newspaper secured with masking tape and spritzed with an adhesive insect spray
- Cardboard sleeve taped shut and smeared with petroleum jelly

Cacti and Succulents, Point by Point

Cacti and succulents are some of the most popular houseplants because they're (mostly) very easy to care for.

An old hose for heavy lifting

If you live in cactus country, you may well landscape with large cacti.

Whenever you need to move a particularly heavy one for any reason, do not drag or roll it. Hold it by the roots, loop a 6-foot section of old garden hose underneath, and lift the cactus with both hands. Of course, you'll need a helper for the largest varieties, including saguaro and cardón cacti.

A gripping newspaper

Protect your fingers when repotting a spiny cactus by making a gripper, or pincer, from a couple of sheets of newspaper. Fold the sheets from top to bottom into a 3-inch paper band. Wrap the band around the middle of the cactus and grip the ends tightly. Then gently tug upward until the plant comes free of the pot.

Dust gently with a soft brush

Gentle is the way to go when dusting potted cacti, so brush them lightly with an old soft toothbrush or shaving brush. In summer, spray the plants lightly with water after brushing.

Rub out pests with alcohol

First, two diagnoses: 1) White wooly spots on your potted cactus or succulent mean mealybugs are doing their thing; 2) small beige or brown bumps on the plant's stems are actually scale insects. If you spy only a small number of either of these pests, kill them by wiping them up with a cotton swab soaked in rubbing alcohol. For heavier infestations, spray the plant with a solution of 1 cup water, 1 teaspoon corn oil, and 1 teaspoon dishwashing liquid.

Take out the sting with tape

Remove tiny cactus prickles from the fingers by firmly pressing adhesive tape on the affected area and then ripping it off. For larger or more stubborn prickles, resort to a pair of tweezers.

Pencil as pusher

Easily remove a small cactus or succulent from a pot by pushing a pencil into the drainage hole, eraser end first. As long as the soil is fairly dry, the root ball should emerge from the pot in one clump.

The All-Important Lawn

Lawn tonics

Some "my-grass-is-greener-than-yours" lawn growers achieve great success with homemade lawn tonics made from ordinary items. Add any of the following ingredients to the reservoir of a 10- or 20-gallon hose end sprayer and water your lawn with the mixture every three weeks or so. Adding 1 cup dishwashing liquid each time will help spread the solution more evenly and make it stick to blades of grass.

- A 12-ounce can of non-diet cola or beer. The sugar in both stimulates microbes that help to break up the soil.
- 1 cup corn syrup or molasses. See note on sugar, above.
- 1 cup household ammonia. Ammonia adds nitrates, the primary ingredient in most fertilizers.
- ½ cup mouthwash. The alcohol in mouthwash kills bacteria and spores and helps deter some pests.

Shoo off skunks and raccoons with camphor

These two furry pests like to raid your lawn at night for grubs, worms, and insects, especially after a rain. The evidence they leave behind? Little round holes. To make your lawn unattractive to the foragers, sprinkle the grass with camphor crystals—an all-natural alternative to toxic moth crystals.

Recycle that grass!

Take a cue from public parks and golf courses and "grasscycle" when you mow your lawn—which means leaving clippings on your lawn

The Lawn Alternative

Ground covers are the low-maintenance alternative to lawns, but don't think you can just plant them and forget them. All plants need watering and fertilizing, though not as often as a picture-perfect lawn. Here's where ground covers really come into their own:

- On hard-to-mow slopes or in tight spaces
- When you want a "natural" garden
- When you're an indifferent mower who's tired of hearing the neighbors complain about your unkempt lawn

English ivy and pachysandra are typical all-green ground covers, but you can also choose flowering vines or spreading plants like aubrieta, periwinkle (*Vinca* spp.), and sun rose (*Helianthemum* spp.).

when you finish. Just mow often enough to make sure no more than one-third of the length of the grass blades is lopped off each time. The resulting clippings serve as beneficial mulch and keeps yard waste out of community landfills.

Three temporary trunk protectors

If you have any fragile tree seedlings that would suffer if you accidentally rammed one with your mower, wrap them up before you mow. Wrap slender trunks in bubble wrap or several sheets of newspaper secured with masking tape or duct tape. An old towel pinned with two or three large safety pins will also work. All three wraps are a snap to put up and take down.

For **greener grass**, try a tonic made with mouthwash or a cup of household ammonia.

Oil your mower blades

Spraying lawnmower blades and the underside of the lawnmower housing with aerosol cooking oil or WD-40 will keep cut grass from building up in your mower, so whip out a can and spray away before you rev up the machine.

Panty hose for your power mower?

Believe it or not, yes. A few layers of panty hose (or, alternatively, two fabric softener sheets) will protect the air intake opening on your power mower—specifically, the carburetor intake horn. Just cut the material to size and secure it to the horn with duct tape.

Coat hanger topiary for ground covers

If you take the low-maintenance route and choose ivy, pachysandra, or ivy over lawn grass, you can ornament the expanse with a mini-topiary or two. Turn wire coat hangers into frames in your shape of choice: a circle, a heart, even your child's initials. Anchor the frame in the soil and train strands of the plants to cover it, using clippers to neaten the growth as necessary. Who knew topiary could be so simple?

Kiddie pool to garden pond

Think it's too expensive to install a small decorative pond in the corner of your lawn? Not if your liner is a child's plastic wading pool. To start, dig a hole to the depth and diameter of the kiddie pool, and make sure the pool sits flat on the bottom of the hole and its top is level with the lawn. To allow drainage during heavy rains, punch holes in the sides of the pool.

Now position the pool in the hole and pack dirt around the sides. Layer the bottom of the pool with a 50/50 mixture of coarse sand and peat moss, and place flat stones around the top edge to camouflage the pool's plastic lip. After using a garden hose to fill the pond, set pots of water plants inside—marsh marigolds, Nymphaea (water lilies), royal ferns—and your pretty new garden feature is complete.

Watering Your Garden

A toothpick time-to-water test

Just as you test a baking cake for doneness by sticking it with a wooden toothpick, you can do the same to see whether a garden bed needs watering. Stick the toothpick into the soil as far as it will go, then examine it. If it comes out clean, it's time to water. If any soil clings to the pick, you can forgo watering and test the soil again the next day.

Milk jug tricklers

Tomatoes aren't the only garden plants that like lots of water. Others with a big thirst include squashes, melons, and rosebushes. How to keep them quenched? Bury plastic milk-jug reservoirs alongside. Start by perforating a jug in several places. Dig a planting hole large enough to accommodate both plant and jug, and bury the jug so its spout is at soil level. After refilling the hole and tamping down the soil, fill the jug with water. Then top it to overflowing at least once a week, and your plant's roots will stay nice and moist.

Water ferns with weak tea

Also, when planting a fern, put a used tea bag in the bottom of the planting hole to act as a reservoir while the fern adapts to its new spot; the roots will draw up a bit more nitrogen. Another drink ferns like: a very weak solution of household ammonia and water (1 tablespoon ammonia to 1 quart water), which also feeds them a little nitrogen.

Borax for sun-sensitive plants

To keep direct sunlight from burning the leaves of ferns, azaleas, yews, hollies, hostas, and herbs such as thyme and chives, add borax to your watering can—1 tablespoon dissolved in 1 gallon water. Wet the leaves of the plants and soak the soil with the solution a couple of times in the spring (more than two treatments is overdoing it), and your plants will be better able to stand up to the sun's hot rays in summer.

Recycle unsalted cooking water

Boiled foods release nutrients of one kind or another, so why pour their cooking water down the drain? Let the water cool, and then use it to give a garden plant or two a healthful drink. But take note: When you cook any of the following, do *not* add salt to the water because salt is harmful to plants.

- **Eggs** Hardboiled eggs leave calcium in the cooking water, so use the liquid to water calcium-loving solanaceous garden plants: tomatoes, potatoes, eggplants, peppers, chayote squash, tomatillos.

A Homemade Rain Gauge

A large plastic soda bottle, preferably the kind *without* a black plastic base, may not be the spiffiest-looking rain gauge in the world—but hey: It doesn't cost a cent, and it works. Just cut off the top third of the bottle, turn the top upside down, and fit it into the larger piece to act as a funnel. Then use waterproof tape to tape the pieces together at the rim.

Lay the bottle on its side and use a ruler and indelible marker to mark off lines ¼ inch apart. Set the gauge in an open area in the yard when you expect rain, then check to see how high the water rises—a clue to how long you should hold off watering your plants.

- **Spinach** Plants need iron, too—and spinach water gives them not only iron but also a decent dose of potassium.
- **Pasta** Starchy water will spur the release of plant nutrients in the soil, meaning starch may be better for plants than for you.
- **Potatoes** Ditto.

A penny splashed ...

You could either take that jar holding six dollars and 21 cents worth of pennies to the coin-roller at the supermarket or use the coins as a splashguard in a window box. Watering plants in window boxes often splatters mud onto windowpanes, as does a driving rain. To solve the problem, simply spread pennies over the soil surface.

Hose punctured?

If water is leaking from a tiny hole in your garden hose, stick a wooden toothpick into the hole and then break it off at surface level. Wrap electrical tape or duct tape around the hose to secure the toothpick, and the leak is history. The wet wood will swell and form a tight seal.

Improving Soil, Making Compost

Hair, hair!

Human hair is by far one of the best nitrogen sources you can add to your compost heap. Six or seven pounds of hair contain a pound of nitrogen—the same amount yielded by *200 pounds* of manure. Check with barbershops to see if they'll give you a boxful of hair; you'll find that many will do so gladly.

Help from Fluffy

Sprinkle unused, alfalfa-based kitty litter onto your compost pile and toss well. Alfalfa is high in nitrogen—an excellent compost activator—which will ultimately hasten decomposition.

Attract earthworms with coffee grounds

The larger the number of earthworms wriggling about in your soil, the better its tilth. Attract the worms to planting beds or other garden areas by digging coffee grounds into the soil.

Solarize soil with clear plastic

What free resource will kill weed seeds, most plant diseases, and nematodes in your soil? The sun. Till the soil and water it, then lay a sheet of clear plastic over the area (a split-open dry cleaning bag will do nicely) and anchor the edges with stones. After four to six weeks, the sun's heat should have rid the soil of most plant menaces.

Composting in a leaf bag

Turn autumn leaves into compost by storing them over the winter in large black plastic leaf bags. When filling the bag with leaves, add a small shovelful of soil and a handful of 10-10-10 fertilizer as an activator. Then direct a stream of water from your garden hose into the bag to saturate the leaves.

Tie the bag closed and bounce it on the ground a few times to mix the contents. Store the bag in a sunny place so that it absorbs the heat of the sun. By spring the leaves will have rotted into rich compost.

COFFEE, TEA, OR COLA?

So your compost pile seems a bit slow in producing the fertile organic matter you want to dig into your garden beds? Speed decomposition of the contents by pouring on **coffee, tea, or non-diet cola**—all three of which will increase the bacterium population that help both soil and compost break down.

Feeding Your Plants

Matchbooks as fertilizer?

Yes! But *only* when you want to add sulfur to the soil to lower the pH for acid-loving plants. Tear out the matches from several matchbooks and toss them into the bottom of planting holes for impatiens, hydrangeas, azaleas, and gardenias.

Fireplace freebie

Hardwood ashes from your fireplace will supply potassium and phosphorous to garden plants. Just make sure not to use wood that has been treated with preservatives or anything else. To fertilize plants, spread a half-inch layer of ashes a few inches from the stem and dig it into the soil.

A couple of caveats: 1) If you store ashes outside, protect them from the rain or their nutrients will be depleted; 2) don't use ashes around potatoes, since ash can promote potato scab.

Limit your plants' coffee consumption

It isn't the caffeine in coffee grounds that garden plants like azaleas and rosebushes and evergreens love but rather the acidity and aeration the grounds provide—not to mention nitrogen, phosphorous, and trace minerals. Just be sure to dig the grounds into the soil to keep them from becoming moldy.

How much to use? Dig about ¾ cup of grounds into the soil near the roots, repeating once a month. And don't overdo it. Fertilizing even acid-loving plants with coffee grounds too frequently could increase soil acidity to undesirable levels.

Tree-feeding drill

To make sure fertilizer reaches a tree's feeder roots, put your power drill to work on some-

Finding Free Manure

Not surprisingly, a lot of farmers and stable owners are more than happy for you to haul manure away from their property for use in your garden (after drying and aging, of course). Also, if your city has a zoo, call the administrative office to see if manure is supplied to gardeners. And when the circus rolls into town … well, you get the picture. A caveat: *Never* use manure from pets as a fertilizer; it often contains roundworms and toxic parasites.

thing besides wood: the soil. Use a bit at least 1 foot long and 1½ inches in diameter, and bore holes in the soil around the drip line—the imaginary circle beneath the outermost tips of the tree canopy. Space the holes about 2 feet apart, then bore a second ring of holes about 2½ feet from the tree trunk. Funnel a slow-release fertilizer into all of the holes, and then plug them with soil and water well.

Add sawdust and leaves to aging manure

Fresh, or raw, manure must be aged so that it won't burn your plants' roots—and only the most committed home gardeners will wait for the six months it takes. If you're one of those gardeners, water a fresh manure pile, cover it with a tarp so the nutrients won't leach out during a rain, and turn the pile with a pitchfork every 10 days or so. To control the odor (especially in summer), add sawdust, dead leaves, or wood chips, forking them evenly into the pile.

Mulches and Such

Free mulch quest

Mulch is usually there for the taking if you know where to look for it. Besides the dead leaves and grass clippings you can collect from your own yard, check with local agricultural businesses and local governments to see if they would like for any waste material to be taken away. In particular, ask for chippable bark, salt marsh hay, prairie hay, pine straw, wheat straw, pecan shells, peanut shells, or cotton burrs or hulls.

Strawberries like sawdust

A sawdust mulch benefits strawberries in two ways: it gives them the acidity they crave and keeps snails and slugs at bay. Raise the foliage of each plant and mound sawdust 2–3 inches high around the stem. But know what you're using: Sawdust from black walnut, cedar, or chemically treated wood contains toxins that do garden plants no favors.

Foil and paper heat-beaters

A single-layer mulch of aluminum foil or brown paper (the latter sprayed with clear shellac) decreases soil temperature because both materials reflect the sun's rays. On very hot days, keep the roots of a favorite specimen cool by laying foil or paper around the base of the plant.

Recycle the tops of root crops

What to do with the leafy tops of the carrots, beets, radishes, and other root vegetables you grow? Once you've harvested the roots, lay the tops between rows of your veggie garden to mulch the crops that remain.

Black plastic for a small space

If you have a tiny garden—say a 4-by-5 foot patch of soil in a paved courtyard—don't bother to buy the black plastic mulch sold at garden centers. (Black plastic is the standard weed-eliminating underlay for bark chip mulches.) Plain black plastic trash bags will do the job equally well. Just spread out the bags side to side—and when it comes time to restyle your small garden months or years later, you can use the bags for their original purpose: to hold trash.

Waging War on Weeds

A pinpointed salt zap

Salt will kill many weeds that can't be pulled up from the roots. Use a garden fork to scrape the soil away from the base of the weed and then cut the stem as close to the ground as possible. Pour salt onto the wound, trying your best not to spill any into the soil.

Drive weeds from cracks with vinegar and salt

If weeds or grass sprout from cracks in your driveway, sidewalk, or any other outdoor paved surface, squirt them with a vinegar and salt solution. To make it, combine 2 cups vinegar, ¼ cup salt, and 2 drops liquid dish detergent in a jar, screw the cap on tightly, and shake well. A simpler alternative is pouring boiling salted water into the cracks. When applying either weed killer, make sure no runoff reaches your garden plants.

Newspaper and plastic smotherers

If part of your garden seems a little too weed-friendly, try one of these mulches to keep undesirable plants from sprouting:

- **Newspapers** Wet several sheets of newspaper so that they cling together, and then set the mat over a patch of weeds. Camouflage the mat by topping it with wood chips or other mulch. Remove it once the weeds are kaput.

- **Trash bags** Split the seams of black plastic trash bags to double their size and use them to blanket the problem spot. Spiff the plastic up with wood chips or such and leave it in place 10–14 days—by which time the weeds should be dead and gone.

---

make your own
Weed Killer

Chemical-laden weed killers do the job, all right, but so do greener alternatives that are easy to make at home. Whatever your views of conventional vs. organic gardening, it's always wise to try weed killers with low toxicity before using harsher poisons.

Vinegar Weed Beater

The acetic acid in vinegar kills the leaves of a weed, not the root—but if you apply this spray often enough it will deplete the weed's stored energy reserves and kill off the intruder.

> 2 cups water
> 1½ cups vinegar (white or cider)
> ½ cup dishwashing liquid

1. Using a funnel, pour all of the ingredients into a 1-quart spray bottle.

2. Shake well to mix.

3. Spray the solution directly on weeds, taking care not to spray any surrounding grass or desirable plants.

A poison ivy–killing cocktail

Poison ivy is one weed you don't want to mess around with. An easy way to kill it? With a spray of vodka and water. Combine 2 tablespoons vodka with 2 cups water and pour the solution into a spray bottle. Vodka's dehydrating action will kill poison ivy soon after the leaves are saturated.

Frost Busters

Coat hanger cold frame

To protect seedlings in heavy planters that you're unable to bring indoors, straighten out two coat hangers and then bend the wire into arcs. Cross them and insert the ends into the planter just inside the rim, leaving headroom for the seedlings. Cover this wire frame with a plastic dry cleaning bag, securing the plastic to the planter by wrapping it with loosely tied twine. Temporarily remove the plastic whenever the seedlings need watering.

Extra insulation

If you're keeping seedlings or hardening off young plants in a cold frame and a hard frost is forecast, line the inside of the frame with sheets of newspaper. Newsprint is a first-rate insulator.

A newspaper blankie

When the weather forecaster predicts a frosty night, tent thinnish sections of the newspaper over seedlings and weight them down at the edges with stones. They'll keep your plants nicely insulated from the cold until the temperature climbs the next day.

Bushels of warmth

In cold climates, old-fashioned bushel baskets make excellent plant protectors, keeping cold winds out while letting in some light. At night, drape the baskets with black plastic for extra protection.

Improvised cloches

The French came up with the idea for the glass cloche, or bell jar, to protect seedlings from frost. Cloches line the shelves at garden centers, but a household substitute will do the job equally well. Some ideas for impromptu plant protectors:

- A tall flower vase, placed upside down over the plant
- A large glass fruit jar
- A 2-liter soda bottle. Slice the bottom off with a sharp knife and place the bottle over the seedling.
- A 1-gallon milk jug, used in the same way as the soda bottle

Warm cozy glow

If frost threatens to damage a large container plant on your patio or perhaps a citrus tree that's bearing young fruit, string incandescent Christmas lights through the branches. Cover the plant with a sheet or drop cloth and turn on the lights. Your plant will stay warm through the night.

Feathered (or Furred) Friends 'n' Foes

Help birds build nests

To attract birds to your yard (they happily feast on leaf-eating insects when not eyeing your veggies or fruits), hang some nest-building materials in a tree. Fill a large-mesh onion bag with dryer lint, hair from your hairbrush, fabric scraps, and short pieces of string or yarn. Then watch your feathered visitors fashion a new home.

A plastic-plate hummingbird feeder

Attract hummingbirds with a fake-flower feeder. Cut a red plastic plate in the shape of a hibiscus flower and poke a hole in the center large enough to accommodate a hamster water bottle. Fill the bottle with sugar water tinted with red food coloring and insert it into the hole, securing it on the back of the "flower" with duct tape. Hang the feeder on a rhododendron bush or a trellis laden with flowers—and even after the real flowers fade, hummingbirds will stop by for a drink.

A real flap

If your property is windier than most, try this trick for keeping birds away from garden plants. Cut plastic garbage bags into "flags" or long strips and staple them to tall wooden stakes with a staple gun. When the plastic whips around in the wind, birds will be scared away by both the movement and the noise.

Scarecrow stuffers

If you decide to put a traditional stand-up, hatted scarecrow in your vegetable plot (as much for nostalgia as anything else), be aware that the stuffing materials for his shirt and pants are probably already in your closet or storeroom.

Anything soft and pliable will do as long as you seal it into a plastic trash bag to keep it dry: old pillows, rags, wadded-up newspaper, bubble wrap, packing peanuts, shower curtains, or drop cloths. And don't forget the old-timey originals: hay, straw, and dead leaves.

Hummingbirds are attracted to the color red!

Guard garden plants with garlic

Encircling a flower bed or vegetable plot with garlic plants will discourage squirrels and other furry pests—including voles, shrews, and field mice—from making a meal of your plants. Space the garlic plants about 6 inches apart to ward off hungry intruders.

Make moles run

Run away from their tunnels, that is. Shoveling used cat litter into the tunnel will announce loud and clear that their territory has been invaded, and moles will leave your yard in a hurry.

Bonus hint: To tell whether holes in your lawn were dug by gophers or moles, "read" the soil mounds alongside. Gophers leave soil piled in a fan or horseshoe shape, while mounds made by moles are more pyramidal.

Oily gopher-and-mole chasers

Soak rags, paper towels, or facial tissues in peanut oil or olive oil and stuff them into gopher or mole holes. The oils will quickly become rancid and stink the critters out of house and home. Or take this less smelly tack: Stick children's pinwheels around the yard and garden; moles and gophers don't like steady clickety-clicking and may escape to a quieter spot.

Go Gophers! (Please)

So your lawn can't compete with Larry's across the street because gophers keep digging tunnels? Maybe Larry knows something you don't: To repel the pests (and their partners in crime, moles) with household ammonia. Do it one of two ways:

- Make a solution to pour down into the tunnel (recipe: 1 cup ammonia to 2 gallons water) and then shovel in some dirt.
- Soak an old dishcloth with undiluted ammonia and stuff it into the tunnel opening.

Rabbit rebuffers

Plenty of repellents will turn rabbits away from your garden plants. Among those to try:

- Talcum powder, dried red pepper flakes, or garlic powder, dusted on and around plants
- Hair from humans, dogs, or cats
- Bars of strong-smelling bath soap placed in vegetable garden rows
- Lemon peels scattered among the plants

Flag down deer

The movement of something white mimics the deer's warning signal that predators or other dangers are imminent: flashing the white underside of its tail. Wind-whipped white "flags" that could keep deer out of your vegetable garden are white plastic grocery bags, rags, or strips of old T-shirts.

Hammer 2- to 3-foot stakes around your plot at 6-foot intervals. Tack plastic grocery bags to the stakes so they'll billow in the wind, or affix white fabric strips long enough to flutter. If you're lucky, deer will run the other way when the white flags fly.

Bring Down Winged Insects

Fool coddling moths with fake apples

The larvae of these moths attack fruits, but you can make sure coddling moths never lay eggs by luring them with fake apples—red Christmas tree balls hung in fruit trees. Start by threading a 12-inch loop of twine through the ball holder, then knot it two or three times. Spray the "apples" on all sides with an adhesive insect spray and hang three or four on fruit tree branches. Coddling moths will zero in on the red targets and get stuck.

Bottle up wasps

Wasps follow their noses to sugar, so set them a sweet trap. Slice the top 3 inches off the top of a large plastic soda bottle and set the necked piece aside. Create a hanger by poking holes on either side of the base near the top. Thread an 18- to 24-inch string through the holes and triple-knot the ends. Place the necked piece into the bottle upside down to form a funnel, taping it tightly.

Pour sugar water into the bottle (use 4 parts water to 1 part sugar, dissolved), and hang your contraption on the branch of a tree favored by wasps. Wasps trying to reach the liquid will either drown or be unable to escape from the bottle.

Repellents in your herb rack

We love our herbs and spices, but most garden pests find them unpalatable or even lethal. Sprinkle any of the following examples around your plants and watch leaf-hungry pests go in search of another spot to dine.

- Powdered cinnamon
- Powdered cloves
- Cayenne pepper
- Black pepper
- Chili powder
- Hot curry powder
- Garlic powder

SUCK 'EM UP

Use a battery-operated **handheld vacuum cleaner** to rid your plants of small leaf-eating insects. Run the vacuum over both sides of the leaves of the affected plant to suck up red spider mites, flea beetles, aphids, whiteflies, and other tiny pests.

- Dried lemon thyme
- Dried bay leaves, crumbled

An aspirin two-fer

The active ingredient in aspirin, salicylic acid, is produced by plants as a natural protection—and that works to the gardener's advantage. Experiments have shown that plants watered with a weak aspirin/water solution not only repel aphids and other sucking insects but also promote strong plant growth.

To make a systemic solution, fill a bucket with 5 gallons water and drop in 3 aspirin tablets (use regular strength, or 325 mg). Stir until the tablets dissolve. Water garden plants as usual with the solution or pour it into a spray bottle to spritz the plants' leaves and stems on all sides. Thereafter, apply the aspirin water every two weeks.

Send bugs to the mothball chamber

If whiteflies, mealybugs, or any other insect pests are attacking your houseplants, sentence them to death by mothball. Put an affected plant (pot, saucer, and all) into a clear plastic dry-cleaning bag. Water the plant and drop five or six mothballs into the bag.

Now tie the bag closed with a twist tie, then move the bagged plant to a bright, though not directly sunlit, spot. Let it sit for a week before taking the plant from the bag and returning it to its usual place. If necessary, repeat the treatment until all of the pests have given up the ghost.

Trap grasshoppers with molasses

To keep grasshoppers from munching on your ornamentals and vegetables, fill several wide-mouth jars half full with a water/molasses solution (8 parts water to 1 part molasses) and place them in problem areas. The pests will be attracted by the smell, dive in, and drown.

---

make your own
Insecticide

Rid garden plants and houseplants of aphids, whiteflies, and other insect pests with this garlic-based spray. If you don't have a sprayer, use a well-rinsed cleaning product spray bottle. No matter your equipment, be sure to cover both sides of the leaves.

Chase-'Em-Off Garlic Spray

Use only dishwashing liquid in this recipe (not laundry or dishwasher detergent) and store the spray as you would any insecticide: in a capped and labeled bottle kept in a childproof cabinet.

    10 garlic cloves, unpeeled
    1 tablespoon vegetable oil
    3 cups hot water
    1 teaspoon dishwashing liquid

1. Puree the garlic (peels and all) in a blender.

2. Strain the mixture through a fine sieve into a quart jar. Add oil, water, and dishwashing liquid, screw the jar cap on tightly, and shake gently to mix. Pour the mixture into a spray bottle.

3. Apply every 3 days for a week to control hatching insect eggs. Repeat as needed after rains or when new infestations occur.

Attract pests with warm colors

Paint milk cartons or plastic dishpans red or orange or yellow, coat with an adhesive insect spray, and set at 12-foot intervals in the garden. Flying insects zoom to them and get stuck fast. To kill aphids in particular, forgo the adhesive and simply fill a yellow container three-quarters full of water. The little green ones will zip straight to the container and end up in a watery grave.

Let toads do it

Toads are among the most insect-hungry garden visitors. Attract them by placing a broken flowerpot or two in a shady spot, then sink a pan filled with water and rocks into the soil so any visiting toads will stick around.

Get a jump on squash borers with kerosene

You can prevent squash borers from attacking squash and melons even before you seed these plants. How, pray tell? By soaking the seeds in kerosene overnight. The seedlings and mature plants will repel borers—but, as you'll no doubt be happy to hear, the kerosene won't infiltrate the fruits.

Eradicate earwig with corn oil

Earwigs are partial to clematis, chrysanthemums, dahlias, and gladiolus—so how do you give the little buggers the brush-off? Not with a whiskbroom but with oil, an earwig non-botanical favorite. Pour a pool of corn oil onto a saucer, set it on the ground amid your flowers, and the pests will crawl into the saucer and drown.

Three Ways to Slay Slugs and Snails

The gastropod gourmets we know as slugs and snails have a special taste for dahlias, delphiniums, hostas, lupines, marigolds, zinnias, and almost any flower or veggie seedling. Luckily, there are ways to deprive them of their meals. Use:

- **Beer** Bury shallow containers (a jar lid is the usual choice) so that the rim is level with the soil, then fill it with beer. Slugs and snails love the yeast in beer and overindulge until they drown.

- **Ashes** Sprinkle wood ashes along garden rows. Like salt, the ashes shrivel the skin of slugs and snails.

- **Fruit rinds** After enjoying half a grapefruit for breakfast, put the rind upside down in the garden. Slugs and snails will gather under it, at which point you can smash the rind with the back of a shovel and add it (and the dead crawlers) to your compost pile. Other citrus rinds work, too.

Protective fabric softener hankies

Keep mosquitoes from dive-bombing you as you work in the garden by tucking a few fabric softener sheets into your clothing. Pin a sheet to a shirt pocket, loop one through a belt loop, and tuck one under the rim of your cap. Once mosquitoes get a whiff of the scented sheets, they'll buzz off in a flash.

Thwart Creepy-Crawlers and Diseases

Repel caterpillars with onion juice

Spray cabbage and other vegetables targeted by caterpillars with onion juice, and watch the pests take a detour. To make a spray, peel 2 medium-size onions, grate them into a large bowl, and add 1 gallon water. Let the mixture sit overnight, then strain it into a spray bottle. To make the plants smelly enough to repel the pests, you may need to spray the leaves twice.

Hunt down hornworms with the hose

While hornworms are the largest of the vegetable garden caterpillars, they're also among the hardest to spot; their pale green color camouflages them as they chomp on the leaves of tomato, potato, and pepper plants. To find hornworms, turn your garden hose nozzle to the fine spray setting and direct the spray to a plant. Any hidden hornworms will thrash about and reveal their whereabouts, at which point you can pick them off and drop them into a bucket of water. The hotter the day, the more of a shock the cold spray will be to a hornworm's system.

Soup can stockades

To keep cutworms and other crawlers from reaching newly planted seedlings, use soup cans as barriers. Cut the top and bottom out of a can, wash it well, and place the can over a seedling. Twist it until the bottom is 2 inches underground, and tender seedlings will gain protection from all directions.

Fight fungus with baking soda

Keep powdery mildew, black spot, and other fungus diseases from infecting your fruit trees, vegetables, gardenias, roses, and such with a baking soda solution. In a large spray bottle, combine 1 teaspoon baking soda, 1 teaspoon dishwashing liquid, and 1 quart warm water. Shake well and spray plant leaves and stems on both sides to discourage fungus diseases from taking hold.

Poison rose black spot with tomatoes

It's long been known that roses grown next to tomatoes are less likely to fall victim to black spot. Make a fungicide by snipping tomato leaves from a plant and whirring them in a blender with a little water; use enough leaves to make 2 cups of slurry. Combine with 1½ quarts water and 2 tablespoons cornstarch and mix well. Store the solution in the fridge, marking it with a warning label. Spray your rosebushes once a week with the fungicide.

On the Patio

Bleach out pots

When repotting patio plants, sterilize flowerpots and planters to keep those newly purchased pygmy roses or Kurume azaleas from succumbing to fusarium wilt or leaf curl. First plug the drainage holes with clay or putty. Then scrub off caked debris with a scrub brush or toothbrush. Rinse the pots and fill with a solution of 1 part household bleach to 4 parts water. Let stand for 2 to 3 hours. Discard the bleach in a laundry room sink (not the yard), rinse the pots with fresh water, and let them air dry.

A bubble wrap warmer for camellias

Camellias grown in containers are particularly sensitive to the cold because of their shallow roots. When winter comes, wrap the pot with thick plastic bubble wrap or several sheets of newspaper and secure the wrap with duct tape. You'll want to turn the pot so the tape is out of the sight line of visitors.

Packing peanuts + plants = smart substitute

Instead of putting rocks or pot shards in the bottom of a patio planter to aid drainage, fill the bottom quarter with packing peanuts. What do they have over rocks? They make the planters lighter and allow you to use less potting soil. And, if the peanuts are made of Styrofoam, you're keeping them out of your local landfill. (Green tip: Biodegradable packing peanuts made from cornstarch can go straight into your compost pile.)

Plastic raincoats for exposed furniture

A big rain is forecast, and you don't have enough indoor space to bring patio or lawn tables and chairs inside. What to do? Cover them with plastic dry cleaning bags. Split the bags lengthwise to double their size, drape them over the furniture, and weight them down with bricks or firewood. Of course, you'll need to save bags in advance; they won't take up much space if you store them folded on a shelf in the garage or garden shed.

make your own
Moss

Want to make a new patio look like it's been around for a while? Whip up a mixture to paint on brick or stone walls or some of your masonry or terra cotta patio planters. First, though, you'll have to go in search of moss and collect a few patches to use as a starter.

Do-It-Yourself Mossifier

A handheld blender works best to puree this mixture, but a long whisking session will do the job in a pinch.

    8–12 ounces moss
    12 ounces beer
    ½ teaspoon sugar

1. Put 8–12 ounces of moss in a pail.

2. Add beer and sugar and puree the mixture until smooth.

3. Using a paintbrush, spread the mixture about ¼-inch thick on masonry planters on the areas you want to mossify. The moss should appear in 4 to 7 days.

Help your pots
drain faster with
packing peanuts!

Bubble away rust with vinegar and baking soda

If you have a concrete patio and metal furniture is leaving rust stains, try this: Pour full-strength white vinegar on the stains, top the puddle with a little baking powder, and leave it for about 10 minutes before wiping it off with an absorbent cloth. Older rust stains may need two or three more applications before they disappear.

Wicker basket to hanging plant

Finally, a use for that wicker basket you've had stuck in the back of the closet for three years! Dig up four or five of the plants in your flower bed and transfer them to the basket—and voila: a hanging plant for the patio. First, though, use an aerosol varnish to weatherproof the basket and line the inside with clear plastic wrap poked with a few drainage holes.

Veg out mosquitoes

To stop mosquitoes and other insect larvae from breeding in birdbaths or rainwater barrels, put a few drops of vegetable oil on top of the water. The oil spreads to form a film over the surface, ensuring that mosquito larvae won't be able to breathe through the water surface. Renew the oil every week through the summer. Light mineral oils also work, but they can make the water unsafe for avian and human consumption.

Herbal mosquito repellents

Steep pennyroyal or fleabane leaves in hot water and let sit for 4–6 minutes. Strain the solution into a spray bottle and spray on patio plants to repel mosquitoes. Or do the same with garlic. Simply simmer 8 to 10 peeled garlic cloves in 2 cups cooking oil for about an hour. Cool, strain into a spray bottle, and spritz away.

Chapter Twelve

Ladies and Gentlemen,
Start Your Engines!

Once upon a time not so very long ago, small-town and suburban streets were lined with car owners at the curb washing their pride and joy—a '48 Nash in Racing Green, or a '57 Chevy in Dusty Pearl—in a glorious Saturday afternoon ritual. Automatic car washes have put a dent in this "analog" practice, but this doesn't mean you can't try some old-fashioned car-care tricks, especially if you like saving money.

Forget expensive car-care contraptions and concoctions and read on: Peanut butter to clean your car? Yes. Vodka? Absolutely. You'll also find ways to keep your wheels in great running condition, be you a driver or a cyclist, and save tons of time (not to mention dough) in the process.

What common, if smelly, substance will eliminate the need for a post-wash waxing? Which baby care item will clean windshields in a jiffy? What fizzy beverage in your fridge has more than one use under the hood? The next 21 pages hold the answers to these questions and more, so let's get on the road.

Cheers to a great
windshield cleaner—
vodka!

Solutions for Car Washers

Baking-soda car cleaner

Prepare in advance for your next few car washes by making your own condensed cleaner base. Pour ¼ cup baking soda into a gallon-size jug, then add ¼ cup dishwashing liquid and enough water to fill the jug almost to the top. Screw on the cap, shake well, and store the concentrate for later use. When it comes time to wash the car, shake the jug vigorously and then pour 1 cup of the cleaner base into a 2-gallon water pail. Fill the pail with warm water, stir to mix, and your homemade cleaning solution is ready to use.

A surprising no-wax washer

Add 1 cup kerosene to a 3-gallon pail filled with water and then sponge the solution over your car. You won't have to spray the car before washing or rinse or wax it once you're done. And the next time it rains, rainwater will bead up and roll off the car, lessening the likelihood of rusting.

Hair conditioner for shine

Wash your car with a hair conditioner containing lanolin. You'll become a believer when you see the freshly waxed look and when you find that the surface will repel rain.

You can see clearly now

Add ¼ cup household ammonia to 1 quart water, pour it into a plastic bottle with a watertight cap, and keep it in your car for washing the windshield and windows. As soon as your windshield begins to get dirty, take out the solution and apply it with a sponge; then dry the windshield with a soft cloth or paper towels.

Banish back-road dirt

In many rural areas, so-called oil roads (some unpaved, others semi-paved) are sprayed with oil to control blowing sand and dust. If you find yourself driving along one of these back roads, your windshield may end up coated with oily grime. To cut through the muck, sprinkle cream of tartar over the windshield, and then wipe the glass down with soapy water, rinse well, and dry.

A one-step window cleaner

Clean your windshield and car windows by rubbing them with baby wipes stored in your glove compartment. What could be easier?

Clean your blades

If your windshield wiper blades get dirty, they'll streak the glass instead of keeping it clean and clear. Make a solution of ¼ cup household ammonia to 1 quart cold water. Gently lift the blades, and wipe both sides with a soft cloth or paper towel soaked in the solution. Then wipe the blades with a dry cloth before lowering them into place.

Fizz windshields clean with cola

When it rains after a long dry spell, a dirty windshield turns into one big mess. Get rid of streaks and blotches by pouring cola over the glass. (Stretch a towel along the bottom of the windshield to protect hood paint.) The bubbles in the cola will fizz away the grime. Just be sure to wash the sticky cola off thoroughly or your cleaning efforts will end up *attracting* dust and dirt.

Vodka on the job

When your windshield-washer reservoir needs filling, raid the liquor cabinet to make your own washing fluid. In a screw-top gallon jug, mix 3 cups vodka (the cheapest you can find) with 4 cups water and 2 teaspoons liquid dishwashing detergent. Screw on the cap and shake well, then pour as much fluid as needed into the reservoir.

No windshield washing fluid?

If the reservoir is empty (and doesn't it always seem to be?), use an unlikely substitute to clean your windshield: feminine hygiene maxi-pads, a box of which you could stash in the trunk. Hold a pad on the sticky side and rub the windshield vigorously. The glass will really shine once you've wiped it to the max.

Shine those car lights

Keep your headlights polished (and yourself, safe) by applying window cleaner and rubbing vigorously with an old pair of panty hose.

---

make your own
Windshield Washer Fluid

Under the hood sits the windshield-washer fluid reservoir that occasionally needs to be topped. And why use a store-bought cleaning fluid when you can mix up your own? With this recipe, you'll not only let your car do the work of keeping the windshield clean, but you may save a few cents.

Keep-It-Bright Windshield Wash

The alcohol in this solution will speed the drying process when the fluid is sprayed onto the windshield—and it helps prevent icing in cold winter weather in the bargain.

    1 tablespoon liquid dishwashing detergent
    3 cups rubbing alcohol
    10 cups water

1. Pour detergent into a clean gallon-size plastic jug with a watertight cap.

2. Add the alcohol and then the water. Cap the bottle and shake it vigorously.

3. Pour as much of the fluid as needed into your car's windshield washer reservoir. Save the rest for later or use it to wash the windows in your house.

Make Metal Gleam

Rid chrome of wax

It's easy to get so excited about waxing your car that you go too far: Wax mars your shiny chrome bumper with smudges that harden and won't come off. WD-40 to the rescue! Spray a little of the lubricant over the dried wax, then wipe it off with a clean soft cloth. The wax will dissolve like magic.

Get wax off rubber with peanut butter

If you're waxing your car and accidentally get white wax on black rubber trim or moldings, wipe the area with peanut butter. The rubber will revert to its original blackness.

De-wax metal trim with ammonia

Car wax mistakenly applied to metal trim can spoil the effect a keen car cleaner strives for. To rid the trim of wax, wipe it with a rag dampened with household ammonia. In a jiffy the trim will sparkle like new.

Baby the trim

Metal trim on your car still not shiny enough for you? Squirt a little baby oil onto a paper towel and polish the metal for a shine worthy of a sterling silver baby cup.

Make chrome glisten

Brighten chrome trim on your car by wiping it with nail polish remover. (Just keep it away from the paint!)

"Let It Shine, Let It Shine, Let It Shine... "

So goes the famous song. If you want to give the chrome on your car a shine to end all shines, simply dampen a clean soft cloth with full-strength white vinegar and gently polish the surface to bring out the natural shine of the chrome.

Two other shine-it-up methods will have the same effect:

- Dampen a pad of ultrafine steel wool (grade 0000), dip it into a little baking soda, and squeeze it until it makes a paste. Then use the pad to scrub the chrome a small section at a time, working with small circular movements. When you've finished, rinse the chrome well and dry it with a clean soft cloth.

- Wash chrome with a cloth soaked in apple cider vinegar. After you've dried it, polish the chrome with baby oil.

Bugs, Smells, and Sticky Stuff

Counterattack on bug splats

If you're at war with the zillions of bugs that seem attracted to the front of your car, plan a little battle strategy. The next time you clean off the bugs, get preventive and spray the front of your car with nonstick cooking spray or vegetable oil or wipe it down with baby oil. Most bugs won't stick around, and the ones that do can be hosed or wiped off more easily.

Mesh away bug messes

Get rid of the bug corpses on your car by squirting a little dishwashing detergent over the spot and scrubbing with a mesh bag—the kind supermarket onions are sold in. The mesh is rough enough to remove bugs, yet not so rough it'll scratch your car paint or windshield. Once you've scrubbed away the bugs, wipe the surface with a clean cloth.

A nutty debugger

To get rid of dead bugs on your windshield or bumper, smear the area with peanut butter (no jelly, please) and let it sit for a while to soften the bug splatters. Then wash off the mess with a cloth soaked in soapy water.

Fight skunk odor with mustard

Get rid of skunk stink by dissolving 1 cup dried mustard in 3 gallons water and splashing the solution over the car's tires and undercarriage, using a spray wand to clean the latter.

Take-It-Easy Bumper Sticker Removal

You say you just can't seem to get around to removing that "Honk if you love whatever" sticker from your back bumper? Once you finally stop slacking off, you may be surprised by how many sticker removers are squirreled away in your cabinets and fridge. Just paint the bumper sticker with one of these four substances and let it soak in for 3 or 4 minutes. Then gently scrape off the sticker with the edge of a credit card.

- Brush the sticker with nail polish remover.
- Apply a thick layer of cold cream.
- Drench the sticker with a citrus-based cleaner.
- Smear it with mayonnaise.

Wax (paper) your radio antenna

If grime clogs your antenna and gets it stuck in an up or down position, extend the antenna to its full height and rub along its length with wax paper. It will be so smooth it'll glide up and down like the arm on a trombone.

Rub Christmas tree sap off the car roof

Got a fresh Christmas tree strapped to the roof of your car? You'll probably end up with sap stuck to the finish—and soap and water won't do the job. Pour a few drops of rubbing alcohol over the sap and rub it with your fingertips.

Tree sap droplets peel off easily with *ice!*

Then wipe it off with an alcohol-dampened rag and let the area air-dry.

Freeze the sticky stuff

Another way of getting rid of sap is to press an ice cube over it for a minute or so. When the sap hardens, simply peel it off of your car, bicycle, or other surface.

Oil away a decal

To remove a decal or sticker from your windshield, spray it with vegetable oil or WD-40 and let the spray soak in for a while. Then scrape the decal off with the edge of a credit card. If bits of it stay stuck, heat the area with a hair dryer and try again.

Take down tar

Road tar can be difficult to remove from your car, but you'll win the battle over black goo fast when you try one of these removal methods, rinsing and drying after each one.

- Try spraying the tar with a laundry pre-wash stain remover. Let it sit for 10–15 minutes and then wipe it off.

- Wet a cloth with linseed oil and apply it to the tar spots. Let the oil soak in for about 10 minutes. Once the tar softens, douse another cloth with linseed oil and wipe the tar away.

- Rub the tar with peanut butter, leave it on for 10 minutes, and then wipe it away with a soft cloth.

- Spray the spots with the old standby WD-40 and let it soak in for 5 minutes. Then wipe the tar away with a soft cloth.

- Pour a cup of carbonated cola on a clean cloth and rub the tar off the car surface.

- Mix 1 cup kerosene with 1 gallon water and scrub the tar away with a rag soaked in the potent solution.

Dealing with Dents and Scratches

Pop goes the dent

If the body of your car is dented, you may be able to pull out the dent with a little suction. Look around your house and find anything with a suction cup attached—for example, the base of an automatic pencil sharpener or a plunger. Place the cup directly over the dent and push it in straight so that the suction engages the metal. Then pull outward gently and firmly. If you're lucky, you'll hear the popping sound that happily tells you the dent is gone.

White out scratches

If your white car gets scratched, use typewriter correction fluid for a touch-up. If your car is another color, try to find a correction fluid or nail polish color to match and apply it as a temporary fix.

Brush out scratches

You can often polish out small scratches in a car's finish with your dental hygiene staples. Squeeze a dollop of toothpaste onto an old toothbrush and work the paste into the scratch. Buff the area with a clean cloth.

Brighten old paint with scouring powder

If your car is old and painted with oxidized paint that's looking dull, try washing it with low-grit bathroom souring powder. Apply the cleanser, wet it with a light spray, and then rub gently with your car-washing mitt. (Test this first on a small area of the car body that isn't front and center.) When you've finished, rinse the car well and wax it.

Wintertime Worry Chasers

Gain traction with bleach

If your car is stuck on an icy patch and can't get enough traction, pour a small amount of undiluted chlorine-based bleach over the tires. The bleach will react chemically to soften both the ice and the rubber, thereby improving traction. Wait for a minute to let the chemical reaction take place, and then try driving away. You can also supply traction by spreading sand, salt, or cat litter over the snow in front of the tires. (Because bleach accelerates tire tread wear, you should only do this in emergency situations.)

Shovel snow with a hubcap

If your car gets mired down in snow, ice, or mud, and you don't have a shovel handy, take off a hubcap and use it to dig the car free.

Use oil to prevent stuck doors

Prevent car and trunk doors from freezing shut in the winter by spraying or wiping the rubber gaskets with a coating of WD-40 or vegetable oil. The oil will seal out any water that could later freeze, while causing no harm to the gaskets.

Tape your door lock at the car wash

Put a strip of tape over your car's door lock before going through a car wash in cold weather. This will keep out water that could later freeze and make the lock inoperable. Once you're out of the car wash, remove the tape.

Thaw door locks with a straw

If the lock on your car door freezes and you can't insert the key, don't get left out in the cold. Try blowing your warm breath into the keyhole through a soda straw. The ice should melt in short order, after which you can unlock the door with ease.

Flame frozen locks

If the lock on your car door is frozen, hold the key in your (preferably gloved) hand and heat it with a match or cigarette lighter. Press the key into the lock and turn it gently without forcing. After a few seconds, the hot metal key will melt the ice, and you'll be able to open the door. Bet-

START YOUR CAR WITH A HAIR DRYER

If you get up one cold morning and your car won't start, connect a **hair dryer** to a long extension cord and direct hot air at the carburetor. Then fire up the engine with ease.

Spray Away Road Salt

Don't you just love the snowfall that makes your town look like the set for a Christmas movie? And don't you hate with a passion the slush your car's wheels throw up as you drive the city streets? You know that the slush is full of the salt the city used to clear the roads, but did you know that salt could rust your car's undercarriage? Not to worry: A cleanup is easier than you think.

All you need is an old garden hose and an ice pick to give your car's undercarriage a salt-cleansing shower. Punch holes in a section of the hose that equals the width of the car body. On a day when the temperature is above freezing, put the hose beneath the car, turn the water on full blast, and let it spray the underside of the car for 10 minutes or so. Move the hose and repeat the process until the entire undercarriage has had a good shower.

ter still, if you have electrical power handy, use a hair dryer to direct hot air into the lock to melt the ice.

A panty hose tree tie

When you buy your Christmas tree, the trick is to get it home without having it scratch the roof of your car or fall off it. Simply line the roof with an old blanket to protect the roof from sap and scratches, then tie the tree in place with a rope made by twisting an old pair of panty hose. Panty hose are strong enough to hold the tree in place, yet soft enough to protect it and the car roof from damage.

Keep ice off wipers

To keep ice from forming on the blades of your car's windshield wipers and hampering their operation in cold weather, wipe each blade with a soft cloth soaked in full-strength rubbing alcohol.

Raw onion windshield rub

No one enjoys scraping ice off the windshield on a freezing cold morning. To avoid the tedious job, slice an onion in half and rub the cut sides against your windshield and car windows the night before a freeze to keep frost from forming.

Shield your windshield with rubber bath mats

To keep your windshield from frosting overnight, position inexpensive rubber bath mats over the glass. Hold them in place with the windshield wipers.

Yogurt cup scraper and scooper

Scrape ice from your windows and windshield using an empty yogurt cup. When you scrape with the edge of the rim, the cup will scoop up the ice. As you scrape, empty the ice onto the ground with a quick flick of the wrist.

Bag your side mirrors

On cold nights, slip plastic bags over your car's side mirrors and hold them in place with clothespins. In the morning, simply remove the bags and your mirrors will be ice-free.

Don't get steamed

Driving can be frustrating in the winter when the inside of your windshield keeps fogging up—not to mention dangerous. Following are three ways to deal with foggy glass:

- Use a clean chalkboard eraser to wipe the inside of the windshield clean.

- Squirt a little shampoo onto a cloth and wipe the glass with it.

- Use "outside air" instead of "recirculated air" and run the defroster.

Checking Under the Hood

Two ways to prevent corrosion

It's not unusual for a car's battery posts to get so corroded that you can't get a proper connection to jump-start the car. So take a little preventative action: Occasionally coat the posts with a bit of petroleum jelly to keep them from corroding. Alternatively, tape a copper penny to the top of the battery so that the corrosion is drawn to the penny and not the battery posts.

Clean corrosion with baking soda

If you fail to keep your battery posts clean, you'll have to deal with corrosion. To clean them, stir 1 tablespoon baking soda into 1 cup water, then pour the solution over the posts. After 4 or 5 minutes, rinse the posts with clear water.

A fuzzy shock protector

When you're working on your car and have to disconnect the negative battery cable, don't let the cable come into contact with the car's metal frame or you'll suffer a nasty shock. One safe way of handling the cable is to make a slit in a tennis ball and push the ball over the end of the cable.

Foot powder leak-spotter

If oil is leaking from your engine and you can't find the leak's source, clean the engine with an aerosol degreaser—say, a silicone spray like WD-40—and then spray its sides and bottom with spray-on foot powder. The leak will reveal itself by turning white.

Dislodge a stubborn oil filter

If you like to change the oil filter yourself but this time it won't budge, a screwdriver and hammer are your saviors. Hammer the screwdriver right through the filter about 2 inches from the engine block. Then grab the screwdriver and use it as a lever to turn the filter counterclockwise. Once you get it started, remove the screwdriver and spin the filter off, making sure there's a pan underneath to catch the leaking oil.

Gum up the works

If the radiator hose in your car springs a leak while you're on the road, chew some gum and stick the wad over the leak. Secure it with adhesive tape. It will hold until you can have a proper repair made (but don't dawdle).

First aid for a fan belt

If the fan belt in your car grows dry, lubricate it with a bit of petroleum jelly. With the engine off, dab the inside edges of the belt with the jelly, then start the engine and let it idle for a couple of minutes. Not only will the petroleum jelly lubricate the belt and keep it from cracking but it will eliminate squealing and slippage.

A cola loosener-upper

If nuts and bolts under the hood refuse to budge, pour a little carbonated cola over the connection or loosen them with a few squirts of WD-40. Give either substance 2–3 minutes to penetrate, after which you should be able to loosen the hardware with a wrench.

Extend a wrench handle with pipe

For a reason known only to toolmakers, some lug wrenches are so short it takes a muscleman to turn them. If you'd prefer not to waste a lot of energy when you tighten a bolt under the hood, slip a short length of slender PVC pipe over the wrench handle and you'll get more than enough leverage to use the tool without strain.

Tape that noisy horn!

If your car horn gets stuck and won't stop bleating, tap the horn button a few times. If that doesn't stop the din, a piece of tape is your solution. Open the hood, disconnect the wire to the horn, and tape down the terminal screw. You'll enjoy blessed silence until you have the horn repaired.

Wash Those Grimy Hands

After working for a good while on a car, your hands are probably as dirty as the hands of a six-year-old kid who's been making mud pies. To get them good and clean, make use of any number of simple household items.

- Before washing your hands, rub them with salt to get rid of any strong odors, including the smell left by gas fumes.

- Pour a little olive oil over your hands and rub them together to dislodge the grease. Then wipe them with paper towels and wash as usual.

- Pour a little laundry presoak stain remover into your palms and work it into a lather. Rinse off the lather, dry your hands with paper towels, and wash them again with soap and water.

- Mix together ½ cup vegetable shortening, ⅓ cup cornmeal, and ¼ cup powdered soap. Then grab a small handful of the mixture, wash your hands under the tap, and rinse with clear water.

- Wet your hands, sprinkle them with dry baking soda, and then wash them as usual with soap and water.

- Pour a bit of vegetable oil over your hands (a tablespoonful will do) and rub it in. Then wash your hands as usual.

- Add a little sugar to some liquid hand soap and wash away.

- To get greasy muck out from under your fingernails, sprinkle baking soda over a damp nailbrush and brush your nails from every angle. If that doesn't do the job, soak your hands in lemon juice for about 10 minutes and then resume the baking-soda brushing.

Wheel and Tire Care

Wheels do make the world go round! Here's how to keep yours in working order.

Oven-cleaner sidewall whitener

To rejuvenate your whitewall tires, spray them with oven cleaner, then thoroughly hose it off. The tires will be sparkling white once more.

Spiff up hubcaps with oven cleaner

Use oven cleaner to remove brake dust, dirt, and grime from your car's aluminum hubcaps. Spray the cleaner onto the hubcap, let it stand for a minute to do its thing, and then rinse it off with a garden hose. Don't use oven cleaner on painted hubcaps, though, since it may take off the paint along with the grunge.

Check for loose wheels

There's a way to see whether vibration has caused the nuts and bolts on your car's wheels to loosen. Simply put a dab of paint on each fastener and another dab right next to it. Then check the dots from time to time. If they're no longer aligned, the fastener is loose. Tighten them all to keep your wheel safe and sound.

Check your tires with a penny

To check the tread depth of a tire, insert a penny into the groove in the tire, head first. If you can see the top of Lincoln's head above the tread rubber, it's worn down to less than $\frac{1}{16}$ inch. Time to replace the tire!

A bubbly hubcap unsticker

If you have trouble removing a hubcap, open a bottle of carbonated cola, hold your thumb over the opening, and shake it up. Then spray the cola around the hubcap's rim. After the cola has soaked in for 2–3 minutes, the hubcap should come off with ease.

Inside Your Car

An odor-eating pair

Deodorize the interior of your car by sprinkling baking soda over everything but the electronic equipment. Take a soft-bristled brush and work the baking soda in well. Close the car up for an hour or so, and then thoroughly vacuum the interior. To keep the car smelling fresh and clean, place a small open container filled with freshly ground coffee beans where it won't get knocked over. The grounds will absorb any strong odors you bring into the car—the smell of fast foods, to name one.

No butts about baking soda

Make good use of the ashtrays in your car by placing about an inch of baking soda in the bottom of each one. If you smoke, it will keep cigarettes from smoldering and stinking up the car even after you've put them out. If you're a nonsmoker, the baking soda will absorb other stale smells.

Baby-wipe your dash

If your car dashboard gets sticky from spilled drinks or greasy hands, clean it with baby wipes. Once it's clean, you can bring a shine to the dashboard with a little baby oil.

Sweeten bad smells with vinegar

To remove the odor left when someone gets carsick, wipe down vinyl upholstery (all of it) with a cloth soaked in a solution of half white vinegar and half water. Then place a bowl of vinegar on the car floor and keep the car closed up tight overnight. In the morning, wipe everything down with a damp cloth.

Upholstery Upkeep

Yes, you *can* make your own cleaners for car seats (and perhaps put the money toward a fun road trip). Here are two recipes, one for vinyl upholstery and the other for leather.

Vinyl Shiner. Mix together ¼ cup liquid soap, ½ cup baking soda, and 2 cups warm water. Dip a clean cloth in the mixture and wipe the seats and trim, then rinse with clear water. If you encounter any tough spots, rub them with a paste made from baking soda and water; let the paste soak in for an hour or more, then wash the entire area with the cleaner and rinse it.

Leather Luxuriator. Mix together ½ cup rubbing alcohol, ½ cup white vinegar, and 1½ cups water. Soak a soft cloth in the solution and clean the upholstery with a circular rubbing motion before butting it dry. To keep the leather from drying out and tearing, occasionally wipe it with a thin layer of baby oil.

Hold taping sessions

Carry a roll of tape in your glove compartment and use it for the following jobs, among others:

- Tape your garage door opener to the underside of the visor on the driver's side of the car. It will be handy, yet out of the way, and it won't fall into your lap as you drive.

- Tape a pen to the dashboard just in case you need one; taping it will keep it from rolling around and getting lost.

- Attach permit stickers to the inside of the windshield instead of using the adhesive on the back. Taping will make the stickers easier to remove.

- Whenever you park at a busy shopping mall, temporarily tape a distinctive paper or cloth pennant to the top of your car's antenna. When you come out laden with packages, you'll be able to spot the car right away.

Magic carpet cleaner

No matter how meticulous you are, you'll eventually end up with greasy stains on the carpet inside your car. When the inevitable happens, mix equal parts of salt and baking soda and sprinkle the mixture over the grease spot. Use a stiff brush to work the powdery white stuff into the spot, and let it sit for 4 or 5 hours. Vacuum it up, and no more stain!

Stop battery drain with a tennis ball

If for some reason you need to keep a car door open for a good while—and the dome light is one of those that won't allow you to switch it off—rely on a trusty tennis ball. Just wedge the ball between the door and the switch. The switch will stay off, your battery will stay charged, and your jumper cables will remain where they belong—in the trunk. If you can't put your hands on a tennis ball, substitute any soft-surfaced small object, like a triangular wedge of scrap wood padded with rags.

Bag a steering wheel

If you have to park in the sun on a really hot summer day, tear a 12-inch strip from one side of a brown paper grocery bag and slip it over the top of the steering wheel, securing it with a piece of tape if necessary. When you return to your car, you'll grab hold of a friendly-to-the-touch wheel.

Adjust air temp with tape

If you have trouble keeping your heat or air conditioning from blowing directly into your face, cover the part of the air vent that's directed at you with duct tape. Just be careful not to cover the entire vent.

Along for the Ride

Laundry basket hold-all

If you tend to collect things in your car and risk drowning in the clutter, here's the simplest way to tidy up: Keep a small plastic laundry basket on the floor behind the driver's seat and use it to hold all those magazines, videos, cleaning supplies, catalogs, maps, and anything else you accumulate. Your clutter will be confined to one spot, and when you give someone a ride, you won't have to scurry to make space for your passenger. You also won't have to fib about how you've been "meaning to clean up all this mess."

Get a (panty-hose) leg up on record storage

It's important to keep your car's registration and the records of mileage, maintenance, and repair warranties where you can put your hands on them quickly. If they regularly get lost in the mess in your glove compartment, store them in the cut-off leg of a pair of panty hose or a self-sealing plastic bag.

Pillbox coin holders

Store spare coins in a used pill bottle and keep it in your car's cup holder. This way, you'll always have the right change ready for paying tolls or using in drink or candy machines along the way. No more, "Can you please give me change for a 20?"

Stock up on trash bags

Keep a number of 30-gallon plastic trash bags in your car for unexpected uses. You never know when you'll need a container for things you acquire on the road or when you'll need to wrap something greasy to keep it from soiling your

The Old Bag

If you're a woman who likes to hold on to her old handbags, you could stash an old oversized one with lots of pockets and zippered compartments in the trunk as an emergency kit. Pack it with a container of motor oil, a can of WD-40, a wrench, bottled water, and any other odds and ends you might need. You could also tape labels to the compartments to let you see at a glance what's where.

upholstery. Likewise, if you spill something on your driver or front passenger seat, simply pull a trash bag over the seat if you have to drive before the offending spill dries. The bags can also protect your upholstery and carpet if your kids or pets pile in the car wet or muddy.

Briefcase to toolbox

If you have a worn briefcase, don't throw it out; put it to good use. Fill it with the tools you need to carry in your car and store it in the trunk. If you get a flat tire or engine trouble on the road, the tools will be neatly packaged and readily at hand.

Take a toy shovel

If you're likely to be driving through snowy areas, keep a shovel handy in case you have to dig out your car. Your best bet? A child's sturdy toy shovel, which works better than you may think for digging out your car—and of course will take up less room in the trunk than a cumbersome full-size snow shovel.

A drink tray for auto fluids

Make a convenient carrier for the various fluids you need to keep on hand for your car, like bottles of motor oil and transmission fluid. Simply take one of those multiple drink carriers from a local fast-food joint and reinforce the bottom with duct tape. It will ensure all of the containers are in one place and keep them from sliding around in the trunk.

Laundry detergent as air freshener

Keep your trunk smelling fresh even on hot summer days when trunks can turn into ovens. Simply snuggle an open box of laundry detergent against the spare tire, and the trunk will smell fresh in any weather. Naturally, you'll want to keep the box no more than half full to prevent spills.

Put on some weight

If you have a pickup truck or a car without four-wheel drive, you'll need to keep something heavy in the trunk to prevent slipping and sliding on icy roads. If your trunk isn't full of heavy tools or the like, fill a couple of pairs of panty hose with bricks and store them in the trunk over the car's rear wheels. The hose will keep the bricks from sliding around, making noise, and scattering dust through the trunk.

Drive a Pickup Truck, SUV, or RV?

"Carpet" a pickup bed

Line the bed of your pickup truck with an old carpet remnant to keep your cargo from rattling or being knocked around and damaged. It'll be easier on your cargo and gentler on your ears.

Shower-curtain rod dividers

A good way to keep things in place in the back of your pickup truck is to set up movable barriers. Fit spring-loaded shower curtain rods at strategic points, wedging them between the sides of the truck bed. You can then move them around to push against any cargo to keep it from rattling or breaking as you rumble along rough roads.

On board catchalls for SUVs

Sometimes the amount of stuff that rattles around in an SUV accommodating a big family knows no bounds. Keep it under control by wedging a plastic milk crate (with padded rim, if the kids are young) or laundry basket in a central spot in the vehicle and urging little riders to keep their playthings and books there when not using them—a long shot, maybe, but worth a try.

Keep a hamper handy in an SUV garage

If you're a parent with young children, how many times have you had to juggle the baby in one arm and shopping bags in the other once you get home? You could make two or three trips between SUV and house, but an easier solution is to keep a laundry hamper handy in the garage. Drop all of your bags (including supermarket bags holding nonperishable goods) into the hamper as soon as you exit the vehicle. Then, once the kids are settled, you can retrieve everything in the hamper at your leisure.

Carry-along car wash for RVs

If you travel in an RV and stay at parks where water to wash your vehicle isn't available, make a batch of washing fluid and carry it with you. Pour ⅓ cup fabric softener into a 1-gallon jug and fill it almost to the top with water. Cap the jug and shake well. When you're ready to wash your RV, put the liquid into a spray bottle and spray the vehicle one 3-foot section at a time. Let it sit for 10 seconds or so, then dry the area with paper towels or a chamois. You can also rely on this mixture during a water shortage, since it uses far less water than standard washing.

Keep mice out of RVs with steel wool

The access slots where you hook up your RV to a cable or hose are "step this way" entries for mice and other small critters. To take up the welcome mat in one fell swoop, wrap the cable or hose in steel wool before connecting it, making sure the scratchy material seals the surrounding gap. With their entry barred, varmints will leave you in peace.

In the Garage and Driveway

Nix nicks with carpet

If your garage is cramped and you tend to bump your door on the sidewall when you get out, attach carpet scraps to the garage wall where the door hits. The carpet will soften the blow and prevent nicks and dents.

Install a bumper bumper

If you need to pull your car all the way into the garage until it almost hits the back wall, affix an old tire on the wall at bumper height. If you do pull in a little too far, your bumper will hit the pliant tire and save the car and the wall from damage.

A combo work seat and tool caddy

If you're tinkering with something on a low part of your car, you'll find it hard to keep squatting or kneeling as you work. But you don't have to. Instead, make an easily constructed combo seat–tool caddy out of a sturdy plastic crate or wood box. Bolt a 1-by-3-inch wood strip onto two parallel sides of the underside of the box or crate. At the ends of each strip, attach screw-cap casters. You can now store your tools inside the crate or box—and unless you weigh three tons you can sit on top of the contraption as you work (just be sure to put the lid on—or top the box with a sheet of plywood). No more achy legs!

Slide right under on vinyl

You don't have to buy a creeper to work under your car. Simply place a 4-by-5-foot scrap of vinyl flooring on your garage floor or driveway pavement—shiny side up—and park the car over it; keep a foot or so of the vinyl protruding from under the car. Lie on your back on the vinyl, and you've got a slippery mat that lets you easily slide underneath the car.

Out, damned spot!

Many garages and driveways are marred by unsightly—and sometimes dangerously slippery—grease stains from oil leaks or greasy tools. Prevent stains when you work by covering the area with newspapers or paper grocery bags. If your car is leaking even a little oil, place an unopened brown paper bag or a flattened cardboard box under the leak. Or scatter cat litter in the area; sweep it up whenever it gets saturated, and replace it with fresh litter as needed.

Contain dust with newspaper

Before you sweep out a really dusty area of your garage, shred a bunch of old newspaper, dampen it with warm water, and scatter it around the area. The soggy paper will keep the dust from rising and resettling as you're sweeping.

Stop garage door seepage with WD-40

If water seeps in through your garage door during a heavy rain, spray the seal on the door with WD-40. The seepage should stop even if the rain doesn't.

Grease Blotters Galore

They're smelly, they're ugly, and they're the automotive equivalent of the banana peel (and not in a good way): the grease spots on the garage floor or driveway. Happily, the self-sufficient methods for making them disappear are many.

Newspaper

Spread several thicknesses of newspaper over spots, thoroughly soak the paper with water, and weight it down. When the paper is dry, remove it—and the stain should come up with it.

Cornmeal

Mix together equal parts of baking soda and cornmeal and sprinkle the mixture over the spot. Let the powder sit and soak up the grease for a couple of hours, then sweep or vacuum the mess away.

Soda

Pour carbonated cola over the spot and hose it off with water.

Baking Soda

For tougher grease spots, sprinkle on baking soda and let it stand for about 3 or 4 hours, then scrub it with warm water and a stiff brush.

Laundry Stain Remover

Spray the area with laundry prewash stain remover. Let sit for about 10 minutes, then sprinkle with powdered detergent and scrub with a broom or stiff brush. Rinse with a hose.

Sawdust, Cat Litter, and Sand

Sprinkle the area with sand, sawdust, or cat litter and leave it 4 or 5 hours to absorb the grease. Then sweep it up.

Paint Thinner

For really tough spots, pour a little paint thinner over the spot and the surrounding area, sprinkle baking soda or cat litter on top, and then cover it with newspapers and let everything sit overnight. In the morning, remove the newspaper and sweep up the mess.

Hints for Cyclists

Shine your bike with furniture polish

Once your bike is nice and clean, you'll want to shine it up and show it off. Instead of using liquid or paste wax and spending time applying the wax to the bike's various tubes, joints, and hard-to-reach spots, all you really need to do is spray the bike all over with a furniture polish that contains wax—something you probably already have around the house.

Salt-and-lemon juice rust buster

Salt can cause metal to rust—yet it can also be used to *remove* rust. (Go figure.) If any rust spots appear on the handlebars or wheel rims of your bike, try this home remedy. In a small container, mix ⅓ cup salt with 2 tablespoons lemon juice to make a paste. Apply the paste to the rusted area with a dry cloth and rub it in. Rinse and dry it thoroughly, and then step back and admire your rust-free bike.

Maintain your chain with WD-40

The hardest part of a bicycle to clean is the chain. But you can make the job easier with WD-40. Turn the bike upside down and spray some WD-40 onto a soft, clean cloth. Rub the chain with the cloth a few links at a time. Move the pedals forward to work on a new section of chain.

Once the entire chain is clean, carefully dislodge it from the chain ring (the metal toothed wheel that engages it) and use a screwdriver or dull knife to remove any gunk that's lodged between the chain ring's teeth. That done, use a cloth to polish between the teeth with a back-and-forth flossing motion, and then reseat the chain.

Proving a Bike Is Yours

You know how susceptible bikes are to theft—and even though your bicycle has a serial number engraved on its frame, thieves can easily file it off. To make sure you can identify your bike should you ever find it in someone else's possession, remove the seat of the bike, roll your business card or a similar ID around a pencil, and push it inside the pipe supporting the seat. Once the seat is back in place, no one will think to look there. And won't the new bike "owner" be surprised when you disassemble the bike seat and pull out your ace in the hole!

Spray for a smooth ride

To keep the chain of your bicycle well lubricated, spray it with WD-40 and wipe off any excess with a soft cloth. You can also spray WD-40 into the cables and bearings to drive out moisture, and then on the springs in the seat to eliminate squeaking. Finally, spray the frame of the bike to keep dust from sticking to it.

Repair a slash with a dollar bill

If a sharp rock or anything else in the roadway slashes your tire, you can patch the puncture in the inner tube—but it will bulge out through the slash in the tire when you try to ride. How to prevent the bulge? After patching the inner tube, fold a dollar bill in quarters and tuck it between the inner tube and the tire slash—a quick fix that should hold you for the ride home.

Bent bike wheel?

If one of your bicycle's wheels gets bent and you don't have any tools at hand, try this temporary fix: Remove the wheel and smack it against a nearby tree. Check it for alignment, and then smack it again if necessary. When the wheel looks reasonably straight, put it back on the bike and, if feasible, ride to the nearest bike shop to have the wheel repaired or buy a new one.

Let Mother Nature help you with a flat tire

If you get a flat tire while cycling and don't have a repair kit with you, completely deflate the tire, turn the bike upside down, and pull one side of the bad tire out from the rim of the wheel. A good way to work it out is with the wide end of a house key, but any dull metal object will do. Once the tire is loose around one side, find some leaves and moss along the roadside and stuff them inside the rim. Then squeeze the tire back into place and ride straight home. The repair will let you ride (carefully) for a while, but not for long—so repair the flat properly as soon as possible.

Baby powder for motorcyclists?

Yes indeed. If you're a motorcyclist who likes to deck yourself out in leather before taking to the highway, sprinkle the seat with baby powder before you mount. The fine powder will make it easier for you to slide freely from side to side on the seat, assuring you of a smooth ride.

Keep your visor unfogged

To keep a motorcycle helmet visor from fogging up on the road, put a drop of dishwashing liquid on the inside, then rub it over the whole surface with your finger until it's no longer visible. Then kiss misty visors good-bye as you mount your bike and speed off.

Motorbike wash-time protectors

If your motorcycle gets caked with mud and road grease, you'll want to hose it down. When you do, be careful to keep the pressurized water stream away from the cables and controls. The easiest way is to cover them with plastic. Save the plastic sleeves that protect your morning newspaper and slip them over the handlebars at wash time. To keep water out of the ignition lock, fix a piece of masking tape over the keyhole.

Chapter Thirteen

Home Repairs Made Easy

In the last few years, do-it-yourself repairing (or upgrading, for that matter) has taken on a status that has elevated it from drudgery to sheer fun, with money-saving and often down-right stylish results. But when push comes to shove, do-it-yourselfers (DIYers, for short) like to fix and upgrade things for two reasons: pure unadulterated enjoyment and savings.

In the coming pages, we'll take everyday DIY-ing to the next level, and show you how you can save even more of the green stuff by using common household items to help you work faster, safer, and more efficiently. You don't have to be particularly handy to make use of our advice: These are basic, simple procedures, whether you're resetting a hinge screw or doing a little plumbing.

Though the emphasis here is on nontoxic alternatives to commercially available chemicals, we recommend you wear gloves, eye protection, and take other safety precautions as necessary.

Silence that squeaky hinge with **shaving cream!**

Window Insights

Rub out window scratches with toothpaste

Squeeze a small amount of toothpaste onto a soft cotton cloth and vigorously polish the scratch for a minute or two. Wipe off the excess with a damp rag and presto! The scratch is gone. Be sure to use plain, white paste—no gels or striped varieties. You can use an extra-whitening toothpaste; most have higher amounts of abrasive.

Stop cracks in their tracks with nail polish

You can buy yourself some time before replacing a cracked window by applying a couple of coats of clear nail polish to both sides of the crack. Once dry, the polish will seal any holes in the glass and contain the damage.

Stifle a rattle with a matchbook

A rattling window is sure to rattle your nerves, especially when you're trying to sleep. How can you ever silence that racket? Easily, with a book of matches. Slide the thin end of the matchbook in between the sash and the loose corner of the window frame. Wedge it in as far as you can, but leave at least a third of the book exposed for easy removal. Then give the window a few light tugs to make sure it won't shake on blustery nights. Sweet dreams!

Plug a drafty window leak

That drafty window is guaranteed to suck out precious heat from your home and raise your fuel bills. What can you do if it's wintertime and the caulk gun is all dried up? Simple. Once you've located the source of the draft (it's often along the top of the lower sash or in a corner between the sash and window frame) take two paper towels, sandwich them together, and fold them up from the bottom an inch at a time until you have a thick padded strip. Lay the pad over the air leak and secure it on all sides with masking tape.

Clip a busted slide

Is a broken corner slide preventing you from opening that window screen or aluminum storm window? Don't scrape your fingers trying to reach the spring. Reach for a paper clip instead. Partly open the clip, then use needle-nose pliers to bend the last $\frac{1}{4}$-inch of the wire to form a right angle. Slide the hook under the sash and use it to grab the slide from below. Push toward the center of the window to free it.

Fast fix for a major screen tear

A window screen is no match for a big dog's big paws. If you can't replace the screening material right away, make a temporary repair by attaching the loose screen to the frame with duct tape. First, clean the area with a cotton ball soaked in rubbing alcohol. Let it dry, then attach two facing strips of tape to the edge of the torn screen, leaving some excess tape along the bottom. Press the strips together, and attach the excess to the inside of the frame with another piece of duct tape. Be sure not to leave any gaps that can allow mosquitoes and other insects to enter.

Repair a Torn Screen

Why replace a whole window screen when its only defect is a few tiny holes?
Here's an easy three-step way to seal those small tears:

1

If possible, remove the screen and lay it on a flat surface on top of a few sheets of newspaper.

2

Use a toothpick or your fingertips to straighten out the torn threads and reduce the gaps between them.

3

Spread a small amount of epoxy, model airplane glue, or clear nail polish over the threads with a match or a piece of a matchbook cover; use the toothpick to open any clogs before the glue hardens.

4

Repeat the process until the glue has saturated the area around the tear. Give it 24 hours to dry, and your screen will be as good as new.

Open Sesame: DIY Door Fixes

Get the lead in

Forget about oil, which can do more harm than good to a stuck lock. The best lubricant for a lock's inner mechanism is graphite, and a good source of graphite is pencil lead. Rub a sharpened, soft lead pencil (No. 1 or No. 2) repeatedly against the companion key, and insert it several times into the lock. Perform this trick twice a year to keep locks in top working condition.

Remove a broken key

It happens all the time: Keys get old and bent and wind up breaking off inside the lock. If you can't enter your house or apartment through another door, run to a neighbor to borrow a couple of items before calling a locksmith. First, try removing the broken piece with tweezers. If that won't work, apply a drop of super glue to the end of the piece that's still on your key chain.

Line it up with the part inside the lock, and carefully insert it. Hold it in place for 40–60 seconds and then slowly pull out the key.

Light up your lock

You know what it's like to come home to a dark porch and have to feel around for the lock on your front door. If you never want to go bump in the night again, dab a few drops of glow-in-the-dark paint around the keyholes of your exterior locks with a cotton swab or small paintbrush. Do the same for any dead-bolt locks on the inside of your house as well, which will make exiting much easier in the event of a power outage or other emergency.

Polish a loose doorknob

A wobbly doorknob is often the result of a loose setscrew (a tiny screw found on the doorknob shank), which keeps the knob firmly in

SILENCE A PERSISTENT SQUEAK

If a freshly oiled door hinge continues to squeak and squawk, the most likely cause is rust, dirt, and other debris on the hinge pin. To silence it for good, use a heavy book to prop the door closed and then remove the offending hinge pin. Give it a good scrubbing with fine-grade **steel wool**, and then blow off any dust or loose steel threads, then rub it with some oil. Tap the hinge pin back into place, then relish the quiet that ensues.

place on the spindle. Everyday usage can cause setscrews to loosen, but you can keep them in place by brushing on a little clear nail polish right after you tighten them.

Pamper a noisy hinge

Is that squeaking door hinge making *you* unhinged? A few drops of baby oil applied around the pin should solve the problem. Can't find the oil, and you're out of WD-40? A bit of cooking spray, petroleum jelly, or even shaving cream can be used to quiet a squeaky hinge.

Reset a hinge screw

A loose hinge will cause a door to stick or become difficult to open or close. Tightening the hinge screws usually solves the problem, but if an undamaged screw won't grip, it means the hole is stripped or stretched out.

To fix it, slide a magazine or two to prop the opened door, if necessary, and then remove the hinge. Loosely fill the screw hole with wooden toothpicks or matchsticks soaked in wood glue. Keep them flush with the frame by carefully trimming off any protruding ends with a utility knife. When you screw back the hinge, the extra wood should hold the screw firmly in place.

Pop goes the rusted bolt

Loosen a rusted bolt by rubbing it with a few tablespoons of carbonated soda.

Unstick a stuck door

If your front door sticks because it rubs against the floor or threshold, try this simple fix. Duct-tape all four edges of a coarse sheet of sandpaper to the floor where the door rubs, then open and close the door over the sandpaper until it swings smoothly.

Curiosity Corner
And You Think *You* Have an Old Door!

It may not be the world's oldest door, but a battered, seldom-used storeroom door in Westminster Abbey was recently declared the oldest door in Great Britain.

. According to a dendrochronology test (the scientific analysis of tree-ring growth patterns), the door's five vertical planks came from a single tree that was felled between 1032 AD and 1064 AD. That date establishes it as part of the original abbey built during the reign of Edward the Confessor and further distinguishes it as the only surviving Anglo-Saxon-era door in England. Some experts additionally believe the door's 6½-foot-high-by-4½-foot-wide size and double-sided form would have made it unique among the Saxon abbey doors, and that it might have even secured the entrance to Edward's chapter house.

Warwick Rodwell, Westminster Abbey's consultant archaeologist, credits the late timber expert Cecil Hewett with inspiring the project. Upon seeing the old door in the 1970s, Hewett observed it could be "very early." Very early indeed!

Walls and Ceilings

Find a wall stud with a razor

Don't have a stud finder? Use an electric razor instead. Switch on the razor and place it flush against the wall. Move it slowly over the wall, and note the sound of its hum. When the razor moves over a stud, the pitch of the buzz will rise.

White-out wall and ceiling flaws

If you've ever used a typewriter, you know how valuable a small bottle of white correction fluid can be. What you may *not* know is that it's even more useful around the home for covering up small stains and blemishes on white walls, moldings, and ceilings. Simply dab it on the defect, and it's gone. When touching up glossy surfaces, coat the dried correction fluid with a little clear nail polish.

Wipe away wallpaper paste

Removing old wallpaper can be a pain, but what's even worse is contending with old wallpaper paste. A window squeegee can make the job a lot easier (and neater). Dip the squeegee in a bucket of very hot water (add 1 cup of vinegar for extra-strength paste). Use the spongy side to apply the solution to the wall; then flip it over and use the blade to remove the glue. Wipe the goop off the blade frequently with a damp rag.

Cover nail holes without spackle

Out of spackle? Before you head over to the hardware store, look in your medicine cabinet—a bit of plain white toothpaste should do the job. You can also fill small holes in plaster and drywall with a paste of equal parts baking soda and white glue. Or you could mix 2 tablespoons salt and 2 tablespoons cornstarch with just enough water to make a stiff putty.

Stick on a patch

Some people think the lack of wall studs makes it far more difficult to patch a hole in drywall. But they're wrong. In fact, all that's needed to set the patch is a couple of paint-mixing sticks (free at most hardware stores)—or, if it's a small hole, Popsicle sticks. Glue the sticks to the back of the wall or attach them with drywall screws. Once the sticks are secure, add the drywall plug, tape, and joint compound.

Secure a screw

An unanchored wall screw may work loose over time as the hole surrounding it expands. Take up the slack by cutting one or two twist ties (the

Find the stud with an *electric razor!*

kind used on bread bags) into strips, equal in length to the screw. Bunch them together in your fingers, stuff the hole, and then reset the screw. If the hole has significantly widened, use steel wool, small pieces of cardboard, or a cotton ball soaked in carpenter's glue or white glue. Let the glue dry for at least 24 hours before placing any weight on the screw.

Banish ceiling stains

Get rid of ugly ceiling stains by donning a pair of goggles and aiming a long-handled sponge mop moistened with equal parts water and chlorine bleach at the ceiling. Then scrub away, keeping at it until the stains are gone.

Fix small cracks

Don't replaster a ceiling just to cover up a few small cracks. Try this instead: Make a paste of equal parts baking soda and white glue and use it to fill in the gaps. It's easier, and it really does the job—but it only works with white ceilings, of course.

Match a patch

When plastering a section of ceiling, it's worth putting in the extra effort to do the job right. Once the plaster is level, try to match the texture of the surrounding ceiling. You can usually come pretty close by applying some gentle touches with a small scrub brush, a pocket comb, or a dry abrasive sponge.

Simple (and Safe) Wallpaper Removal

You don't have to rent a commercial steamer or use toxic chemicals to strip your old wall covering. Here are two easy methods that are not only nontoxic but surprisingly inexpensive, too.

1

Fill two-thirds of a spray bottle with hot water and one-third with liquid fabric softener. Spray a section of wallpaper until it's saturated. Let the solution soak in for 15–30 minutes, peel or scrape off the covering, and repeat. Keep the bottle warm by storing it in a pot of hot water between uses.

2

Use a garden sprayer or a paint roller to apply a solution of equal parts white vinegar and hot water. Saturate an area of wallpaper, wait 10 minutes, then peel it off. For extensive jobs, work with the windows open; vinegar is nontoxic but has a strong odor.

Flooring Fix-Ups

Give scratched floors the boot

Light scratches in wood flooring can often be successfully camouflaged with shoe polish. Just be sure to shop around and find the best color match for your floor. Apply the polish with a soft cloth, let it dry, then buff with a slightly dampened rag. Now that's a quick 'n' easy cover-up!

Dealing with dents

An easy repair for shallow dents on wood floors is to fill them with clear nail polish or clear shellac. Allow at least 24 hours for it to dry. The wood's natural color will show through, causing the blemish to vanish.

Iron off a broken tile

To lift a damaged vinyl tile, cover it with a cloth, then give it a rubdown with a clothes iron on a medium setting. Use slow, even strokes. The heat from the iron will eventually loosen the glue and the tile, making it easy for you to pry it up with a putty knife. If you don't have an iron at hand, try using a hair dryer.

Wash away carpet glue

Removed your carpet only to find old glue stuck to the subfloor? Don't scrape it off; instead, mix a solution of 3 parts hot water and 1 part vinegar. Spread the mixture over the subfloor and let sit for 30 minutes. The softened glue will come right off with a putty knife.

Stick up a rug

If your favorite braided rug is coming apart at the seams, grab the epoxy or hot glue gun. Apply a small amount of adhesive to the outside edges of the separated braids and pinch them together until the glue dries. A similar approach is used to repair slight pulls in a Berber carpet. Squeeze a bit of glue into the base of the loose stitch and push it back into place. If the pulled stitch is very long, you can trim it down with a sharp knife or scissors before gluing. The weaves of looped Berbers may require you to thread a toothpick through a loop to keep it free of glue.

Renew a burned carpet

To remove slight burns and singes from carpeting, use a tweezers to lift the threads and then carefully slice off the charred tips with a sharp scissors, razor blade, or utility knife. Trim the threads as little as possible to avoid leaving an indentation. The longer and denser the material, the better your results are likely to be.

Stone-cold clean

Tools covered with flooring adhesive can be a royal pain in the neck to clean. So instead of scrubbing and scouring, place them in a plastic bag and put it in the freezer overnight. In the morning, the glue will be rock solid and easily chipped off with a hammer and wedge. Just be sure to wear goggles to protect your eyes from any airborne shards.

A GRATER FIX FOR GASHED VINYL

Gash in your vinyl floor? Find a small, spare piece of vinyl and grind it down with a **cheese grater**. Remove any chunks and mix the gratings with clear nail polish. Use the mixture to fill in the dent.

Heating Up, Cooling Down

Do like Grandma used to do

Increase the warmth and moisture inside your home on bitterly cold days by just simmering a large pot of water on the stove. Don't forget to periodically check the pot, and refill the water as needed. Toss a few cloves, some orange peel, and one or two cinnamon sticks into the pot, and you'll have a delightful air freshener as well.

Get incensed about drafts

To pinpoint the often mysterious source of house drafts—and where you'll need to add or renew your weather stripping—wait for a windy day, then light a stick of incense. Start with the window or door nearest the draft. Hold the incense in a bottom corner of the frame and slowly raise it. The smoke should travel up in a straight line; when it moves sharply in one direction or another, you've located a leak. Repeat the process for all the sealed openings around the house.

Block door drafts

A drafty door can raise your fuel bills all year round. Until you can replace the weather stripping, try blocking the air leak with a homemade draft shield. Get an old tube sock, or cut a sleeve off an old shirt or jacket, and fill it with sand, rice, or foam padding weighed down with a few small stones. Sew the open ends and keep it against the crack at the bottom of the door. For safety's sake, prevent stumbles by spray-painting the draft-blocker a bright color.

Free Window Insulation (and More)

Hold on to the soft foam packing material used for toys, sporting goods, and electronics items. It can come in handy when insulating the gaps around window fans and air-conditioning units.

Even your air conditioner's old foam filters can be called back into duty as insulation material; just be sure to wash them well in some soapy water and let them dry completely before using.

Also, don't forget to recycle those large pieces of rigid foam packing from major appliances and other products. When you store your air conditioner for the winter, place sections of foam under the corners to protect floors from gouges and scratches.

Straighten a bent fin

Bent condenser or evaporator fins restrict air circulation and cause room air conditioners to operate less efficiently. The problem is easily preventable, however. Remove the outside grille and inspect the foil-like fins on the machine at least once a year. Straighten any bent ones by inserting a spatula or pocket comb alongside and running it up and down.

Keep air conditioners running clean

A dirty filter obstructs a room air conditioner's airflow, which decreases cooling, increases power consumption, and results in higher utility bills. Check your air conditioner filters every four weeks and clean them when most of the surface is matted with dust. You can clean "slide-out" mesh filters simply by spraying them with a garden hose. Wash pliable soft foam filters in a bucket of warm water mixed with 2 tablespoons baking soda. Wring filters out well when done and let them air-dry thoroughly before reinserting them.

Degrease a dirty fan

Even occasional use can cause a rotating fan to collect dust and grime on its blades and grilles. Besides spreading allergens throughout your home, the built-up dirt reduces the fan's air output and places unwanted stress on the motor.

To clean a dirty fan (which you should do twice a year), unplug the power cord, and remove the housing. Vacuum off any loose dust using a soft brush attachment, then wipe down the blade and grilles with a rag or sponge dipped in solution of ¼ cup household ammonia and ¼ teaspoon dishwashing liquid in 1 gallon warm water. Make sure all the parts are dry before you reassemble them.

Household Superstar!

12 Neat Home Repair Uses for Nail Polish

1. Mark off liquid measurement levels (pint, quart, etc.) inside a bucket.

2. Mix with ground vinyl dust to repair a gash in vinyl flooring.

3. Fill in light dents in wood floors and wooden furniture.

4. Fill in imprinted numbers on hand tools to make them easier to read.

5. Keep knobs on dressers and cabinets from loosening by dipping screws into clear nail polish before tightening.

6. Coat brass handles and knobs with clear nail polish to prevent tarnish.

7. Paint the buttons of a remote control or the edges of a keyhole with glow-in-the-dark nail polish to make them easier to spot.

8. Stop rust from forming on screws, nails, and fasteners by covering them with clear nail polish.

9. Coat scratches on metal appliances to prevent rust.

10. Apply to the bottoms of shaving cream cans and other metal containers to keep them from leaving rust marks.

11. Indicate measurements on the handle of a hammer.

12. Use clear nail polish to seal small tears in window shades and window screens.

Finessing Furniture

That light through yonder window is damaging

Sunlight can wreak havoc on your furniture, but you can restore it to its former luster with plain old petroleum jelly. Use a soft cloth to rub a good amount into the wood until the finish perks up. Remove any leftover ointment with a clean cloth, and then polish the wood to renew its shine.

Tea time for grime

To remove accumulated grime on wooden furniture, put two tea bags in a quart of boiling water, and let it cool. Dip a soft cloth into the solution, wring it out, and then test it in an inconspicuous area on the table. If you're pleased with the results, wipe down one section of the piece at a time. Continue dipping, wringing, and wiping until all the old polish has been removed. Let it dry, buff with a soft dry cloth, then stand back and watch it glow.

Steam out a dent

You can usually repair a small, shallow dent in wood furniture with a warm, damp cloth and a steam iron. Fold the cloth and place it over the dent, then press down with the tip of a warm iron for several seconds. If the dent doesn't swell, repeat the process, but don't overdo it. The idea is to provide just enough moisture to swell the wood back to its original size.

Repair veneer edging with an iron

If veneer stripping or edging is bulging or popping up from the surface of a piece of furniture, lay a warm, damp cloth over it, and press down with the tip of a warm iron for several seconds. Once it's flattened, roll it with a rolling pin.

Unstick a drawer

Wooden drawers can become stuck for all sorts of reasons, but the most common cause is excessive humidity. Although you can't see it, the wood fibers actually swell from the extra moisture in the air. To shrink them back to their original size, use a hair dryer on a warm setting, directing it to the drawer slides and the drawer itself—which should open with ease after a few minutes. For stubborn stuck drawers, try rubbing the sides, bottom edges, and slides with lip balm, a bar of soap or paraffin wax, or beeswax.

Lubricate metal drawer runners

Rust and other deposits can cause metal drawer runners to lock up or to move unevenly. Keep them running smoothly and rust-free by lubricating them occasionally with petroleum jelly or WD-40.

Hassle-free hardware

Want to keep the shine in your decorative brass handles and knobs? Give them a coat of clear nail polish or clear lacquer. This simple task will provide years of protection against skin oils and tarnishing.

Revive sagging cane seats

The more use it gets, the more a cane seat is likely to sag. To tighten it, first soak two or three dishtowels in hot water and wring them out lightly. Now turn the chair over and lay the hot towels on the bottom of the seat for about 30 minutes. Remove the towels and let the seat air-dry, and then give the cane at least 12 hours to shrink back into place.

Wipe Out Water Rings

All it takes is one sweating glass or steamy plate and you'll be forever reminded of it in the form of an ugly white water ring on your wood tabletop.

You can often dry up a fresh ring using a hair dryer on a low setting. Most established rings, however, require some form of abrasion. Here are five time-tested methods.

Ashes and Mayonnaise

Mix the ash from one cigarette in a table-spoon of mayonnaise. Dip a rough cloth in the mixture and rub it vigorously into the ring. Polish when done.

Salt and Lemon Oil

Pour a little lemon oil onto a rag and dip it in ½ tea-spoon of salt. Gently rub the rag over the spot. If the ring starts to lighten, repeat the process using vine-gar instead of lemon oil. (Not recommended for shellac finishes.)

Lemon Oil and Steel Wool

Lightly rub the stain with #0000 extra-fine–grade steel wool dipped in lemon oil. Once the ring is gone, polish the table with lemon oil and buff with a clean cloth.

Salt and Corn Oil

Mix equal parts of corn oil and salt, rub it into the ring, and then polish it off with a clean cloth.

Baking Soda and Toothpaste

Mix equal amounts of white toothpaste and baking soda and apply it to a rag. Rub in the paste moving parallel to the wood grain, wipe it off, and then pol-ish with lemon oil.

Tighten loose joints

A bit of wood glue is usually all you need to secure a wobbly chair leg or rail. If the joint is too loose, however, glue alone may not do the job. An easy way to solve the problem is to increase the width of the tenon (the contoured end of the loose piece) by coating it with wood glue and wrapping it with cotton thread or a wood shaving. (If you decide on the latter, choose a shaving that's uniformly thick for a consistent fit). Let it dry, then glue the tenon back into the mortise.

Reglue it right

Most wobbly furniture can be fixed by simply regluing the parts back together—but since new glue won't stick to old dried glue, the key is to get rid of the old stuff. One of the best tools for getting rid of dried glue is the small wire-bristle brush you use for cleaning battery posts and terminals. The external brush (shaped like a pine tree) is ideal for removing glue from mortises and holes, while the internal brush (shaped like a cup) is perfect for scraping dried glue from tenons and dowel ends.

Paste over a minor burn

Although fewer people smoke in their homes these days, burn marks on wooden furniture are a more common problem than you might think. If the scorch doesn't go below the finish, you can usually rub it out with a paste made of fine firewood ash and lemon juice (2 parts ash to 1 part juice). Wipe the area clean, then polish and wax.

Sticky Business

The list of items that can wind up stuck on a tabletop is as long as it is varied. About the only thing that's true in all cases, though, is that you should never simply yank off the offending object, because you may wind up damaging the tabletop's finish. To unstick something, follow these instructions:

- A piece of paper placed under a wet or hot object can stick like glue. First, carefully peel off as much of the paper as possible, then dab the remainder with a rag dipped in some olive oil. Let the oil soak in several minutes, and wipe away the residue with the dry side of the rag.

- If the youngest member of the family has decorated your tabletop with stickers or postage stamps, cover them with a coat of petroleum jelly and let it sit for 2–4 hours. Use an old credit card to gently scrape off the stickers. Repeat if necessary; polish when done.

- If said child parks her lollipop on the table, scrape away as much of the candy as you can, then squirt a little baby oil on top of what's left. Give it a few minutes to soak in before sliding off the residue. Buff it to a shine. Baby oil also works well for bubble gum, stuck glassware, and candle wax.

- Dried airplane glue, epoxy, and other types of household cement are notoriously difficult to remove, but they can sometimes be softened with an application of cold cream, peanut butter, or vegetable oil.

Scratch Begone!

Instant fix for scratched woodwork

Your guests will be walking through the door any minute when you happen to notice several fresh, light scratches on your dark-wood wall unit. What can you possibly do on such short notice? Rush to the kitchen, fetch a small cup or container, and mix 1 teaspoon of instant coffee in 1 tablespoon vegetable oil or water. Apply the mixture with a cotton ball and let it dry. (Not recommended for valuable antiques or shellac finishes.)

Cover scratches in leather

Camouflage those unsightly scratches in leather furniture with a like colored permanent marker. Before you start, test the marker on an inconspicuous part of the couch to make sure it's a good match. Work slowly and carefully when tracing over the scratch. Medium or fine-point markers work best overall; extra-fine tips may deepen a scratch while thick markers often leave a visible "edging" around repairs.

Fill cracks with coffee

Is that small crack, nick, or gouge all you can see each time you look at your dark wood dresser? Reach for the instant coffee. Mix 2–3 tablespoons with just enough water to make a thick paste; for wood with red tones, add a few drops of iodine. Put the paste on a small putty knife or a disposable plastic knife and use it to fill the crack. Remove any excess around the edges with a barely damp cloth. Let the paste dry completely, then buff with furniture wax.

"Homeopathic" scratch care

Most light scratches on wood can be repaired without a trip to the hardware store. That's

---

make your own
Leather Rejuvenator

Heat, sunlight, and simple wear and tear can cause leather furniture to dry out and crack. Restore some of the lost pliability and prevent the cracks from spreading by cleaning, oiling, and polishing.

Liven-It-Up Leather Lotion

Olive oil rubbed into the leather is left to soak in overnight before you restore leather upholstery to its original shine.

> 1 cup water
> 1 cup white vinegar
> 1 teaspoon household ammonia
> ½ to 1 cup olive oil
> Furniture cream

1. Combine water, vinegar, and ammonia in a pail and stir to mix. Pour olive oil into a small bowl.

2. Dip a sponge into the water and vinegar solution, wring it out, and use it to wet a section of upholstery.

3. Rub oil into the wet leather with your fingertips, a rag, or a cotton ball. Let soak in overnight.

4. The next day, shine leather with furniture cream and buff with a soft cloth.

---

because masking a scratch is simply a matter of covering it up or adequately lubricating the exposed wood fibers. What's truly amazing is the number of items you probably already have around your home that can get the job done.

Nuts to
wood scratches!

Regardless of which method you use, wax the surface when done.

- Conceal scratches with closely matched shoe polish, a melted crayon, a permanent marker, or some iodine.

- Use the meat of a Brazil nut, walnut, or pecan. Rub the nut over the scratch several times, then vigorously massage the oil into the scrape with your thumb.

- Can't find the nutcracker? Rub in a little peanut butter or mayonnaise instead. Wipe it off with a damp rag after 30 minutes or so.

- If that's too messy, try a little baby oil, or mix 1 tablespoon olive oil or vegetable oil with 1 tablespoon lemon juice. Apply it with a soft cloth, then buff it off after 30–45 minutes.

- Cover scratches with a generous amount of petroleum jelly. Let it soak for 24 hours, then remove the excess with a soft cloth.

Wax away hairline scratches

High-gloss lacquer finishes are prone to developing hairline scratches when dishes or other items are slid across the surface. You can often get rid of these light scratches with car wax, which contains a light abrasive. Test the wax first on a bottom edge or other inconspicuous area to make sure it won't discolor or damage the finish. Once you're set, apply the wax to a soft cloth and polish using a steady circular motion.

Woodworking Tips

Make customized wood putty

When working with specific types of wood, save some of the finest sawdust produced by your sanders. Mix a handful of the sawdust with ordinary white wood glue until it becomes a thick paste, then overfill the crack. Let dry, then lightly sand. Note: Cracks filled with adhesive-based putty will not accept stain the same way that solid wood does.

Instant wood putty

Need some wood putty in a hurry for an emergency repair on an inexpensive piece of furniture? Mix a couple tablespoons of spackling paste with instant coffee until you achieve the desired shade of brown. Fill in the crack and smooth with a damp rag.

Pluck some putty

An old guitar pick makes a great tool for applying small amounts of putty to fill nail holes and small cracks in wood. An easy solution with no strings attached!

Soften wood filler

Acetone-based cellulose wood fillers (one being Plastic Wood) are designed to dry quickly. If you notice that your acetone filler has started to stiffen in the can, you can soften it by adding a little acetone nail polish remover. Stir in just enough to bring the filler to the right consistency or it will become too runny to use. Note: There's no saving filler that's already hardened.

Get rid of glue with vinegar

Don't despair when you get a hardened glob of glue on your woodwork. Cover it with a

How to Identify Finishes

If you're about to strip a piece of furniture but don't know how it's finished, do this test to see which solvent to use. (Note: Test solvents first on a hidden section if you don't intend to strip the whole thing.)

1. Start by moistening a rag with some rubbing alcohol and rubbing vigorously. If the finish softens, it's shellac.
2. If the finish is unaffected, brush on one or two coats of turpentine. If the turpentine loosens the finish, it's varnish.
3. Still not budging? Try a coat of lacquer thinner. If that does the job, it's a lacquer finish.
4. If alcohol, turpentine, and lacquer thinner won't work, the piece has a polyurethane finish and requires a chemical stripper.

rag soaked in warm white vinegar and leave it overnight. The glue will slide off with ease in the morning. Vinegar will also soften old glued joints—and even that last bit of white or yellow glue that's hardening in the bottom of the bottle. Just add a few drops of vinegar to the bottle and let it sit for an hour or two. Shake well, drain the vinegar, and repeat the process as necessary.

The last straw for glue spills

Keep a bunch of plastic drinking straws nearby when working in the wood shop; they come in handy when working with adhesives and lubricants. If you use too much wood glue along a seam, for instance, simply fold a straw in half and use the folded edge to scoop up the excess.

Stop stripper drips

The next time you need to strip a table or a chair, place the legs inside recycled tuna cans or aluminum pie pans. The containers will catch the drips, which, besides keeping your work-space cleaner, will let you recycle the stripper for a second coat.

Flip a stripped finish

Stop off in the kitchen before stripping that next piece of furniture. The flat, flexible blade on an old plastic spatula is exactly what you've been looking for to scrape off used stripper. Hold the spatula from the blade in a reverse position and push it in a straight, steady motion to remove the old finish.

Better ways to stain

Put those old pairs of panty hose to work when staining furniture. A rolled up piece of nylon hose makes a great alternative to a cotton cloth or a rag. Not only does it drip less, but it won't leave behind any lint.

A leftover paint roller also makes a terrific stain applicator. Cut a 9-inch roller into three equal pieces. Whether affixed to an applicator or held in your hand, a roller holds more stain than a brush and applies it more evenly than a rag.

Baby the end grain

Want to save a few dollars? Don't spend them on a commercial sealer when finishing your next woodworking project. Instead, seal the end grain with baby oil (or its unscented cousin, mineral oil). It will work just as well as the stuff you get from the hardware store when it comes to keeping the color uniform by preventing the end from soaking up too much stain.

Rust Busters

In the workshop …

Remove rust from knives, screwdrivers, and other tools by rubbing them with a slice of **raw potato** dipped in salt.

Scour rusty tools and machine parts with a steel wool soap pad dipped in **turpentine**.

Dip a rag into a paste made from 4 tablespoons **salt** and 2 tablespoons **lemon juice** to remove rust spots on chrome and other metallic surfaces.

Apply a thin coat of **WD-40** or **petroleum jelly** to wrenches, saw blades, screwdrivers, shears, or pliers to keep them rust-free during extended periods of non-use.

Rub down tools with **hair conditioner** to help prevent rusting.

Drop in a few recycled **silica gel packs** (the kind found in a new pair of shoes and other leather products) to keep rust out your toolbox. Ditto a few pieces of **blackboard chalk** or **charcoal briquettes** wherever you store tools in your workshop.

Around the house …

Rub rust marks on stainless steel with **lighter fluid**, then scrub with a damp sponge sprinkled with scouring powder. Rinse thoroughly.

Plunge a rusty kitchen knife into a large **onion** a few times, and it may end up rust-free.

Brush rust stains on porcelain with **toothpaste** (tool of choice: old toothbrush).

Mix **salt** with **turpentine** to remove rust on most surfaces.

Remove rust stains left by metal furniture on patio paving stones by wetting the stain and topping it with **powder** used to make citrus-flavored drinks (think lemon or orange Kool-Aid).

Coat a nick on a metal appliance with clear **nail polish** to keep it from rusting.

Rub rust rings from metal cans off of kitchen and bathroom countertops with **car wax**.

Put a **coffee filter** in a cast iron skillet to absorb moisture and prevent rust.

Help Around the Kitchen

Rub out scorch marks

If you spot a scorch mark on your laminate countertop, don't reach for the abrasive cleanser; chances are you'll only remove the finish. If the burn isn't too deep, buff it out with car wax or a mixture of toothpaste and baking soda.

A fast fix for dents

If the color hasn't been altered, you can disguise dents and scratches on practically any kitchen surface—including wood, glass, and even some types of tile—with clear nail polish. Brush on the polish in thin coats, letting it dry between applications. When you're done, smooth the polish with a piece of very fine grit sandpaper, then buff the area with a soft cloth.

Save a rusty dishwasher rack

But how? With pieces of flexible, clear plastic tubing sold at hardware stores. For most racks, tubing with an inside diameter of ⅛ inch works best. Cut the tubing into ¼-inch lengths and slip them over the rack tops.

Check the fridge gasket

If your frost-free refrigerator/freezer is more than five years old, inspect its rubber gaskets for leaks at least once a year. The easiest method is to place a bill of currency halfway inside, shut the door, and tug on the bill. Repeat the process in several spots around the seal. The bill should hold firmly; if it's easy to pull out, the gasket needs to be repaired or replaced.

Add ballast to your freezer

Freezers work at maximum efficiency only when they are at least two-thirds full. If you

What's the Story?
The Mother of All Dishwashers

Homeowners the world over owe a debt of gratitude to Josephine Garis Cochrane of Shelbyville, Illinois. In 1886, Cochrane, a Victorian-era socialite, invented the first automatic dishwasher to prevent her servants from breaking the family china when they hand washed it. Interestingly, Cochrane was not the first inventor in her family; her maternal great-grandfather, John Fitch, received a patent for the steamboat in 1791. (The "father of steam navigation," Robert Fulton, didn't build his first steamship until nine years after Fitch's death in 1798.)

At a time when women were all but shut out of commerce and trade, Cochrane's hand-operated Garis Cochrane Dishwashing Machine was the hit of the 1893 World's Columbian Exposition in Chicago and subsequently became a staple in many hotels and restaurants.

It wasn't long before Cochrane's invention spawned numerous imitators and competitors, both in the United States and overseas. Yet, her Crescent Washing Machine Company continued producing dishwashers according to her designs well after her death in 1913. In 1926, Crescent was purchased by Hobart Manufacturing Co., which later sold dishwashers under the KitchenAid name, a brand now owned by Whirlpool.

Test the seal on your refrigerator door with a **dollar bill!**

don't have enough food to freeze, add some bulk by filling a few plastic soda bottles or milk jugs with water and placing them in your freezer. You can easily remove the ice ballast when you get food to replace it.

No-stick kitchen drawers

Most kitchen drawers work on a guide-and-track system. That is, rounded guides on the drawer keep it moving back and forth on tracks mounted inside the cabinet. Accumulations of dust and other impediments can slow down drawers or cause them to stick. Keep them moving freely by spraying the tracks and guides with a little WD-40 once or twice a year.

Cabinet doors banging?

If your wooden cabinet doors always close with a bit of a bang, soften the blow by sticking bumpers at each door's top and bottom corners. Inexpensive door bumpers are one solution, but perhaps a little too obvious for the creative do-it-yourselfer. Instead, try pressing small circular bandages (also called spot bandages) into service, testing to see if you need a double layer for each bumper to silence the bang.

Repair instead of replacing

If you've ever bought a replacement part for a kitchen appliance, you're probably still recovering from sticker shock. The truth is many nonmechanical parts can be easily repaired for just pennies. For instance, a broken handle on a microwave oven or a cracked dishwasher arm can often be easily reattached with some two-part epoxy. Likewise, a little caulk can be used to patch a small crack in your refrigerator's rubber gasket, while a few strips of duct tape can usually mend a busted tab on a refrigerator door shelf. Remember: Replace only that which can't be fixed.

Plumbing Secrets

No plunger, no problem

Use a rubber ball or tennis ball instead. Secure the ball in a vise and cut it in half with a hacksaw or a utility knife. Fit the concave side over the drain and press down with your palms or the base of your thumbs to create suction.

Clamp down on loose plungers

A plunger with a loose handle makes every job more difficult and can even be dangerous if the handle slips out or breaks off. If your plunger handle is easily separated from the suction cup, tighten it by placing an adjustable hose clamp around the base of the cup.

Saucer as sink shield

Don't let your work go down the drain! Before you take apart a faucet or nearby fixture, take a small plate or saucer out of the kitchen cabinet. Then simply place it upside down over the sink drain to prevent any small pieces from getting lost.

Loosen a stuck faucet

You've tried everything, but that faucet handle won't budge. Relax and have a cool soft drink. After a few sips, pour out several ounces over the faucet. Give the carbonation 5–10 minutes to loosen any rust or corrosion around the faucet—followed by a few gentle strikes with a mallet. Mission accomplished.

Plug pipes before soldering

It's almost impossible to solder a crack in a copper water pipe; the heat turns the dripping water to steam, which keeps solder from adhering. An easy way to overcome the problem is to stuff a piece of white bread 8–10 inches down

---

make your own
Drain Cleaner

Even if you clean out your dirty pots and pans before washing them, grease can still collect inside the drain. Ditto for conditioners and other hair products used in the shower. Use this potent nontoxic mixture twice a month in your kitchen and bathroom drains to help keep them clog-free.

Aunt Ida's Grease Buster

This powder gets its powerful punch from the chemical reaction between the alkalinity of the baking soda and the acidity of the cream of tartar. Be sure to keep your face pointed away from the drain when adding the water, which triggers the reaction.

    1 cup baking soda
    1 cup salt
    ¼ up cream of tartar
    1 cup boiling water

1. Put baking soda, salt, and cream of tartar in a glass canister, put the lid on tight, and shake well to mix.

2. Pour ¼ cup of the mixture down a dry drain and follow it with 1 cup boiling water.

3. Wait for the bubbles to subside, then flush with cold water for 3–4 minutes.

Blow-dry a *frozen water pipe* to get things moving

the pipe before you start. The bread will soak up the water, giving you time to solder the pipe. It will also break up and be flushed away once the water is turned back on.

Hose off pipe leaks

Need a quick patch for a leaking water pipe? Cut off a section of old garden hose or rubber tubing that's several inches wider than the affected area of pipe. Slice it lengthwise, then wrap the hose around the leak. Attach it with three hose clamps: one on each end and one in the middle.

Blow-dry a frozen pipe

If a water pipe freezes in the winter cold, close the shutoff valve and open the nearest faucet. Then, starting at the faucet, use a hair dryer on a medium setting to thaw the pipe. Be sure to keep the dryer moving so the pipe won't get too hot in one spot; a sudden shift in temperature can cause pipes to crack. After it thaws, wrap the pipe in fiberglass or foam insulation to keep it from freezing in the future.

Prevent pipes from freezing in winter

Cold snap on the way? You can keep pipes from freezing during the winter months by pouring 1 cup of salt followed by 1 quart of boiling water down your drains once every week or so.

Bathroom Basics

Fix scratched surfaces

Scratches in your acrylic bathtub? Pick up some metal polish. Apply it with a soft cloth using a circular motion. The light abrasive in the polish lifts out most fine scratches. To smooth out deeper nicks and scrapes, dampen them with a bit of water and then gently rub with a piece of very fine wet-dry sandpaper before polishing.

Scratches on enamel tubs and surfaces can be covered with a few thin coats of epoxy-based touch-up paint (available at most hardware stores) or liquid paper. Clean the damaged area with some rubbing alcohol on a cotton ball. Let the alcohol thoroughly evaporate before applying the paint.

Fill tubs before caulking

Before you caulk a seam around a bathtub, fill the tub with water. The extra weight will widen the gap in the joint between the tub and the wall, which makes for a thicker seal that's less likely to crack or tear later on. Just make sure you can reach all the way around the tub before turning on the water.

A smarter, simpler way to save water

Some folks put bricks inside their toilet tanks to reduce the amount of water per flush. It's a good way to conserve water, but it can be lousy for the toilet because bricks submerged in water often break up and cause leaks. A better option is to use recycled plastic bottles filled with sand or water. Remove any labels and check that the bottle is tightly sealed before placing it in the tank.

Detect Toilet Tank Leaks

A continuously running toilet is telling you that something is leaking, so don't ignore it. It might be annoying, but it's also wasting up to 2 gallons of water per minute and can cost you plenty in higher water bills.

To check for leaks, lift off the tank cover and make sure the water level isn't too high. Gently bend the float arm downward (or use a screwdriver to turn the ballcock adjustment screw counterclockwise). If that doesn't stop the water from running, you can easily pinpoint the source of the leak by adding 1–2 teaspoons of food coloring to the tank water. Don't flush the toilet for an hour or two.

- If the food coloring appears in the water inside the bowl, the leak is coming through the valve—in which case the flapper needs to be repaired or replaced.

- If the water collects outside the bowl, look in the tank and make sure the refill tube is properly attached (a loose or misdirected tube can shoot water under the lid). If the tube isn't the problem, the tank itself is leaking. Eureka!

Down in the Basement

Sound off on circuits

Labeling the breaker box is often one of those perpetual chores on homeowners' to-do lists—and for good reason, since an unlabeled breaker box forces you to locate circuits by trial and error. Here's a trick to speed the process: Before heading down to the basement, plug a radio into an outlet on the same circuit you need to switch off. You'll know you've found the right one when you hear the radio go silent. (Give that song a 10!) A vacuum cleaner will also work as a noise source.

Touch up a scratched washer or dryer

Metal buckles, zippers, and clasps can leave dings and scratches on both washing machines and clothes dryers—marks that will surely rust when exposed to moisture and wet clothing. Don't wait to repair the damage, or you'll regret it. First, clean the area with a cotton ball dipped in rubbing alcohol. When the alcohol has dried (a few seconds at most), cover the scratch with a thin coat of clear nail polish or like-colored auto body touchup paint, available from auto supply stores.

Catch the ripper

If your clothes come out of the wash with small rips or snags, it's likely that something inside the washer is the guilty party. Rub a wad of recycled panty hose over the agitator and tub to detect any coarse edges that snag. Then smooth over the rough spots with a piece of very fine grit sandpaper or epoxy.

Keep washer lint at bay

Does it seem like you're forever clearing washer lint out of your basement sink drain? There's an easy way to solve the problem: Make a lint catcher. Place an old tube sock or the foot section from an old pair of panty hose over the end of the washing machine's drain hose. Attach it

PILOT, WE HAVE IGNITION!

Do you wince at the mere notion of having to rekindle the pilot light on your gas burner? A match-holder could make the job a lot less stressful. Get an old telescoping radio or TV antenna and cut off the tip. Then use pliers to crimp an alligator clip onto the end. You could also straighten a **wire hanger** and use needle-nose pliers to form a small loop at the end, or attach a small spring from a pen at the end to hold the match.

Soak up musty smells with *kitty litter.*

with thick rubber bands or tie it with sections cut from the panty hose's elastic waistband. Leave enough slack in the catcher to prevent the lint from clogging the hose.

A great stand-up routine

Why go through a balancing act every time you need to stand up a mop, duster, or broom? Cut off the finger sections from some old latex gloves and slip them over the ends of all those long wooden handles. The rubber provides enough traction to stop a pole from sliding whenever you lean it against a wall.

Air out a basement

You don't have to live with that musty-smelling basement. Once you've taken care of the source of the moisture, combat any lingering odor by mixing 4 pounds kitty litter with 2 pounds of baking soda in a large container. Then fill several coffee cans to the brim and place them around your basement. Replace with fresh mixture as needed.

Hang up insulation

When insulating the floor above an unheated basement or crawl space, use wire strips cut from recycled metal hangers to keep the fiberglass batts in place. Cut pieces slightly wider than the batt, and place them about 17 inches apart between the floor joists. Although the wires should hold the batts firmly in place, make sure they don't compress the fiberglass.

Exterior Repairs

Get a better handle on glass

Need to move a large pane of glass? Wish there were some way to get a better grip on the big sharp slab? Well, there is. Cut off two short sections from an old garden hose (four sections for a two-person job). Use a sharp knife or scissors to slit each piece down the middle, and then slip them onto the top and bottom edges of the glass.

Bag a lock

Give your outside padlocks some needed protection in winter by covering them with plastic sandwich bags. The plastic wards off rust and prevents damage when moisture seeps inside the lock and repeatedly freezes and thaws.

Bonus hint: When a lock does ice up, you can usually open it by warming the key for several seconds with a match or lighter before inserting it. (Whack forehead and say, "But of course!")

Juice out those concrete patio rust stains

Unsightly orange rust stains defacing your concrete or stone patio? Remove them with the citric acid found in powdered lemonade, lemon-lime, or orangeade drink mixes. Wet the surface with water, then pour the powder over the stain. Cover it with a sheet of plastic to keep the moisture from evaporating, and put a weight on top to hold it in place. After 30 minutes or so, remove the plastic, scrub with a stiff-bristled brush, and rinse. Repeat if necessary.

Weather shingles with soda

Worn or broken wooden roof shingles should be replaced as soon as possible, but it may be years before the new shakes blend in with their

Save the Chlorine for the Pool

Forget what "they" say: Skip the chlorine bleach when removing moss or algae from roofing shingles. Chlorine can strip the color from some materials and corrode metal gutter parts, and the runoff will kill any vegetation growing down below. Oxygen bleach powder, on the other hand, is completely nontoxic and much gentler on roofing materials—yet it's just as effective as chlorine bleach, if not more so.

Following the manufacturer's directions, mix enough powder and water to make 2 to 4 gallons of bleach solution (less for spot treatments). Apply it with a bristle brush on a pole, moving in a downward motion; the bleach will foam up as it's working. Keep the surface wet for 20 minutes, then hose off the debris. (Caution: Working on a roof is dangerous. Be sure to wear appropriate footwear and take all necessary precautions.)

This same procedure can be used to clean algae, moss, or mildew off a wooden deck. It's also an excellent way to prepare a deck for sealing.

New Life for an Old Garden Hose

Don't throw out that leaky old garden hose. Instead use a thin drill bit to punch a few more holes, crimp the end, and presto!—a terrific soaker hose. Don't need a soaker hose? There are still lots of terrific uses for a retired hose around the house.

Slice open a section of hose and use it as a protective cover for a chain saw's teeth or a circular saw blade between uses.

Cut a piece long enough to cover the tines of a metal rake. (Use a utility knife to slit the hose, but don't cut through to the ends.) Slip it over the rake and use as a squeegee to clear away puddles on decks, patios, and walkways.

Use it to cover a fraying length of rope to keep it from getting worse.

Staple small, diagonally sliced pieces to the overhead joists in your basement workshop to keep power cords out of your way.

Slit a short piece down the middle and put it over the shoulder of a shovel blade to cushion your foot and improve traction as you step down on it.

Slip a small section over a wire bucket handle for a more comfortable grip.

surroundings. One way to speed things up is to "age" them beforehand using a solution of water and baking soda. In a large bucket, mix 1 pound of baking soda in ½ gallon of warm water. Either dip the shingles in the bucket, or apply the solution with a paintbrush. Let them dry for a few hours, and they'll take on a weathered, gray appearance. Don't forget to coat your new "old" shingles with a wood preservative before installing them.

Make a gutter scoop
The next time you need to clean the leaves out of your gutters, don't waste your money on a new gutter scoop. Instead, take a plastic oil container and cut the bottom off diagonally. It's the perfect width for any gutter, and it comes equipped with a spout that serves as a handgrip.

Foil a leaking gutter
If your steel gutter has sprung a leak, patch the hole by applying a generous coating of roofing cement to the hole or crack and then covering it with a piece of heavy-duty aluminum foil. Repeat the process and finish off the job with a top coat of cement. Now that's a seal!

Chisel with care
Cushion your hand while chiseling cracked concrete. An ordinary sponge ball wrapped around the chisel makes a handy shock absorber. To shield your eyes and face from any stray fragments, push the chisel through a piece of window screen before you start chipping away.

Quick fix for a loose brick
You don't need to mix up a fresh batch of mortar just to replace a single loose brick in a retaining wall, porch step, or outdoor grill. Simply get out two-part epoxy and apply it to the sides of the brick where the mortar has come loose. Let it cure for 24 hours, then seal any remaining gaps with urethane or silicone caulk.

Instant aging for new mortar
If you think those new mortar joints are going to stand out like a sore thumb against the old cement, "age" them to match by dabbing the wet mortar with a damp black tea bag. (You may need to experiment a bit to obtain the right shade.)

Pour your own stepping-stones
Looking to put that leftover cement to good use? Why not make a few concrete stepping-stones? Your molds? A couple of garbage can lids. Coat the inside of the lids with a thin, even layer of motor oil so the cured concrete will slide out. You can even add your own decorative touches by etching shapes in the wet cement using leaves or other objects.

Cover cement with hay to keep it from setting up
Every builder who works out-of-doors has had the frustrating experience of working with cement when the temperature dips. To minimize problems, keep the area covered with hay before the pour, then after the concrete is placed and smoothed, cover it with plastic sheeting followed by hay.

Insider Tool Tips

Sharpen blades with a matchbook

Don't have a whetstone? You can still restore a dull blade on a small craft or utility knife by rubbing it a few times on the striking surface of a matchbook or, if one is handy, an emery board. Be sure to sharpen both sides of the cutting edge.

Be carpet scrap happy

As handy as they are for repairing tears and burns in carpeting, carpet remnants may be even more useful around the workshop. You can:

- Glue them to the inside of your toolbox to cushion tools in transit.
- Tack them to the tops of sawhorses and workbench surfaces to prevent scratching furniture finishes.
- Staple several remnants inside a narrow cabinet to form cushy cradles for drills and other power tools.
- Staple remnants (one at a time) to a small block of wood to make a reusable contact-cement applicator.

Hands-on handles

You'll get a firmer (and more comfortable) grip on hammers, wrenches, screwdrivers, and other tools if you wrap the handles with adhesive tape or flat foam weather stripping. Hard tools, now soft to the touch.

Extend an oilcan's reach

Need to lubricate a difficult-to-reach gear or joint? Tape a piece of broom straw to the oilcan's spout. The drops of oil will travel along the straw to their distant destination.

Nail-pulling protectors

Have you ever pulled a nail out of a piece of wood only to discover the hammerhead marred the grain? You can easily prevent it from happening by slipping the brim of a baseball cap under the head of the hammer before you start pulling. Can't find a cap? A plastic spatula or a large guitar pick will work just as well.

Shield wood from hammers

Protect wood from accidental hammer blows with this homemade hammer guard. Take the lid from a small plastic container and cut a small hole (one large enough to fit over the nail head) in the center. Place the lid over each nail before hammering it in. To prevent wood from splitting, blunt the tips of your nails with a hammer before using them.

Pliers as flashlight holder

Trying to hold a flashlight and work at the same time is a juggling act you don't want to perform. But you can still get the illumination you need if you don't have a helper to hold the light. Just place the flashlight between the jaws of a pair of pliers and position it at the required angle. Slip a thick rubber band around the handles of the pliers to keep the flashlight from slipping.

Fizz away corrosion

Loosen a rusty nut or bolt by covering it with a rag soaked in hydrogen peroxide, vinegar, or club soda. Let it sit for an hour to give the liquid time to work into the corrosion. The carbonation in club soda or soft drinks has another workshop application as well: It will unfreeze a rusted padlock or cabinet lock.

Caulking and Adhesives

Cold weather caulking

Need to do some caulking on a crisp, cool day? Keep your caulk pliable and running smoothly by wrapping the tubes in a heating pad for 30–45 minutes before using them. Trap the heat by wrapping each tube in plastic wrap before inserting it into the caulk gun.

Stick it to caulk

Don't use your finger to tool a bead of silicone or butyl rubber caulk unless you don't mind wearing it for a while. A Popsicle stick or the back of a plastic or old teaspoon is a much better way to go about it; both have smooth, rounded edges and are easy to hold without getting the caulk on your skin.

Improve your aim

It can be difficult to maneuver a caulk gun in a tight spot or to properly seal a crevice that's out of reach. But an effective extension tool may be as near as a kitchen cabinet or drawer: a plastic drinking straw. Attach the straw (or any plastic tube of the right size) to the nozzle of the caulk tube. Keep your impromptu extender from slipping off by securing it with duct tape.

Mix it up

Recycled bottle caps and jar lids are ideal for mixing two-part epoxy. The raised edge keeps the adhesive from spreading out as you're mixing it, and the limited interior space prevents you from using too much.

In the bag

Looking for an easy way to mix *and* apply two-part epoxy? Venture no farther than the pantry. Grab a plastic sandwich bag and pour as much adhesive as you'll need into a corner section. Tie off the rest of the bag and mix the epoxy by rolling it between your fingers. Use a pin to put one or more small holes in the bag and gently squeeze the epoxy out.

Undo the glue

You shouldn't have to fight to get glue out of a bottle or tube. Declare a truce by dabbing a little petroleum jelly on the inside of the glue lid or on the tip of the tube before replacing the cap. It will prevent the glue from sticking to the cover, and you'll have one less frustration to face.

TAPE A TUBE

Wrapping caulk tubes in **duct tape** can help you work more neatly and efficiently. The tape helps tubes fit more snuggly in the caulk gun and prevents the sticky mess that follows when tubes swell and collapse as the plunger squeezes out the caulk.

Clamping and Sanding

Clamps from the car

Got an old beat-up jumper cable that's just lying around collecting dust? Cut off the battery clips and bring them down to your workshop. They make dandy spring clamps and can accommodate widths up to 1½-inches thick. You could also use an automotive hose clamp to secure a cracked wooden leg or spindle. Just be sure to put a piece of cloth between the clamp and the wood so you won't risk gouging the surface.

Pour on the pressure

It's impossible to clamp some irregularly shaped items and fragile objects to do repairs, but you can still provide adequate pressure. Fill a small plastic bag with sand to weigh down repairs on small, fragile items; use a larger bag for big, sturdier items.

True grit

Want to extend the life of your sanding belts and get the most use out of each sheet of sandpaper? Then back either with strips of duct tape. The tape will prevent the paper from tearing and take some of the stress off the belts. Write down the grit of the paper and the direction of the belt on the tape using a permanent marker.

Resizing sandpaper

There's no rule that says you have to use a whole sheet of sandpaper for every job. In fact, many sanding jobs require you to cut the paper to odd shapes or sizes. Figuring out what to use in place of a block is the tricky part. Here are a few common household items you can use to get the job done (some will require you to glue or tack on the sandpaper):

What's the Story?
Sandpaper's Sojourn

The first recorded use of sandpaper took place in thirteenth-century China, when ancient artisans used natural gum to bond crushed shells, seeds, and sand to parchment. Still, up until the nineteenth century most woodworkers and cabinet-makers relied on dried sheets of sharkskin to smooth their wooden wares.

In the 1800s the fish skins were replaced by "glass paper," made by gluing small particles of glass by hand onto sheets of paper. Commercial production of glass paper began in London in 1833 when John Oakey, a onetime piano manufacturer's apprentice, developed a way to mass produce it. A year later, Isaac Fisher Jr. of Springfield, Vermont, obtained four patents for coating and manufacturing what he called "sandpaper."

Sandpaper jumped in popularity in 1921 when 3M introduced Wetordry, the world's first waterproof sandpaper, after purchasing the patent from its unsung inventor. The product, first used for repainting automobiles, is still sold today—a case of "if it ain't broke, don't fix it."

- A box of playing cards
- Pencils and pencil erasers
- Section of garden hose
- Kitchen sponges
- Wooden clothespins
- A wood block secured to a sponge mop holder (for walls and ceilings)

Ladder Lowdown

Stuck on top

Few things are quite as vexing as dropping a needed screw or tool from the top of a ladder. One way to put the kibosh on such mishaps is to glue a magnet strip to the top rung of your ladder. It will safely hold on to all your fasteners and small tools until you need them. When it comes to larger tools, secure them to the ladder's tool shelf with large rubber bands or tubing.

Off on the right foot

A scrap of outdoor carpet wrapped around the bottom rung of a ladder makes a handy mat for wiping the soles of your shoes before you ascend. It will also let you know you've reached bottom when climbing down. Secure the carpet scrap with duct tape and replace with a fresh piece when needed.

Boot up a ladder

Set the feet of a ladder in a pair of old rubber boots to give it a skid-free footing on smooth surfaces.

Don't leave your mark

Cushion the tops of a ladder's rails with an old pair of socks, gloves, or a couple of bunched up T-shirts to prevent it from damaging vinyl siding and wood shingles or leaving marks or scratches on interior walls. One less thing to repair!

The Clever Homemaker's
crisis center

When a grease splatter burns your hand, the advice in emergency guides (and this book) is to race to the nearest faucet and hold the burn under cold running water for 15 minutes. But what about all those other problems we encounter in daily life? The kind that aren't necessarily emergencies but need a quick fix nonetheless. Ants taking over the kitchen, a makeup spill on your white silk blouse, diaper rash causing your baby dire distress—you can take care of them all by using the common household items and suggestions that fill the previous chapters in this book. This section, however, will provide you with emergency fixes that will help you quickly avert virtually any crisis that may come up in your home. Culled from a vast well of folk remedies and ages-old common sense, it speaks to the imagination of ordinary do-it-yourselfers possessing an extraordinary knack for solving problems great and small.

Body Repairs

A cold is coming on like gangbusters.
Set your hair dryer to warm, hold in front of face, and breathe in the warm air. *(Fire up the hair dryer, page 154)*

You have a cold or allergy, and your stuffy nose feels like it may explode.
Peel and halve a clove of garlic and hold it on your tongue as long as you can, taking

fumes into throat and lungs.

Inhale a pinch of ground pepper to precipitate sneezing and clearing.

Add ¼ cup vinegar to the water in a vaporizer.

Your head is pounding like a steel drum.
Soak your feet in hot water laced with mustard powder to calm a vascular headache. *(Head-to-toe headache remedy, page 161)*

Tie a scarf, bandana, or necktie tightly around your head at forehead level. *(Wear a headband, page 161)*

You're coming down with the flu.
Drink a cup of elderberry tea or a glass of water with 20–30 drops of elderberry tincture. *(Swat the flu bug with elderberry, page 156)*

A painful toothache or gum infection is killing you.
Mix 2–3 teaspoons of table salt in a glass of warm water; vigorously

swish in mouth. *(Saltwater rinse for toothaches, page 163)*

Clamp down on a cotton ball wetted with several drops of clove oil and get to the dentist. *(Clove oil to the rescue! page 163)*

Make a pain-relieving mouthwash with 6 ounces water, ¼ teaspoon salt, and 6–8 drops clove oil. *(Ditto)*

Your ear aches.
Use a clean eyedropper to drop 3 percent hydrogen peroxide into your ear and let it bubble for 3–5 minutes. *(Bubble away ear trouble, page 162)*

You have a cold sore that looks (and feels) terrible. Dab it with yogurt or vinegar throughout the day.

You overdid it, and now your back muscles are screaming.
Position a cold, unopened soft drink can between a wall and the painful area, and then move from side to side to massage it. *(Tin can massage, page 164)*

Leg cramps wake you and send you out of bed hopping like a frog. Stand on a cold stone or ceramic tile floor to slow blood flow and relax tightened, cramped muscles. *(Painful leg cramp relievers, page 164)*

You burned your tongue on that first bite of hot pizza. Sprinkle a pinch or two of sugar on your tongue to ease the pain.

Constipation— 'nuff said. Take 1 tablespoon blackstrap molasses before bed. *(Grease the skids with blackstrap molasses, page 166)*

Take 1–2 teaspoons castor oil for relief in about 8 hours. *(Old-timey constipation cure, page 166)*

Diarrhea is keeping you on the run. Make an infusion from the berries or dried leaves of blackberry, blueberry, or bilberry plants. *(Treat diarrhea with berries, page 166)*

Puree a whole lemon in a blender, add salt, and take 1 teaspoon two or three times a day.

An upset stomach is upsetting your day. Brew infusions from angelica, anise, caraway seed, chamomile, cinnamon, fennel seed, ginger, marjoram, oregano, or peppermint. *(Stomach soothers, page 165)*

Drink cold club soda with a dash of bitters.

Your hiccups aren't responding to the usual cures. Eat some peanut butter and take your time before swallowing it. *(Peanut butter for hiccups, page 180)*

You need a quick treatment for an ordinary skin cut. Place a peeled, bruised half-clove of garlic over a cleaned cut, secure with a bandage, and leave for up to 10 minutes. *(Treat a cut with garlic, page 171)*

Use mouthwash to disinfect the cut.

Apply a substantial amount of black pepper directly to the cut. *(Black pepper stops bleeding, page 171)*

You banged your arm or leg so hard it's going to bruise. Immediately press an onion on the spot for 15 minutes to reduce discoloration. *(Lessen bruising with an onion, page 171)*

Don't Scratch That Itch!

Whatever the cause—animal, vegetable, or mineral—itchy skin can drive you nuts. But scratching can result in infections and scarring. Control your instinct, and try one of these itch-stopping remedies instead.

Mosquito and other insect bites Saturate a clean cloth with white or cider vinegar or rubbing alcohol, and dab bites. A few drops of ammonia or a generous dab of chest rub applied directly to the bite (not bleeding or open sores) will also quell itching.

Chigger bites Soothe itching with a saltwater soak; then coat the rash with vegetable oil or lard.

Poison ivy or poison oak Apply a paste of 3 teaspoons baking soda and 1 teaspoon water to the rash. Vinegar also takes the sting out.

Athlete's foot Soak the affected foot in a saltwater footbath. (Beat athlete's foot, page 170). Dust feet, socks, and shoes with baking powder to dry the infection. For stronger relief, make a salve of 1 teaspoon baking soda and ½ teaspoon water; rub between toes and leave for about 15 minutes. Rinsing feet with undiluted cider vinegar three or four times daily will also calm itching.

Itchy sunburn Make a lotion of 1 part powdered milk, 2 parts water, and a couple pinches of salt, and dab on burned areas. Or treat sunburn with strong green tea. (Soothe sunburn with green tea, page 171)

Apply a banana peel, inside down, on the bruise and secure it with a bandage.

Apply cotton gauze soaked in cider vinegar for an hour.

An inflamed boil needs draining. Cover boil with a wet tea bag and secure with a bandage, then leave on overnight.

A wasp or bee sting threatens to ruin a day in the sun. Apply a paste of 2 parts baking soda to 1 part vinegar. (*Double-duty paste for bee stings, page 172*)

Pour on undiluted vinegar and scrape away stinger with a credit card.

Dab on a paste of meat tenderizer and water. (*Papaya milk [sort of] for stings, page 172*)

Place an onion slice over the sting.

Spray the sting with WD-40 or a window cleaner containing ammonia.

Your toddler has a sudden nosebleed. Set her on your lap, leaning slightly forward, and gently pinch her nostrils closed. (*Stopping Baby's nosebleed, page 179*)

Baby has a sudden, painful case of diaper rash. Apply honey, which will absorb liquid and keep skin dry. (*Diaper rash soothers, page 178*)

Quicken healing by sealing out moisture with petroleum jelly or vegetable shortening or toasted cornstarch. (*Ditto*)

Apply the spice fenugreek. (*A spicy baby powder substitute, page 178*)

Nothing seems to help your colicky infant get comfortable. Give him several sips of fennel seed or peppermint tea to help expel gas and relieve cramps. (*Two herbal teas for colic, page 179*)

Your baby gets a cut or scrape. Use a baby wipe or hand wipe to clean a dirty cut or scrape when no water is available.

Squeeze lemon juice, mouthwash, vinegar, or hard liquor directly on the injury, cover with a napkin, and hold in place for a minute or two to stop bleeding.

Your child's baby tooth just came out, and the blood is flowing. Squeeze excess liquid out of a cool used tea bag and press the bag onto the empty tooth socket. Hold for 1–2 minutes, then reapply as necessary to stop bleeding.

Those beautiful new shoes gave you an ugly new blister. Slice open an aloe leaf and scoop out the gel. Apply gel and bandage blister. (*Aloe for blisters, page 174*)

Household Help Line

A water pipe in the basement is leaking. Make a temporary patch using a garden hose or rubber tubing that's larger in diameter than the pipe. (*Hose off pipe leaks, page 349*)

You arrive at your country cabin to find the water pipes frozen. Blow warm air from a hair dryer on a pipe until it thaws. (*Blow-dry a frozen pipe, page 349*)

You forgot to cover the outdoor faucets, and a freeze is predicted. Shut off valves and then open taps and drain remaining water. Wrap spigots and any exposed pipe in several sheets of newspaper to insulate against cold, and cover with plastic bags secured with duct tape.

A tear in a window screen is letting the bugs in. Apply a few dabs of clear epoxy glue, model

10 Grooming and Clothing Mishaps

Appearance matters, and keeping yourself looking good means knowing what to do when trouble rears its not-so-pretty head.

1. **Too much scent** You went a little wild with the cologne, and the scent is overpowering. Dab a little vodka on the spots where scent was applied.

2. **No lipstick** When you changed purses, you forgot it. Use a brown eyebrow pencil to add a little color to your lips. *(Emergency lip color, page 188)*

3. **No mousse** There's no hair mousse in the bottle, and you're not one to wear bangs. Mix a little shaving cream with a drop of rubbing alcohol and rub into the hair where needed. *(Run out of hair mousse? page 189)*

4. **Paint in hair** While you're painting the ceiling, paint drips onto your hair. Rub olive oil on the spots until all paint traces are gone.

5. **Chlorine-damaged hair** Swimming in the pool turns your blonde tresses green. Massage ketchup or undiluted tomato juice into your hair. Cover with a shower cap (not a towel) and leave on for 10–15 minutes before rinsing.

6. **Blood on clothes** You cut your hand, and the blood drips onto your khaki pants. Soak stained portion overnight in carbonated soft drink, then wash as usual. *(Pop out bloodstains, page 198)*

7. **Chocolate stains** Your three-year-old smears chocolate on her shirt to wipe her hands. Cover the stain with meat tenderizer, leave for an hour, brush away powder, and wash.

8. **Lipstick marks** Lipstick stains mar your shirt or blouse. Remove the center from a piece of white bread and knead into a ball. Blot the stain with the bread ball until lipstick is mostly gone. Wash as usual. *(Lipstick smear remover 2: Bread!, page 197)*

9. **Scorch marks** Your favorite white cotton shirt has a prominent scorch mark. Dab the mark with a white cotton cloth moistened with 3 percent hydrogen peroxide, then wash as usual.

10. **Stuck ring** You tried on your friend's new ring and can't get it off. Apply mayonnaise liberally to ring and finger to aid the ring's slide. *(Unstick a stuck ring, page 204)*

airplane glue, or nail polish over and around the hole. *(Repair a Torn Screen, page 329)*

Use duct tape for temporary repairs when a screen has detached from the frame or has large rips and tears. *(Fast fix for a major screen tear, page 328)*

Your house key broke off in the lock. Try to extract the broken part with tweezers or needle-nose pliers. Use Super Glue to join the key's two parts. *(Remove a broken key, page 330)*

Someone very young left pencil or ink doodles on your wall. Rub pencil marks with a piece of rye bread or a clean art gum eraser.

For ink marks, dab on white vinegar with clean cloth or sponge, then continue until marks are gone.

Your child decorated your wall with crayons. Rub lightly with a clean fabric softener sheet. Rub vigorously with a clean art gum eraser.

Scrub with shaving cream and a soft toothbrush or nailbrush.

Soften marks with a hair dryer and remove with baby oil on a cloth. *(Erasing crayon marks from walls, page 72)*

Scrub gently with a damp cloth dipped in baking soda or white toothpaste.

For crayon on wallpaper, very lightly

skim the surface with a steel wool soap pad, stroking in one direction, until marks disappear.

You've spilled paint on your beautiful wood floor. Stir 1½ teaspoons vinegar and 1½ teaspoons laundry detergent into 2 cups warm water and sponge up remaining paint. *(Clean up paint spills with vinegar, page 74)*

You spot a glob of butter or sour cream on your rug. Scoop up with a spoon, blot with a paper towel, and pour on baking soda, talcum powder, cornstarch, or cornmeal. Leave for up to six hours to absorb grease, then vacuum and repeat as needed.

You dropped a contact lens or earring stud on the rug and can't find it. Tightly attach a couple layers of cheesecloth, a piece of panty hose, or a fabric softener sheet over the crevice tool of your vacuum cleaner with a rubber band or tape. Slowly and carefully vacuum the rug, checking the covered nozzle until the lost item appears.

You just noticed an ugly white water ring on your wooden table. If the ring is still wet, use a hair dryer on low to dry it quickly.

For darker woods, mix ashes from one cigarette in a tablespoon of mayonnaise and rub into the spot until color is restored. *(Wipe Out Water Rings, page 339)*

For a nonshellac finish, pour a little lemon oil on a rag, dip it in salt, and gently rub the spot. *(Ditto)*

Lightly rub the ring with fine (#0000) steel wool dipped in lemon oil. *(Ditto)*

Mix equal amounts white toothpaste and baking soda and rub in, going with the wood grain. *(Get rid of water rings and spots, page 76)*

Coming to Your Pet's Rescue

Kitty, Rover, and assorted other pets have their own share of problems—among them, these five plights.

Your DOG swallowed something that wasn't food. Induce vomiting by giving Poochie 1–2 tablespoons of hydrogen peroxide. *(Hydrogen peroxide for an upset stomach, page 226)*

FIDO's doghouse is Flea City. Wash down interior walls, plus dog bed and any bedding, with strong salt water. Repeat treatment every few weeks to keep your best friend's home flea-free.

Fluffy the CAT rolled in some sticky stuff. Mix 1 teaspoon mild shampoo or dishwashing liquid with ¼ to ½ cup warm water, massage it into the sticky patch and remove residue with a wire-toothed brush. *(Unsticking something sticky, page 236)*

Pee-yew! **Your pet had a run-in with a SKUNK.** Wash your pet in a bath of equal parts white vinegar and water. *(De-skunk your pet with vinegar, page 236)*

Your pet SNAKE is not where he's supposed to be. Lay sheets of aluminum foil, bubble wrap, or crinkly cellophane in potential hiding places so that you can hear him moving. *(Your pet snake is lost? page 243)*

Guests are coming, and you notice **scratches on your serving table.** Apply 2-3 tablespoons instant coffee mixed with just enough water to make a thick paste. *(Instant fix for scratched woodwork, page 341)*

See "Homeopathic" scratch care *(page 341)* and proceed as directed.

A vinyl or cork **tile is about to pop out** of the kitchen floor. Cover the tile with aluminum foil and iron with a hot iron to heat the glue. Weigh down tile with books, bricks, or other heavy flat object until the glue resets.

Your interior decorator uncle is due for an overnight stay, and a piece of **wood furniture** in the guest room somehow got gouged. Make ersatz wood putty by adding instant coffee to 2 tablespoons spackling paste to get the desired color. (*Instant wood putty, page 343*)

The kitchen **sink is clogged,** and you have no plunger. Use a tennis ball or small rubber ball cut in half as a suction cup. (*No plunger, no problem, page 348*)

Put any of the following into the drain, let sit for 10–15 minutes, and then flush with boiling water:

1 cup baking soda and 1 cup hot white vinegar.

½ cup borax, then boiling water added slowly.
2 Alka-Seltzer tablets or 3 denture tablets followed by 1 cup vinegar.

1 cup salt, 1 cup baking soda, and ½ cup white vinegar to rid drain of hair clogs.

Your **washing machine is doing the shake, rattle, and roll.** Use a flashlight to peek under the machine when it's in action. If one of the washer feet isn't resting firmly on the floor, place a wood shim, small carpet scrap, or piece of linoleum tile under the unsteady foot.

A **drinking glass crashed** to the bathroom floor, and you're worried you'll miss the tiniest pieces. First, wear gloves to pick up large pieces. Then choose one of these methods:

Press the area with wet newspaper to take up tiny bits of glass.

Press a slice of bread or a wad of adhesive tape over tiny slivers and glass dust to remove them from the floor.

Ants are swarming over your kitchen counters.

Sugar Make an ant trap by dissolving 2–3 teaspoons sugar in 1 cup water, moisten paper towels or sponges in sugar water and set out overnight. Next morning, sweep trap and ants into a dustpan. (*Lure ants with sugar, page 90*)

White vinegar Spray windowsills, door thresholds, counters, cabinets, and other surfaces with a mixture of equal parts white vinegar and water. (*Repel ants with vinegar, page 90*)

Cayenne pepper and cinnamon Sprinkle these substances on surfaces where ants gather. (*Spicy ant repellents, page 52*)

Grits, flour, or ashes Spread over ant trails, and ants will soon find somewhere else to walk. (*Ants hate grits, page 51*)

Lemon juice, etc. Outside the house, pour lemon juice on thresholds, sills, cracks, and holes where ants can enter. Scatter lemon rinds around door entrances. Or use borax, powdered chalk, salt, talcum power, cream of tartar, powdered sulfur, or oil of clove in the same way.

Petroleum jelly Apply around the rims of pets' food bowls to keep ants at bay.

Roaches. Anywhere, anytime.

Mix equal parts baking soda and sugar and scatter where roaches are seen.

Making sure there's no danger to children and pets, sprinkle boric acid powder into cracks and crevices and under appliances where roaches lurk.

Seal off roach entrances with equal parts cornstarch and plaster of Paris mixed with enough water to make a thick paste.

If you're fast, you can kill a scurrying roach with a spray of WD-40.

Your house is invaded by fleas. If the invasion isn't too severe, place bowls of salt in areas where fleas are to attract and trap them.)

Set a plate containing a little water and a few drops of dishwashing liquid on the floor, place a gooseneck lamp alongside, and bend the bulb close to the water to attract fleas.

Wash floors with the juice and rinds of 4 lemons in ½ gallon water to repel fleas.

Vacuum rugs often to remove flea eggs.

On the Road

It's a cold morning, and the car won't start. Get your hair dryer and a long extension cord. Pop the car hood. Now blow hot air directly at the carburetor to warm the engine for easy ignition. *(Start your car with a hair dryer, page 312)*

The fan belt just broke. Help! For a temporary fix, twist a pair of panty hose into a long rope, thread it around the fan pulleys, and knot tightly.

Your auto horn won't shut up. Stop the incessant blaring by raising the hood and taping down the terminal screw. *(Tape that noisy horn! page 315)*

You backed into a post, and your taillight cover cracked. If the light itself is okay, you can temporarily repair the translucent cover with red or yellow duct tape. Cut tape and adhere to cover cracks, then turn on the light to be certain it's clearly visible.

It's a dark and stormy night, and your headlight goes out. Covering the dead headlight with reflector tape will help get you home safely.

Your wheels are spinning on an ice patch. Pour undiluted chlorine bleach over your tires. *(Gain traction with bleach, page 312)*

Lay a large piece of scrap carpet or a thick pad of newspaper (two or three sections of the average daily) where the wheel hits the icy road.

Your car wheels are bogged in snow or mud. Make a shovel dig more efficiently by spraying it with WD-40.

Your car's temperature gauge suddenly goes into the danger zone. Check under the hood after the engine cools. If you see a cracked or broken water hose, you can probably make a short-term repair—just long enough to get to an expert—by wrapping the hose with duct tape.

Acknowledgments

The writers and editors who produced this book wish to thank the following people and organizations, all of whom graciously shared their knowledge or expertise. American Society of Travel Agents; Arizona Cooperative Extension, Mojave County; Larry Buchwald; Jim Buie; Andrew R. Byers; Trevor Cole; Vicki Coombs; Pat Courtney; Marilyn Dale; Marianne Dervish; Polly DuBose; Carolyn Jackson; Dan Janssen; Pamela Johnson; Marilyn and Gene Kalet; Barbara Kaye; Madelon Konopka; John J. Ligon; Dr. Sandra McCurdy; Marty Malone; Men's Garden Club of America; Montana State U. Extension Service, Park County; North Carolina Cooperative Extension, Henderson County; Maurice Ogutu; Oregon State U. Extension Service, Lane County; Penn State Cooperative Extension, Indiana County; Mary Kay Pleyer; Bob Pollock; Angela Ponce; Julia Pryor; Jack Reagor; Linda Renslow; Derek Scasta; Barbara Scott; Aliza Schiff; Hannah Schiff; Mary Skinner; Martha A. Smith; Jim Sorrenti; John Teague; Texas AgriLIFE Extension Service (Texas A & M System), Navarro County; Diane Turner; Sara Beth Warne; Sean Whalen; U. of Illinois Extension, Countryside Extension Center; U. of Nebraska Extension-Lincoln, Lancaster County; U. of Tennessee Extension, Bedford County

Index

Page numbers in *italics* refer to illustrations.

green-conscious curtain rods, 89
greens, 37, 38
    see also lettuce
green tea, 162, 171, 184
grilled cheese sandwiches, 17
grime, removal of, 85, 87
grits, 51
grocery bags, 117, 202
    as pooper-scoopers, 230
    for scaring off deer, 297
    storage of, 66, 67
grommet dies, 136
grooming, of pets, 228, 233
grosgrain belts, 235
ground covers, 287
grout, 87, 142
guinea pigs, 242
gum, 314, 340
gutters, rain, 114, 355

H

hair, in gardening, 291, 297
hair accessories, 102, 112, 215, 217
hairballs, 233
hair care, 189–91, 221
    for pets, 228, 236, 241
hair conditioner, 185, 189,
    306, 345
hair dryers, 72, 135, 191, 201, 310
    colds as stunted by, 152, 154
    for dusting plants, 278
    for gum removal, 74
    as salad green dryer, 37
    smoothing shirt wrinkles
        with, 194
    starting car with, 312
    thawing car locks with, 313
    thawing frozen pipes
        with, 349
    unsticking drawers with, 338
hairline frizzies, 190
hairspray, 190
    on eyeglasses, 205
    for holding zippers, 194
    homemade, 190
    for static cling, 193
    for straw hats, *183*, 202
Halloween door wreath, 139
ham, 22, 43
hamburgers, 20
hammers, hammering, 337, 356
hammocks, 115
    for lizards, 243
hampers, laundry, 91, 321
hamsters, 242
handbags, 202, 319
handkerchiefs, cleaning of, 199
hand lotion, homemade, 200
handsaws, for separating ribs, 37
hanger racks, 101

hangers, 104, 136, 193, 195
hangnails, 192
hang-tiered baskets, 111
harboiled eggs, 25
hard rolls, 45
hardwood floors, cleaning of,
    70, 72
hat boxes, for storage, 98, 109
hat racks, 101
hats, 95, *183*, 202
hay fever, 158
headaches, *153*, 160–61, *161*, 167
headbands, 160, 193, 202
headboards, 128, 141
headlights, cleaning of, 307
hearts-and-flowers
    centerpieces, 139
heating, of house, 336
heat rashes, 178, 209
heel marks, cleaning of, 71
helmets, motorcycle, 325
hemorrhoid cream, 187
hemorrhoids, 177
hepatitis, 180
herbal hair rinse, 190
herbal remedies, 152–60, 162,
    163, 165–68, 170–80
herbs, 20, 254
    as bug repellents,
        298–99, 303
    chopping of, 37
    growing of, 167, 168, 222,
        270, 289
    for litter box odor, 231
    see also specific herbs
hermit crabs, 244
herpes, 167, 181
hiccups, 180–81
high-heel shoes, 201
hiking, 253, 259, 260, 262
hinges, 136, *327*, 330, 331
histamines, 160
hives, 173
hockey sticks, 222
holiday cards, 120
holiday decorations, 149–51
    lighting up fireplace mantels
        and, 137
    protecting from pets and, 138
    storage of, 98, 119–21
    and using kitchen supplies for
        tree decorating, 217
hollies, 289
home office, managing clutter in,
    116–18
honey, 30, 157, 158, 181
    for diaper rash, 178
    in facials, 200
    in hand lotion, 200
    for skin maintenance, 184–85

for sore throats, 155
honeydews, 281
hoof dressing, 240, 241
hooks, 139
hops pillows, 176
hops shampoo, 189
horns, car, 315
hornworms, 301
horse care, 240–41
horseradish, 157, 280
hostas, 300
hot feet, 170
hot pepper, 51, 156
houseplant hints, 278–79
    hubcaps, 312, 316
hula hoops, for portable
    cubicles, 266
humidifiers, odor removal from, 80
hummingbird feeders, 296, *296*
hydrangeas, 277
hydration drinks, 180
hydrogen peroxide, 86
    clearing earwax with, 162
    corrosion removal with, 356
    for dog's upset stomach, 226
    for scorch marks, 199
    for tomato sauce stains, 197
hygiene tips, for children, 221
hypericin, 176
hypnotic suggestion, 175
hyponatremia, 168

I

ibuprofen, 160
ice cream, 17, 41
ice cubes, 42
    baking bread with, 30
    candle wax removal with,
        76, 77
    for cleaning of garbage
        disposals, 49
    sap removal with, 310, *310*
    skimming fat with, 15
    storing of, 41
    watering plants with, 278
ice cube trays, for storage, 99,
    105, 115
ice packs, 265, 267
ice picks, 313
ice scrapers, 55
icing, 32
incense, locating drafts with, 336
indigestion, 160, 165, 166, 167
indolebutyric acid (IBA), 271
infant seats, as bathing aid, 208
infusions, 159, 165, 167
ink, "invisible," 213
ink stains, 94, 197
insect bites, 167, 181, 209
insecticide, *see* bug repellents